Sunset

Things You Can Make for Children

By the Editors of Sunset Books
and Sunset Magazine

DARROW M. WATT

Snuggly sock dolls appear in
Children's Clothes & Toys, page 72.

Lane Publishing Co. • Menlo Park, California

All the ingredients of a happy childhood

From bibs, blocks, beanbags, and bunks to easels, kites, and a tooth fairy doll—all the makings for a fun-filled childhood are right here.

For many people, the desire to share and relive special moments of childhood is irresistible. One way to experience this pleasure is by enriching a child's world with playthings, furniture, clothing, and attractive room accessories.

So, we decided to join the fun by combining three of our best-sellers that focus on children's environments. Adults and kids alike have always looked to *Sunset* for great ideas, designs, and easy-to-follow projects. Here they are by the dozen—for babies, toddlers, grade schoolers, teenagers, and you, too.

Cover: This easy-to-build structure for sleep and play appears on page 54 of *Children's Furniture.* Photograph by Stephen Marley.

Sunset Books
    Editor: David E. Clark
    Managing Editor: Elizabeth L. Hogan

First printing October 1986

DARROW M. WATT

Rolling sand table is from *Children's Rooms & Play Yards,* page 74.

CONTENTS

Children's Furniture

For the person who loves to build with wood—and has a special child in mind—we offer a wide range of imaginative and practical projects for children of all ages. Whether it's a rocking horse or a canopy bed, a toy box or a playroom set, the designs are sure to delight any youngster.

Children's Rooms & Play Yards

Children's rooms are beehives of creative activity, as are their outdoor play yards, where sand, grass, and simple equipment are transformed into hours of fantasy. Here, we offer lots of good ideas for enriching both environments.

Children's Clothes & Toys

These projects feature stylish looks in jackets and vests, birthday banners, and other colorful fabrications. Step-by-step instructions show you how to sew your own creations for children to wear, hug, nap upon, play with, or display on the wall.

Sunset
Children's Furniture

By the Editors of Sunset Books and Sunset Magazine

Lane Publishing Co. • Menlo Park, California

Book Editors
Scott Fitzgerrell
Don Vandervort

Developmental Editor
Fran Feldman

Contributing Editor
Scott Atkinson

Coordinating Editor
Michael Green

Design
Roger Flanagan

Illustrations
Bill Oetinger

Photography
Stephen Marley

Photo Stylist
JoAnn Masaoka

Just for kids…

All children love a place that's theirs alone—a special realm where everything is child-size, where dreams, imagination, and whimsy hold sway. The best furnishings and playthings for children reflect the spirit, as well as the scale, of that magical world.

If you've always wanted to create something special for a child—a piece of furniture or a plaything that combines charm and fancy with practicality and good craftsmanship—this is the book for you. Here, we present a delightful array of one-of-a-kind woodworking designs just right for a child-size world.

Whether you're an experienced woodworker or an enthusiastic beginner, there's a project here for you. From the simple and lovable rocking lion to the stylish teen bed-desk-wardrobe combination, you're sure to find a design among the more than 30 on these pages that's both tailored to your skills and a perfect fit for the special child you have in mind.

There's plenty here to inspire you, but we don't leave you up in the clouds—we offer down-to-earth, practical information, too. A complete materials list accompanies each project, and detailed instructions and drawings guide you each step of the way, from cutting out the pieces to painting on the last curlicue. In addition, special features scattered throughout the book tell you all about the tools, materials, and techniques you'll need to complete the projects.

We hope you'll derive many hours of pleasure from building these projects, and that you'll think of our book as your partner in creating something truly special. We supply the plans; you supply what money can't buy—the time,

the talent, and most importantly, the loving touch.

We gratefully acknowledge the many woodworkers who helped us test projects and prepare them for the camera—especially John Jones of J & W Wood Products, David Pederson, Phil Puccinelli, Peter Santulli, Paul Staley of Modern Cabinet Systems, and Jim Thomson. For their generosity in sharing props for use in our photographs, we thank Bear Comforts, Cotton Works, The Dollhouse Factory, The Hammock Way, Palo Alto Sport Shop & Toy World, Strouds Linen Warehouse, Toyhouse Schoolhouse, Velveteen Rabbit, and Wherehouse for Bedspreads. We also extend special thanks to copy editor Scott Lowe and photographic assistant Greg Anderson.

Cover: Pulled up front-and-center is our snappy Race Car Bed (page 82); beyond, the elegant Heirloom Rocking Horse (page 8) stands saddled and ready to ride. The Modular Wall System (page 39) provides a place for everything and keeps everything in its place. Photograph by Stephen Marley. Cover design by JoAnn Masaoka.

Sunset Books
　　Editor: David E. Clark
　　Managing Editor: Elizabeth L. Hogan

Second printing October 1986

CONTENTS

Delight a young artist with this
easy-to-build Folding Easel (page 15).

Special features

Childscale

Few pleasures compare with that of making something special for a child you love. If you're a woodworker—or would like to be—you're in an enviable position: the satisfaction you derive from your hobby can go hand in hand with the pleasure you'll get from delighting that child.

Children live in a world of adult-scale furnishings, furnishings that don't fit them either physically or psychologically. Even very young children need—and appreciate—furnishings scaled to their growing bodies and minds.

This book can help. It's a collection of child-scale projects—both furniture and playthings—designed to meet the needs of children. But we haven't thought only of pleasing them: everything in the book has been selected to appeal to the woodworker as well as the child. After all, homemade projects should be fun for the builder, too.

Most of the projects were created especially for this book, and we applied a test to each one before including it: either it had to save money over its commercial counterpart or it had to be unavailable commercially.

In addition, we felt that the projects should address a broad range of woodworking abilities, though none should demand professional expertise. For this reason, you'll find a considerable range in the amount of time, talent, and financial resources required to complete the projects.

A brief overview of all the projects in the book, as well as the special features, follows. Also, be sure to note the hints we give on the facing page about how to use the book.

About the projects

Tailoring furniture to a child's physical needs is a bit like trying to hit a moving target, since children are constantly changing. You can build items that fit a certain range of ages, you can make more specialized things that can be set aside or passed on when outgrown, or you can build furniture and toys that are adjustable and grow with the child. You'll find examples of all three approaches among the projects in this book.

Tailoring to a child's marvelous sense of magic and wonder deserves equal attention. In selecting and designing projects for this book, we made sure to stock it well with imagination and magic.

The book begins with a selection of playthings and room accessories—projects that are part furniture, part toy. The rocking lion and horse (pages 6–9) exemplify the book's range within a single subject: the lion is quick and easy to build, the horse takes longer and requires more skill.

You'll find a customized van toybox and a finely crafted wooden wagon paired up on pages 22–25. The former is easy to build; the latter is more involved, but like the horse, it's an heirloom that's well worth the time and effort it requires.

The animal-shaped chairs on pages 34–35 are pure whimsy—an easily built set of simple chairs made from a single sheet of plywood and some pieces of solid lumber. Less fanciful, but no less practical, are the fold-down stepstool and the versatile multiposition chair on pages 30–33.

The easel (pages 14–15) and the workbench (pages 26–27) are quick, inexpensive projects designed to give years of service. The play kitchen and doll house cabinets (pages 18–21) work as hard as they play, and each can be used for storage after it's outgrown.

The sports rack, mirrored organizer, and clothes rack on pages 10–13 are all business (but not at the expense of attractive design), and each is easy to build.

The modular wall and closet systems (pages 38–41) offer plenty of organization at minimal expense. Their elegant, uncluttered designs will complement any child's room.

Two sharply contrasting playsets come next. The hardwood table and stools (pages 42–43) are simple, clean, and contemporary; the charming country styling of the painted table, bench, and chairs on pages 46–49 recalls an earlier day. Both projects are easy to build.

Two folk-art cradles follow on pages 50–53. These designs embody the timeless traditions of Scandinavian and Shaker craftsmanship. Each requires a modest store of tools and experience. In contrast, the all-in-one sleep and play structure on pages 54–57 is an easy project designed to be a complete "environment" for a young child.

On pages 58–61 you'll find a pair of contemporary bunk beds. The first unstacks into individual twin beds; the second features an adjustable desk within its L-shaped configuration. Both projects fall into the easy-to-moderate

Building furniture & playthings for children

skill range and both are less expensive than equivalent commercially produced furniture.

If your child sleeps in a metal-framed twin bed, try dressing it up with a little headboard magic—or enhance its usefulness with underbed drawers; the projects on pages 62–65 show you how. If you'd rather start from scratch, consider the chest bed on pages 66–69; within its twin-size frame you can store the contents of a large dresser.

Canopy beds are perennial favorites, and the one on pages 70–71 is no exception. It's also an exceptional value—easy to build and quite inexpensive.

Three fantasy beds are next. On pages 74–77, budding astronauts will find a craft suitable for night flights into dreamland—a space shuttle built from plywood and plastic planters. The tent-topped wagon bed on pages 78–81 evokes everything from a campground to a circus wagon. For the speed demon in your midst, there's the race car bed on pages 82–85. Its startlingly authentic lines will make it look like it's setting lap records right in the middle of your child's room.

An easy-to-build loft bed with desk and wardrobe follows this trio (pages 86–89). Especially effective for a small room, it combines sleep, study, and storage functions in a sleek, stylish package that takes up very little floor space.

The book concludes with three adjustable projects that combine to make a "room that grows up" (pages 90–95). There's a table that can be positioned at three different heights, a convertible crib-to-youth bed with dresser, and a two-position desk. All three share a clean, contemporary look and require moderate woodworking skill; all will save you money over equivalent commercial designs.

About the special features

Throughout the book you'll find a series of special features beginning with the selection and purchase of materials and ending with finishing. Though it's beyond the scope of this book to offer a complete course in basic woodworking, these features will orient you if you're a beginner and jog your memory if you're an expert. Each one is tailored to the projects in the book.

In "Basic materials" (pages 16–17), we discuss the materials recommended for the projects and guide you in their purchase. "Tools of the trade" (pages 28–29) helps you through the numerous choices you'll need to make when acquiring and using tools. In "Marking, cutting & drilling" (pages 36–37) you'll find many useful tips that will aid you in building your project.

"Joinery" (pages 44–45) is an outline account of a craft within a craft: the creation and assembly of wood joints, connections that are crucial to the structural integrity of the project.

Since some wood joints can be very difficult to make, we've restricted the types of joints used in our projects to the simpler ones. These are all accounted for here.

The final feature, "Finishing your project" (pages 72–73), is a guide to the finishes we used on the projects, as shown in the photographs. These finishes are both easy to apply and extremely durable.

In this feature we explain the techniques you'll need to know, including how to prepare the wood, how to apply each of the various finishes, and how to cut and attach plastic laminate.

Using this book

After you've decided on a project, read all the instructions and study the illustrations and materials list before starting to build. We've designed these elements to streamline your work: you can shop directly from the list, and the alphabetical labels on the pieces will help you move back and forth between the instructions, the drawings, and the list without any confusion.

Look up any unfamiliar operations in the special features. If you don't have all the tools you need, borrow or rent what you lack. Or consider buying new tools that you can use again and again. Enrolling in an adult education program in woodworking, if it's available in your community, offers an excellent solution to the problem of an inadequate workshop or tool kit.

Once you've marshalled your resources and you understand the procedures, you're ready to begin. Turn the page—and have fun!

These two spirited mounts are off and running. The rocking lion is so quick and easy to build that even young lion tamers can help with construction. The rocking horse is a solid hardwood heirloom that requires more time and effort. Each is a sturdy design and will carry its rider many miles.

Rocking lion

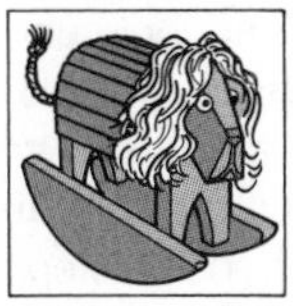

Much like its jungle counterpart, this time-tested rocking lion rarely fails to capture the imaginations of young and old alike. This project can be turned out in a few hours—and a child can help, too.

1. Cut all pieces to size. (Note: The lengths given for neck pieces **D** and **E**, which are cut at a 45° angle at one end, are for the longest sides.) Cut the tops of ends **A** to a 4⅝-inch radius and cut the arches between the legs as shown. Cut twenty-eight 2-inch and twelve 3-inch lengths of dowel. Mark and drill ⅜-inch holes in body pieces **B** as shown.

2. Starting at the top of ends **A**, attach pieces **B** with 2-inch dowels and glue. Use the holes in **B** as guides for drilling corresponding holes in **A**, keeping ends **A** parallel to each other and perpendicular to pieces **B**.

3. Rip the rounded edges from head pieces **C**, then join them by gluing and clamping. Cut the profiles in the head. Glue and nail pieces **D** and **E** to **C**.

4. Drill ⅜-inch head mounting holes in front end **A**. Hold the head in position and drill corresponding holes in **D** and **E**. Attach the head with glue and 3-inch dowels.

5. Cut rockers **F** as shown in the detail drawing; drill the top front mounting hole in each. Mark and drill a corresponding hole in each leg of front end **A** and temporarily assemble with dowels. Clamp the rear legs to the rockers and adjust the body until level. Drill the remaining mounting holes and fasten rockers **F** to legs **A** with glue and dowels.

6. Trim the dowels, round over all edges, and sand. Attach the pulls with glue and dowels. Finish, coloring the nose and eyes with a pen. Nail on the mane and attach the tail (pass it through a 1-inch hole drilled in back end **A**).

Design: Rick Morrall.

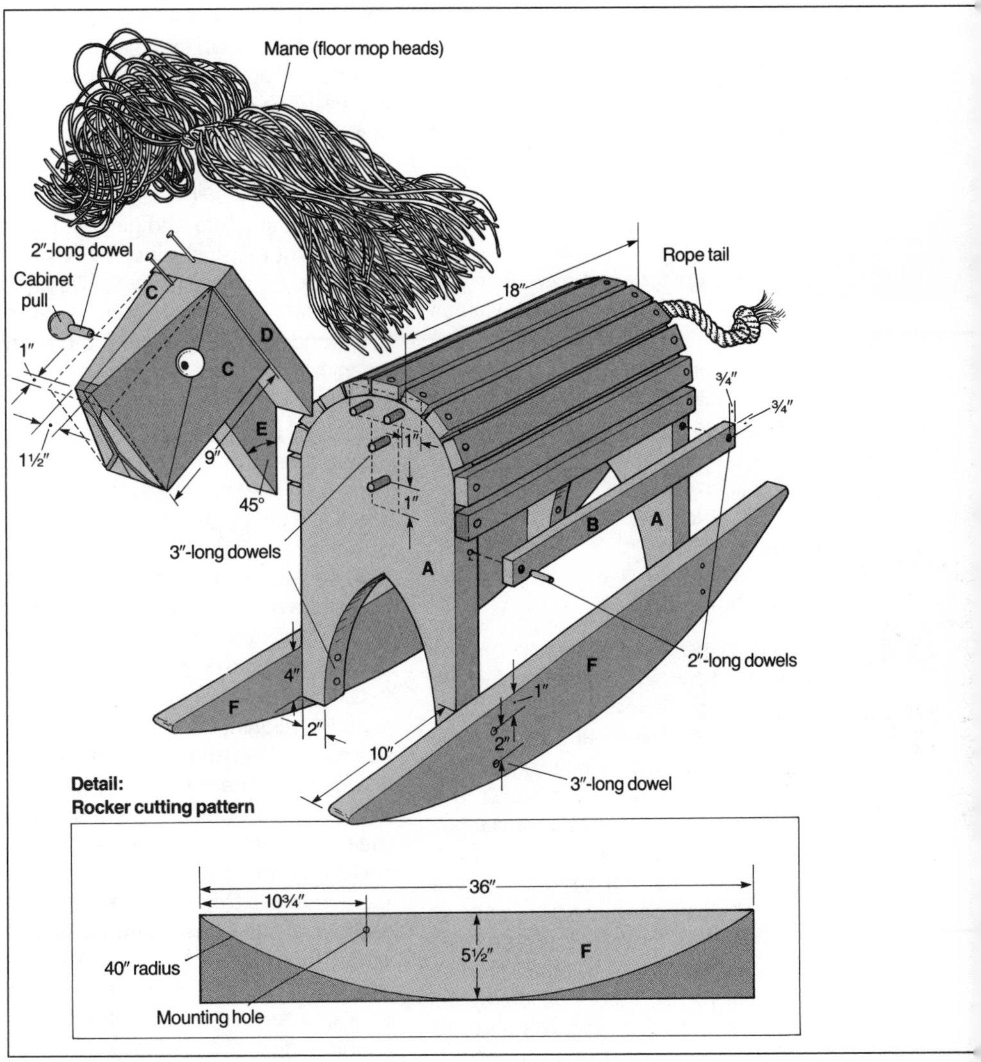
Mane (floor mop heads)
2″-long dowel
Cabinet pull
1″
1½″
C
D
C
E
9″
45°
3″-long dowels
18″
Rope tail
¾″
¾″
1″
1″
B
A
A
2″-long dowels
F
F
4″
2″
1″
2″
10″
3″-long dowel
Detail:
Rocker cutting pattern
36″
10¾″
5½″
F
40″ radius
Mounting hole

BUY		TO MAKE			
Clear fir					
1	3-foot 2 by 10	2	Ends	**A**:	1½″ by 9¼″ by 16″
1	16-foot 1 by 2	10	Body pieces	**B**:	¾″ by 1½″ by 18″
1	6-foot 1 by 2	3	Body pieces	**B**:	¾″ by 1½″ by 18″
1	8-foot 2 by 6	2	Head pieces	**C**:	1½″ by 5½″ by 9″
		2	Rockers	**F**:	1½″ by 5½″ by 36″
1	2-foot 2 by 4	1	Neck piece	**D**:	1½″ by 3½″ by 9½″
		1	Neck piece	**E**:	1½″ by 3½″ by 7½″

MISCELLANEOUS

8′ of ⅜″ hardwood dowel • 2′ of 1″ braided rope • 2 floor mop heads
10d nails • 2 wood cabinet pulls • Wood glue • Clear nontoxic finish • Black felt-tip pen

Heirloom rocking horse

The simple elegance of this fine hardwood rocking horse will make it a source of delight for all ages. If you're a moderately experienced woodworker, you won't find the project difficult. The beauty and durability of the completed horse, pictured on page 6, will repay your investment in time and materials many times over.

In addition to basic tools, you'll need a saber saw, router, and a radial-arm or table saw to build the horse as shown; a band saw and belt sander are helpful. Both the level of difficulty and the tools needed are somewhat "adjustable," however; you could, for example, omit the inlaid bridle and girth—and the router they require.

1. Using the grid-enlargement method described on page 36, transfer the cutting patterns (Details 1 and 3) to heavy paper and cut them out. Edge-join the boards by gluing and clamping to make "blanks" for body **A**, rockers **D**, and saddle halves **J** (see detail drawings). Cut the ⅜-inch dowel into 40 pieces, each 1½ inches long. Blind dowel (see page 45) the body blank where shown in Detail 3. If you're not using a band saw, cut the saddle-half profiles before gluing; if you're using a band saw, cut the profiles after gluing. (Be sure the halves mirror each other.)

Pieces **K** and **L** and the optional bridle and girth inlays are ¼ inch thick. Rip these pieces from a dark hardwood (ours are walnut), or use ash or oak and stain it darker.

Trace the patterns for body **A**, legs **B** and **C** (made from single boards), and saddle halves **J**, then cut all pieces. Use a beam compass or, preferably, the saber-saw jig shown on page 36 to cut the rocker blank as shown in Detail 2; move the pivot point up 3¼ inches for each cut. Add reinforcing dowels to the feet and rockers where shown and shape the rocker ends. Cut pieces **E**–

I, **K**, and **L**. Mortise rocker ends ¼ inch deep where shown in Detail 3, tracing around the end of a foot support **E** to establish the size; be sure the centers of the mortises are 32 inches apart. Cut the four leg wedges from the 1 by 6 as shown in Detail 3.

To add the bridle and girth inlays, if desired, rout 3⁄16-inch-deep by ¾-inch-wide grooves where shown in Detail 3; then glue ¼-inch by ¾-inch strips of hardwood in each groove. Sand flush when the glue has cured.

2. Unless otherwise indicated, assemble all the pieces with glue and the appropriate screws as shown in the exploded drawing. Drill counterbore holes and plug with screw hole buttons or dowels as indicated. Be careful to drill adequate shank-clearance and pilot holes to avoid splitting the hardwood. Before assembling the horse, round over all exposed edges and sand.

Glue the leg wedges in place on legs **B** and **C**, aligning as shown in Detail 3. (Be sure to keep the left and right pairs of legs sorted as you work.) Place two legs on one side of the body, sanding their upper edges so they lie flat and positioning them by means of the alignment marks in Detail 3. Check that the centers of the hooves are 32 inches apart; then fasten the legs in place, observing the right or left-side screw locations as shown. Add the two remaining legs to the other side in the same way.

3. Assemble rockers **D** and foot supports **E**. Add footrests **F**, gluing and doweling them in place as shown in Detail 3 and the exploded drawing. If your buckaroo needs a booster step, build it by gluing and doweling step **G** to supports **H**; use screws and two pieces **I** to lock the step assembly in place. Center the horse on the supports and screw the feet to the foot supports as shown.

4. Fasten one saddle half **J** to the body with 1½-inch screws, then add its mate, using 2½ and 3-inch screws (see exploded drawing and Detail 1). Glue and clamp the two remaining pieces **I** to the horse's head to act as mounts for the leather ears. Drill holes in mounts **I** where shown. Glue and clamp trim pieces **K** and **L** in position. Add ½-inch screw hole buttons for eyes. Round one end of each of the 1-inch dowel handles and drill the other end as shown. Drill holes in **A** and **K** (see Detail 3). Use the threaded rod to connect the handles and body.

5. Shape and sand the saddle, using the photo as a guide. Do any final shaping, rounding, and finish sanding, then apply two or three coats of varnish or penetrating oil finish. Cut and roll the leather ears, insert them in ear mounts **I**, and secure them with toothpicks glued in 1⁄16-inch holes drilled through the mounts and ears.

Design: Louis Jewell.

BUY		TO MAKE	
Ash, oak, or walnut			
18	board feet of ¾-inch stock	Pieces **A–D**, **H**, and **J–L** (see text and drawings for sizes)	
		2	Foot supports **E**: ¾″ by 2″ by 14½″
		3	Footrests **F**: ¾″ by 2″ by 15½″
		1	Step **G**: ¾″ by 2″ by 14″
		4	Pieces **I**: ¾″ by ¾″ by 2½″

MISCELLANEOUS

6′ of ⅜″ hardwood dowel • 2 pieces of 1″ hardwood dowel, each 3″ long
24 sq. inches of leather • Screw hole buttons: 20 at ⅜″, 2 at ½″
4′ of 1 by 6 pine or fir • 2 round toothpicks • 4½″ of ¼″ threaded rod • Wood glue
#12 flathead woodscrews: 24 at 1½″, 4 at 1¾″, 1 at 2½″, 3 at 3″ • Finish

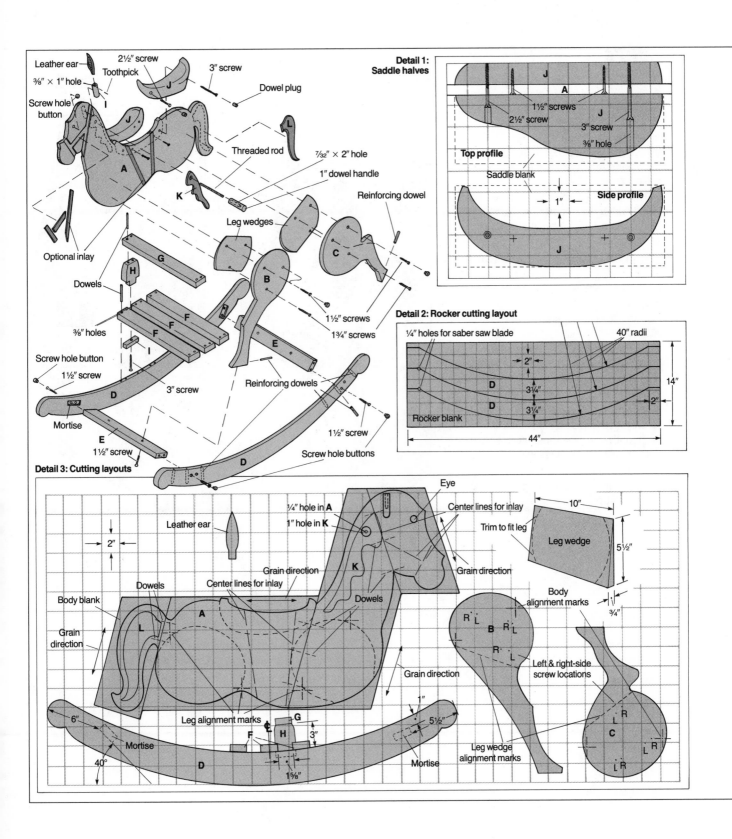

Leather ear
Toothpick
2½" screw
3" screw
⅜" × 1" hole
Dowel plug
Screw hole button
J
I
J
J
Threaded rod
⁷⁄₃₂" × 2" hole
L
1" dowel handle
A
Reinforcing dowel
K
Leg wedges
Optional inlay
Dowels
H
G
C
Reinforcing dowel
⅜" holes
F
F
B
Screw hole button
F
I
1½" screw
E
3" screw
1½" screws
D
1¾" screws
Mortise
Reinforcing dowels
E
1½" screw
1½" screw
D
Screw hole buttons

Detail 1: Saddle halves

J
A
1½" screws
2½" screw
J
3" screw
⅜" hole
Top profile
Saddle blank
1"
Side profile
J

Detail 2: Rocker cutting layout

¼" holes for saber saw blade
40" radii
2"
D
3¼"
D
3¼"
14"
2"
Rocker blank
44"

Detail 3: Cutting layouts

Leather ear
Eye
¼" hole in **A**
1" hole in **K**
Center lines for inlay
Trim to fit leg
10"
Grain direction
Leg wedge
5½"
Grain direction
Body alignment marks
Grain direction
K
¾"
Body blank
A
Dowels
Center lines for inlay
Dowels
Grain direction
R L
B
R L
2"
L
Left & right-side screw locations
L
R L
Grain direction
Grain direction
Leg wedge alignment marks
6"
1"
G
5½"
Mortise
F
H
3"
L R
C
Mortise
Leg alignment marks
40°
D
1⅝"
L R

FORM & FUNCTION

Sports rack (below)
Mirrored organizer (page 12)
Freestanding clothes rack (page 13)

Sports rack

This easy-to-make rack keeps the clutter of sports equipment out of closet corners. Baseball bats dangle from pegs, skis and other long items stand upright, shoes go on shelves, sports clothing hangs from pegs, and balls are stored in the base.

The perfect project for a novice woodworker, this sports rack requires only basic tools and skills for its construction.

1. Cut all pieces to size. Mark and drill 1½-inch-deep holes for the dowels in top **C** where shown. Cut the angle along sides **A** as shown in the detail drawing. Cut the dowel into eight pieces, each 5½ inches long.

2. Glue and nail sides **A** to base **B** and top **C**. Add shelves **D** and front **E**. Glue one end of each dowel and tap them into the holes in **C**.

3. Set the nails and fill the holes. Sand all surfaces and apply one coat of finish. Lightly sand the inner face of back **F** and recoat it. Let the pieces dry.

4. Nail on the back, dropping it down ¾ inch from the upper edge of top **C** and overlapping each side **A** ⅜ inch.

Design: Don Vandervort.

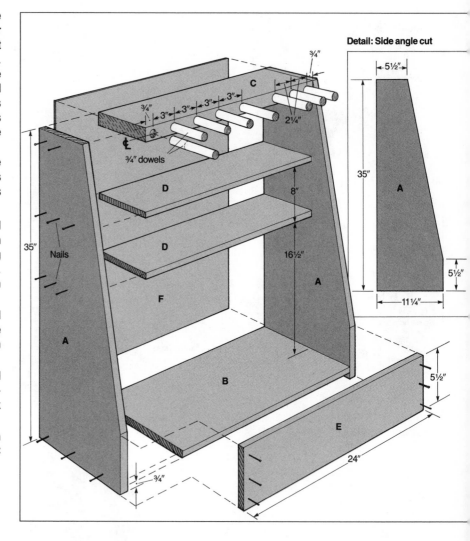

Detail: Side angle cut

BUY		TO MAKE		
Knotty (#3) pine				
1	8-foot 1 by 12	2	Sides **A**:	¾" by 11¼" by 35"
		1	Base **B**:	¾" by 11¼" by 22½"
1	6-foot 1 by 6	2	Shelves **D**:	¾" by 5½" by 22½"
		1	Front **E**:	¾" by 5½" by 24"
1	2-foot 2 by 6	1	Top **C**:	1½" by 5½" by 22½"
Hardboard				
1	¼-inch 2 by 4-foot piece	1	Back **F**:	¼" by 23¼" by 33⅛"

MISCELLANEOUS
4' of ¾" hardwood dowel • 5d finishing nails • Wood glue • Wood putty
Clear satin polyurethane finish

Practical, good-looking, and easily built accessories include (from left to right) a sports rack, a mirrored organizer, and a clothes rack. Each is made from standard-dimension pine and requires little more than basic tools.

Mirrored organizer

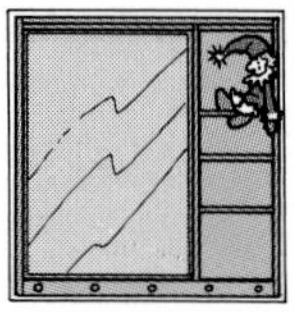

This simple, wall-mounted unit (see photo on page 11) offers a mirror, shelves for display or organization, and pegs for backpacks, jackets, and the like. The case, made from standard-dimension lumber, is glued and screwed together. Order the mirror from a glass dealer before you begin the case.

Cut the plugs for the screw holes from scrap lumber, using a plug cutter.

1. Cut all pieces to size. Cut the dowel into five pieces, each 3½ inches long. Mark and drill 1-inch-deep holes for the dowels in base **B** where shown.

2. Drill counterbore and pilot holes for screws. Glue all joints. Using 1¼-inch screws, join sides **A** to base **B** and top **C**. Screw divider **D** in place, spacing it from the right side with shelves **E** (use two 2½-inch screws to attach **D** to base **B**). Attach the shelves, screwing through **A** and **D** as shown.

3. Using glue and brads, attach back **F**, leaving a ¼-inch border all around. Glue one end of each dowel and tap the dowels into the holes in base **B**.

4. Glue and screw mounting strips **G** and **H** against the back, screwing down through top **C** with 1¼-inch screws.

5. Plug the screw holes. Sand and finish all the wood, including the quarter-round molding.

6. With the unit on its back, set the mirror in place. Cut the quarter-round to fit around the mirror, mitering the ends. Carefully toenail the pieces with brads. Set the heads and fill the holes.

7. Drill countersink and pilot holes through mounting strips **G** and **H** and screw the unit to wall studs, using two 2½-inch screws.

Design: Don Vandervort.

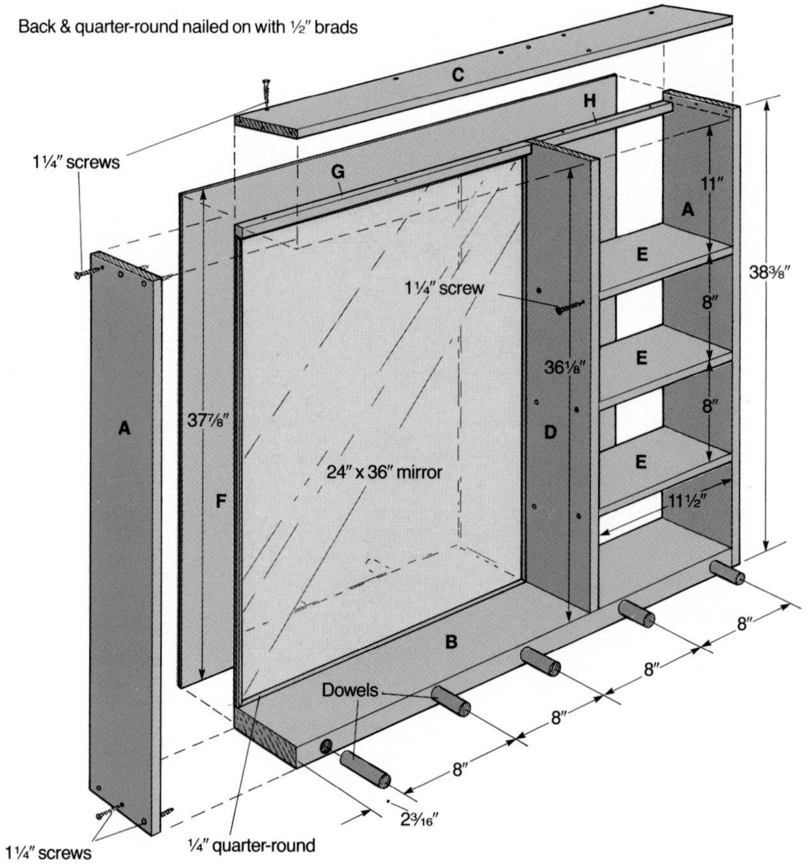

Back & quarter-round nailed on with ½″ brads
C
H
1¼″ screws
G
A
11″
E
38⅜″
1¼″ screw
8″
E
36⅛″
8″
A
37⅞″
D
E
24″ x 36″ mirror
F
11½″
B
8″
8″
Dowels
8″
8″
2³⁄₁₆″
1¼″ screws
¼″ quarter-round

BUY		TO MAKE
Clear pine		
1	10-foot 1 by 6	2 Sides **A**: ¾″ by 5½″ by 38⅜″
		1 Top **C**: ¾″ by 5½″ by 36⅜″
1	8-foot 1 by 6	1 Divider **D**: ¾″ by 5½″ by 36⅛″
		3 Shelves **E**: ¾″ by 5½″ by 11½″
1	4-foot 2 by 6	1 Base **B**: 1½″ by 5½″ by 36⅜″
1	3-foot 1 by 1	1 Mounting strip **G**: ½″ by ¾″ by 24⅛″
		1 Mounting strip **H**: ½″ by ¾″ by 11½″
Birch plywood (shop grade)		
1	¼-inch 4 by 4-foot sheet	1 Back **F**: ¼″ by 37⅜″ by 37⅞″

MISCELLANEOUS

¼″ by 24″ by 36″ mirror • 12′ of ¼″ quarter-round clear pine molding
31 1¼″ by #6 drywall screws • 4 2½″ by #6 drywall screws • ½″ brads • Wood glue
Wood putty • Clear satin polyurethane finish • 2′ of ¾″ hardwood dowel

Freestanding clothes rack

Add a decorative element and plenty of additional storage to a child's room with this freestanding clothes rack, pictured on page 11. It offers a 3½-foot closet pole and two shelves—one below for shoes and skates, and one above for books, toys, and other treasures.

Because construction is so simple, a child can help you build the rack. In addition to basic tools, you'll need a saber saw or band saw for making the curved cuts. A router is helpful for rounding over edges.

1. Cut the pieces to size. Using the grid-enlargement method described on page 36, cut out feet **E** and hearts **F** (see detail drawing) and round over their edges. Sand the curves smooth. If you wish to finish the feet and hearts to contrast with the frame, as shown in the photo, stain them now.

2. Glue and screw all joints; countersink the screws. Attach top **B** to sides **A**, then attach sides **A** to base **C** and shelf **D**. Fasten shelf **D** to base **C**. Mount the closet pole brackets where shown. Cut the fir round to fit between the closet pole brackets and install it.

3. Fill all holes and sand the unfinished pieces. Finish all pieces, including the feet and hearts, with the clear finish of your choice.

4. Using three screws for each foot, glue and screw on the feet, starting the screws from the inside of sides **A**; be careful not to countersink the screws too deeply. Attach the hearts in the same manner.

Design: Heidi Merry.

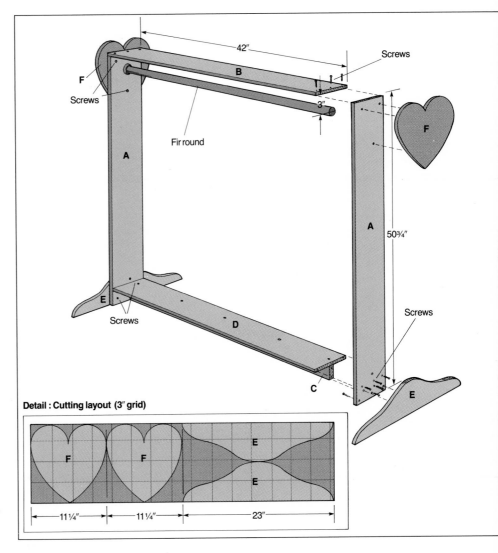

Detail : Cutting layout (3″ grid)

BUY		TO MAKE	
Knotty (#3) pine			
2	6-foot 1 by 8s	2	Sides **A**: ¾″ by 7¼″ by 50″
		1	Top **B**: ¾″ by 7¼″ by 42″
1	4-foot 1 by 8	1	Shelf **D**: ¾″ by 7¼″ by 40½″
1	4-foot 1 by 4	1	Base **C**: ¾″ by 3½″ by 40½″
1	4-foot 1 by 12	2	Feet **E** (see detail drawing)
		2	Hearts **F** (see detail drawing)

MISCELLANEOUS
33 drywall screws, 1¼″ by #6 • 4′ of 1⅜″ fir round • 1 pair closet pole brackets with screws
Wood glue • Wood putty • Maple stain • Clear finish

To paint a masterpiece, every artist needs the right equipment. This sturdy, versatile easel fills the bill—and it's equally well adapted to chalk and marker work. As the inset photos show, the easel folds up compactly once the masterpiece is finished.

Folding easel

Young artists will like this versatile easel: its adjustable art boards provide generous space for creativity, and its large tray holds plenty of chalk, paint, and markers. Parents will appreciate its easy-to-build folding design: the easel is compact when folded and rigid when set up.

1. Cut all pieces to size. Mark and drill holes for pivot screws in tray sides **A** and two legs **E**; mark and drill holes for locking dowels in remaining legs **E** (see Details 1 and 2). Drill holes in one crosspiece **C** as shown. Cut the dowel in half.

2. Join tray sides **A** and **B** with glue and 6d nails spaced 3 inches apart. Add crosspieces **C**, using glue and 4d nails. Set the nails and fill the holes. Cut the molding in half and glue in place where shown. Attach tray bottom **D** with glue and 2d nails, leaving a ¼-inch border all around.

3. Join legs **E** in pairs with hinges. Round over all wood edges, sand, and apply two coats of gloss polyurethane to all wood pieces, tray bottom, and one art board **F**. Paint the other board with chalkboard paint.

4. Attach the legs to tray sides **A** with 1½-inch screws and finish washers, leaving the screws just loose enough to permit easy movement. Glue the dowels in opposite legs (see Detail 1).

5. Stand the easel up and open the legs, resting the tray on the dowels. When the tray is level, mark the outline of each dowel on the tray underside. Cut away the tray within the outlines with a craft knife or chisel. Install the mending plates as shown in Detail 1 (they should pivot to lock and unlock the dowels in their notches). Using ¾-inch screws, attach art boards **F** and chalkboard spacers **G** to the legs as shown, setting their height as desired.

Design: Scott Fitzgerrell.

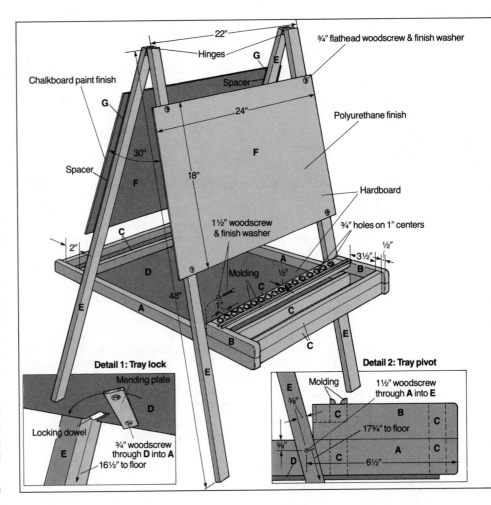

BUY		TO MAKE	
Clear fir or pine			
4	8-foot 1 by 2s	2	Tray sides **A**: ¾″ by 1½″ by 28″
		2	Tray sides **B**: ¾″ by 1½″ by 6¼″
		6	Tray crosspieces **C**: ¾″ by 1½″ by 17½″
		4	Legs **E**: ¾″ by 1½″ by 48″
Tempered hardboard			
1	¼-inch 4 by 4-foot sheet	1	Tray bottom **D**: ¼″ by 18½″ by 26½″
		2	Art boards **F**: ¼″ by 18″ by 24″
		2	Chalkboard spacers **G**: ¼″ by 1½″ by 18″

MISCELLANEOUS
3′ of ¼″ quarter-round molding • 3″ of ¼″ hardwood dowel
10 brass flathead woodscrews, ¾″ by #8, with finish washers
2 1½″ butt hinges with screws • 2 brass flathead woodscrews, 1½″ by #8, with finish washers
2d, 4d, and 6d finishing nails • 2 mending plates, ¾″ by 1½″
Wood glue • Wood putty • Chalkboard paint • Gloss polyurethane finish

Though quality lumber and fasteners alone won't ensure a project's success, it's difficult to come up with first-rate results using less than first-rate materials. Here's a guide to choosing the best.

Shopping for lumber

Lumber is divided into softwoods and hardwoods, terms that refer to the origin of the wood. Hardwoods, such as ash, birch, maple, and oak, come from deciduous trees; softwoods, such as fir, pine, redwood, and cedar, come from conifers. As a rule, softwoods are less expensive and more readily available. (To find hardwoods, look in the Yellow Pages under "Hardwoods.")

Lumber sizing. Though it's often assumed that a 2 by 4 is 2 inches thick and 4 inches wide, it's not. These numbers give the *nominal* size of the lumber—before it's dried and surfaced (planed). The chart at right lists the nominal sizes of softwood lumber and the standard surfaced dimensions for each. The lumber is sold in lengths ranging from 6 to 20 feet in increments of 2 feet.

Buying hardwoods can be tricky; they usually come in random widths and lengths, in odd thicknesses, and often with rough edges. You may see the designations S1S, S2S, S3S, and S4S, which mean "surfaced one side," "surfaced two sides," and so on. The term "four-quarter," or 4/4, represents the nominal thickness of a board. An unsurfaced 4/4 board is between 1 and 1¼ inches thick, an 8/4 board around 2 inches thick, and so on. The surfaced size will be somewhat less.

Unless you have a planer, you'll probably need to have your hardwood lumber milled at the lumberyard. And to fit the wood on hand, you may need to resize your lumber slightly or fine-tune the project dimensions. For minor resizing jobs, a table saw equipped with a carbide-tipped blade is usually sufficient.

Moisture content. When wood is sawn, it's still "green." Before it's ready to use, most lumber is either air-dried or kiln-dried. Kiln-drying, the more expensive process, reduces moisture content to less than 8 percent. To avoid warping or shrinking, use kiln-dried lumber whenever possible.

Grading. Lumber of the same species and size is graded on a sliding scale: the top grades are virtually flawless, the bottom grades virtually unusable. Even within the same grade, you'll often find striking differences between pieces. Let your eye be the final judge.

If you're using softwood and want a perfect, natural finish, choose Clear, B and better, Superior finish, Clear allheart (redwood only), or Supreme (Idaho white pine). If you plan to paint, you can substitute a less expensive wood, since paint hides many defects. Number 2 and 3 pines are often chosen specifically for their tight knot patterns.

Top hardwood grades include Firsts, Seconds, and a mix of the two called FAS. Next comes Select. Between FAS and Select are two subgrades: FAS 1 face and Select and better. The former, graded FAS on one face but No. 1 Common (the next lower grade) on the other, may be an economical choice if only one side will show.

Choosing plywood

Plywood, a man-made product, offers several advantages over solid lumber: exceptional strength, availability in large sheets, and, in most cases, lower cost.

Softwood plywood. Though softwood plywood may be manufactured from up to 70 species, Douglas fir and Southern pine are the most common. The standard sheet size is 4 by 8 feet, but many lumberyards sell half sheets.

Both the face and the back of a plywood panel are graded by appearance (letters A through D designate the standard grades). Generally, an A face is suitable for a natural finish, a B face for stain, and a repaired C face (called "C-plugged") for paint. If both sides of a panel will be exposed, use AB plywood. An AD panel is an economical choice where only one side will show.

Standard dimensions of surfaced lumber

NOMINAL SIZE	SURFACED (Actual Size)
1 by 2	¾″ by 1½″
1 by 3	¾″ by 2½″
1 by 4	¾″ by 3½″
1 by 6	¾″ by 5½″
1 by 8	¾″ by 7¼″
1 by 10	¾″ by 9¼″
1 by 12	¾″ by 11¼″
2 by 3	1½″ by 2½″
2 by 4	1½″ by 3½″
2 by 6	1½″ by 5½″
2 by 8	1½″ by 7¼″
2 by 10	1½″ by 9¼″
2 by 12	1½″ by 11¼″
4 by 4	3½″ by 3½″

Hardwood plywood. Popular domestic hardwood plywoods include ash, birch, black walnut, cherry, maple, and oak. A number of imported woods are also available. We've selected birch for many of the projects; it's durable and attractive, tools cleanly, and is one of the lowest-priced hardwood plywoods. You can increase your savings by using "shop grade" birch plywood—panels with very slight defects that won't meet grading standards. Standard panel size is 4 by 8 feet.

If you're planning to clear-finish plywood edges or simply looking for extra strength in thin sheets, opt for Baltic or Finnish plywood, birch panels made up of many very thin, solid veneers. They're available in 5 by 5 or 8 by 4-foot sheets (the grain runs across the width).

Hardwood plywoods have their own grades: Premium, the top of the line, is the best choice for a natural finish. Good grade (sometimes designated "Number 1") normally looks best when stained. Sound grade (Number 2) is best when painted. Grades lower than Sound are generally not worth using.

Fasteners

Nails, screws, bolts, and adhesives—these fasteners hold together all the other materials featured in the projects. Here's a closer look at each.

Nails. *Box* nails have wide, flat heads to spread the load and resist pull-through. When you don't want the nail's head to show, use a *finishing* nail and sink the head with a nailset.

"Penny" (abbreviated as "d") indicates a nail's length. Here are some equivalents in inches: 2d = 1", 3d = 1¼", 4d = 1½", 6d = 2".

Screws. Not all screws are created equal. Many projects call for hardened bugle-head *drywall* screws, now widely available as "multipurpose" screws. These versatile fasteners are an improvement over traditional woodscrews. If you substitute woodscrews, choose the next larger gauge number (diameter) in each case.

For a decorative touch, turn to *brass flathead* woodscrews with finishing washers. The heavy-duty *lag* screw is used with a flat washer and should be driven with a ratchet and socket.

Bolts. The *machine* bolt's square or hexagonal head is driven with a ratchet. *Carriage* bolts have self-anchoring heads that dig into wood as you tighten the nut.

To complement your bolts, use the standard "hex" nuts, T-nuts, wing nuts, or nylon-insert locknuts as specified.

Machine bolts need a flat washer at each end; carriage bolts require only one washer, inside the nut.

Adhesives. Adhesives vary according to strength, resistance to heat and water, and setting time.

Yellow (aliphatic resin) glue, often labeled "carpenter's glue" or "wood glue," is a good all-purpose adhesive. Though similar to white household glue, yellow glue has a higher resistance to heat, sets up faster, and is stronger.

Attach plastic laminate to wood surfaces with *contact cement.* It bonds immediately and needs no clamps. The older type of contact cement is highly flammable; buy the newer, water-base type if you can.

To position patterns and stencils, use artist's *spray-mount;* it's readily available in aerosol cans from art and hobby stores.

Fasteners for furniture

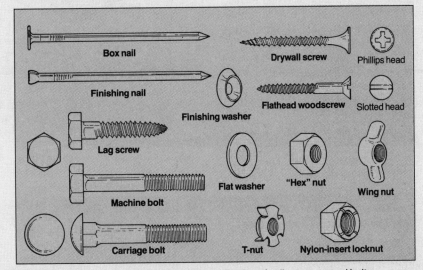

Box nail • Drywall screw • Phillips head • Finishing nail • Finishing washer • Flathead woodscrew • Slotted head • Lag screw • Flat washer • "Hex" nut • Wing nut • Machine bolt • Carriage bolt • T-nut • Nylon-insert locknut

Choose fasteners for your projects from this collection of nails, screws, and bolts.

Play kitchen

Transform a corner of your child's room into a scaled-down kitchen. Sized for children, this kitchen set includes a range with a peekaboo door, a sink cabinet with a plastic sink, and a refrigerator with shelves.

Each piece is actually a cabinet. All three are constructed in the same way, except for the mounting of the doors. The cabinets are made from ½-inch birch plywood with ¼-inch hardboard backs.

1. Cut all plywood pieces to size. Lay out backs **D** and **E** on the hardboard sheet and cut them to size.

Using a saber saw, make the cutout in one cabinet top **C** for the sink tub, making sure the hole is dimensioned to hold the tub securely. Also make the cutout in oven door **G** for the "window."

2. Assemble each cabinet with glue and nails, spacing nails 2 to 3 inches apart. Attach sides **A** or **B** to top **C**; attach bottom shelf **C** so its top surface is 2 inches up from the bottom of **A**. Add intermediate shelf **C** (two shelves for the refrigerator) and back **D** or **E**. Attach toekick **F**. Hang door **G** or **H** as shown in the large drawing, using a continuous hinge cut to fit (see Detail 1). Trim the range door slightly for a good fit.

3. Set the nails, fill the holes, and sand all surfaces. Apply a base coat of paint, then sand and dust well. Apply a top coat. When it's dry, paint circles on the rangetop with black enamel.

4. Screw on the door pulls and magnetic catches. Drop the tub in place.

Design: Don Vandervort.

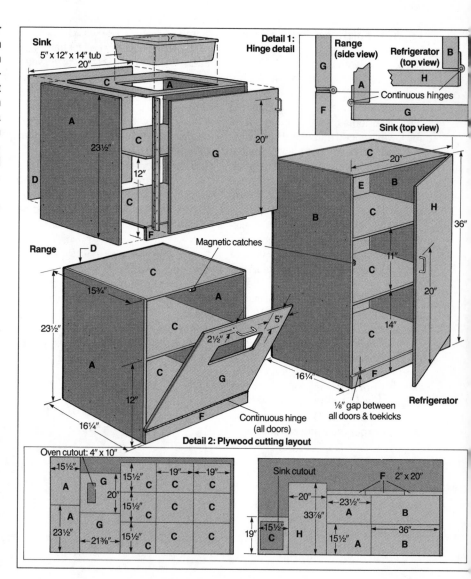

BUY		TO MAKE
Birch plywood (shop grade)		
2	½-inch 4 by 8-foot sheets	Pieces **A–C** and **F–H** (see plywood cutting layout)
Hardboard		
1	¼-inch 4 by 4-foot sheet	2 Backs **D**: ¼" by 20" by 23½"
		1 Back **E**: ¼" by 20" by 36"

MISCELLANEOUS
3d finishing nails • 2 continuous hinges, one 1¹⁄₁₆" by 36" and one 1¹⁄₁₆" by 48", with ½" screws
3 magnetic catches • Plastic sink tub, 5" by 12" by 14"
3 cabinet pulls • Wood glue • Wood putty • Nontoxic enamel

Both the doll house cabinets and the play kitchen components start from simple plywood boxes. The sink, range, and refrigerator, largely unadorned except for paint, can be built in a day. The town and country houses, dressed in 1/12-scale finery, are a bit more involved, yet each is an easy weekend project.

Doll house cabinets

Here's a pair of doll houses that your child won't outgrow: each sturdy house doubles as a roomy storage cabinet. Shown are two versions of the same basic structure—one a charming country cottage, the other a sophisticated town house (see the photo on page 19). Each is realistic without being time-consuming to build; construction is easy.

Both houses permit great freedom of decoration—let your imagination be your guide. Though each uses materials available at doll house specialty shops, you can fashion the decorative details from bits of standard molding or workshop scrap. Only basic tools are required, though a table saw is helpful for cutting the plywood.

1. For either house, cut all pieces to size.

2. Glue and nail all joints, spacing the nails 2 to 3 inches apart. Assemble sides **A**, floors **B**, and back **C**; mount front **C** with a continuous hinge (for the country house, cut the hinge down to 21 inches). This completes the town house.

To complete the country house, glue **E1** to **E2**, letting **E2** overlap; then glue

and nail the pieces to the back. Nail through **E1** and **E2** into sides **A**; glue reinforcing pieces **F** in position as shown. Add four spacers **G**, trimming the hinge-side piece for door clearance.

3. To decorate the completed structure, take it to a doll house specialty shop or a hobby shop and experiment with the various items you'll find there: scale doors and windows, siding, shingles, fancy trim, and the like. Or decorate your house with pieces of standard molding.

Once you've chosen your materials, unscrew front **C**, and mark and cut openings for doors and windows. Size the openings to the manufacturer's specifications or, if you're building from scratch, size them to a scale of one inch per foot.

Prefinish the roof, walls, and trim, then glue the trim in place. To finish the country house as shown, whittle, finish, and attach half-timbering; then "plaster" the plywood with all-purpose patching compound, texturing by hand and with a whisk broom or stiff brush. Paint the shingles after attaching; paint the "plaster" when it's dry. Paint the interior, then glue walls **D** where desired. Reattach front **C**; add the catch.

Design: Scott Fitzgerrell.

Detail: Plywood cutting layout

Country house

A   C   21½"   A
10"   19"   37"   4"
18"   F   F   B
B   10"
22½"   G   B
5½" × 1"
E1   6½"   D
23"   C   D
E2   Cut at 67°

Town house

B   19"   C
10"   32"
B   18"   C
B   10"   A
A
B
D
D   6½"
D

BUY	TO MAKE
Fir plywood (grade AB)	
1 ½-inch 4 by 8-foot sheet	Pieces **A–G** for country house or pieces **A–D** for town house (see plywood cutting layout)

MISCELLANEOUS
1 continuous hinge, 1 1/16" by 30", with ½" screws • Magnetic catch • 2d finishing nails
Wood glue • Trim and finish (see below)

TRIM & FINISH
Country house: 550 sq. in. fish-scale shingle strips • 4' of 1" half-round molding for rakes
Ready-made windows • Ready-made door trim • All-purpose patching compound
15' of ¼" by 1½" pine for half-timbering, door, chimney, and chimney pots
Ivory and slate gray enamel • Medium oak stain • Scale brick paper
Town house: 8' of ¼" by 1½" pine for parapet, step, and curb
30" of scale dentil cornice molding • Ready-made windows and door with classical trim
60" of scale decorative band molding • 128" of scale dentil molding for quoins
Navajo white spray enamel • Scale brick paper

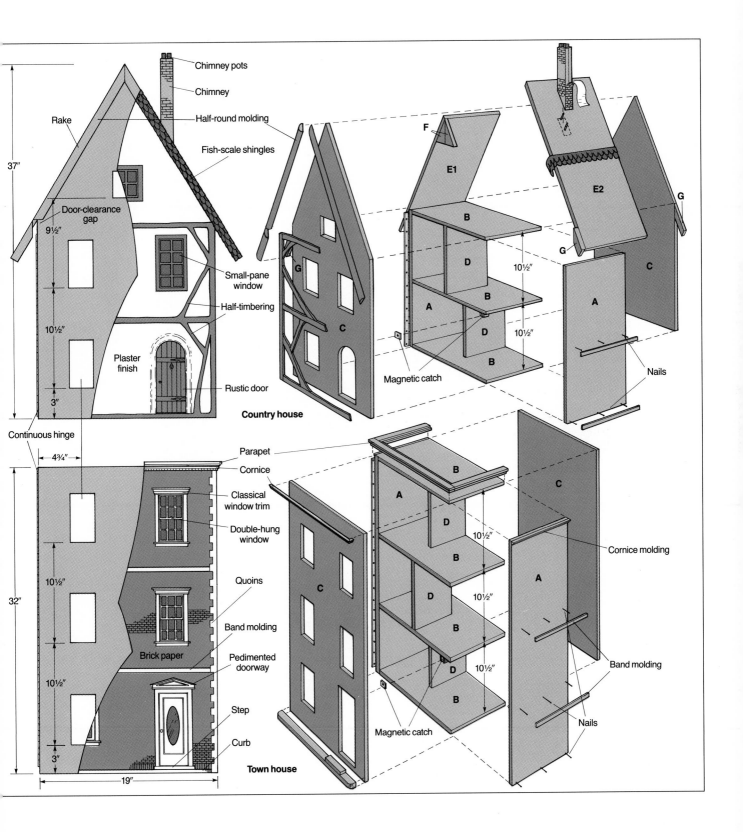

Chimney pots

Chimney

Half-round molding

Fish-scale shingles

Rake

37″

Door-clearance gap

9½″

Small-pane window

Half-timbering

10½″

Plaster finish

3″

Rustic door

Country house

Continuous hinge

4¾″

F

E1

B

G

D

B

A

10½″

D

10½″

B

Magnetic catch

C

E2

G

G

C

A

Nails

Parapet

Cornice

Classical window trim

Double-hung window

Quoins

Band molding

Brick paper

Pedimented doorway

Step

Curb

Town house

32″

10½″

10½″

3″

19″

B

A

D

10½″

B

D

10½″

B

D

10½″

B

C

C

A

Cornice molding

Band molding

Nails

Magnetic catch

A capacious cargo hauler, the bright, bold van toybox on the left is easy to build and can be decorated to suit your fancy. On the right is the wooden wagon, an elegant, solid-oak heirloom designed to last for generations.

Custom van toybox

Building this plywood van—by yourself or with a child—is just part of the fun. Its expansive, flat sides offer great opportunities for custom decoration. And its ample capacity ensures its usefulness when cleanup time rolls around.

1. Lay out and cut sides **A**, back **B**, bottom **C**, and front **D** (see Detail 1). Lay out windshield **E** and cut to length only. Cut the molding into two fillers **G** and two bumpers **H** as shown. Cut axles **I** and mark center lines for them on **C**, 4 inches from each end.

2. Glue and nail the axles to the bottom, then add **A**, **B**, and **D**. Glue the fillers in place as shown.

3. Cut one long edge of windshield **E** at a 75° angle as shown. Hold it in position against **D**, mark its width, then cut the other long edge at a 75° angle. Glue and nail it in place.

4. Measure the top of the van and cut lid **F** in one piece. Cut the front edge at a 75° angle and cut the 3-inch hole as shown; then saw the piece in half. Cut the continuous hinge in half. Center it on each side and use it to attach the lids. Add weatherstripping where shown in the photo (this protects little fingers from being pinched). Attach the friction lid supports (use the manufacturer's instructions and the photo as guides; the lids should open just past vertical).

5. Round over all edges, set the nails, and fill the holes; then paint. Paint the windows and grille, following the layout in Detail 2. Finish bumpers **H** and attach. Trim the van as desired. We used automotive striping tape and vinyl letters from a stationery store. A word of caution: These materials can be peeled off and possibly ingested. An alternative is to use nontoxic paint for the trim. Finally, drill ⅜-inch pilot holes in the axles and add the wheels as shown.

Design: Bill Oetinger.

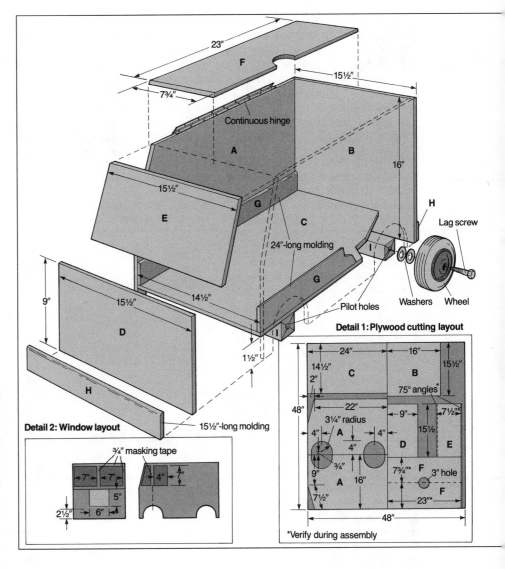

BUY		TO MAKE
Douglas fir plywood (grade AB)		
1	½-inch 4 by 4-foot sheet	Parts **A–F** (see Detail 1)
Clear pine, fir, or other softwood		
1	3-foot 2 by 2	2 Axles **I**: 1½" by 1½" by 14½"

MISCELLANEOUS
8' of ⅜" by 2¼" pine molding • 1 continuous hinge, 1¹⁄₁₆" by 30", with ½" screws
2 friction lid supports • Vinyl weatherstripping, ⅜" by 8'
4 wheels, 1½" by 6" in diameter with a ½" hub • 4 lag screws, ½" by 3", with 2 washers each
3d finishing nails • Wood glue • Wood putty • Nontoxic paint
Striping tape and vinyl letters (optional)

Heirloom wooden wagon

Oak construction makes this classic wagon as rugged as it is good-looking. To build it, you'll need a moderate level of woodworking skill, a radial-arm or table saw with a dado blade, and components for the steamer (see Detail 1).

1. Cut all pieces to size. Rabbet sides **A** and dado sides **A** and ends **B**. Use Detail 3 to locate and mark half-lap joints between yoke top **N** and yoke extensions **P**; cut the joints to fit (see large drawing). Rabbet the ends of **N**. Cut profiles and drill axle holes in axle supports **L** and **O** (see Details 5 and 6). Shape the ends of yoke extensions **P** (see Detail 3); drill ¼-inch bolt holes. Cut the dowel into twelve 1½-inch pieces.

2. Glue and dowel sides **A** and one end **B** (use three dowels per joint). Slip in bottom **C**; add remaining end **B**. Using glue and brads, fasten spacer blocks **D** and **E** (see large drawing and Detail 3). Glue stake supports **F** and **G** to the blocks.

3. To make each stake section, glue and screw together four stakes **H** and two stake connectors **I** as shown; countersink the screws and slightly bevel the lower ends of the stakes.

4. Glue and screw crosspiece **J** to support **K**; add axle supports **L** (see large drawing and Detail 5). Glue and screw support **M** to the underside of bottom **C** where shown in Detail 3 (**M** corresponds to the position of the front undercarriage). Center and drill a ⅛-inch hole through **M** and **C** and use as a guide to counterbore and drill **C** and **M** for the machine screw. Add the roller glides (see Detail 3).

Glue and screw yoke top **N** to axle supports **O** and yoke extensions **P**; add crosspiece **Q**. Drill a 5/16-inch hole in the center of **N**. Cut and screw an aluminum angle along each inside edge of **P** and trim flush at the ends.

5. Nail together and cut bending form halves **R** (see Detail 1). Make the steamer as shown, pour in about a quart of water, and bring to a boil. Add pieces **S**, cover, and steam for about 4 hours or until pliable (check water supply periodically). Put the pieces in the form as shown, making sure the long edges are flush. Tightly clamp and leave overnight. Release, apply glue to all mating surfaces, and reclamp; leave overnight.

6. Glue handle pieces **T** and **U** to the tongue (see Detail 2). Shape as shown.

Trim and round over the other end of the tongue; drill the ¼-inch bolt hole. Plug all visible screws, round over sharp edges, sand, and apply two finish coats.

7. Drill four counterbore holes in bottom **C** for the carriage bolts (see Detail 3); attach the rear undercarriage. Attach the front undercarriage (see Detail 4) and the tongue. Cut axles to length from the rods and install; mount the wheels as shown and attach the axle caps. Add the rubber mat and the stake sides.

Design: Don Vandervort.

BUY		TO MAKE		
Oak (grade to suit)				
9	board feet of 4/4 stock	2	Sides **A**:	13/16″ by 5″ by 36″
		2	Ends **B**:	13/16″ by 5″ by 17⅛″
		2	Rear axle supports **L**:	13/16″ by 5″ by 12⅛″
		1	Rear support **K**:	13/16″ by 5″ by 12⅜″
		1	Rear crosspiece **J**:	13/16″ by 5″ by 12⅜″
		1	Front support **M**:	13/16″ by 5″ by 14″
		1	Yoke top **N**:	13/16″ by 5″ by 14″
		2	Front axle supports **O**:	13/16″ by 5″ by 7½″
		2	Yoke extensions **P**:	13/16″ by 2″ by 15″
		1	Front crosspiece **Q**:	13/16″ by 2½″ by 12⅜″
Oak flooring				
6	5/16-inch by 2-inch by 12-foot pieces	8	Spacer blocks **D**:	5/16″ by 2″ by 1 15/16″
		2	Spacer blocks **E**:	5/16″ by 2″ by 4½″
		2	Stake supports **F**:	5/16″ by 2″ by 36⅝″
		2	Stake supports **G**:	5/16″ by 2″ by 19¼″
		24	Stakes **H**:	5/16″ by 2″ by 16″
		12	Stake connectors **I**:	5/16″ by 2″ by 14″
		3	Tongue pieces **S**:	5/16″ by 1¾″ by 29½″
		2	Handle pieces **T**:	5/16″ by 1¾″ by 8¼″
		2	Handle pieces **U**:	5/16″ by 1¾″ by 3¼″
Douglas fir (construction grade)				
1	6-foot 2 by 6	2	Bending form halves **R**:	1½″ by 5½″ by 36″
Fir plywood (grade AD)				
1	⅝-inch 2 by 3-foot piece	1	Bottom **C**:	⅝″ by 17⅛″ by 35⅛″

MISCELLANEOUS

2′ of ⅜″ hardwood dowel • 2 pieces of aluminum angle, each ¾″ by ¾″ by 10″
4 roller glides, ¾″ in diameter • 2 galvanized steel rods, each ½″ by 18″ • 8 ½″ washers
4 wheels, 10″ in diameter, with ½″ hubs • 4 knock-on axle caps, ½″ in diameter
96 brass flathead woodscrews, ½″ by #6 • 10 flathead woodscrews, ¾″ by #6
28 drywall screws, 1¼″ by #6 • Brads • 4 carriage bolts, ¼″ by 1½″, with nuts and washers
1 machine bolt, ¼″ by 4″, with locknut and 2 washers
1 machine screw, 5/16″ by 3½″, with 2 locknuts and 2 washers
Wood glue • Wood putty • Clear penetrating oil finish • Black rubber mat, 34⅜″ by 16⅜″

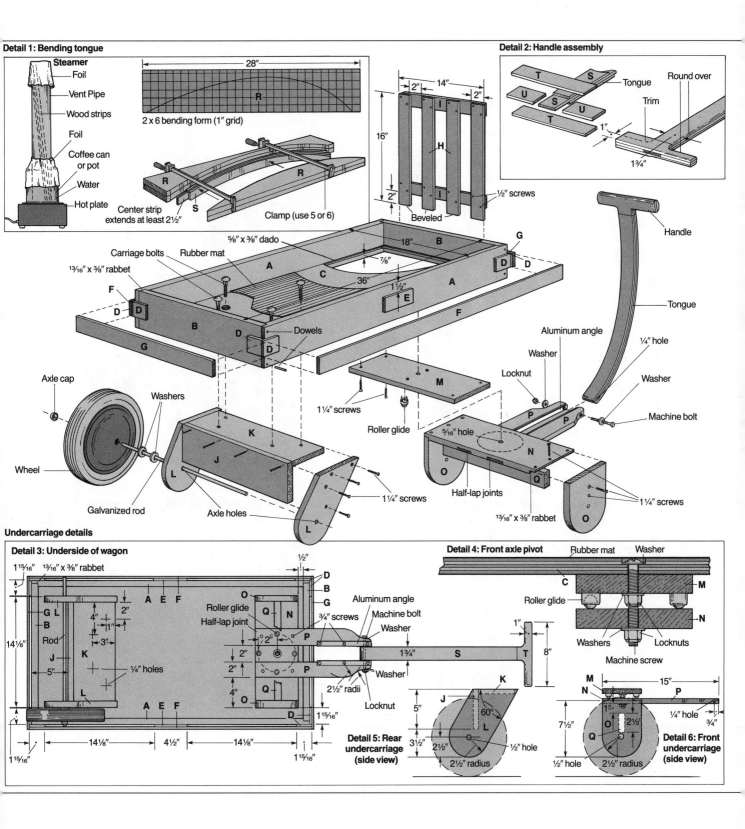

Detail 1: Bending tongue

Steamer
- Foil
- Vent Pipe
- Wood strips
- Foil
- Coffee can or pot
- Water
- Hot plate

28″

2 x 6 bending form (1″ grid)

R

Center strip extends at least 2½″

R R S

Clamp (use 5 or 6)

Detail 2: Handle assembly

T S
U S U
T T

Tongue
Round over
Trim
1″
1¾″

Handle

Tongue

⅝″ x ⅜″ dado
Carriage bolts
Rubber mat
¹³⁄₁₆″ x ⅜″ rabbet
F
D D
G

2″ 14″ 2″
16″
2″
Beveled
½″ screws
I
H
I

18″ B
7⁄8″
C
36″
1½″
E
A
F
D D
G

A
B
D
Dowels

¼″ hole
Washer
Aluminum angle
Washer
Locknut
Machine bolt

Axle cap
Washers
Wheel
Galvanized rod
Axle holes

K
J
L
L

1¼″ screws
Roller glide
M
1¼″ screws

P P
N
⁵⁄₁₆″ hole
O
Q
Half-lap joints
¹³⁄₁₆″ x ⅜″ rabbet
O
1¼″ screws

Undercarriage details

Detail 3: Underside of wagon

1¹⁵⁄₁₆″ ¹³⁄₁₆″ x ⅜″ rabbet
½″
D
B
14⅛″
A E F
G
G L
B
Rod
J K
5″
¼″ holes
L
A E F
D
1¹⁵⁄₁₆″

4″ 2″
1″
3″

O
Q N
Roller glide
Half-lap joint
¾″ screws
Aluminum angle
Machine bolt
Washer
P
2″
2″
2″
P
4″
Q
O
D
2½″ radii
Washer
Locknut

1¾″
S
1″
T
8″

14⅛″ 4½″ 14⅛″
1¹⁵⁄₁₆″ 1¹⁵⁄₁₆″

Detail 4: Front axle pivot

Rubber mat Washer
C
Roller glide
Washers Locknuts
Machine screw
M
N

Detail 5: Rear undercarriage (side view)

K
J
60°
L
5″
3½″
2½″
2½″ radius
½″ hole

Detail 6: Front undercarriage (side view)

M 15″
N
1″
P
¼″ hole
¾″
7½″
Q
O 2½″
½″ hole 2½″ radius

Sturdy workbench

If you have an up-and-coming builder in the family, this project is for you. You'll find that a small investment in time and materials is repaid many times over by a workbench that's rigid, durable, and versatile.

Key features include simple construction, a replaceable top that overhangs its base for easy mounting of vises and clamps, and a convenient tool rack. The design is also adaptable: you can vary the length of the detachable legs to suit the user, or scale up the entire structure if you wish—right up to adult size.

1. Cut all pieces to size (see detail drawing). Glue and screw ends **B** to sides **A**, good sides out, as shown. Check the frame as the glue dries to be sure it's square. Then add one top **C**, aligning it flush with the edge of **A** on the tool-holder side as shown. (The top overhangs the other three sides by 1½ inches.) Fasten **C** to the frame with glue and 10 screws. Countersink the screws.

2. With the unit upside down, clamp legs **F** in place, drill ⁵⁄₁₆-inch holes through sides **A** and the legs where shown, and fasten each leg to the frame with two carriage bolts. Turn the unit right side up. Add the second top **C**, good side up, but do not glue; instead, attach it with 10 screws spaced a little inside those underneath. Countersink the screws.

3. Screw spacer **D** in place, then add tool rack **E**, fastening it with paired screws. Don't glue **E** in place—you'll need to remove it to change to longer legs as your little carpenter grows.

Design: Scott Fitzgerrell.

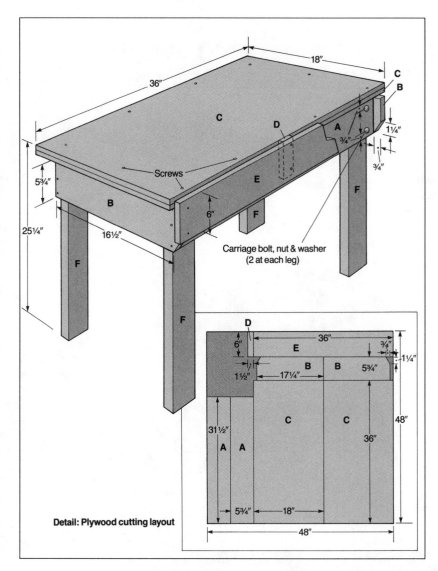

Carriage bolt, nut & washer (2 at each leg)

Detail: Plywood cutting layout

BUY	TO MAKE
Douglas fir plywood (grade AD)	
1 ¾-inch 4 by 4-foot sheet	Parts **A–E** (see detail drawing)
Standard and better fir	
1 8-foot 2 by 4	4 Legs **F**: 1½" by 3½" by 23¾"*

MISCELLANEOUS

8 carriage bolts, ⁵⁄₁₆" by 2½", with nuts and washers
40 drywall screws, 1¼" by #6 • Wood glue

*Cut the legs shorter if desired; for longer legs, use a 10 or 12-foot 2 by 4 instead.

A half-sheet of plywood, a 2 by 4, basic tools, and an hour of time are about all it takes to build this solid little workbench. Young carpenters will appreciate its scaled-down proportions—and it's a simple matter to raise the height of the bench as the carpenter grows.

TOOLS OF THE TRADE

What tools do you need to build the projects in this book? Among the basics are a tape measure, try or combination square, compass, crosscut saw, electric drill and twist bits, hammer, screwdriver, adjustable wrench, vise, and C-clamps. Two standard carpentry tools, a carpenter's square and chalkline, will help you lay out cutting lines or grids when a try or combination square is too small.

Today's woodworkers also consider the following tools basic:

Portable circular saw. Using a circular saw and the correct blade, you can cut faster and more accurately than with a handsaw. The popular 7¼-inch model cuts through surfaced 2-by lumber at any angle from 45° to 90°. Combination and plywood blades handle basic cutting chores.

Portable saber saw. This easy-to-use saw specializes in curves and cutouts. The variable-speed models allow fine control when cutting tight curves or different types of wood. Look for a saw with a tilting baseplate for cutting bevels to a 45° angle. Stock up on blades for rough cutting and tight curves.

Table and radial-arm saws. Real timesavers when you're doing a lot of cutting, these stationary machines can handle such precision cuts as rabbets and dadoes. The 10-inch models can crosscut 4-by lumber.

A table saw, a circular saw that's permanently mounted in a table, has locking rip fences and miter gauges that make it the saw of choice for crosscutting short lengths of wood or for ripping.

A radial-arm saw is mounted on an arm above the table and drawn across the material. You can raise, lower, tilt, and even swivel the saw for miter cuts or narrow rip cuts. Though you can crosscut long pieces with ease, ripping—or even crosscutting—large sheets is difficult.

Miter box. If you're cutting trim or narrow stock with a handsaw, use a miter box to guide the saw at a fixed 45° or 90° angle.

The woodworker's tool kit

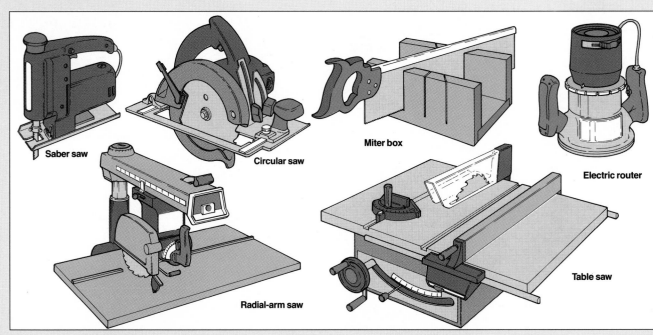

Saber saw · Circular saw · Miter box · Electric router · Radial-arm saw · Table saw

These power and specialty tools make clean, quick work of cutting, drilling, and finishing.

Electric router. A router equipped with the proper bit makes short work of dadoes, rabbets, and other grooves; it will also round or bevel the edges of a board and trim plastic laminate in a single pass. Straight, rabbeting, rounding-over, chamfer, cove, core-box, and laminate-trimming bits are the ones used in the projects.

Butt chisel. A sharp butt chisel helps pare notches, smooth the bottoms of grooves, and square rounded edges. A ¾-inch-wide blade is a good general-purpose size.

Jack plane. To smooth and square-up board faces and sides, choose a 14-inch-long jack plane.

Four-in-hand. Files and rasps shape and smooth wood to its final form. The four-in-hand has file and rasp teeth on both sides of its half-round profile.

Electric drill bits. The following bits produce larger holes and cleaner results than twist bits:

• *Spade bits* are the standard for holes from ⅜ to 1½ inches in diameter.

• *Brad point bits* (¼ to 1 inch) are preferred when appearance counts.

• *Hole saws* bore holes up to 4 inches in diameter.

• *Pilot bits* drill countersink and counterbore holes simultaneously.

• *Standard* and *Phillips screwdriver bits* drive screws effortlessly.

Spring and pipe clamps. Spring clamps excel at fixing guides for sawing. Buy a pair with at least 2-inch jaw capacity. For clamping tabletops and other wide assemblies, attach pipe clamps to any length of ½ or ¾-inch steel pipe that suits your job.

Ratchet and socket set. These are essential for tightening countersunk or counterbored bolts and lag screws. A ⅜-inch-drive ratchet and matching 12-point socket set is your best bet.

Belt and finishing sanders. Large belt sanders abrade wood quickly—they're best for shaping, rounding, and smoothing over large areas. For a finer finish, choose a finishing sander.

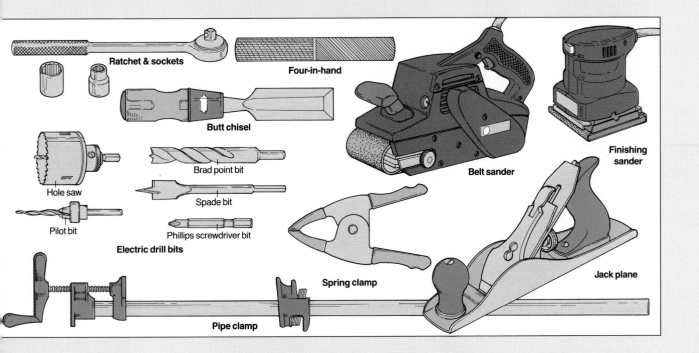

Ratchet & sockets

Four-in-hand

Butt chisel

Hole saw

Brad point bit

Spade bit

Pilot bit

Phillips screwdriver bit

Electric drill bits

Belt sander

Finishing sander

Spring clamp

Jack plane

Pipe clamp

The toddler is sitting on the fold-down stepstool. His bear buddy is trying the rocker side of the multiposition chair (the other chairs show two other positions). Both projects are easy to build.

Multiposition chair

This simple chair offers a small child a variety of options. Rotating it from one side to another changes it from a low rocker to a chair to a stepstool to a stool (see the illustrations below).

Construction is easy—simply cut out the parts, and glue and nail them together. You'll need only basic tools and a saber saw to build the chair.

You might also consider making several of the chairs at once. Since so little lumber is required for each chair, and since most suppliers sell the necessary 1 by 12s and 1 by 8s in minimum 6-foot lengths, you'll almost certainly have enough wood to build at least two. And because construction is so easy, a child can help you—perhaps in making one as a present for a friend or younger sibling.

1. Cut all pieces to size. Cut the curve along one long edge of each side **A** with a saber saw. (Note: The curve has a 35¾-inch radius. Use a yardstick tacked to a workbench to help you mark the arc.) Also cut the 86° angle at one end of each side **A** (see the detail drawing).

2. To make each hand-hold, drill a pair of 1-inch holes on 3-inch centers. Using a saber saw, cut from one hole to its mate.

3. Mark the placement of seat boards **B** on the sides where shown. Glue and nail the sides to one seat board, then to the other. Nail through the back of one board into the edge of the other as shown in the detail drawing, spacing nails every 3 inches.

4. Set the nails and fill the holes. Sand all surfaces, easing the edges, and finish.

Design: Don Vandervort.

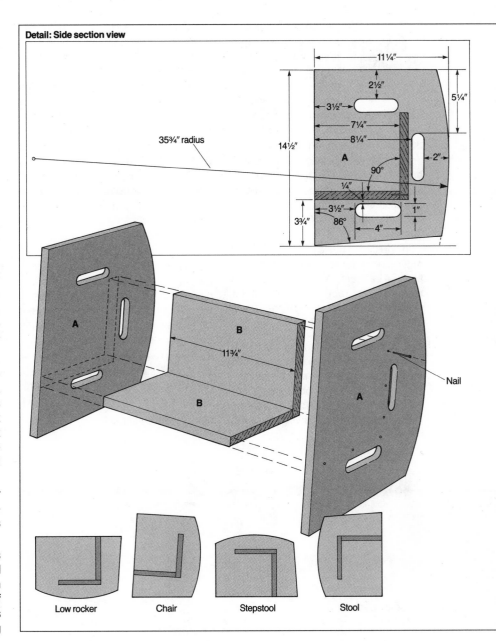

Detail: Side section view

Low rocker • Chair • Stepstool • Stool

BUY		TO MAKE	
Clear pine			
1	3-foot 1 by 12	2	Sides **A**: ¾" by 11¼" by 14½"
1	2-foot 1 by 8	2	Seat boards **B**: ¾" by 7¼" by 11¾"

MISCELLANEOUS
5d finishing nails • Wood glue • Wood putty • Clear penetrating oil finish

Fold-down stepstool

Any child will appreciate the boost this handy little stepstool can give. It's invaluable for reaching such adult-height items as water faucets, countertops, and cookie jars. The stepstool, pictured on page 30, is also light enough for easy toting.

Construction (from pine or fir, and hardwood dowel) is quick, inexpensive, and strong. Take special care to cut accurately, though, for this is the key to the stepstool's strength and easy operation.

In addition to basic tools, you'll find a radial-arm or table saw helpful for cutting the rabbets. A router, which can also cut the rabbets, is useful for rounding over edges—an important detail for a project such as this.

1. Cut all pieces to size. Cut the handhold in top **B** as shown in Detail 3. Cut the profiles in sides **A** and **D**; cut rabbets in **A** and **D** and drill three flat-bottomed holes in each side **A** and one in each side **D** (see the large drawing and Details 1 and 2). Drill holes for one brace **C** through sides **D** as shown. (Note: Sides **A** are paired and must mirror each other; likewise, sides **D**. Keep track of their proper orientation as you work.) Finally, mark all screw locations on sides **A** and **D** as shown, and drill countersink and pilot holes.

2. Assemble the pivoting step pieces **D**, **E**, and **F** with glue and screws. Putty the screw heads, then round over all edges; sand smooth. Fit one brace **C** through the holes in sides **D** and make sure that it rotates freely; if not, sand either the dowel or the holes.

3. Assemble the completed step, stool sides **A**, and remaining braces **C** with glue and screws as shown. Fit top **B** in place. Mark the position and angle of the rip cut on its forward edge (see large drawing). Cut the top and fasten it with glue and screws as shown.

4. Round over all remaining edges, fill the holes, sand carefully, and finish. (We used two coats of satin polyurethane for a durable, washable surface.)

Design: Bill Oetinger.

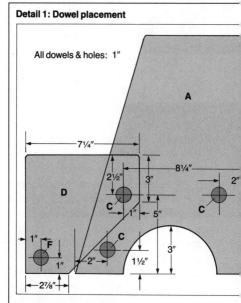

Detail 1: Dowel placement

All dowels & holes: 1"

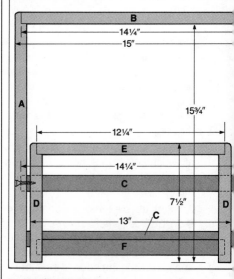

Detail 2: Front elevation

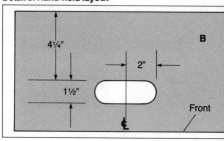

Detail 3: Hand-hold layout

BUY		TO MAKE		
Clear pine or fir				
1	3-foot 1 by 12	2	Stool sides **A**:	¾" by 11¼" by 15¾"
1	4-foot 1 by 8	1	Stool top **B**:	¾" by 7¼" by 14¼"
		2	Step sides **D**:	¾" by 7¼" by 7½"
		1	Step top **E**:	¾" by 7¼" by 12¼"
Hardwood dowel				
1	5-foot or 2 3-foot 1-inch-diameter pieces	3	Braces **C**:	1" by 14¼"
		1	Brace **F**:	1" by 12¼"

MISCELLANEOUS
24 drywall screws, 1¼" by #6 • Wood glue • Wood putty • Clear nontoxic finish

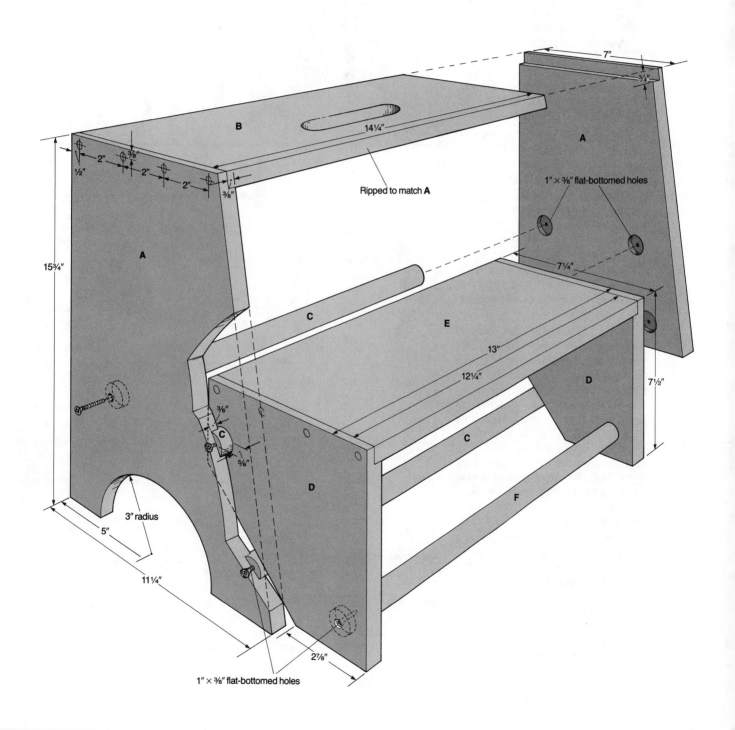

B

A

14¼"

Ripped to match **A**

2"

⅜"

½"

2"

2"

⅜"

7"

¾"

A

1" × ⅜" flat-bottomed holes

15¾"

A

C

7¼"

E

13"

12¼"

D

7½"

C

⅜"

C

1"

⅝"

D

C

3" radius

5"

D

F

11¼"

2⅞"

1" × ⅜" flat-bottomed holes

33

Chair menagerie

Here's a happy collection of animals guaranteed to capture any child's imagination. You can build this set of chairs with just basic tools and a saber saw. You'll need a steady hand for the paint job, but the patterns are simple and even beginners should get good results.

1. Cut all pieces to size (to transfer grid patterns, see page 36). Cut finger holes in seat backs **E** and drill countersink and pilot holes in cleats **D** and **F** (see Detail 1). Round over all exposed edges, either by hand or with a router and ½-inch rounding-over bit set ⅜ inch high. Putty all plywood edges and sand all parts.

2. Glue and nail elements **B** to profiles **A**, cleats **D** to seats **C**, and cleats **F** to seat backs **E**. Set the nails and fill the holes; then sand.

3. Screw (do not glue) the seats and backs to profiles **A** without drilling pilot holes in **A** (set the seat height to suit your child, but stay within the seat-mounting area indicated on each plan). For the nonrocking chairs, keep the seats level and the backs angled as shown in Detail 1. On the swan rocker, angle the backward-facing seat 5° to 10° and attach the back at a 90° angle to the seat. To guard against tipping over backward, fasten the seat back as close to the rear edge of the swan's neck as possible.

4. With the chairs assembled, paint the background color on all surfaces. Let the paint dry; then disassemble the chairs. Paint the designs as shown, either freehand or using a paper stencil attached with spray mounting adhesive—let the adhesive dry before applying the stencil. After the paint dries, reassemble the chairs, this time using glue as well as screws.

Design: Sandra Popovich & Scott Fitzgerrell.

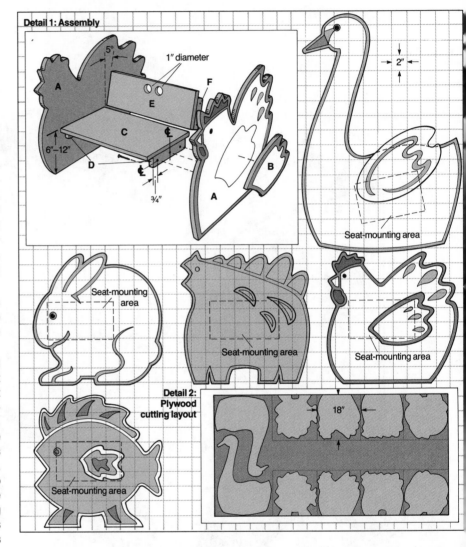

BUY		TO MAKE		
Birch plywood (shop grade)				
1	¾-inch 4 by 8-foot sheet	10	Animal profiles **A** (see Detail 2)	
			Applied elements **B** (cut from scrap)	
Pine or fir				
1	6-foot 1 by 10	5	Seats **C**:	¾" by 9¼" by 12"
1	6-foot 1 by 6	5	Seat backs **E**:	¾" by 5½" by 12"
1	10-foot 1 by 2	10	Cleats **D**:	¾" by 1½" by 8"
		10	Cleats **F**:	¾" by 1½" by 3¾"

MISCELLANEOUS
4d nails • 50 drywall screws, 1¼" by #6 • Wood glue • Wood putty • Nontoxic enamel

Fish, fowl, swan, bunny, or dinosaur—it's hard to choose a seat from such an appealing group. You can mix or match designs and adjust seat heights to fit the child.

MARKING, CUTTING & DRILLING

Marking, cutting, and drilling are fundamental to virtually every woodworking project. Here are some tips to help you achieve clean, accurate results the first time around.

Caution: Whenever you use power tools, be sure to wear safety goggles.

Layout techniques

For most layout tasks, you need only a tape measure, combination square, and pencil. Add more specialized tools—such as a carpenter's square, chalkline, or compass—as you need them.

One note: The symbol ℄, used on some project drawings, indicates the center line of the element shown.

Marking straight lines. When measuring cutting lines on solid lumber, lay the tape along the edge of the material and always pull the tape taut against the end hook. Mark the distance, then draw the line with the help of a try or combination square (make sure the thickness of the line lies on the waste side of the material).

Measure and mark wide sheet materials at several points, then connect the marks with a carpenter's square or chalkline. To use a chalkline, pull out the cord and stretch it between the end marks. Then, holding the chalkline toward one end, lift it and release quickly so it snaps down sharply.

If you're cutting out several identical components, mark and cut the first, check it, then use it as a pattern to trace each additional piece.

Marking circles and arcs. A simple compass draws limited circles and arcs; wing dividers, available in larger sizes, are more precise. For large curves and circles, make a beam compass: tack one end of a thin board or yardstick to the material, hold a pencil at the desired radius, and pivot.

Transferring grids. To transfer gridded patterns, mark the edges of the material at the scale indicated in the plan and connect the marks with straight lines. Mark the intersections of a curving line from square to square, then connect the marks with freehand lines, or use a French or flexible curve (available in art or drafting supply stores).

For clean cuts

The number of teeth per inch along a saw blade determines the kind of cut it makes. The more teeth, the smoother—but slower—the cut. To hide the splintering that occurs where saw teeth

Three techniques for clean cutting

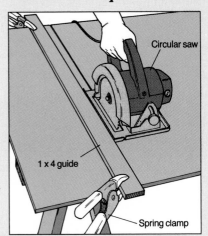

For long, straight cuts, clamp a scrap guide to the material and let the saw ride against it.

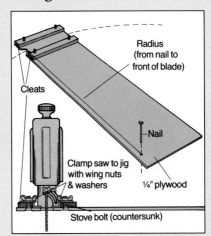

Cut large arcs and circles with a saber saw and jig. Adapt the basic design to fit your saw's baseplate.

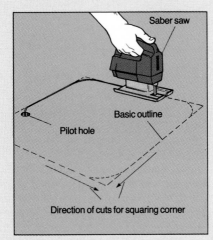

To make rectangular cutouts, drill a pilot hole for the saw's blade, cut the basic outline, then square each corner.

exit, cut with the good side *up* when using a handsaw, table saw, or when crosscutting with a radial-arm saw; if you're using a portable circular saw or saber saw, or ripping with a radial-arm saw, cut with the good side *down*.

Sawing straight lines. The key to sawing straight is using a guide. If your saw doesn't have one, improvise a guide from a *straight* length of scrap lumber and two clamps, as shown on the facing page. Cushion the jaws of the clamp to protect the work. Be sure to allow for the thickness of the blade—or "kerf"—when cutting; otherwise, the finished piece will be too short.

Sawing curves, circles, and cutouts. Arcs, curves, and circles are all jobs for a saber saw. When cutting curves, use the finest blade you can. The tighter the curve, the more slowly you should cut.

You can execute a circle with a radius up to 6 or 7 inches with the help of a circle guide. To cut larger arcs and circles, such as the rockers for the projects on pages 6–9 and the wheels for the wagon bed on pages 78–81, try building your own saber saw jig from a straight board or plywood strip, pivoting pin (such as a nail), and some type of sturdy attachment between the jig and baseplate (see facing page).

For cutouts inside a panel, first drill a pilot hole in the waste area for the saber saw blade, as shown on the facing page. Cut the basic outline. If the corners must be square, round them off on the first pass, then finish by sawing into the corners. If they must be tightly curved, first drill the arcs with an electric drill and brad point bit or hole saw (see page 29).

Drilling tips

Be sure to clamp down small materials before drilling. If possible, match the drill speed to the job: highest speeds for small bits and softwoods, slowest speeds for large bits and hardwoods. When drilling large holes in tough materials, first make a small lead hole.

Drilling pilot holes. Screws require predrilled pilot holes in all but the softest materials. For *drywall screws,* use a 3/32-inch bit for #6 screws, a 1/8-inch bit for #8 screws. In softwoods, drill half as deep as the screw's length, two-thirds to three-quarters the length in hardwoods. For *woodscrews,* pick a drill bit the diameter of the screw's unthreaded shank and drill as deep as the shank's length.

Flathead screws are typically countersunk to sit flush or just below the surface; often, they're counterbored, then covered with putty or a wood plug (see below). To drill these holes, choose either a second bit (5/16-inch for #6 drywall screws, 3/8-inch for #8) or a special pilot bit (see page 29).

Solving drilling problems. To drill straight holes in a board's face, use a portable drill stand; a doweling jig works well along edges (see below). Or drill a scrap block and then use the block for a guide.

To keep the back side of the wood from breaking away, lay or clamp a wood scrap firmly against the back of your work and drill through the piece into the scrap.

To stop a drill bit at a specified depth, use a pilot bit, wrap electrical or masking tape around the bit at the correct depth, or buy a stop collar specially designed for the purpose.

Pilot hole profiles

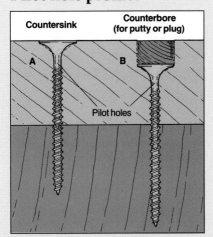

Drilling screw holes: Countersink hole (A) lets the screw sit at or just below the surface; counterbore hole (B) hides screw.

Guides for drilling

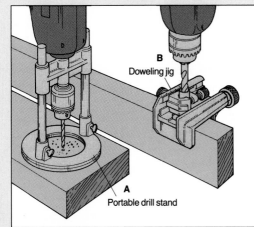

To keep a drill bit moving in the right path, use a portable drill stand (A) or a doweling jig (B).

Modular design is the key to these two storage systems: each is basically two large cabinets connected by smaller cabinets or shelves. The closet organizer at left can be customized to fit available closet space. The modular wall unit at right can tame the most unruly room.

Modular wall system

Order from chaos—that's what this modular wall system can create. The adjustable shelves and rolling cart store treasures, books, and toys neatly and accessibly.

The wall system is made of two tall cabinets joined by two small cabinets. Adjustable shelves between the cabinets, as well as inside them, offer plenty of flexible storage. The rolling cart, garaged between the two tall cabinets, provides handy storage for laundry or oversized toys.

Components are built from standard-dimension softwood and birch

BUY		TO MAKE	
Clear pine or Douglas fir			
1	4-foot 1 by 3	2	Toekicks **F**: ¾″ by 2½″ by 23¼″
4	6-foot 1 by 12s	4	Uprights **A**: ¾″ by 11¼″ by 72″
2	12-foot 1 by 12s	10	Fixed shelves **B**: ¾″ by 11¼″ by 24″
1	10-foot 1 by 12	4	Sides **C**: ¾″ by 11¼″ by 12¾″
		2	Adjustable shelves **H**: ¾″ by 11¼″ by 24½″
2	10-foot 1 by 12s	10	Adjustable shelves **G**: ¾″ by 11¼″ by 23″
Birch plywood (shop grade)			
1	¼-inch 4 by 8-foot sheet		Backs **D** and **E** (see Detail 1)
1	¾-inch 4 by 4-foot sheet		Cart pieces **I–M** (see Detail 1)

MISCELLANEOUS

48 shelf pegs • 4 1¾″ plate-mounted casters with screws • 5d finishing nails
2d nails • 4 woodscrews, 2½″ by #8
Wood glue • Wood putty • Clear penetrating oil finish
8 carriage bolts, ¼″ by 1¼″, with nuts and washers

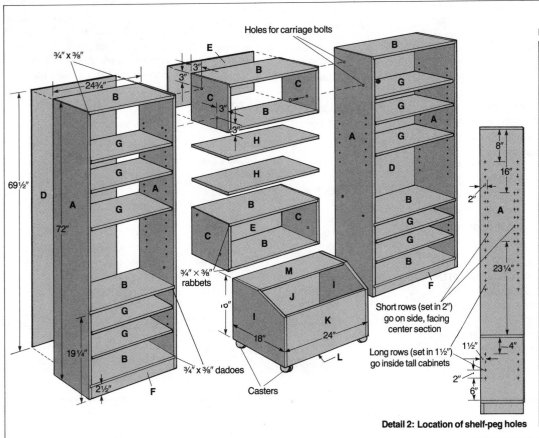

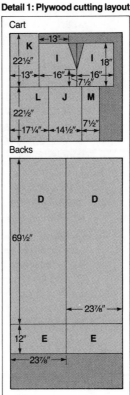

. . . Modular wall system

plywood. In addition to basic tools, you'll need a radial-arm or table saw for cutting rabbets and dadoes.

Refer to the drawings on page 39 as you work.

1. Cut all pieces to size (see Detail 1). Rabbet and dado uprights **A** and rabbet sides **C** where shown.

2. Label each upright **A** to remember its position. Mark for placement of shelf-peg holes (see Detail 2) and drill. (Note: The two center uprights are drilled on both sides. The holes on the inside of the cabinets are 1½ inches from the edges. The holes on the outside are spaced 2 inches from the edges so they're offset from the holes on the inside. The vertical spacing for all holes is 2 inches; the depth is ½ inch.)

3. To assemble the cabinets, glue and nail uprights **A** and sides **C** to fixed shelves **B** with 5d nails spaced 3 inches apart; set the nails. Letting backs **D** and **E** overlap the uprights 5/16 inch and letting **E** overlap shelves **B** 3/8 inch, attach the backs with glue and 2d nails spaced 5 inches apart. Attach toekicks **F** with glue and 5d nails; set the nails. Drill counterbores and holes for carriage bolts in sides **C**, align with the center uprights, and mark and drill counterbores and holes in the uprights.

4. Glue and nail together cart pieces **I–M**, using 5d nails spaced 3 inches apart. Screw casters to the bottom.

5. Fill holes, sand, and finish.

6. Stand up the tall cabinets in place and bolt the small cabinets to them. Add shelf pegs and adjustable shelves **G** and **H**. Using two woodscrews for each, fasten the tall cabinets to wall studs through the top of the backs. Store the cart in the center section.

Design: Don Vandervort.

Closet organizer

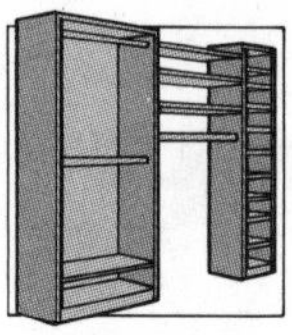

Standard closets waste space when used to store children's clothes. Blouses, shirts, and pants often hang out of a child's reach on the closet pole, leaving unused space below.

This closet organizer, pictured on page 38, is a simple adaptation of the modular wall system. It offers two levels of hanging space, the lower one easily reached by children. In addition, the organizer presents a column of shelves for shoes, sweaters, and such.

The unit shown is for a closet about 5 feet wide. For closets of other sizes, you can change the dimensions of the shelves and closet poles that connect the two cabinets—and even the cabinets themselves. (However, don't span more than 4 feet with the closet poles.)

1. Cut all lumber to size except center shelves **L** and closet poles **H** and **I**. Rabbet and dado uprights **A** where shown.

2. Label each upright **A** to remember its position; then mark for placement of the ½-inch-deep shelf-peg holes (as shown in the detail drawings) and drill. (Note: The two center uprights are drilled on both sides; the holes on the inside of the narrow cabinet are spaced 1½ inches from the edges so they're offset from those on the outside.)

3. To assemble the cabinets, glue and nail uprights **A** to fixed shelves **B** and **C** with 5d finishing nails; set the nails. Letting backs **J** and **K** overlap the uprights 3/8 inch, attach the backs with glue and 2d nails spaced 5 inches apart. Attach toekicks **F** and **G** with glue and 5d nails; set the nails.

4. Fill holes, sand, and finish.

5. Stand up the cabinets in the closet. Measure the distance between them and cut shelves **L** and closet poles **H** and **I** to fit, allowing for pole brackets and shelf pegs. Mount the brackets on the sides of the cabinets. Add closet poles **H** and **I**, shelf pegs, and adjustable shelves **D**, **E**, and **L**. Using two woodscrews for each, fasten the cabinets to wall studs through the top of the backs.

Design: Don Vandervort.

BUY		TO MAKE		
Clear pine or Douglas fir				
1	3-foot 1 by 3	1	Toekick **F**:	¾″ by 2½″ by 23¼″
		1	Toekick **G**:	¾″ by 2½″ by 11¼″
4	6-foot 1 by 12s	4	Uprights **A**:	¾″ by 11¼″ by 72″
1	8-foot 1 by 12	2	Fixed shelves **B**:	¾″ by 11¼″ by 24″
		2	Fixed shelves **C**:	¾″ by 11¼″ by 12″
2	8-foot 1 by 12s	8	Adjustable shelves **D**:	¾″ by 11¼″ by 10⅞″
		1	Adjustable shelf **E**:	¾″ by 11¼″ by 22⅞″
		3	Adjustable shelves **L**:	Cut to fit (up to 24″)
Closet pole round				
1	6-foot by 1⅜-inch diameter	2	Closet poles **H**:	Cut to fit
		1	Closet pole **I**:	Cut to fit (up to 24″)
Birch plywood (shop grade)				
1	¼-inch 4 by 8-foot sheet	1	Back **J**:	¼″ by 24″ by 69½″
		1	Back **K**:	¼″ by 12″ by 69½″

MISCELLANEOUS
3 pairs closet pole brackets • 48 shelf pegs • 5d finishing nails
2d nails • 4 woodscrews, 2½″ by #8
Wood glue • Wood putty • Clear penetrating oil finish

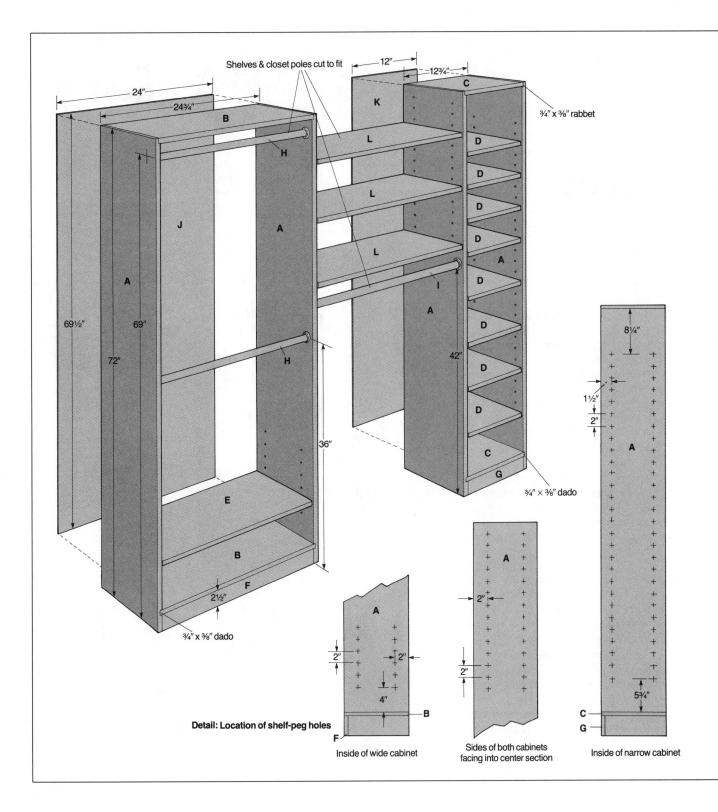

Shelves & closet poles cut to fit

24"

24¾"

B

H

12"

12¾"

K

L

C

¾" x ⅜" rabbet

D

D

D

D

A

D

A

J

A

L

L

A

I

A

¾" x ⅜" dado

8¼"

1½"

2"

A

69½"

69"

72"

42"

36"

H

E

B

F

2½"

¾" x ⅜" dado

A

2"

C

G

5¾"

C

G

A

2"

2"

4"

2"

B

F

Detail: Location of shelf-peg holes

Inside of wide cabinet

Sides of both cabinets facing into center section

Inside of narrow cabinet

Maple table & stools

This strikingly simple playroom set is easy to build if you have the right tools and materials. Because the leg attachment needs to be very strong, you must use maple or another dense, split-resistant hardwood and make the mating surfaces absolutely flat.

We show laminated maple countertop for the table and edge-joined maple boards for the stools, but the materials can be used interchangeably. You can also vary the sizes of both the tops and the legs. In fact, it's best to customize their dimensions to suit both the child and the materials available. You'll need a plug cutter to cut the plugs.

1. Cut table and stool tops **A**, **C**, and **E** to size, or make the tops by edge-joining individual boards (see page 45). Round the corners as shown. Cut legs **B**, **D**, and **F** to length, making sure all cuts are square and mating surfaces are absolutely flat. Round over all long edges as shown (a router with a ½-inch or ¾-inch rounding-over bit is ideal for this).

2. Mark leg locations on the underside of each top, and mark screw locations on the upper surface (see Detail 1). For each table leg only, add a third screw, dead center. With the legs held in position, drill counterbore and pilot holes as shown in Detail 2. Glue the mating surfaces and screws, then drive in the screws (a hand brace or an electric drill with a screwdriver bit is extremely helpful here). Cut ½-inch-diameter walnut plugs and glue them over the screws.

3. When the glue has cured, trim the plugs a little "proud" of the surface, then sand them flush. Finally, sand all surfaces and finish. (Note: Maple countertop often comes pre-oiled. If you want other than an oil finish, you'll need to sand down to bare wood.)

Design: Robert Zumwalt.

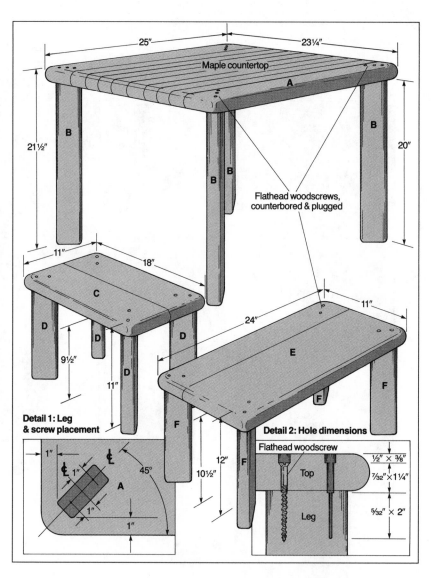

BUY		TO MAKE		
Maple (or other hardwood)				
Countertop or random-width boards (see text), 1½ inches thick	1	Table top	**A**:	23¼″ by 25″ (or to suit)
	1	Stool top	**C**:	11″ by 18″ (or to suit)
	1	Stool top	**E**:	11″ by 24″ (or to suit)
Random-length 2 by 4s	4	Table legs	**B**:	20″ (or to suit)
	4	Stool legs	**D**:	9½″ (or to suit)
	4	Stool legs	**F**:	10½″ (or to suit)

MISCELLANEOUS

¾-inch walnut (or other hardwood in a contrasting color) sufficient for 28 ½″ plugs
28 flathead woodscrews, 3½″ by #12 • Wood glue • Clear nontoxic finish

Elegant in its simplicity, this sturdy playset will stand up to years of use. Solid hardwood and careful construction are the essentials for its success.

JOINERY

Joinery—the craft of assembling pieces of wood accurately and securely—is a crucial step for the success of your project.

The basic joints

The following guide explains the use and construction of the basic joints used in our projects.

Butt joints. To make these simple joints, first check that the mating surfaces are smooth and flat. Then butt one board against the other, glue and clamp, and fasten with screws, nails, or dowels (see facing page).

Miter joints. Two pieces cut and joined at a 45° angle make up the miter joint. Radial-arm and table saws have adjustable blades and guides that make mitering a cinch. If you're cutting miters with a handsaw, a miter box (see page 28) will aid you enormously.

Dado joints. Dadoes—rectangular grooves along a board's face—make strong, rigid joints widely used to construct drawers and join shelves to uprights.

Power tools work best for cutting dadoes. An electric router equipped with a straight bit smooths the cut as it goes (clamp a guide onto the work for the baseplate to follow).

To cut dadoes with a standard power saw blade, set the blade at the correct depth, cut the borders (using a guide), and make repeated passes through the waste wood until it virtually falls out. Finish each groove with light chisel strokes. Dado blades, available for both table and radial-arm saws, can cut a dado in one pass.

Rabbet joints. Rabbets, grooves cut along board edges, are commonly used for corners. The rabbets minimize the amount of visible end and edge grain, and because of the extra surface they offer for gluing, the joints are very strong.

It's nearly impossible to execute a long rabbet with a handsaw. Instead, use either a router fitted with a self-piloting rabbeting bit or a stationary power saw equipped with a dado or standard blade. If you're using the standard blade, cut the inside border first, then remove the waste as described above for dado joints.

To make a *stopped* rabbet, first drill the stopped end of the rabbet to the correct depth and width, then cut the rabbet. Square off the stopped rabbet's rounded end with a sharp chisel.

Doweling

Dowels don't make joints, they reinforce them. For *through* doweling, such as for the rocking lion on pages 6–7 and the table and desk on pages 90–91 and 94–95, choose a drill bit the same diameter as the dowel and bore holes slightly shallower than the dow-

Close-up of the four basic joints

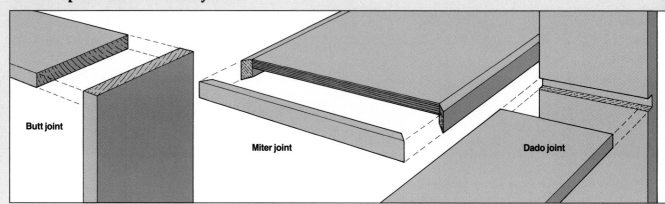

Butt joint

Miter joint

Dado joint

Butt, miter, dado, and rabbet are the basic joints used to assemble pieces of wood. Techniques for fastening the joints after they're cut are explained on the facing page.

el's length. Cut small lengthwise grooves in the dowel so excess glue can escape. Then coat the dowel with glue and, using a mallet or lightweight hammer, tap it into place. To finish the dowel, see at right.

Blind doweling is often used to edge-join boards when making wide panels, as required for the rocking horse on pages 8–9 and the table and stools on pages 42–43. Here, the dowels don't show; the trick is drilling straight, matching holes in the two pieces to be joined. You can do this in one of two ways. Either lay the two surfaces face to face and mark across both edges at once, then drill both holes slightly deeper than half the dowel length; or drill one hole, insert a dowel center in the hole, and press the pieces together. The dowel center marks where the second hole should be drilled. Glue the dowels as for through doweling.

A doweling jig (see page 37) makes the whole process much easier and more accurate.

Fastening techniques

Tips for fastening joints neatly and securely appear below. For information on fasteners, see page 17.

Gluing and clamping. Before applying any adhesive, always test the fit of the pieces to be glued by assembling them while dry. Make any necessary adjustments at this point.

Make sure that the pieces to be glued are clean and dry. Spread the adhesive evenly on both surfaces to be joined. The end grain of wood, which is usually more porous, may absorb extra glue; add a second coat.

Most adhesives allow for some adjustment of pieces during assembly. Check angles with a square and adjust them before the glue sets. Temporary braces made from scrap wood can be tacked on to fix angles.

When clamping, cushion the jaws of the clamp with pieces of scrap wood to avoid marring the material. Tighten the clamps until snug (but not too tight).

"Finishing" your fasteners. In most cases, fasteners need to be driven flush or concealed below the surface.

Drive finishing nails within ⅛ inch of the surface with a hammer, then tap the nail head below the surface with the point of a nailset. Conceal the resulting hole with wood putty.

Flathead and drywall screws can be countersunk or counterbored (see page 37) and covered with putty or plugs. Cut plugs from matching or contrasting wood with a plug cutter, available from many woodworking retailers.

Bolts and lag screws look best when counterbored. To drill the counterbore hole, use a bit that's the same diameter as the washer below the bolt head or nut. Drive the bolt home with a ratchet and socket.

To finish off dowel ends, trim them with a handsaw or sharp chisel, then sand them flush with the surface.

Doweling techniques

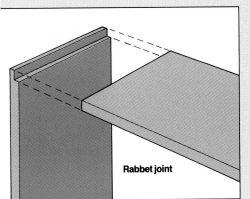

Rabbet joint

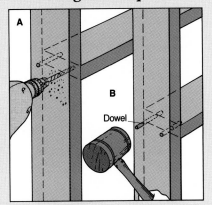

Through doweling reinforces basic joints. First drill the holes (A), then coat the dowels with glue and tap them in (B).

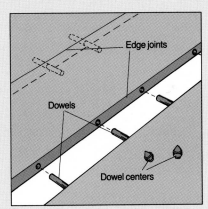

Blind doweling strengthens edge-joined boards. The trick is lining up the holes; dowel centers can help.

Baltic birch plywood and interlocking construction make this playset strong, lightweight, and durable; country-style pierced and painted decorations make it delightful. You can build the set from a single sheet of plywood using only basic tools and a saber saw.

Slot-together playroom set

If you prefer to spend time as a decorative painter rather than as a furniture builder, this project is for you. You can mark, cut, and assemble the entire playroom set in a day. The real fun, though, is painting the completed set.

The simple charm of folk-style furniture is evoked in each piece, and each provides plenty of "blank canvas" for decorative painting. You can use the handpainted country patterns we show or develop your own motifs. The set is ideally suited for stencil work, découpage, or the like. Each piece also knocks down easily for storage or even for shipping, which raises the interesting possibility of building the set as a gift for someone far away.

You'll need only a saber saw and basic tools; a table saw will make short work of cutting the pieces, and a router is helpful for rounding over edges, but neither is required. Refer to the drawings on pages 48–49 as you work.

Marking & cutting

1. Transfer the patterns shown in Drawing 2 to heavy paper, using the grid-enlargement technique outlined on page 36. If you wish to decorate your set as shown, transfer the leaf and apple patterns to graph paper. Cut all patterns.

2. Trace the plywood patterns onto the plywood in the areas shown in the detail drawing, then cut all pieces to size. Make angled cuts at the top of all trestles: 82° for the table trestles, 77° for the others. Cut all slots and the piercedwork apples. Round the corners of the tabletop and benchtops as shown in Drawing 1. Round over all edges, including the edges of the apple cutouts (if you have a router, use a ⅜-inch rounding-over bit set ¼ inch high). Don't round over the angled trestle tops or the slots in the trestles and chair seats.

Assembling the table & bench

1. Using stretchers **A** as patterns, mark and cut the angles at each end of bench cleat **C** and the angles at the ends of table cleats **C**. Assemble stretcher **A**, trestles **B**, and cleats **C** with screws (see Drawing 1); use ⁹⁄₃₂-inch pilot holes and countersink the screws. For the second table cleat **C**, drill counterbore holes where shown and ⅛-inch pilot holes for the 2½-inch screws.

2. Invert tops **D** and the **ABC** assemblies; center and mark each **ABC** assembly on its top. Remove the **ABC** assemblies and apply glue to cleats **C** only; then fasten the **ABC** assemblies to the tops with five 2d nails through each cleat, driving the nails flush (do not set the heads).

Assembling the chair

1. For each chair, make cleat **C** by ripping the 1 by 4 as shown in Drawing 1 (side view). Using stretcher **A** as a pattern, mark and cut the angles at each end of the cleat. Assemble stretcher **A**, trestles **B**, and cleat **C** as shown, drilling countersink and ⁹⁄₃₂-inch pilot holes for the 1¼-inch screws.

2. With a file or rasp, cut back the front underside edge of the slot in chair seat **D** until chair back **E** can be angled at 77° (see Drawing 1). With all parts inverted and correctly positioned, mark the position of the **ABC** assembly on the underside of the seat; be sure chair back **E** fits snugly against cleat **C**. Remove the back and the **ABC** assembly, and apply glue to cleat **C** only; then fasten the **ABC** assembly to seat **D** with 2d nails through the cleat, driving the nails flush (do not set the heads). Using a 1¼-inch screw, fasten back **E** to cleat **C** as shown.

Finishing the set

To finish your set as shown, you'll need 2-inch alphabet stencils and ½-inch number stencils (both available at stationery stores); enamel undercoat and flat blue enamel; red, white, green, and brown artist's acrylics or oils; and matte varnish. Be sure all paints and the varnish are nontoxic.

1. Disassemble each piece. Apply undercoat and one or two coats of blue enamel to tops **D**, seats **D**, and backs **E**. When the paint is dry, apply a coat of matte varnish to all surfaces of each piece. Allow the varnish to dry thoroughly.

BUY		TO MAKE		
Baltic birch plywood				
1	½-inch 8 by 4-foot sheet	Pieces **A**, **B**, **D**, and **E** (see plywood cutting layout)		
Pine or fir (grade to suit)				
1	8-foot 1 by 3	2	Table cleats **C**:	¾" by 2½" (see text for length)
		1	Bench cleat **C**:	¾" by 2½" (see text for length)
1	2-foot 1 by 4	2	Chair cleats **C**:	¾" (see text for width and length)
MISCELLANEOUS				
29 drywall screws, 1¼" by #6 • 3 drywall screws, 2½" by #8 • 2d finishing nails				
Wood glue • Finish (see text)				

2. Using the photo and Drawing 2 as guides, tape the leaf and apple patterns in position, then trace lightly around each pattern with a pencil. Remove the patterns and, using the photo for reference, paint in the red, white, and green portions of the designs. Let the paint dry; then use a little brown to create shadowing on the apples, and give each one a white highlight as well.

3. When all the paint is dry, tape the alphabet and number stencils in place and paint in each character with red. Paint all exposed plywood edges red as shown. Let the paint dry.

If you have a steady hand, box in the tabletop and benchtop apples with light, ruled pencil lines, then paint over your marks with red (see the photo for guidance).

4. After all the decorative painting is completely dry, apply two coats of matte varnish to protect your work. Follow the manufacturer's instructions, but omit sanding between coats.

Design: Pamela Silin Palmer & Karen Kariya of Faunus Designs.

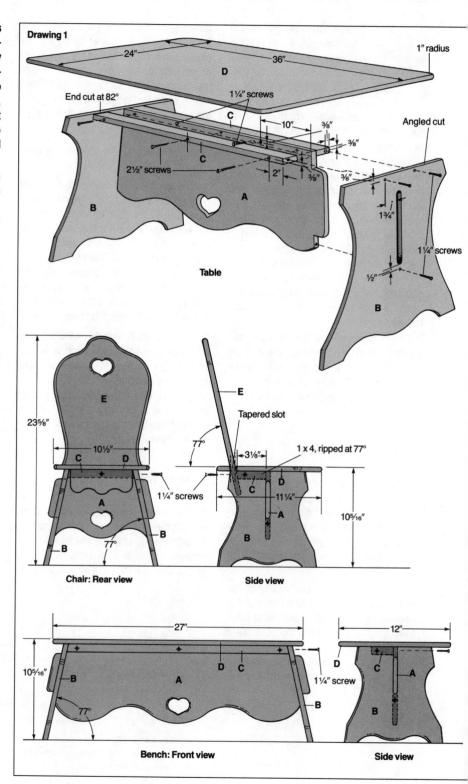

Drawing 1

Table

Chair: Rear view

Side view

Bench: Front view

Side view

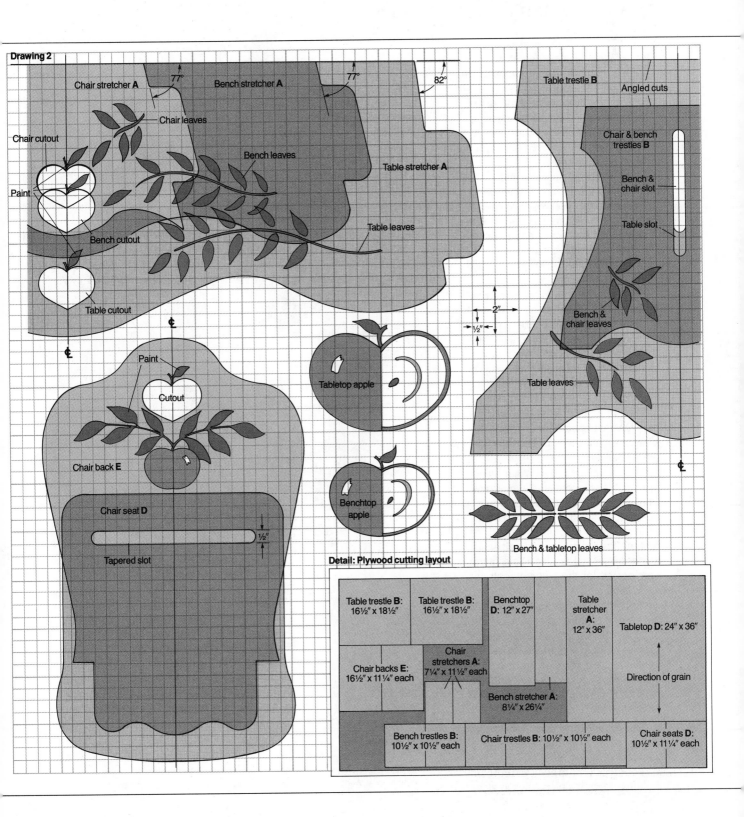

Drawing 2

Chair stretcher **A**

77°

Bench stretcher **A**

77°

82°

Table trestle **B**

Angled cuts

Chair leaves

Chair cutout

Bench leaves

Paint

Table stretcher **A**

Chair & bench trestles **B**

Bench & chair slot

Table slot

Bench cutout

Table leaves

Table cutout

Bench & chair leaves

₵

₵

Table leaves

Paint

Cutout

Tabletop apple

Chair back **E**

2"

½"

Chair seat **D**

Benchtop apple

Bench & tabletop leaves

½"

Tapered slot

Detail: Plywood cutting layout

Table trestle **B**: 16½" x 18½"	Table trestle **B**: 16½" x 18½"	Benchtop **D**: 12" x 27"	Table stretcher **A**: 12" x 36"	Tabletop **D**: 24" x 36"
Chair backs **E**: 16½" x 11¼" each	Chair stretchers **A**: 7¼" x 11½" each		Direction of grain	
		Bench stretcher **A**: 8¼" x 26¼"		
Bench trestles **B**: 10½" x 10½" each	Chair trestles **B**: 10½" x 10½" each			Chair seats **D**: 10½" x 11¼" each

Scandinavian rocking cradle

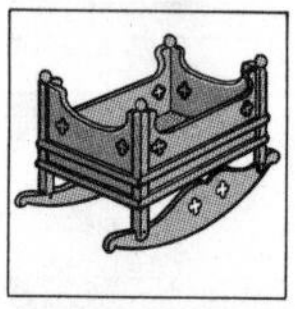

This pretty cradle takes its design from traditional Norwegian folk cradles. It features graceful curves, pierced decoration, and a soothing end-to-end rocking motion that mimics the rise and fall of a boat on a gentle swell.

We've specified clear pine and a clear finish, but there are many other possibilities you might consider. Old Norwegian cradles were often painted or were finished with both paint and a natural finish. Sometimes, a decorative band of carved or painted patterns was added at the base of the cradle.

Our design allows for all these possibilities. For example, you might want to paint or stain your cradle—translucent colors that let the grain show through are especially attractive. If you're fond of stenciling, carving, or decorative painting, consider attaching the band at the bottom of the cradle.

Even though we've specified clear pine for best appearance, almost any kiln-dried grade will do; just select the pieces carefully.

The cradle is sized to take a standard 18 by 36-inch cradle mattress. Construction is simple and requires only basic tools. A radial-arm or table saw, or a router, is helpful for cutting the rabbets; the router also makes it easier to round over edges. Use a hole saw or Forstner bit for the pierced quatrefoil decorations.

The only tricky cut in the project is the stopped rabbet in each post; see page 44 for instructions. Take special care in cutting and rabbeting all the cradle pieces. Opposite sides must match exactly, and the rocker bottoms must have identical curves for a smooth rocking action.

1. Cut all pieces to size. Transfer the cutting patterns to heavy paper (see page 36) and cut them out. Then use the paper patterns to mark and cut both the left and right-side profiles in sides

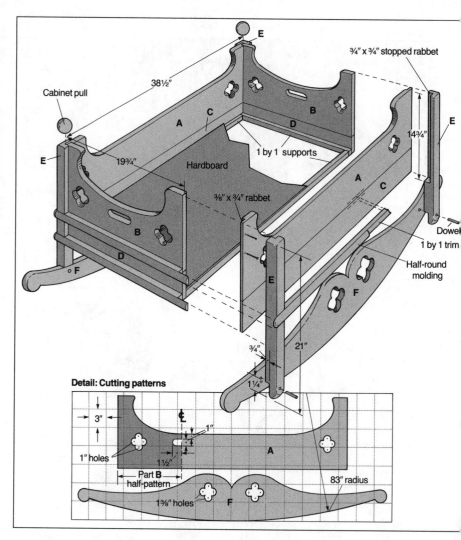

BUY			TO MAKE		
Clear pine					
2	6-foot 1 by 12s		2 Sides	**A**:	¾″ by 11¼″ by 38½″
			2 Ends	**B**:	¾″ by 11¼″ by 19¾″
2	6-foot 1 by 4s		2 Sides	**C**:	¾″ by 3½″ by 38½″
			2 Ends	**D**:	¾″ by 3½″ by 19¾″
1	8-foot 2 by 2		4 Posts	**E**:	1½″ by 1½″ by 21″
1	10-foot 1 by 8		2 Rockers	**F**:	¾″ by 7¼″ by 51″
6	6-foot 1 by 1s		Trim and hardboard supports (see text)		

MISCELLANEOUS

4 pieces of ¾″ half-round pine molding, each 6′ long • 9″ of ½″ hardwood dowel
4 cabinet pulls, 1½″ in diameter • 1 piece of ¼″ hardboard, 18¾″ by 36¾″
3d finishing nails • Wood glue • Clear nontoxic finish • Cradle mattress, 18″ by 36″

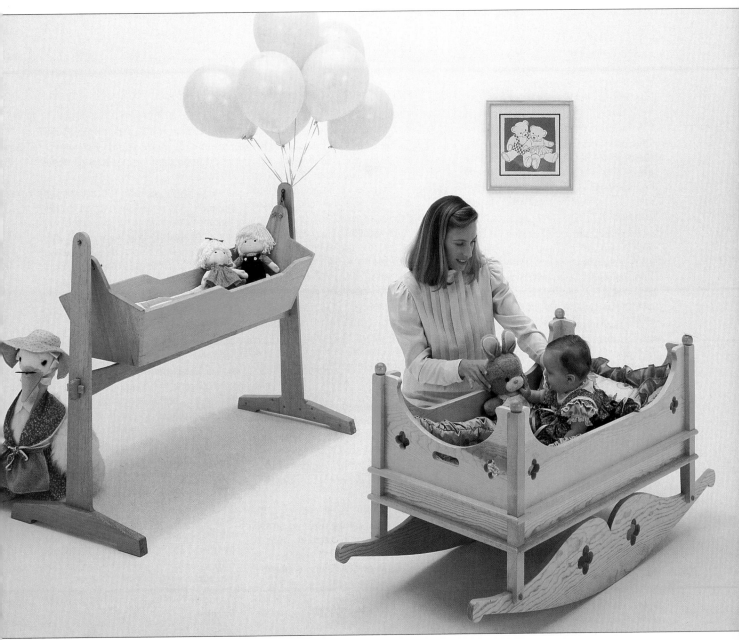

These two cradles are based on timeless designs from two different cultures: at left, a graceful, Shaker-style hanging cradle made from clear fir; at right, a cozy, Scandinavian rocking cradle made from clear pine. Each is direct and simple in both concept and construction.

...Scandinavian rocking cradle

A, ends **B**, and rockers **F** (flip the paper patterns over to get the right-side profiles of ends **B**). Mark and cut quatrefoils in **A**, **B**, and **F**. Rabbet sides **A** and **C** and posts **E**. Round the bottoms of the posts as shown and cut hand-holds in ends **B**.

2. Glue and nail together sides **A** and ends **B**; repeat for **C** and **D**. Square-up the resulting frames and let the glue cure. Glue posts **E** to the **CD** box, then add the **AB** box, gluing it to posts **E** and the **CD** box. Let the glue cure.

3. Measure and cut the 1 by 1s and half-round trim to fit as shown, allowing the longer half-rounds to extend ½ inch beyond the edge. (Note: You may need to rip the 1 by 1s to get an exact fit between the cradle sides and the half-rounds.) Glue all the trim in place. When the glue has cured, trim and round over the protruding half-rounds. Use the remaining 1 by 1s to provide hardboard supports as shown. Glue and nail the supports flush with the bottom of the sides and ends.

4. Clamp rockers **F** in place, then mark and drill **E** and **F** where shown for dowel connectors. Cut four 2-inch dowel pieces and round over one end of each. Glue and dowel the rockers to the posts. Glue a cabinet pull to the top of each post. Sand, then apply the finish of your choice. When the finish is dry, drop in the hardboard mattress support and add the mattress.

Design: Scott Fitzgerrell.

Shaker-style hanging cradle

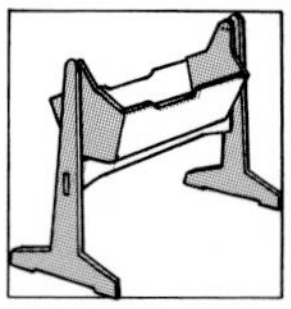

This traditional cradle adapts the simple lines of old Shaker cradles, lines that make it at once easy to build and easy to look at. Like many antique cradles, it uses a long, narrow mattress that helps restrain very young infants and provides room at the foot for toys and extra bedding. The cradle, pictured on page 51, unclips from its stand; the stand knocks down for travel or storage.

To make the cradle, you'll need basic tools and a saber or circular saw—or preferably a radial-arm or table saw. Construction, though requiring precision, is essentially easy.

1. Rip one eased edge from the 6-foot 1 by 10. Cut all pieces to size; cut the dowel into six 2-inch and two 2¼-inch pieces. Edge-join ends **A** to make two 17 by 18¼-inch panels, blind doweling with the 2-inch dowels (see Detail 3 and page 45).

Referring to the large drawing and Details 2 and 3, make bevel and profile cuts in ends **AA** and sides **B**, bottom **C**, and stretcher **G**. Drill two ¼-inch holes in each end **AA** where shown. Add dowels in the ends of stretcher **G** (see Detail 2). With ½-inch and ¾-inch drill bits and a chisel, file, or rasp, make

rectangular mortises in uprights **D** and stretcher **G** where shown. From scrap wood, make four wedges as shown in Detail 2.

2. Spacing nails every 2 to 3 inches, glue and nail ends **AA** to sides **B**, then fasten bottom **C** in place. Glue and screw uprights **D** to crosspieces **E**, then glue and nail crosspieces **F** in place as shown. When the glue has cured, mark and cut the foot and upright profiles as shown in the large drawing and Detail 1. Drill ¼-inch holes in the uprights where shown.

3. Round over all edges (except the wedges), then set the nails and fill the holes. Sand smooth. Apply the finish of your choice (we used polyurethane). When the finish is dry, bolt the snap hooks in place; cut the bolt ends flush with the nuts and peen smooth.

4. To assemble, insert stretcher **G** in uprights **D** and gently tap in the wedges. For extra security, add screws (see Detail 2), countersinking the heads. Add loops of rope to the cradle, adjusting the length so the cradle bottom clears the stretcher; secure each end with overhand knots. (Heat the rope ends with a match to prevent fraying.) Clip the cradle in place and add the mattress.

Design: Randall Fleming & Scott Fitzgerrell.

BUY		TO MAKE			
Clear fir or pine					
1	6-foot 1 by 10	4	Ends	**A**:	¾″ by 9⅛″ by 17″
1	10-foot 1 by 10	2	Sides	**B**:	¾″ by 9¼″ by 39″
		1	Bottom	**C**:	¾″ by 9¼″ by 36″
2	8-foot 1 by 6s	2	Uprights	**D**:	¾″ by 5½″ by 40″
		2	Crosspieces	**E**:	¾″ by 5½″ by 24″
		4	Crosspieces	**F**:	¾″ by 5½″ by 9¼″
1	6-foot 1 by 4	1	Stretcher	**G**:	¾″ by 3½″ by 50½″

MISCELLANEOUS

2 bronze snap hooks, 2¼″ long • 2′ of ¼″ hardwood dowel
3′ of ¼″ bronze-colored nylon rope (check marine supply stores)
2 roundhead brass bolts, ¼″ by 1½″, with nuts and washers
10 drywall screws, 1¼″ by #6 • 3d finishing nails • Wood putty • Wood glue
Clear nontoxic finish • Foam mattress, 2″ by 8½″ by 33″

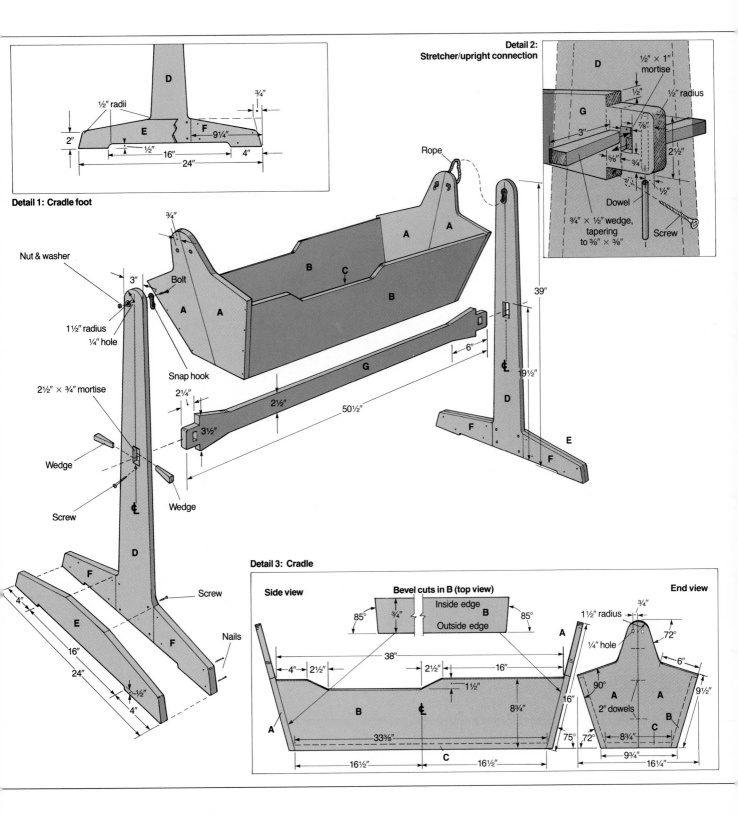

Detail 1: Cradle foot

D
½" radii
¾"
2"
E
½"
F
9¼"
16"
4"
24"

Detail 2: Stretcher/upright connection

D
½" × 1" mortise
½"
½" radius
G
7/8"
3"
5/8"
2½"
¾"
Dowel
Screw
¾" × ½" wedge, tapering to 3/8" × 3/8"

Rope

Nut & washer
¾"
3"
Bolt
A
A
B
C
B
A
A
39"
1½" radius
¼" hole
Snap hook
2½" × ¾" mortise
6"
19½"
D
2¼"
2½"
50½"
G
3½"
F
E
Wedge
Screw
Wedge
℄
D
F
Screw
4"
Nails
E
F
16"
24"
½"
4"

Detail 3: Cradle

Side view

Bevel cuts in B (top view)
85°
¾"
Inside edge
B
Outside edge
85°

End view
¾"
1½" radius
72"
¼" hole
6"
90°
A
A
B
2" dowels
C
75°
72"
8¾"
9¾"
16¼"
9½"

A
4"
2½"
38"
2½"
16"
A
16"
B
℄
8¾"
1½"
16½"
C
16½"

53

This easy-to-build system allows for plenty of imaginative play for active minds and bodies, and its three components can be arranged to fit in almost any room. The bed accepts a standard crib mattress, which is large enough for children up to early school age; a second crib mattress hides under the loft platform, ready to be set out for an overnight guest. The ramp and loft take on different identities with every new game.

Sleep & play structure

Transform an ordinary room into a fort, a castle, or any other magical place your child's imagination might create. This play/sleep structure, consisting of a loft, a bed, and a ramp/slide for traveling between the two, sets the stage for creative play and sweet dreams.

Because the bed uses a crib mattress, it's suitable only for children up to early elementary school age. When your child outgrows the bed, you can replace it with a larger one.

The bed can fit completely under the loft or be pulled out into the room as shown. A second mattress, stored under the loft platform, nestles into the loft for friends sleeping over.

In addition to basic tools, you'll need a radial-arm or table saw and a router for rounding over sharp edges. A dado blade would be helpful.

Refer to the drawings on pages 56–57 as you work.

The ramp

1. Cut ramp pieces **A–H** to size. Dado a ⅜-inch-deep by ½-inch-wide groove along the length of side rails **D** where shown. Make the angled cuts on legs **A** and **B** and side rails **D** (see detail drawing). With a ⅜-inch-radius bit, round over the upper edges of **D**.

2. Apply glue along the dadoes and insert ramp base **E**. Glue supports **F** to base **E**; then screw through the side rails **D** into the ends of **F**. Glue and nail one ramp foot **C** to ramp legs **A**, then attach the other **C** to ramp legs **B**, using 6d nails. Glue and screw ramp supports **G** to ramp legs **A** and **B**. Countersink the screws.

3. Glue and nail the feet assemblies to **D**, setting the nails. Cut one long edge of ramp end **H** at a 75° angle, then glue and nail it in place as shown.

4. Fill the nail holes, sand, and finish.

The bed

1. Cut bed pieces **I–M** to size. Glue and nail supports **K** and **L** to sides **I** and **J** as shown.

2. Glue and nail **I** to **J** at the corners, using 6d nails spaced 3 inches apart. Set the nails and fill the holes.

3. Drop bed base **M** in place.

4. Sand and finish to match the ramp; add a crib mattress.

The loft

1. Cut loft pieces **N–T** to size. Mark legs **N** for placement of all connecting rails. Drill countersink and pilot holes in rails **O** and **R** where shown. Glue and screw rails **O** and **R** in place. Countersink the screws. Glue and screw rail **S** at the bottom of one long side. Countersink the screws.

2. Drill screw holes for rails **P** and **Q** (do not attach). Notch loft base **T** as shown to fit around the legs.

3. Sand and finish to match the ramp and bed.

4. Move all the pieces into the room; then screw rails **P** and **Q** to the legs. Countersink the screws. Attach a pair of screw-eyes to the inside of each rail **O** as shown. Stretch shock cords across to hold the extra mattress. Add base **T**.

Design: Don Vandervort.

BUY		TO MAKE	
Clear pine or Douglas fir			
1	10-foot 1 by 2	2	Bed supports **L**: ¾″ by 1½″ by 51″
1	6-foot 1 by 2	2	Bed supports **K**: ¾″ by 1½″ by 28½″
1	6-foot 1 by 3	1	Loft rail **S**: ¾″ by 2½″ by 54½″
1	2-foot 1 by 4	1	Ramp end **H**: ¾″ by 3½″ by 22½″
3	10-foot 1 by 6s	4	Loft rails **R**: ¾″ by 5½″ by 54½″
		2	Loft rails **Q**: ¾″ by 5½″ by 34½″
		2	Ramp feet **C**: ¾″ by 5½″ by 21″
2	10-foot 1 by 6s	2	Ramp rails **D**: ¾″ by 5½″ by 97½″
1	10-foot 1 by 8	2	Loft rails **O**: ¾″ by 7¼″ by 54½″
1	6-foot 1 by 8	2	Loft rails **P**: ¾″ by 7¼″ by 34½″
2	8-foot 1 by 12s	2	Bed sides **J**: ¾″ by 11¼″ by 54″
		2	Bed sides **I**: ¾″ by 11¼″ by 28½″
1	10-foot 2 by 2	3	Ramp supports **F**: 1½″ by 1½″ by 21″
		2	Ramp supports **G**: 1½″ by 1½″ by 18″
4	6-foot 2 by 3s	4	Loft legs **N**: 1½″ by 2½″ by 70¼″
1	8-foot 2 by 6	2	Ramp legs **A**: 1½″ by 5½″ by 32¼″
		2	Ramp legs **B**: 1½″ by 5½″ by 9¾″
Fir plywood (grade AD)			
3	½-inch 4 by 8-foot sheets	1	Ramp base **E**: ½″ by 21¾″ by 96″
		1	Bed base **M**: ½″ by 28½″ by 52½″
		1	Loft base **T**: ½″ by 34½″ by 56″

MISCELLANEOUS

4d finishing nails • 6d finishing nails • 50 drywall screws, 2″ by #6
4 2″ screw-eyes • Wood glue • 2 elastic shock cords
Wood putty • Clear penetrating oil finish • 2 crib mattresses, each 27¼″ by 52″

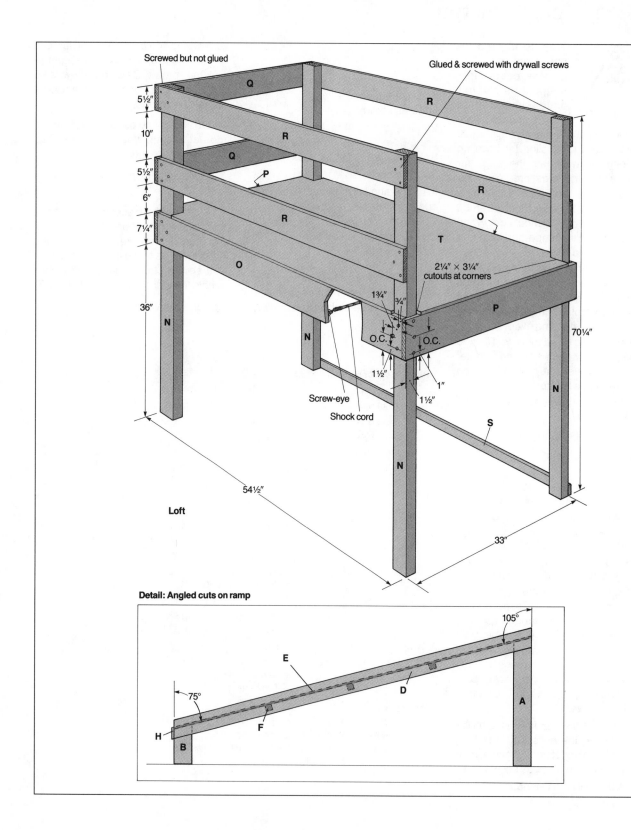

Screwed but not glued

Glued & screwed with drywall screws

Q

R

5½"

10"

R

Q

5½"

P

6"

R

R

7¼"

O

T

O

2¼" × 3¼"
cutouts at corners

1¾"   ¾"

36"

70¼"

N

P

N

O.C.   P   O.C.

1½"

N

Screw-eye

1"

Shock cord

1½"

S

N

54½"

Loft

33"

Detail: Angled cuts on ramp

105°

E

75°

D

A

H

F

B

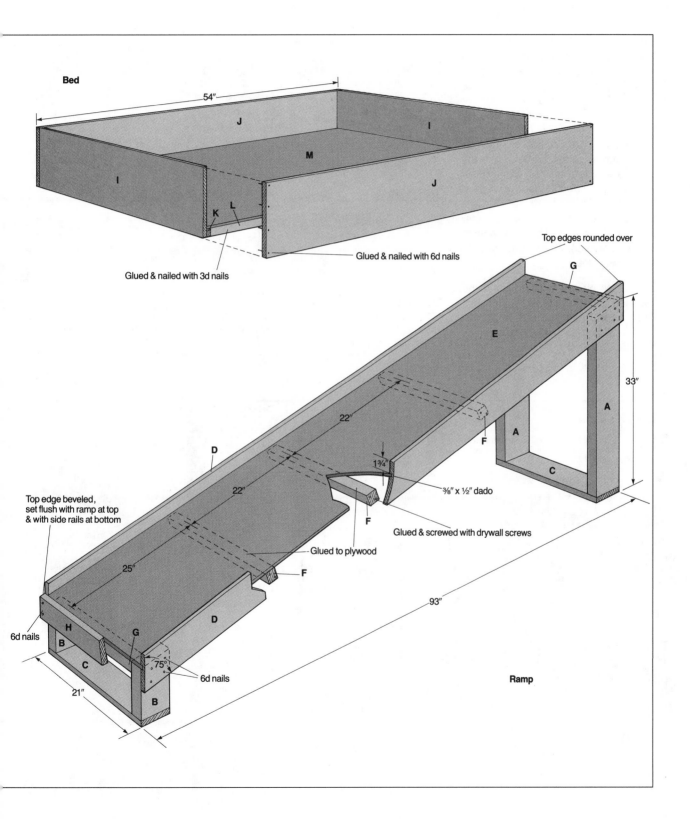

Bed

54"

J

I

M

I

J

K L

Glued & nailed with 6d nails

Glued & nailed with 3d nails

Top edges rounded over

G

E

A

33"

F

A

C

D

22"

1¾"

⅜" x ½" dado

22"

F

Glued & screwed with drywall screws

Top edge beveled,
set flush with ramp at top
& with side rails at bottom

25"

Glued to plywood

F

D

6d nails

H

G

B

C

75"

6d nails

21"

B

93"

Ramp

Stacking bunk beds

This bunk bed is actually two separate beds that unstack easily when the kids want a change or move into their own rooms.

The beds connect with ¾-inch dowels that are fitted into holes in the tops and bottoms of the posts. When the beds are unstacked, you can remove the safety rail and ladder and fit caps onto the tops of the posts.

For this project, you'll need a router and a radial-arm or table saw (a dado blade is helpful). Use a plug cutter to make the plugs.

1. Cut all pieces to size except the plywood mattress supports **F**. Note that ladder legs **J** are cut at a 78° angle. Rip ⅛ inch off both long edges of end rails **C** and side rails **B**.

BUY		TO MAKE		
Clear pine or Douglas fir				
4	10-foot 1 by 2s	4	Bed cleats **D**:	¾″ by 1½″ by 76½″
		4	Bed cleats **E**:	¾″ by 1½″ by 39″
4	8-foot 1 by 6s	8	End rails **C**:	¾″ by 5½″ by 47½″
1	8-foot 1 by 6	5	Steps **K**:	¾″ by 5½″ by 16″
1	10-foot 2 by 3	2	Ladder legs **J**:	1½″ by 2½″ by 60″
2	14-foot 2 by 6s	4	Side rails **B**:	1½″ by 5½″ by 76½″
1	4-foot 2 by 6	1	Safety rail **G**:	1½″ by 5½″ by 44″
4	8-foot 4 by 4s	8	Posts **A**:	3½″ by 3½″ by 40″
		8	Post caps **L**:	3½″ by 3½″ by 4½″
Fir plywood (grade AD)				
2	¾-inch 4 by 8-foot sheets	2	Mattress supports **F**:	Cut to fit
Hardwood dowel				
2	¾-inch by 36-inch lengths	2	Safety rail connectors **H**:	11″
		8	Post connectors **I**:	5″

MISCELLANEOUS
52 drywall screws, 2″ by #6 • 24 lag screws, ¼″ by 3″, with washers
3d finishing nails • Wood glue • Wood putty • Clear penetrating oil finish
2 twin mattresses, each 39″ by 75″

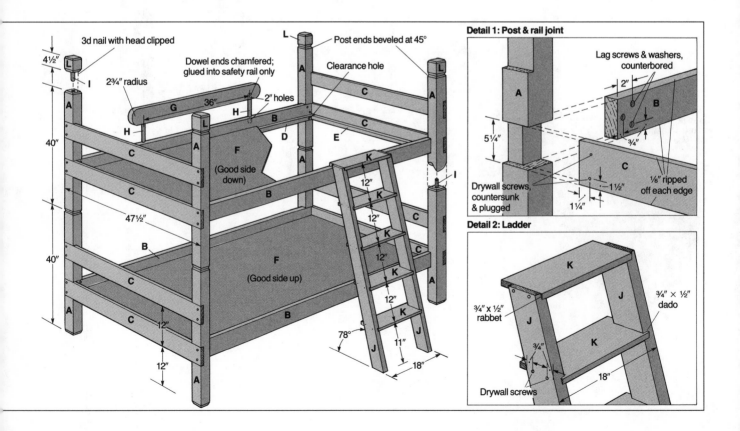

The classic over-and-under combination gets two different treatments here. At left, the handsome solid-wood bunks come apart to make a pair of twin beds; at right, the lower bunk is set at a right angle to the upper one, creating space for an adjustable corner desk.

. . . *Stacking bunk beds*

2. Dado posts **A** to receive rails **B** and **C**—two posts as shown in Detail 1 and two posts in the mirror image for each bed. Center and bore 3-inch-deep, ¾-inch-diameter holes into both ends of all the posts. Slightly bevel all post ends with a router and chamfer bit.

3. Drill counterbore and pilot holes for lag screws in side rails **B** and countersink holes for drywall screws in end rails **C**. Glue and screw rails **C** to posts **A**; cover the screws with plugs cut from pieces of scrap lumber. Temporarily lag screw side rails **B** in place. Drill ¾-inch clearance holes for lag screws in cleats **D** as shown. Then glue and nail cleats **D** and **E** to rails **B** and **C**. Cut mattress supports **F** to fit.

4. Dado and rabbet ladder legs **J** for steps **K** at a 78° angle as shown in the large drawing and Detail 2. Glue and screw the steps in place.

5. Round the ends of safety rail **G** at a 2¾-inch radius, drill holes, and glue in safety rail connectors **H** where shown. Center and drill matching holes in one long side rail **B** to receive the dowels.

6. Insert four post cap connectors **I** into four post caps **L**. Add a nail next to the dowel in each and clip off the head (this keeps the cap from turning).

7. Sand and finish.

8. Move the bed to the room after removing the mattress supports and long rails. Reattach the rails to the end assemblies and add the mattress supports. Insert the remaining post connectors **I** into the tops of the posts of the lower bunk bed. Stack the beds. Add the post caps and the twin-size mattresses.

Design: Don Vandervort.

L-shaped bunks with adjustable desk

The L-shaped configuration of these bunk beds makes maximum use of minimum floor space. Not only is there the usual pair of beds, but there's also a corner desk that adjusts in height.

Construction is easy. A socket wrench, a saber or circular saw, and basic tools are all you need.

1. Cut all pieces to size. Mark and drill the counterbore and bolt holes as shown in Detail 1. Make cutouts, holes, and slots in uprights **F** and **G** and braces **K** and **M** where shown. Cut the fir round 81½ inches long; cut the dowel in half. Divide the corner guard molding into four equal lengths.

2. Except where noted, all screw connections are counterbored and filled. Glue and screw the upper and lower bed frames together as shown. Cut 1 by 2 cleats to fit each frame as shown; glue and nail them in place. Nail mattress supports **O** in position. Glue and screw legs **E** to the lower bunk.

3. Using glue and nails spaced 3 to 4 inches apart, build **HIJ** (position **J** 2¼

inches back from the rear edges of **H** and **I**), **KLMN**, and **NMN** assemblies (see Detail 3). Glue and toenail all assemblies together as shown; set the nails. Cut the screen molding as indicated and fasten with glue and brads.

4. Fill the screw holes and finish as desired. (We used satin polyurethane and semigloss enamel.) Fasten the corner guard with glue and brads.

5. Move the components into the room. With the unit on its back, position the upper bed frame and uprights **F** and **G**. Drill through the bolt holes and plywood with a ⅛-inch bit, then back through the plywood with a ¼-inch bit. Bolt the frame in place. Screw side **A3** in position where shown. Stand the unit up and attach the lower bed frame just as you did the upper one. Position the unit, locate the studs, and fasten side **A2** to the studs with lag screws. Add the fir round and secure it with dowel pins in ½-inch holes.

Drill holes for the desk-mounting bolts in upright **F** and side **D1** as you did the bunks. Bolt the desk in position. Add the mattresses.

Design: Scott Fitzgerrell.

BUY		TO MAKE		
Douglas fir (Select Structural grade)				
7	8-foot 2 by 8s	3	Sides **A**:	1½" by 7¼" by 80"
		2	Ends **B**:	1½" by 7¼" by 41"
		2	Ends **C**:	1½" by 7¼" by 44"
		2	Sides **D**:	1½" by 7¼" by 77"
Birch plywood (shop grade)				
2	¾-inch 4 by 8-foot sheets	Pieces **E–N** (see Detail 2)		
Douglas fir plywood (AD grade)				
2	¾-inch 4 by 8-foot sheets	2	Supports **O**:	¾" by 40¾" by 76¾"

MISCELLANEOUS
Fir round, 1⅜" by 8' • Pine or fir corner guard molding, ¾" by ¾" by 6'
2 pieces of ¼" by ¾" pine or fir screen molding, each 6' long • 4" of ½" hardwood dowel
4 pieces of pine or fir 1 by 2, each 12' long • 30 drywall screws, 3" by #8
8 drywall screws, 1¼" by #6 • 14 carriage bolts, ¼" by 2" • 3 carriage bolts, ¼" by 2½"
19 ¼" washers • 14 ¼" nuts • 3 ¼" wing nuts • 2 lag screws, ¼" by 3"
3d finishing nails • Brads • Wood glue • Wood putty • Finish
2 twin mattresses, each 39" by 75"

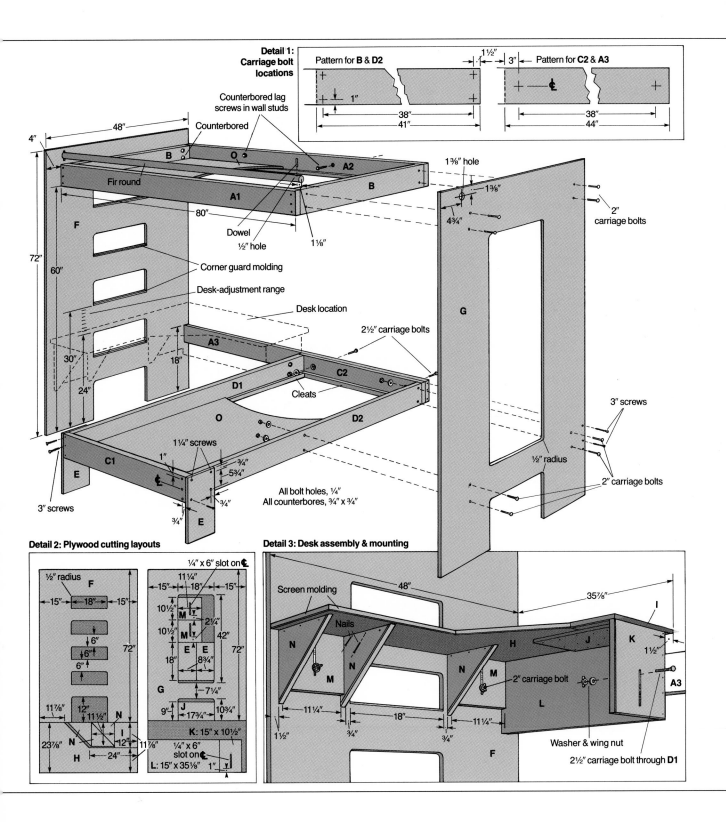

Detail 1:
Carriage bolt locations

Pattern for **B** & **D2**

1½″ 3″ Pattern for **C2** & **A3**

1″

38″
41″

38″
44″

48″

4″

Counterbored lag screws in wall studs

Counterbored

B   O

Fir round

A2

B

A1

80″

Dowel

½″ hole

1⅛″

1⅜″ hole

1⅜″

4¾″

2″ carriage bolts

F

72″

60″

Corner guard molding

Desk-adjustment range

Desk location

G

2½″ carriage bolts

A3

30″

18″

24″

C2

D1

Cleats

O

D2

1¼″ screws

1″

¾″

5¾″

3″ screws

¾″

3″ screws

½″ radius

2″ carriage bolts

E

C1

E

¾″

All bolt holes, ¼″
All counterbores, ¾″ x ¾″

Detail 2: Plywood cutting layouts

½″ radius

F

15″ 18″ 15″

6″

6″

6″

72″

11⅞″

12″

11½″

N

23⅞″

12″

N

H

24″

11⅞″

I

¼″ x 6″ slot on ₵

11¼″

15″ 18″ 15″

10½″

M

10½″

M

2¼″

E   E

18″

8¾″

42″

72″

G

7¼″

J

9″

17¾″

10¾″

K: 15″ x 10½″

¼″ x 6″
slot on ₵

L: 15″ x 35⅛″ 1″

Detail 3: Desk assembly & mounting

48″

35⅞″

Screen molding

Nails

N

N

M

H

J

K

I

1½″

M

N

M

2″ carriage bolt

L

A3

11¼″

18″

11¼″

1½″

¾″

¾″

F

Washer & wing nut

2½″ carriage bolt through **D1**

61

Make the most of a standard metal bed frame with these two projects: underbed drawers provide useful storage in a space that's usually lost; adaptable headboards make bold graphic statements—you can use one of our motifs or design your own.

Rolling drawers

These low-profile drawers roll underneath a bed and reclaim space otherwise occupied by unmatched socks and dust balls. The drawers are perfect for storing small toys (they can be rolled to a play area) or seasonal clothing.

The feet of the bed frame must be at least 5 feet apart for all three drawers to fit underneath. If your opening is smaller, you can either change the dimensions of the fronts, backs, and bottoms of the drawers or make two wider drawers. The drawers shown use most of the depth available with a twin bed, but you can make them any depth you like. You might even make two sets, one set accessible from each side of the bed. You could also make one to fit at the end of the bed.

All three drawers are made from one sheet of ½-inch plywood. In addition to basic tools, you'll need a radial-arm or table saw. A dado blade would be helpful.

1. Cut all pieces to size (see plywood cutting layout and materials list). Cut ½-inch-wide by ¼-inch-deep dadoes along sides **A** and backs **B** where shown.

2. For each drawer, glue and nail sides **A** to back **B** and inner front **C** as shown, keeping the upper edges flush. Glue along the dadoes and slide bottom **D** into the grooves. Nail the bottom to the underside of the inner front.

3. Drill pilot holes and screw through inner front **C** into front **E**, keeping all edges flush. Countersink the screws.

4. Set all nails and fill the nail and screw holes. Sand and finish. Screw a caster to the bottom at each corner. (Note: Though the drawers can be gripped under the front, you can add a pull to each for convenience.)

Design: Don Vandervort.

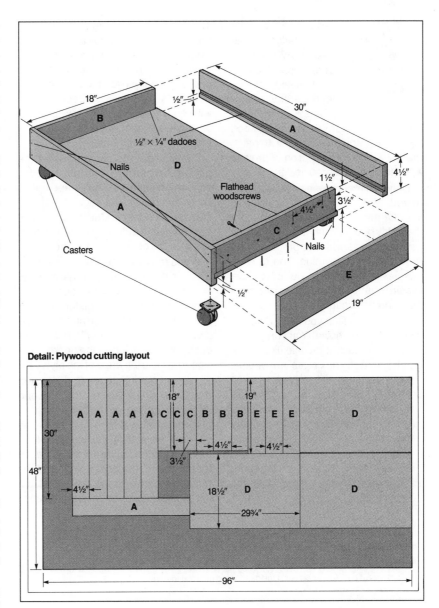

Detail: Plywood cutting layout

BUY (For three drawers)	TO MAKE
Birch plywood (shop grade)	
1 ½-inch 4 by 8-foot sheet	Pieces **A–E** (see plywood cutting layout)

MISCELLANEOUS
3d finishing nails • 12 flathead woodscrews, ¾" by #6
12 1¾" plate-mounted casters with screws • Wood glue • Wood putty
Paint • 3 drawer pulls (optional)

Easy custom headboards

Here's a quick cure for a characterless metal-framed twin bed—dress it up with a bold and beautiful custom headboard as shown in the photo on page 62. Each headboard is made from a sheet of plywood contour cut and dressed up with paint; the posts, which are optional, provide a frame for the painted design.

Only minimal carpentry skills are required. The level of painting is up to you. Of the four designs shown, both the teddy bear and landscape are fairly freeform—open to interpretation and not too time-consuming. The crayon-box design and the fanciful locomotive require numerous ruled lines and are a bit harder to execute.

You needn't limit yourself to the designs that are shown. You can just as easily reproduce a favorite illustration or photograph, or create an original design right on the plywood—even something as simple as your child's name or initials in big block letters or a graceful script can be wonderfully appealing.

You can construct the headboard with only basic tools, though you'll need a saber saw to make easy work of the contour cutting.

1. Choose your design and cut the plywood to the length indicated. (If you're working with an original design, divide its width into 12 equal segments, then use this interval to mark off vertical segments as required. Each square will equal 4 inches on the plywood. Be sure to leave sufficient clearance at the bottom for the mattress.)

Transfer the top contour, using the grid-enlargement techniques described on page 36 (you'll need only a beam compass—see page 36—for the crayon-box design). Cut the top profile; then sand and putty any edges that will show on the completed headboard.

If you're using the posts, measure and cut the 1 by 3s and the molding (see the detail drawing for construction information), but don't fasten them in place. If you're not using the posts, you can round the "shoulder" provided in each pattern and carry the nearest design line out to the edge of the plywood.

2. Undercoat all pieces and let them dry. Draw a line across the plywood sheet 18 inches up from the bottom and mark off a 4-inch grid from this point to the top of the sheet. (Note: Eighteen inches allows 6 inches each for the frame, the box spring, and the mattress; measure the bed you're using and adjust this dimension as needed

so that the painted design begins just below mattress level.) Use a pencil to transfer the gridded pattern (yours or ours) to the plywood.

3. Paint the headboard as desired. The samples shown were painted with interior semigloss enamel. Hobby-shop enamels, available in smaller quantities than house paints, are also a good choice.

We used browns, greens, yellows, pale blue, white, and red for the landscape. The locomotive was done in mossy green, crimson, black, gray, and brown; the yellow lines are vinyl pinstriping tape purchased at an automotive supply store. The tape is a real timesaver—but don't use it unless your child is past the age of peeling it off and ingesting it.

For the crayon-box design, we used a light mustard yellow, dark green, a rainbow of crayon colors, and black pinstriping tape. The teddy bear was done in tan, medium brown, white, green, and blue. Colors were mixed freely on all headboards to achieve pastels and intermediate shades; experiment with your own colors.

4. When the paint is thoroughly dry, glue and nail the post pieces in place. Drill holes for the knobs where shown in the detail drawing and glue them in place. Set the nails and fill the holes; then touch up the paint. When it's dry, you can apply one or two coats of matte or satin polyurethane or varnish to all surfaces, if you like, for maximum protection and durability.

5. Spacing the headboard ¾ inch up from the floor, use the headboard-mounting flanges on the metal bed frame as templates for marking and drilling ¼-inch mounting holes in the headboard for four carriage bolts. Bolt the headboard in place as shown. Or you can fasten the headboard directly to the wall, using hollow-wall fasteners.

Design: Sandra Popovich & Scott Fitzgerrell.

BUY	TO MAKE
Birch plywood (shop grade)	
1 ¾-inch 4 by 8-foot sheet	One headboard (see text for size and shape)

MISCELLANEOUS

4 carriage bolts, ¼" by 1½", with nuts and washers • Wood putty • Finish
Twin-size metal bed frame with mattress and box spring • Hollow-wall fasteners (optional)
For optional posts: 4 pine or fir 1 by 3s, 6' long • 2 pieces of pine molding, ⅜" by 1¾" by 6'
2 wood knobs or decorative finials • Wood glue • 3d nails

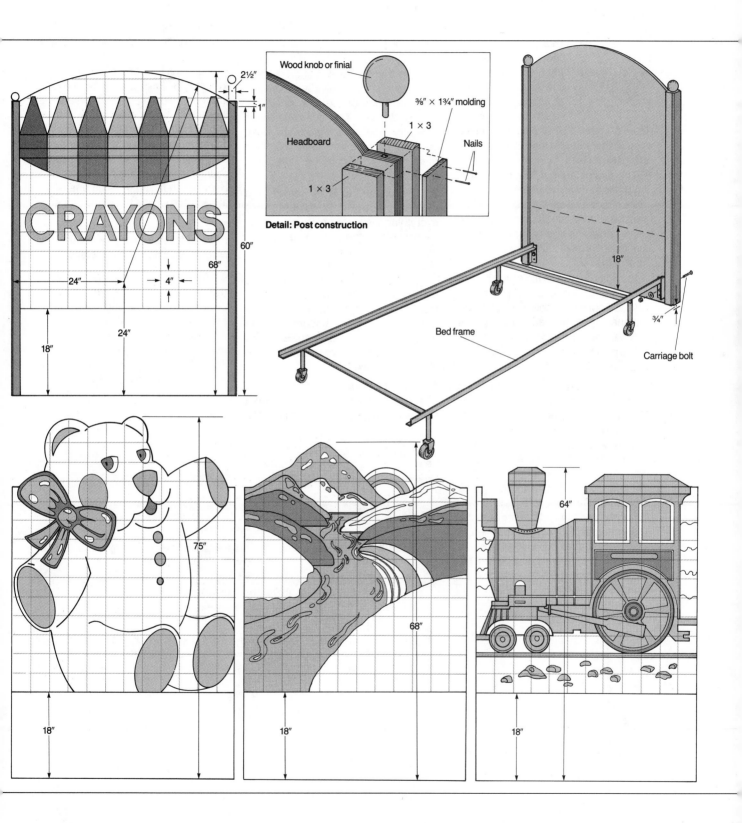

CRAYONS

2½"
1"
60"
68"
24"
4"
24"
18"

Wood knob or finial

⅜" × 1¾" molding

1 × 3

Headboard

Nails

1 × 3

Detail: Post construction

18"

¾"

Bed frame

Carriage bolt

75"

64"

68"

18"

18"

18"

Chest bed

This handsome chest bed is a real worker when it comes to storage. In addition to the generous drawers visible in the photo, there's a deep bin in the back for linens (you lift the twin-size mattress and open the lid to get to it).

The pieces are cut from good-looking Baltic birch plywood where appearance counts; where it doesn't, less expensive shop-grade stock is used. Solid cherry rails and cherry veneer behind the open drawer pulls dress up the front of the bed.

In addition to basic tools, you'll need a router and either a radial-arm or table saw. Except where noted, all joints are fastened with glue and countersunk screws spaced about 6 inches apart.

Refer to the drawings on pages 68–69 as you work.

1. Cut all pieces to size. Dado and round over top rail **N** as shown in Detail 2. Cut rabbets and dadoes in drawer pieces **G**, **H**, and **I** as shown in the large drawing and Detail 4. (Note: The length of fronts **H** and backs **I** presumes a ½-inch clearance for the drawer glides. This is standard, but check your glides to be sure.) Cut holes for pulls in drawer facings **J** and bin lid **F**. Using a router with a ½-inch rounding-over bit set ⅜ inch high, rout all plywood edges that will show. With a cove or core-box bit, rout the drawer pulls in facings **J** as

shown in Detail 3. Cut the cherry veneer into ten 3-inch squares.

2. Join long divider **A** to short dividers **B**, spacing the short dividers 25 inches from the ends of the long one. Join ends **C** to back **D**. Square-up these assemblies and let the glue cure. Then cut nine 1 by 2 cleats to fit, fastening them where indicated in the large drawing.

3. Join ends **C** to **A** as shown. Add mattress support **E**, making sure everything is square before driving the screws. Attach the continuous hinge to bin lid **F**, then fasten the lid in place. Glue top rail **N** to the mattress support; then fasten it to each end **C** with two screws on center line, spaced about ½ inch from the top and bottom of the rail (see Detail 2). Glue bottom rail **O** to ends **C** and short partitions **B**; screw through **C** into the rail, following the directions above.

4. For each drawer, attach sides **G** to back **I**, slide in drawer bottom **K** (it's not necessary to glue it), then add front **H**.

Square-up the frame and let the glue cure. Glue veneer squares on the inside of each drawer facing **J** as shown in Detail 3. Finally, glue facings **J** to fronts **H**, allowing ¾-inch overlaps at the sides, 1-inch overlaps at the top and bottom of the large drawer, and 1¹⁄₁₆-inch overlaps at the top and bottom of each small drawer. Drive six countersunk screws through each front **H** into each facing **J**, using one screw at each corner and two in the center.

5. Fill all holes, sand, and apply two coats of finish. Add bin bottoms **L** and **M** (they don't need to be fastened).

6. Attach the drawer glides, following the manufacturer's directions. The drawers overlap the ends and dividers by ¼ inch, the top rail by ⅝ inch, and the bottom rail by ½ inch. Mount the middle drawer first, then use it as a guide for aligning the small drawers. Allow a ¼-inch space between each pair of small drawers.

Design: Robert Zumwalt.

BUY		TO MAKE
Baltic birch plywood		
1	¾-inch 8 by 4-foot sheet	Pieces **C** and **J** (see Detail 1)
Birch plywood (shop grade)		
3	¾-inch 4 by 8-foot sheets	Pieces **A**, **B**, and **D–I** (see Detail 1)
Tempered hardboard		
1	¼-inch 4 by 8-foot sheet	Pieces **K–M** (see Detail 1)
Cherry		
1	2 by 4	Top rail **N**: 1½" by 3¼" by 76½"
1	2 by 3	Bottom rail **O**: 1½" by 2" by 76½"

MISCELLANEOUS
Cherry veneer sufficient for ten 3" squares • 35′ of 1 by 2 pine or fir (for cleats)
5 pairs of 22" full-extension drawer glides • 1 continuous hinge, 1½" by 72"
1 lb. (about 200) drywall screws, 1¼" by #6 • Wood glue • Wood putty
Clear nontoxic finish

When it comes to packing a great deal of storage into a small space, it's hard to beat this twin-size chest bed. Baltic birch plywood combines attractively with cherry accents, and construction is strong and straightforward.

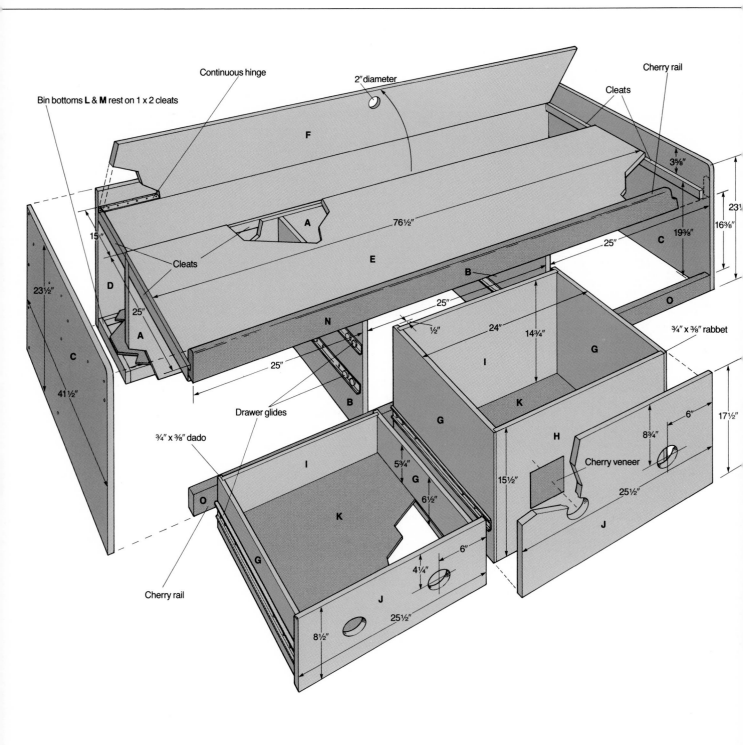

Continuous hinge

Bin bottoms **L** & **M** rest on 1 x 2 cleats

2" diameter

Cherry rail

Cleats

F

3⅝"

23½"

76½"

15"

16⅜"

19⅜"

A

Cleats

E

25"

C

D

B

A

23½"

25"

O

N

25"

C

½"

24"

14¾"

¾" x ⅜" rabbet

41½"

I

G

B

K

Drawer glides

G

H

17½"

¾" x ⅜" dado

G

6"

I

5¾"

8¾"

Cherry veneer

O

G

K

6½"

15½"

25½"

J

Cherry rail

G

6"

4¼"

J

25½"

8½"

Detail 1: Cutting layouts

3/4″ Baltic birch plywood

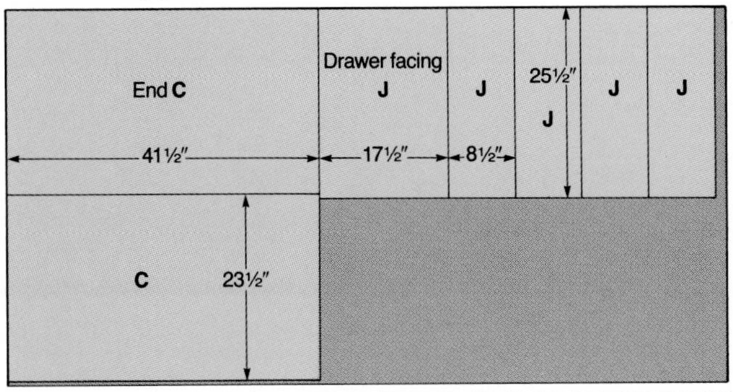
End C
Drawer facing J
J
25½″
J
J
J
41½″
17½″
8½″
C
23½″

Birch plywood (shop grade)

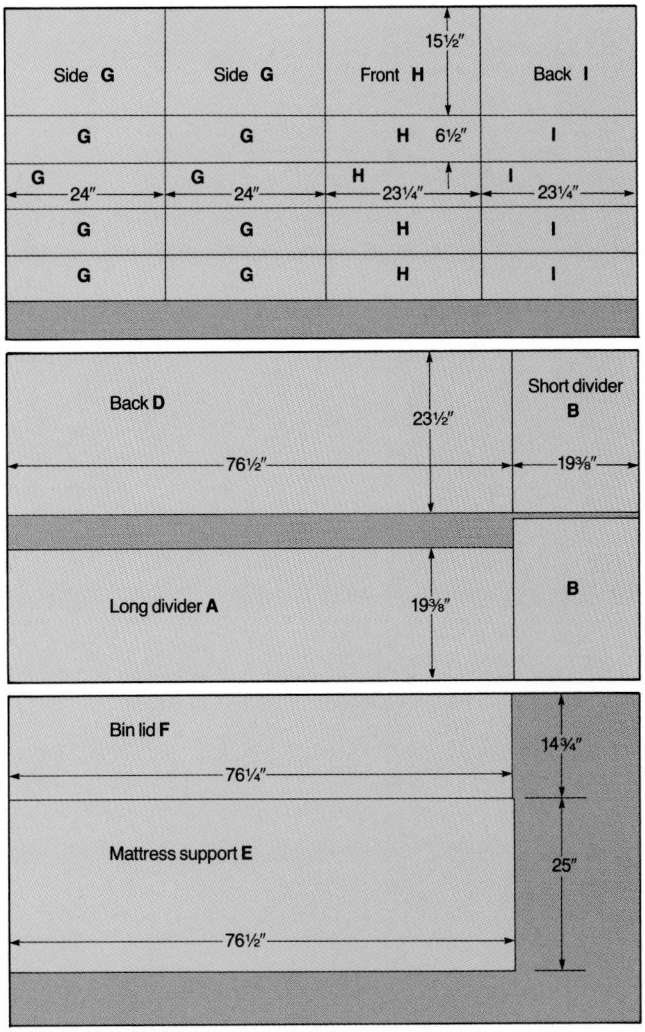
Side G
Side G
Front H
15½″
Back I
G
G
H 6½″
I
24″
24″
23¼″
23¼″
Back D
23½″
Short divider B
76½″
19⅜″
Long divider A
19⅜″
B
Bin lid F
14¾″
76¼″
Mattress support E
25″
76½″

Tempered hardboard

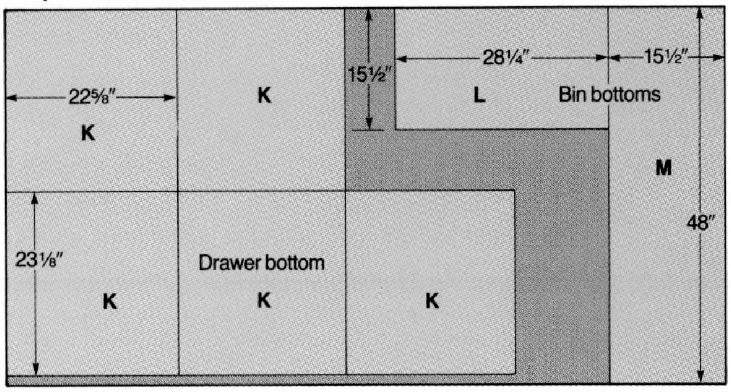
15½″
28¼″
15½″
22⅝″
K
K
L
Bin bottoms
M
48″
23⅛″
Drawer bottom
K
K
K

Detail 2: Top-rail joint (side section view)

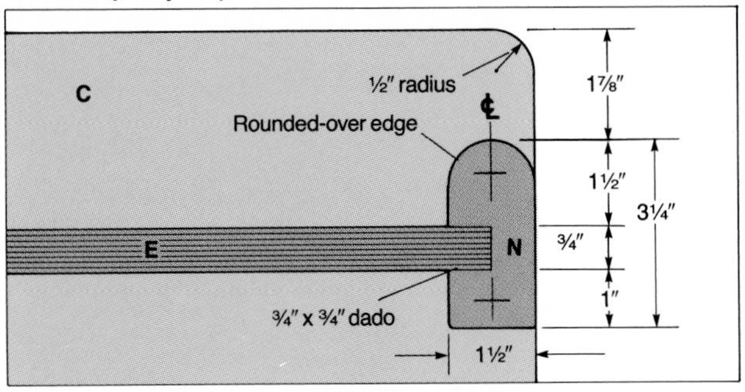
C
½″ radius
Rounded-over edge
1⅞″
1½″
3¼″
E
N
¾″
1″
¾″ x ¾″ dado
1½″

Detail 3: Drawer-pull routing (front elevation & side section view)

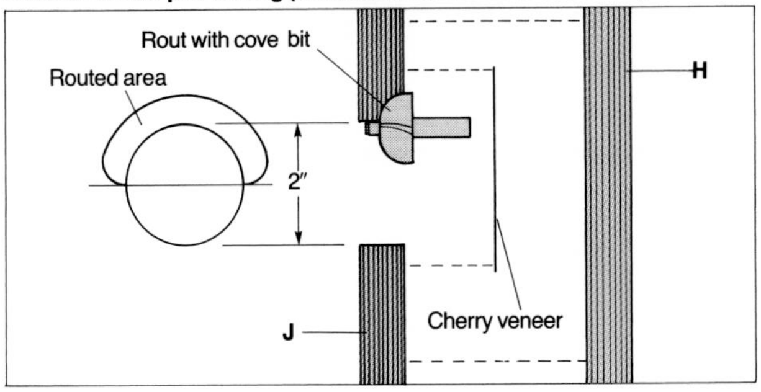
Rout with cove bit
Routed area
H
2″
J
Cherry veneer

Detail 4: Drawer-bottom dadoes

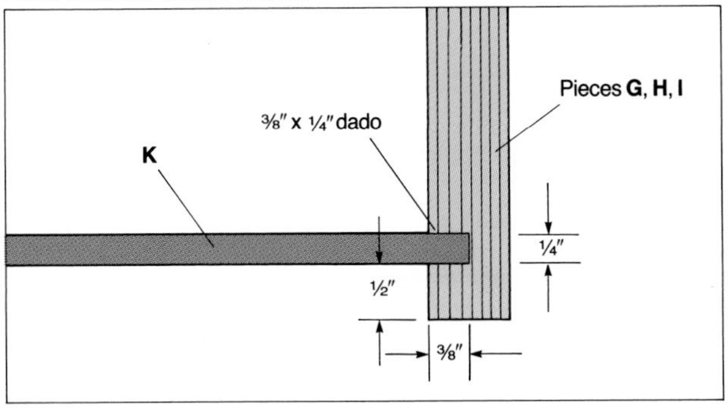
Pieces G, H, I
⅜″ x ¼″ dado
K
¼″
½″
⅜″

This enchanting canopy bed will gladden the heart of any would-be princess—and its simple, inexpensive construction will please the court carpenter as well.

Romantic canopy bed

This fanciful canopy bed, an easy weekend project that requires only basic tools to build, is essentially two frames connected by posts. One frame holds a twin-size box spring and mattress; the other supports four pairs of ready-made rod-pocket curtains (available at department stores).

1. Cut all pieces to size. Mark and drill holes in uprights **A** for finials, casters, and carriage bolts. Using the uprights as guides, drill holes for the carriage bolts in frame sides **C**.

2. Using glue and countersunk screws for all connections, attach uprights **A** to ends **B** with three screws at each joint. Then attach two cleats **D** to each side **C** (use six screws for each cleat). Assemble top frame supports **E** and **F** as shown, square the completed frame, and let the glue cure.

3. Apply the finish of your choice (we painted all plywood parts and used gold paint for the finials and clear satin polyurethane on the posts and top frame supports). When the finish is dry, attach the curtain-rod brackets (see Detail 1).

4. Move the pieces to the room and assemble sides **C** to the uprights with carriage bolts as shown. Attach the top frame to the uprights with countersunk screws (do not glue). Staple the gauze fabric to the top frame supports, letting it settle slightly between the frame members (see photo). Trim the gauze flush with the edges. Cut small holes in the gauze for the finials and insert them in the uprights. Add the box spring and mattress.

Run one curtain rod through each pair of curtains. Hang the curtains, attach the tiebacks, and add the casters.

Design: Scott Fitzgerrell.

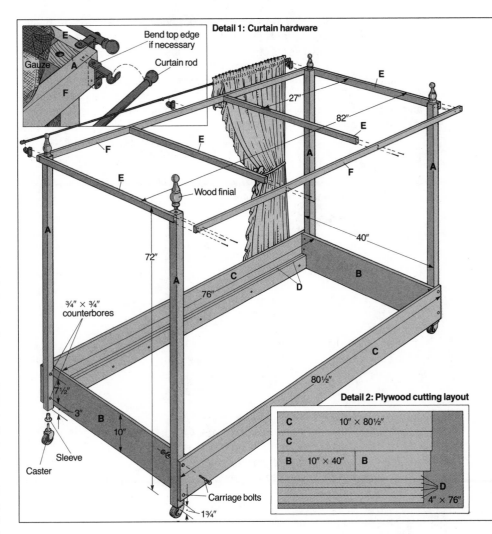

Detail 1: Curtain hardware

Bend top edge if necessary
Curtain rod
Gauze
27″
82″
Wood finial
72″
40″
¾″ × ¾″ counterbores
76″
80½″
7½″
3″
10″
Sleeve
Caster
Carriage bolts
1¾″

Detail 2: Plywood cutting layout

C	10″ × 80½″
C	
B	10″ × 40″	B
		D
	4″ × 76″

BUY		TO MAKE		
Clear fir or pine				
4	6-foot 2 by 2s	4	Uprights **A**:	1½″ by 1½″ by 72″
4	8-foot 1 by 2s	4	Top frame supports **E**:	¾″ by 1½″ by 40″
		2	Top frame supports **F**:	¾″ by 1½″ by 82″
Fir plywood (grade AD)				
1	¾-inch 4 by 8-foot sheet	Pieces **B**, **C**, and **D** (see Detail 2)		

MISCELLANEOUS

4 stem-type casters, 2″ in diameter • 4 wood finials
4 pairs rod-pocket curtains with attached valances and tiebacks, 100″ wide by 72″ long
4 curtain rods • 10 curtain-rod brackets • 2½ yds. gauze fabric, at least 42″ wide
56 drywall screws, 1¼″ by #6 • 8 carriage bolts, ¼″ by 2″, with nuts and washers
Staples or tacks • Wood glue • Finish • Twin box spring and mattress, 39″ by 75″

FINISHING YOUR PROJECT

A good finish enhances fine wood and hides the defects in lesser grades. It also keeps dirt and moisture out of wood pores and grain and wards off dents and scratches. The products used in our projects include clear finishes, enamel, and plastic laminate. Here's how to achieve good results with each one.

Preparing the wood

Before you can finish it, the wood must be carefully patched and sanded. You may also choose to seal or stain your project.

Filling and patching. Cracks, hammer marks, and fastener holes should be filled with wood putty before sanding. Spread wood putty with a putty knife or, for nail holes, your finger. Build up each patch slightly above the surface, then sand it level. When filling large or deep holes, build up the patch in layers.

Water-base wood putty, sold in powder form, allows you to "model" a surface; it's also good for filling plywood edges. Mix it with water, wet the wood surface slightly, then apply the mixture with a putty knife or your hand. The putty dries in less than an hour and sands readily.

If you plan to paint, the color of the patch isn't critical. But for a clear finish, pick a putty the same shade as the wood. If you'll be staining, choose a patch the same color as the final finish. To be sure of the best match, test the combination on a scrap of the same wood.

Sanding. The three stages in sanding are rough, preparatory, and finish. Dry, surfaced lumber doesn't require much rough sanding. Nor do the better grades of plywood—too much sanding will wear down the face veneer. A good, sharp saw blade keeps edge sanding to a minimum.

For general smoothing, choose 120-grit sandpaper; use 220-grit for finishing. For a super-smooth surface or to sand between finish coats, look for 400 or 600-grit "wet-or-dry" paper.

Sand either by hand or with a power sander. Hand sanding provides the finest finish. To provide a flat surface for the sandpaper, use a sanding block. Always sand with the wood grain; cross-grain marks will show up as ugly scratches when finished.

When the surface is smooth, dust it with a brush or vacuum, then wipe the surface with a rag moistened with mineral spirits.

Sealing. Sometimes applied to sanded wood before stain or clear finish coats, a sealer reduces moisture absorption so these later coats go on more evenly.

Shellac diluted with denatured alcohol is often used as a sealer. You'll also find a variety of special products in home improvement centers. Since sealers react differently with various stains and materials, test the combination on a wood scrap or ask your dealer.

Staining. Used for coloring wood to enhance the natural grain or make it look aged, stain also hides minor defects.

The simplest to use are pigmented oil and penetrating oil stains. Pigmented oil stains produce an opaque surface that's best for making one wood species look like another. Commonly known as colored Danish oil or colored penetrating oil, penetrating oil stains (see facing page) have become popular because they simultaneously provide color and finish coats while allowing the natural wood grain to show through.

A woodworker's finishing kit

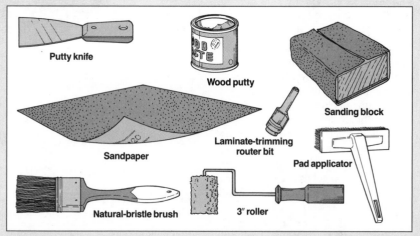

Putty knife

Wood putty

Sanding block

Sandpaper

Laminate-trimming router bit

Pad applicator

Natural-bristle brush

3″ roller

These finishing aids help you prepare, smooth, and finish wood surfaces.

Finishing techniques

Modern finishing techniques offer a wide range of appearances, from the natural look of penetrating oil to the brightest, glossiest enamel. Here's an introduction to several types. Follow the instructions on the can or ask your supplier for information on the particular product you're using.

Penetrating oil. This finish soaks into wood pores to give a natural look and feel to furniture surfaces. It's the simplest, most foolproof clear finish around.

Typically, you just spread penetrating oil on the wood with a brush or rag, wait half an hour, and wipe off the remaining surface liquid with a clean rag. A second—or even a third—application is usually a good idea, especially if the wood is very porous. The more oil absorbed by the wood, the tougher the finish coating.

If you'd like greater surface luster or extra protection, apply two or more coats of a good paste wax.

Polyurethane. A clear surface finish similar to varnish, polyurethane is extremely durable, as well as water and heat-resistant. It's available in satin and gloss finishes.

Apply polyurethane with a natural-bristle brush. To avoid a thick "plastic" look, use it sparingly, applying no more than two or three coats. Between coats, sand lightly with 600-grit wet-or-dry sandpaper or 4/0 steel wool for better adhesion. To cut excess gloss, rub the final coat with steel wool.

Lacquer. A fast-drying, high-luster finish similar to shellac, lacquer has superior durability and hardness. But its drying speed is a liability: be sure you choose a *brushing* lacquer, which dries relatively slowly.

Brush on lacquer liberally, using long strokes. Work rapidly with a wider than normal brush to speed things along. Keep your working area small and finish one area before moving on to the next.

The optimum time to wait before sanding or applying a second coat is 4 hours. After the final coat of lacquer has dried overnight, you can rub the already glossy surface with pumice or rottenstone and oil for an even higher gloss, or cut the gloss with 4/0 steel wool.

Enamel. For bright, solid colors—and for masking lower grades of wood—choose enamel, preferably oil base. It's available in flat, semigloss, and gloss finishes, and in a wide range of colors. If you need only a small quantity of enamel for a project, buy enamels in a hobby shop rather than in a paint store.

Always start your paint job with an undercoat or "primer." Not only does the undercoat seal the wood (allowing the finish coats to go on much more easily), but it also serves as an "indicator" to any remaining surface flaws, which can then be puttied or sanded. After priming, smooth the surface with 220-grit sandpaper.

Apply finish coats with a high-quality, natural-bristle brush. The trick is to spread the paint generously onto the wood, then feather it out with lighter strokes in the direction of the grain. Another technique useful for larger areas is to lay on the paint with a small (about 3-inch) paint roller, then smooth it out with light brush strokes. Pad applicators also work very well on large areas.

Let the first finish coat dry (refer to the paint can for drying time), then sand lightly with 220-grit sandpaper before applying a second, final coat.

Working with plastic laminate

If you're looking for a colorful, tough, washable surface, consider applying a layer of "childproof" 1/16-inch-thick plastic laminate. No special tools are required for the job.

First measure the surface to be laminated, adding 1/4 to 1/2 inch on all sides as a margin for error. Mark the cutting line on the laminate, then score it with a sharp utility knife. Cut with a fine-toothed saw (face up if you're using a handsaw, face down if you're using a power saw).

Apply contact cement to both surfaces to be joined and let the cement dry (normally 20 to 30 minutes). Cover the base material with heavy brown wrapping paper and lay the glued side of the laminate down on the paper. The glue, if dry enough, should not stick to the paper.

Carefully position the laminate before joining the two surfaces (once joined, the laminate can't be moved). Slowly pull the paper out, pressing the plastic down as you go. Then use a roller or rolling pin to press down the laminate.

If you're applying laminate to the edges as well as to the top surface, first attach the edge pieces, then add the top piece.

Trim the laminate to the exact size with an electric router and self-piloting laminate-trimming bit; or, if you're working with hand tools, shave it to size with a block plane, then dress it with a fine-toothed file.

Space shuttle bed

Like its NASA namesake, this sleek spaceship is both practical and attractive. It's at once a bed, a plaything, and a storage center. Hovering above a recessed base, the frame cradles a 33 by 66-inch standard youth mattress—a size that makes the bed compact overall, yet still suits it for children up through age 10 or 11. The base contains a drawer that can move around the room.

For all its visual impact, the bed is easy to build—it's basically just a tapered plywood box with tail fins and a curved top. Only basic tools are required, though a router, a power sander, and hand and stationary power saws are very helpful. Take time in finishing—effort expended here will pay handsomely in sculptural effect.

Refer to the drawings on pages 76–77 as you work.

1. Cut all pieces to size. Note that except for curves, you need not grid the plywood. Instead, just grid and cut one inner side **A** and use it as a pattern for cutting its mate and both outer sides **B**. Use the grids as guides for measuring the remaining pieces. The patterns do not take saw kerfs into account, since the dimensions of braces **O** aren't critical. Simply cut them from the areas shown after you've cut the other pieces. Also note that though Detail 3 gives exact measurements for the unbreak-able planters used for the rocket engines, almost any similar size will do.

2. Unless otherwise indicated, all joints are made with glue and countersunk screws set in ¹⁄₁₆-inch pilot holes and spaced 3 to 5 inches apart. Assemble inner sides **A**, outer sides **B**, back **C**, and platform **D**. Add front bulkhead **E** after marking and cutting its angled top. Make the angled cuts on **B**.

Add side thruster mounts **F** after fitting and cutting them for best exposure of the thrusters. On each side, hold one reinforcing piece **I** in place against **A** and **F** where shown in the large drawing and Detail 3; mark and cut its junction with **B**. Set these pieces **I** on platform **D** within each thruster housing; then mark and cut each to match the curved contour of the platform. Use the completed pieces **I** as patterns for the two remaining pieces **I**.

3. Cut the 2 by 6 in thirds and glue the pieces together to form nose block **G**. Cut and shape the nose (see Detail 2); then fasten it in place.

4. Set the tips of top **H** in the tail slots. Use pieces **I** to mark and cut matching curves in the ends of **H** (**H** will overhang sides **A** and **B**; don't attempt to align it). Glue **H** into the slots, then glue and screw it to sides **A** and **B** and thruster mounts **F**, working from back to front and stopping where the downward curve begins. Space screws 4 inches apart. Glue and clamp pieces **I** in place.

Cut fifty 1-inch squares or circles from leftover ¼-inch plywood to serve as pressure pads that help bend the top. Apply glue to front bulkhead **E** and sides **A** and **B** from **E** rearward. Working from back to front, finish fastening top **H**, using screws spaced 2 to 3 inches apart and passing each screw through a pad before fastening. Let the glue cure, then remove the screws and refasten them at every other hole, omitting the pads and countersinking the screws. Repeat for the remaining length of top **H**. Trim all overhanging edges.

5. Trim the corners on main engine mounts **J** and install (see Detail 3). Glue and nail trim **K** (cut from half-round molding) in place, working from each side around to the end and cutting the pieces to fit. Butt the joints at the corners, then round them over (see the photo) with a rasp or sander. Cut louvers **L** from quarter-round molding and glue in place where shown.

6. Assemble supports **M** and **N**. Glue and nail together braces **O** and **P**, then attach to the supports as shown. Assemble drawer front and back **Q**, sides **R**, and bottom **S**. (Note: The drawer rests directly on the floor. If your floor is not carpeted, attach nonmarring furniture glides or a 2 by 4-foot piece of carpet to the underside of the drawer.)

7. Round over and putty all edges; sand well. Shape, putty, and sand the nose so **B**, **D**, **G**, and **H** all meet "seamlessly." Putty the inside angles of the thruster housings and the intersections of the tail fins and top **H**; shape the putty with your fingers or a dowel to give a coved appearance.

8. Paint carefully (see page 73). We painted our ship gloss white, the base and drawer flat black, and the engines gloss black. Decals and vinyl letters completed the job. After the paint is dry, screw the planter-engines to their mounts and add the drawer pulls.

Assemble the bed in place, attaching the supports where indicated with screws only. Drop in the mattress.

Design: Scott Fitzgerrell.

BUY		TO MAKE
Birch plywood (shop grade)		
2	¾-inch 4 by 8-foot sheets	Pieces **A–F**, **J**, and **M–R** (see Detail 1)
1	¼-inch 4 by 8-foot sheet	Pieces **H**, **I**, and **S** (see Detail 1)

MISCELLANEOUS

1 pine 2 by 6, 10' long • 14' of 1" half-round molding
8' of ¼" quarter-round molding • 5 unbreakable plastic planters (see Detail 3)
2 drawer pulls • 1 lb. (about 200) drywall screws, 1¼" by #6 • 3d finishing nails
Wood glue • Water-base powdered wood putty • Nontoxic enamel • Decals and letters
1 youth mattress, 33" by 66", 4" to 6" thick

It's a straight trajectory from lumberyard to liftoff with this sleek spacecraft: you'll need little more than three sheets of plywood and basic tools. The cargo is a youth-size mattress (which keeps the overall dimensions compact). A large drawer built into the base adds valuable storage.

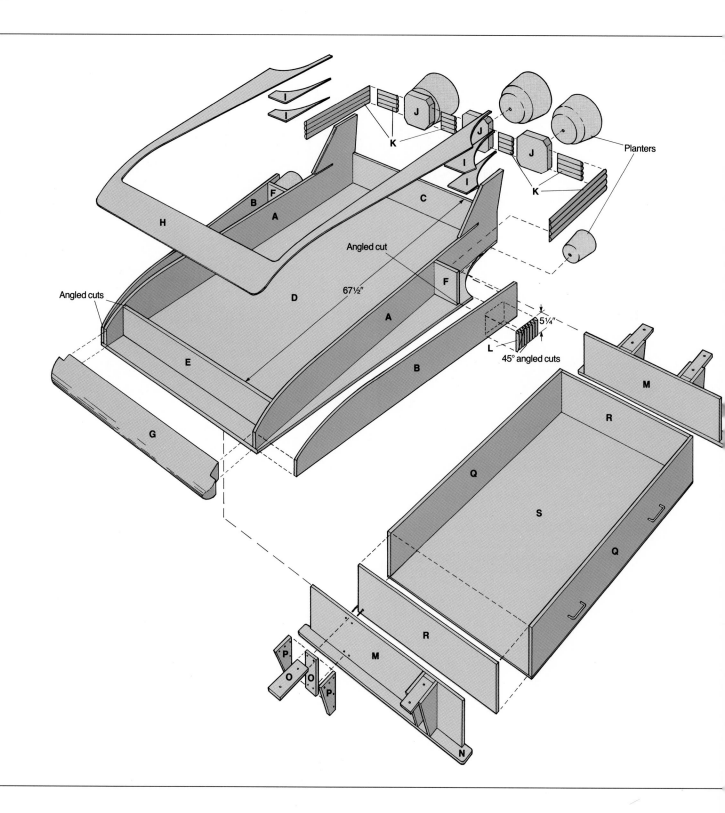

Detail 1: Plywood cutting layouts (1 square = 3″)

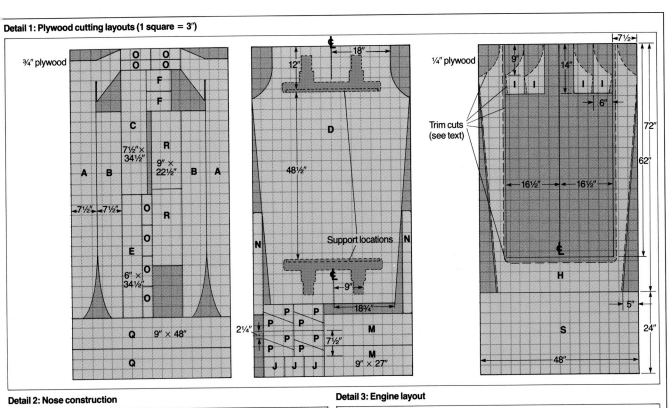

¾″ plywood

O O O O
F
F
C
7½″ × 34½″
R
9″ × 22½″
A B B A
7½″ 7½″
O
R
O
O
E
6″ × 34½″
O
O
Q 9″ × 48″
Q

¢
18″
12″
D
48½″
N N
¢
9″
Support locations
18¾″
2¼″
P P
P P
P P
P P
7½″
J J J
M
M
9″ × 27″

¼″ plywood
7½″
9″
14″
6″
Trim cuts (see text)
I I I I
72″
62″
16½″ 16½″
¢
H
S
5″
24″
48″

Detail 2: Nose construction

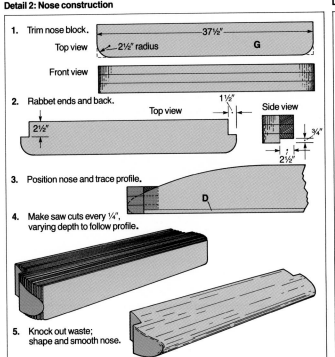

1. Trim nose block.
   Top view
   37½″
   2½″ radius G
   Front view

2. Rabbet ends and back.
   Top view
   1½″
   Side view
   2½″
   ¾″
   2½″

3. Position nose and trace profile.
   D

4. Make saw cuts every ¼″, varying depth to follow profile.

5. Knock out waste; shape and smooth nose.

Detail 3: Engine layout

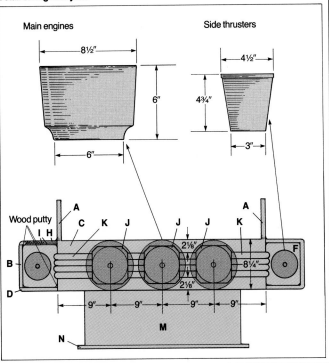

Main engines
8½″
6″
6″

Side thrusters
4½″
4¾″
3″

Wood putty
A A
I H C K J J J K F
B
2⅛″
8¼″
D
2⅛″
9″ 9″ 9″ 9″
M
N

This tent-topped fantasy wagon has instant appeal for kids of all ages. Best suited to large spaces, it comes apart to facilitate transit between workshop and bedroom. Building the wagon is easy, but you'll need some skill to handle the tent construction.

Fantasy wagon bed

This bed conjures up a different image in the mind of each beholder. Is it a circus wagon? A camping tent? In any case, one thing is certain: the bed creates a private, almost magical place that's part bed, part clubhouse, part sanctuary.

The bed is best suited to large rooms where its bulk isn't overwhelming. It takes a twin-size mattress, but is substantially larger than a twin bed.

It's a fairly ambitious project, though only the tent construction calls for special skills. The rest of the structure is essentially a series of simple subassemblies. In addition to basic tools, you'll need a grommet tool, a sewing machine, a saber saw, and a radial-arm or table saw with dado blades. A router is also helpful.

Refer to the drawings on pages 80–81 as you work.

1. Cut all pieces to size. Using Detail 1 as a guide, drill 1¾-inch holes in frame pieces **B**. Shape the ends of handles **H** and dado the ends of legs **G**; bevel **H** and **G** where shown. Rabbet the ends of posts **L** and **M** as shown in Detail 2 (note that posts **M** should mirror each other).

For the wheels, cut the CD, CDX, and ¾-inch birch plywood into circles as shown in the large drawing (see page 37 for an easy method for cutting). From birch plywood scraps, make six 5½-inch spacers as shown, then cut a 1¾-inch hole in the center of each wheel and spacer.

2. Cut the AD plywood to 48 by 83 inches for platform **D**. Glue and nail together frame pieces **A** and **B**, using 6d nails. Square it up. Using 3d nails, glue and nail platform **D** in place, then add frame pieces **C**. Add plates **E** and **F**, fastening with glue and 6d nails. Fasten legs **G** in place where shown in Detail 1, using counterbored lag screws; do not glue. Level the platform by placing its rear edge on a sawhorse.

3. Build half-walls by gluing and nailing together **IJI** and **KJK** subassemblies as shown, using 4d nails. Glue and nail posts **M** to the **IJI** subassemblies where shown. Drilling ¼-inch holes for the bolts and 5⁄16-inch holes for the T-nuts, fasten the half-walls to the platform with bolts and T-nuts (see half-wall framing plan in Detail 1). Glue and nail each end of the **KJK** assembly to posts **M**. Fasten posts **L** with bolts and T-nuts (see large drawing and Detail 1).

4. Measure and cut ¼-inch birch plywood for cladding to fit inside and outside the platform and half-walls as shown, butting sheets where they meet.

Fasten them with glue and brads, but don't fasten the cladding to posts **L** and don't fasten the half-wall cladding to the platform. From the 8-foot 1 by 6s, rip rail caps to fit as shown (note the mitered corners). Fasten them with 3d nails, set the nails, and fill the holes. Round over the top edges. Notch the front of the completed platform for handles **H** (see large drawing and Detail 1) and fasten the handles in place with lag screws.

5. Glue and screw together roof supports **N** and **O**. Fasten this frame to the posts with counterbored bolts and T-nuts as shown. Glue and screw together roof pieces **P** and **Q**; make an-

BUY		TO MAKE		
Fir (Clear or Select structural grade)				
2	6-foot 1 by 6s	2	Frame pieces **A**:	¾" by 5½" by 48"
		2	Frame pieces **C**:	¾" by 5½" by 11⅞"
4	8-foot 1 by 6s	4	Frame pieces **B**:	¾" by 5½" by 81½"
1	14-foot 1 by 4	4	Wall pieces **I**:	¾" by 3½" by 37"
2	8-foot 1 by 4s	2	Wall pieces **K**:	¾" by 3½" by 41"
		2	Roof supports **N**:	¾" by 3½" by 48½"
2	8-foot 1 by 4s	10	Wall pieces **J**:	¾" by 3½" by 16½"
3	8-foot 4 by 4s	2	Legs **G**	3½" by 3½" by 20¾"
		2	Handles **H**:	3½" by 3½" by 36"
		2	Posts **L**:	3½" by 3½" by 38½"
		2	Posts **M**:	3½" by 3½" by 38½"
5	8-foot 2 by 4s	2	Plates **E**:	1½" by 3½" by 48"
		4	Plates **F**:	1½" by 3½" by 35½"
		2	Roof supports **O**:	1½" by 3½" by 82"
6	8-foot 1 by 2s	3	Roof pieces **P**:	¾" by 1½" by 83½"
		5	Roof pieces **Q**:	¾" by 1½" by 47"
2	12-foot 1 by 2s	10	Roof pieces **R**:	¾" by 1½" by 28½"

MISCELLANEOUS

3 fir 1 by 6s, each 8' long • 3 4' by 8' sheets of ¾" fir plywood: grades AD, CD, and CDX
2 4' by 8' sheets of ¼" birch plywood and 1 4' by 8' sheet of ¾" birch plywood, all shop grade
1¾" fir round, 5' long • 2 pieces of ½" hardwood dowel, each 3" long
1⅜" fir round: 2 pieces 44" long, 1 piece 50" long • 25' of 5⁄16" nylon rope
75' of 3⁄16" nylon cord • 2' of ½" nylon webbing • 15 yards of 10 oz. cotton canvas, 36" wide
6 nylon fairleads and 3 horn cleats, all with mounting screws
Heavy thread • 13 ⅜" grommets • 12 2¼" bronze snaps (check marine supply stores)
12 hollow-wall fasteners, ¼" drill, ⅛"–½" grip range • 12 #10 washers
¼" bolts: 9 at 1½", 4 at 3½", 4 at 4", all with washers and T-nuts
8 lag screws, ¼" by 3", with washers • ¼ lb. (about 50) drywall screws, 1¼" by #6
6d and 4d box nails • 3d finishing nails • Brads • 4 sq. inches of leather • Wood glue
Wood putty • Finish • Twin mattress, 39" by 75"

gled cuts in roof pieces **R** and attach to **P** (see Detail 1). Glue and screw **PQ** and **PR** together and fasten the truss to **N** and **O** with screws counterbored ¾ inch. Do not glue.

6. To measure for the tent panels, use the large drawing and Detail 2 as guides, allowing at least ¾ inch at each edge for seams, 1 inch and ½ inch for hems where shown, and about 6 inches at the bottoms of the three roll-up panels. Make the hems, then sew pockets to fit the 1⅜-inch rollers. Cut six 3-inch discs from 1 by 4 scrap.

Join the panels with either simple or lapped and felled seams. Cut reinforcing triangles from the leather and attach where shown. Cut 2-inch pieces of webbing, then loop and stitch in place where shown. Install grommets in the bottom of the half-wall panels (see large drawing and Detail 2).

7. Build the wheels as shown, gluing and nailing them with 3d nails; round over the edges. Assemble the axle, spacers, and wheels; drill for and install the dowel retaining pins.

Detach the wheels and roof-truss assembly and finish all parts as desired. (We used enamel on the plywood and clear penetrating oil on the solid wood.) Glue the rope in place on the wheels, butting the ends and fastening with 3d nails if necessary.

8. Detach posts **L** and the half-wall subassembly, move all parts to the room, and reassemble. Place the tent on the frame and install the bronze snaps, fastening them as shown in Detail 2 (use the photo as a guide to spacing; fasten one snap to each post **L** with a 1¼-inch screw). Lace the tent in place with rope as shown in the photo.

Install the rollers and screw a 3-inch disc at each end. Install the cords, fairleads, and horn cleats as shown in the large drawing and Detail 2. Add the mattress.

Architect: Richard Fernau.

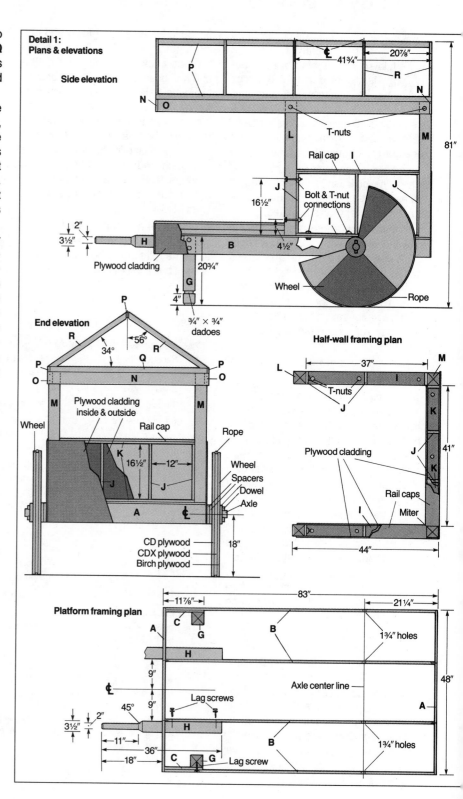

Detail 1: Plans & elevations

Side elevation

End elevation

Half-wall framing plan

Platform framing plan

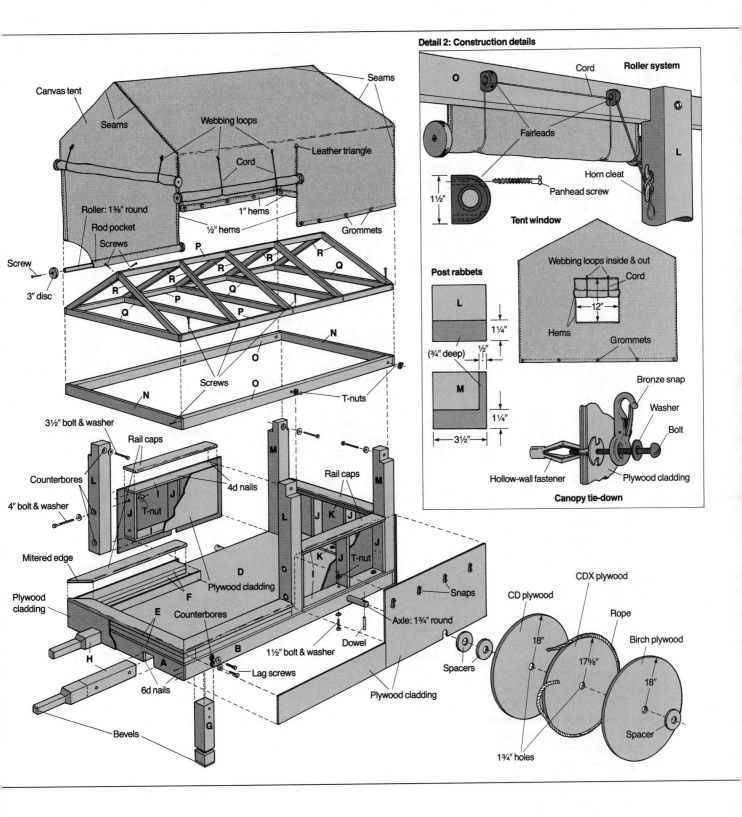

Detail 2: Construction details

Canvas tent

Seams

Seams

Webbing loops

Cord

Leather triangle

Roller: 1⅜" round

Rod pocket

Screws

1" hems

½" hems

Grommets

Screw

3" disc

P

R

R

R

R

Q

R

P

Q

Q

P

P

N

Screws

O

O

O

N

T-nuts

3½" bolt & washer

Rail caps

Counterbores

L

4" bolt & washer

Mitered edge

Plywood
cladding

E

H

A

B

6d nails

Bevels

G

Counterbores

F

D

Plywood cladding

J

I

J

T-nut

I

4d nails

M

L

J

K

J

Rail caps

M

J

K

J

T-nut

I

1½" bolt & washer

Dowel

Lag screws

Axle: 1¾" round

Snaps

Spacers

Plywood cladding

Roller system

O

Cord

Fairleads

L

1½"

Panhead screw

Horn cleat

Tent window

Post rabbets

L

1¼"

(¾" deep)

½"

M

1¼"

3½"

Webbing loops inside & out

Cord

12"

Hems

Grommets

Bronze snap

Washer

Bolt

Hollow-wall fastener

Plywood cladding

Canopy tie-down

CDX plywood

CD plywood

Rope

18"

Birch plywood

17⅝"

18"

Spacer

1¾" holes

TRACK STAR

Race car bed

This bed is guaranteed to fire the imagination of the most avid car fan, young or old. Styled after the famous Can-Am racers, it sports an air dam and rear wing, fender flares, and ground-effects skirts.

The structure is similar to that of the space shuttle bed (pages 74–77); it's based on a youth mattress. The bed's joinery isn't difficult, but the bed can be time-consuming to build. You'll need basic tools plus a saber saw and a router. A radial-arm or table saw also helps.

The drawings are on pages 84–85.

1. Cut all plywood pieces to size. Note: Grid only one outer side **D** (to transfer the contours, see page 36); use this piece **D** as a pattern for cutting its mate. Make only the straight cuts in inner sides **G** and all but the angled cuts on bulkheads **E** and **F**. Cut tires **T** and **U**, and shape the wheels in outer sides **D** (see Detail 3).

Rip the 1 by 4 to 3 inches wide. Rip the 6-foot 2 by 6s to 4¾ inches wide; crosscut to make three pieces, each 48 inches long; four pieces, each 6¾ inches long; and four pieces, each 1½ inches long. Crosscut the 10-foot 2 by 6 to make two 49½-inch-long pieces.

2. Unless otherwise noted, all connections are made with glue and countersunk screws set in ¹⁄₁₆-inch pilot holes and spaced 3 to 5 inches apart. Assemble supports **A** and feet **B** as shown. Fasten these assemblies on base **C** according to the guidelines in Detail 1.

3. Position one outer side **D** and bulkheads **E** and **F**; mark **E** and **F** for the angled cuts noted in the large drawing and cut. Attach outer sides **D**, rear bulkhead **E**, and front bulkhead **F**, as shown in the large drawing and Detail 5, resting sides **D** on the projections of feet **B** (see Detail 5). Glue pieces **J** in position as shown in the large drawing. Rest the unfinished inner sides **G** on base **C** and against outer sides **D**; trace

the top contours. Referring to Details 1 and 5, mark the contours of the notched wing supports and complete the cutting of sides **G**. Fasten them in place on the guidelines (see Detail 1). Add braces **H**.

4. Build nose **O** from pieces cut from the 2 by 6s (see Detail 2). Fasten the nose in place on front bulkhead **F**. Smooth the top of the nose.

5. Attach fender flares **K** and **M**, side skirts **L** (cut to fit from the 1 by 4), and corner pieces **N**. Rout the continuous chamfer in the flares, skirts, corner pieces, and air dam as shown in Detail 4. Hold pieces **I** in position and trace the outline of each vent opening in outer sides **D**. Cut pieces of quarter-round molding to fit within these outlines and glue them in place on **I** (see Detail 5).

6. Cut fifty 1-inch squares or circles from leftover ¼-inch plywood to serve as pressure pads that help bend the top. Glue top **P** in the slots in inner sides **G** (note that **P** will overhang sides **D** and **G**—don't attempt to align it).

Working from back to front in increments of two feet or so, glue and screw top **P** to sides **D** and **G** and braces **H**, spacing screws 2 to 3 inches apart and passing each one through a pad before fastening. Let the glue cure, then remove the screws and refasten them at every other hole, omitting the pads and countersinking the screws. Repeat for the remaining length of top **P** (note that **P** is intentionally long). Trim the edges of **P** all the way around flush with the outside and inside framework.

7. Round over the leading and trailing edges of wing **Q** and all edges of end plates **R**; assemble **Q** and **R** as shown in Detail 5. Fasten the wing to the wing supports, then add support **S** after rounding over its exposed edges. Assemble tires **T** and **U** as shown in the large drawing and round over (see Detail 3). From the plastic pipe, cut, shape, and drill the four exhaust pipes **V** as shown in Detail 5.

8. Round over and putty all edges; fill the screw holes. Shape, putty, and sand the nose so **D**, **O**, and **P** all meet "seamlessly." Putty the inside angles of the nose, flares, skirts, wing, and wing supports; shape the putty with your fingers or a dowel to give a coved appearance (see photo).

Sand well and paint carefully (see pages 72–73). We painted our racer with a variety of enamels: high-gloss red for the body and louvers; flat black for pieces **I** and **J**, the tires, and any exposed areas of the supports and bulkhead **F**; gold metal spray paint for the wheels; and chrome spray paint for the exhaust pipes and the chair glides used as hubs and lug nuts. We trimmed our car with automotive striping tape and vinyl letters and numbers.

After the paint is dry, glue on the louver panels and tires. Install the four exhaust pipes **V** as shown in Detail 5, attaching each one with two ¾-inch screws inserted through the holes drilled in the pipe. Nail the chair glides to the wheels.

Design: Scott Fitzgerrell.

BUY	TO MAKE
Birch plywood (shop grade)	
2 ¾-inch 4 by 8-foot sheets	Pieces **A–H**, **K**, **M**, **N**, and **Q–S** (see Detail 1)
1 ¼-inch 4 by 8-foot sheet	Pieces **I**, **J**, **P**, **T**, **U**, and router base (see Detail 1)

MISCELLANEOUS

3 pine 2 by 6s, each 6' long • 1 pine 2 by 6, 10' long • 1 pine 1 by 4, 6' long
4' of 2" plastic pipe • 6' of ½" quarter-round molding • 8 flathead woodscrews, ¾" by #8
Nylon chair glides: 4 at 1⅞" diameter and 16 at ⅝" diameter • Water-base powdered wood putty
1 lb. (about 200) drywall screws, 1¼" by #6 • Wood glue • Nontoxic enamel
Automotive striping tape • Vinyl letters and numbers • 1 youth mattress, 33" by 66", 4" thick

Sleek, sculptural lines belie the humble plywood origins of this dramatic race car bed. Its youth-size mattress makes it suitable for even a small bedroom. With a little time, some basic tools, and a router, you can build one for your own Grand Prix driver.

Detail 1: Plywood cutting patterns (3″ grid)

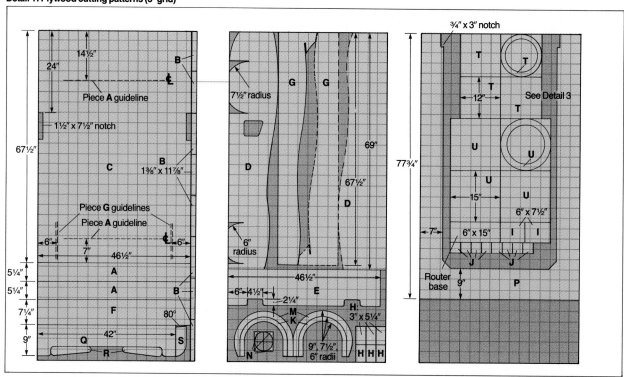

24″
14½″
B
Piece **A** guideline
1½″ x 7½″ notch
67½″
C
B
1⅜″ x 11⅞″
Piece **G** guidelines
Piece **A** guideline
6″
7″
46½″
6″
5¼″
A
5¼″
A
B
7¼″
F
80°
9″
42″
Q
S
R

7½″ radius
G
G
D
69″
67½″
D
6″
radius
46½″
6″ 4½″
E
2¼″
H
3″ x 5¼″
M
K
9″, 7½″,
6″ radii
N
H H H

¾″ x 3″ notch
T
T
12″
See Detail 3
T
U
U
77¾″
U
U
6″ x 7½″
6″ x 15″
I I
7″
J
J
Router
base
9″
P

Detail 2: Nose assembly

1. Using glue, make upper and middle subassemblies from pieces cut from 6′ 2 x 6 (see drawing at bottom). Trace side profile onto ends of upper subassembly (see Detail 5); make saw cuts as shown and knock out waste area. Round over edges of middle subassembly as indicated. Trim corners of both subassemblies to a 3″ radius (see plan view).

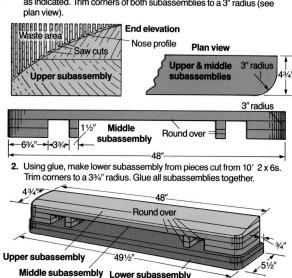

Waste area
End elevation
Nose profile
Saw cuts
Plan view
Upper subassembly
Upper & middle subassemblies
3″ radius
4¾″
3″ radius
1½″
Middle subassembly
Round over
6¾″ 3¾″
48″

2. Using glue, make lower subassembly from pieces cut from 10′ 2 x 6s. Trim corners to a 3¾″ radius. Glue all subassemblies together.

4¾″
48″
Round over
49½″
¾″
5½″
Upper subassembly
Middle subassembly **Lower subassembly**

Detail 3: Wheel routing

1. Remove router baseplate; use as a pattern to make bit and mounting holes in the plywood base. Mount router.

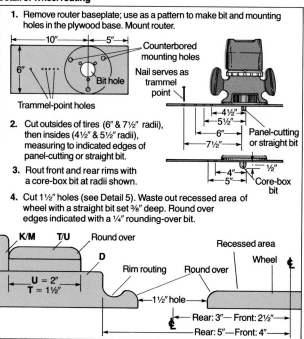

10″
5″
6″
Counterbored mounting holes
Nail serves as trammel point
Bit hole
Trammel-point holes
4½″
5½″
6″
Panel-cutting or straight bit
7½″
½″
4″
5″
Core-box bit

2. Cut outsides of tires (6″ & 7½″ radii), then insides (4½″ & 5½″ radii), measuring to indicated edges of panel-cutting or straight bit.

3. Rout front and rear rims with a core-box bit at radii shown.

4. Cut 1½″ holes (see Detail 5). Waste out recessed area of wheel with a straight bit set ⅜″ deep. Round over edges indicated with a ¼″ rounding-over bit.

K/M
T/U
Round over
D
Recessed area
Wheel
Rim routing
Round over
U = 2″
T = 1½″
1½″ hole
Rear: 3″ — Front: 2½″
Rear: 5″ — Front: 4″

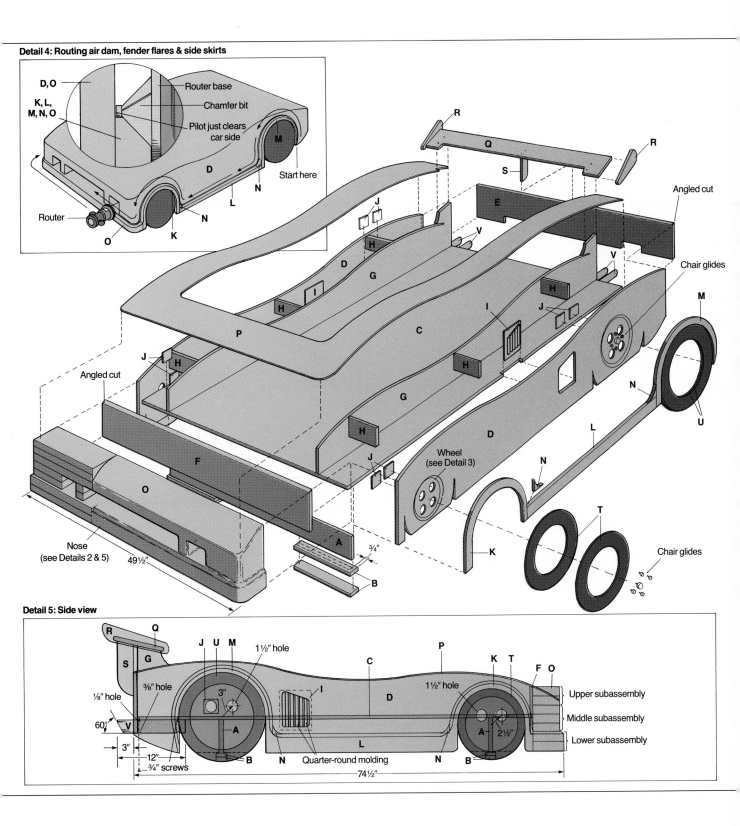

Detail 4: Routing air dam, fender flares & side skirts

D,O

K, L,
M, N, O

Router base

Chamfer bit

Pilot just clears
car side

M

D

N

L

N

K

Router

O

Start here

R

Q

R

S

E

V

V

Angled cut

Chair glides

M

J

H

D

G

I

H

I

H

J

H

C

N

J

H

G

U

P

J

H

D

L

N

H

G

J

Wheel
(see Detail 3)

D

A

¾"

B

Angled cut

F

O

T

Chair glides

Nose
(see Details 2 & 5)

49½"

K

Detail 5: Side view

R

Q

J U M

1½" hole

P

K T

F O

G

S

⅜" hole

3"

C

1½" hole

Upper subassembly

⅛" hole

I

D

Middle subassembly

60°

V

A

N

A

2½"

Lower subassembly

3"

12"

B

Quarter-round molding

N

B

¾" screws

74½"

Occupying little more space than a twin bed, this multipurpose structure provides room for sleep, study, and storage. The elevated bed is low enough to ensure sitting headroom for older children, the adjustable desktop has ample area for serious study, and the handy wardrobe catches the closet overflow.

Teen loft bed with desk & wardrobe

Maximize a teenager's room with this all-in-one environment. In little more space than that taken by a twin bed, this structure offers a broad desk, several shelves, closet space, and a lofty twin bed.

For this project, you'll need basic tools, a saber saw, and a radial-arm or table saw. Use a plug cutter to cut the plugs from scrap wood.

Refer to the drawings on pages 88–89 as you work.

1. Cut all pieces to size. For the fir plywood, no layouts are needed—cut platform **O** and desk top **P** from one sheet each, then cut cleats **K**, **L**, **N**, **Q**, and **R** from the remaining pieces.

Round the upper corners of closet sides **A** and uprights **E** at the radius shown in Detail 2. Cut the triangular ladder holes in one upright **E** (see Detail 2). Cut the screen molding to fit across the horizontal edge of each triangular hole and attach the pieces with brads.

Notch the corners of closet back **B** as shown in the cutting layout. Also notch both ends of notched rail **J** to fit over side rails **H** as shown.

2. To assemble the closet cabinet, glue and nail closet base **C** to two supports **D**. Then glue and screw closet back **B** to support **D**, using 2-inch screws. Glue and screw closet sides **A** to back **B** and supports **D**.

3. To assemble the other side, glue and nail one shelf **G** to two supports **D**. Glue and screw end support **F** to support **D**, then add uprights **E** (be sure to place the upright with the cutouts on the side of the bed that will face forward). Screw remaining shelf **G** in position as shown.

4. For the bed frame, round one end of each side rail **H** at the radius shown. Glue and screw end rail **I** into the side rails, using 3½-inch screws. Countersink the screws. Glue and nail cleats **K** and **L** onto the inner faces of side rails **H** and end rail **I**. Glue and screw through rails **H** into bed supports **M** as shown. Countersink the screws. Measure, then cut and attach short cleats **N** with nails.

5. Nail platform **O** to the cleats and bed supports. Screw through rails **H** into notched rail **J**, resting the lower edge of **J** on the platform support.

6. Determine the desired desk height. Then drill holes for carriage bolts through remaining two supports **D**, back **B**, and end support **F** as shown. Attach the supports with carriage bolts.

7. Glue and nail desk cleats **Q** and **R** around the edge of desk top **P**. Apply the plastic laminate to the desk top with contact cement and trim the edges (for instructions, see page 73). Drill coun-

tersink and pilot holes in desk trim **S**. Attach the trim.

8. Drill holes for the carriage bolts that connect the uprights to the bed frame. Drill counterbore holes inside the frame for the washers and nuts.

9. Plug all screw holes. Set all nails and fill the holes. Sand as required. Seal, then apply two coats of paint to all outer plywood surfaces as shown in Detail 2. Finish remaining areas with two coats of clear finish, sanding between the coats.

10. With a helper, move the components into the room. Lay the end cabinets on their sides and bolt the bed frame to them. Stand the assembly upright. Bolt the desk in place and add the mattress. Attach the closet pole end brackets; trim and add the closet pole. Mount the mirror where shown in Detail 2.

Design: Don Vandervort.

BUY		TO MAKE	
Birch plywood (shop grade)			
3	¾-inch 4 by 8-foot sheets	Pieces **A–C** and **E–G** (see Detail 1)	
Clear pine or Douglas fir			
3	8-foot 2 by 8s	2 Side rails **H**:	1½″ by 7¼″ by 85″
		1 End rail **I**:	1½″ by 7¼″ by 43½″
		1 Notched rail **J**:	1½″ by 7¼″ by 43½″
4	8-foot 2 by 3s	6 Supports **D**:	1½″ by 2½″ by 43½″
		2 Bed supports **M**:	1½″ by 2½″ by 40½″
1	6-foot 1 by 2	1 Desk trim **S**:	¾″ by 1½″ by 62⅝″
Fir plywood (grade AD)			
2	¾-inch 4 by 8-foot sheets	2 Cleats **K**:	¾″ by 1½″ by 62⅝″
		1 Cleat **L**:	¾″ by 1½″ by 40½″
		2 Cleats **N**:	¾″ by 1½″—cut to length
		1 Platform **O**:	¾″ by 40½″ by 85″
		1 Desk top **P**:	¾″ by 42¾″ by 63⅜″
		2 Desk cleats **Q**:	¾″ by 1½″ by 39¾″
		2 Desk cleats **R**:	¾″ by 1½″ by 63⅜″

MISCELLANEOUS

4′ of ¼″ by ¾″ screen molding • 4′ of 1⅜″ closet pole round
Closet pole end brackets with screws • Brads • 4d finishing nails • 2″ by #6 drywall screws
3½″ by #8 drywall screws • 4′ by 6′ sheet of plastic laminate
20 carriage bolts, ¼″ by 2″, with nuts and washers
Contact cement • Wood glue • Wood putty • Enamel • Clear penetrating oil finish
1 twin mattress, 39″ by 75″ • 15½″ by 55½″ framed mirror with mounting cleats or 4 ¾″ screws

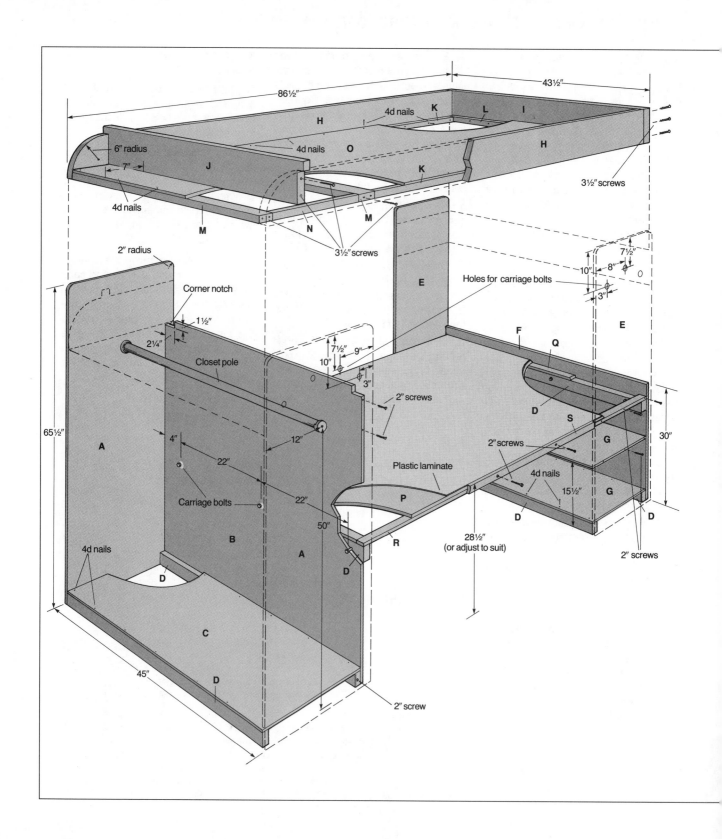

Detail 1: Plywood cutting layout

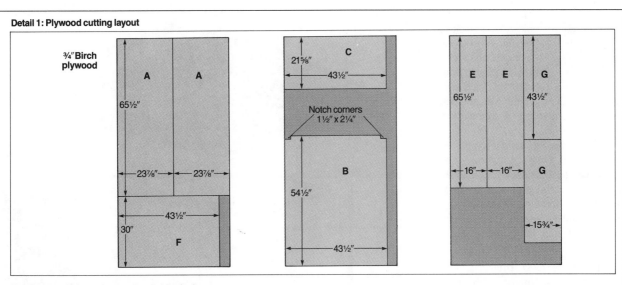

¾″ Birch plywood

A A

65½″

23⅞″ 23⅞″

43½″

30″

F

C

21⅝″

43½″

Notch corners
1½″ x 2¼″

B

54½″

43½″

E E G

65½″ 43½″

16″ 16″ G

15¾″

Detail 2: Paint & ladder layout (front elevation)

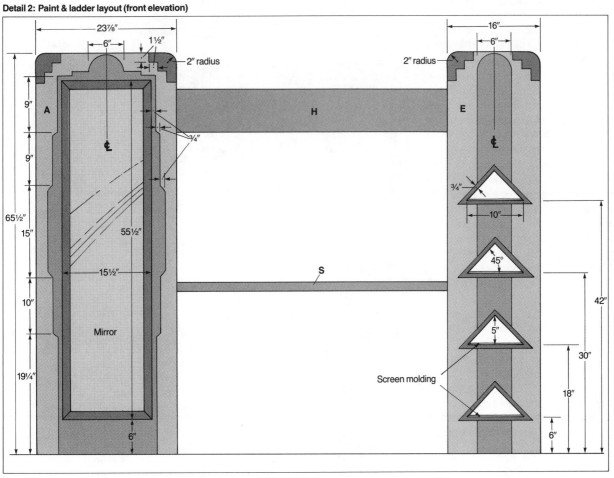

23⅞″

6″

1½″

2″ radius

16″

6″

2″ radius

9″

A

H

E

9″

¾″

65½″

15″

¾″

55½″

10″

15½″

S

10″

45°

Mirror

5″

19¼″

Screen molding

6″

42″

30″

18″

6″

A ROOM THAT GROWS UP

Adjustable table (below)
Crib-to-youth bed (page 92)
Adjustable desk (page 95)

Adjustable table

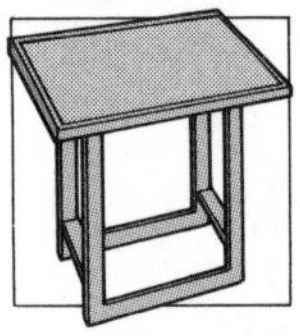

This easy-to-make table adjusts quickly to three different heights, making it useful for all ages, toddler to adult. A sturdy hardwood frame "tumbles" into three positions and supports an easy-care plastic laminate top.

All you'll need to build the table is a basic tool kit. One note on materials: Though we list the cross-sectional size of the frame pieces as ¾ inch by 1½ inches, available hardwood is likely to be fractionally different. Use any similar size for your table; just keep the overall dimensions accurate.

1. Cut pieces **A–D** to size. Cut the dowel into 32 pieces, each 1⅜ inches long. From the 1 by 1 pine or fir, cut eight positioning blocks, each 2¾ inches long. Cut a piece from the plastic laminate 33 inches square.

2. Glue and blind dowel frame pieces **A** to frame pieces **B**, as shown in the large drawing and Detail 1 (see page 45). Join the **AB** assemblies by gluing and through doweling (see page 44) frame connectors **C** where shown.

3. Apply the plastic laminate to table top **D** with contact cement and trim the edges (for instructions, see page 73). A bevelled trim cut is also fine; it leaves an attractive "reveal" around the table top once the edging is applied. Mark and cut trim pieces **E** for either miter or butt joints as desired; then glue and nail the trim in place. Set the nails and fill the holes.

4. Round or chamfer all the edges, sand, and apply a finish of your choice (we used lacquer).

5. Invert the top, center the frame in its lowest position (see Detail 2), and trace its outline. Mark the locations for the positioning blocks and double check their locations by trying the frame in its other positions. Glue the blocks in place.

Design: Scott Fitzgerrell.

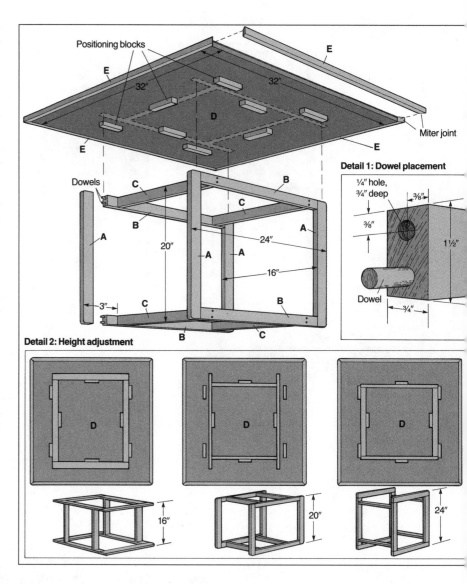

Detail 1: Dowel placement

Detail 2: Height adjustment

BUY		TO MAKE		
Maple or birch				
Random-length 1 by 2s	4	Frame pieces	**A**:	¾" by 1½" by 20"
	4	Frame pieces	**B**:	¾" by 1½" by 21"
	4	Frame connectors	**C**:	¾" by 1½" by 14½"
Random-length 1 by 1s	4	Trim pieces	**E**:	⅞" by ⅞" by 34"
Particleboard				
1	¾-inch 4 by 4-foot sheet	1	Table top **D**:	32" by 32"

MISCELLANEOUS

4' by 4' sheet of plastic laminate • 2' of 1 by 1 pine or fir • 48" of ¼" hardwood dowel
Contact cement • 3d finishing nails • Wood glue • Wood putty • Clear nontoxic finish

All three of these cleverly designed pieces can be tailored to fit a child from infancy right through high school and beyond. In this baby's room, the adjustable table rests in its lowest position; the crib-to-youth bed is configured as a crib, with its dresser resting on the mattress support and the crib rails in place; and the adjustable desk is set in its high position, allowing an adult to work close by baby's side. For a look into the future, see page 94.

Crib-to-youth bed

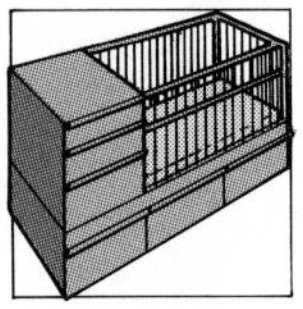

Both sleep and storage are provided for in this well-designed crib-to-youth bed. For baby, the bed is fitted with rails and a crib-size mattress. A stack of drawers nestles at the foot of the bed.

When your child outgrows the crib, the rails come off, the drawer stack moves to the floor, and—with the addition of a bunk-size mattress—the set serves through the teen-age years.

In addition to basic tools, you'll need a radial-arm or table saw equipped with a dado blade.

1. Cut all pieces to size. Cut a ¾-inch by ⅜-inch rabbet in one long edge of each cabinet side **I**. Cut 1¼-inch by ¾-inch corner notches in both ends of interior supports **G**. Cut ½-inch-wide by ¼-inch-deep dadoes in drawer sides **N** (see Detail 1 and large drawing).

Cut a ¾-inch by 2-inch rabbet in the end of each post **R**. Rip one rail **U** in half and mortise for hinges where shown. Mark and drill ⅝-inch-diameter by ½-inch-deep holes for dowels in rails **S**, **T**, and **U** where shown (mark the rails together, side by side). Note: For safety, be sure to follow the specifications in the large drawing for the spacing of the dowel bars.

2. Unless otherwise specified, glue and nail all joints, spacing nails 4 to 6 inches apart. First attach sides **A** to back **B**, then to front panel **C**. Add bed cleats **D** and **E**, positioning them 2¾ inches down from the top edges. Add cleats **F** to the inner surfaces of sides **A**. Attach interior supports **G**. Add mattress support **H** and fasten it to **D**, **E**, and **G**.

3. Attach cabinet sides **I** to top **J**; then add cabinet back **K**. Add bases **L** and **M** (the base projects 2 inches below cabinet pieces **I**), fastening as shown. Mark and cut the plastic laminate to fit over top **J**. Attach it with contact cement and trim the edges (for instructions, see page 73).

4. Assemble the six drawers as shown in the large drawing and Detail 1; cut the drawer pulls from the ¾-inch stock and bevel them as shown. Mount the drawer glides, following the manufacturer's directions and allowing ⅛-inch clearance between cabinet drawers. Add casters to the bottoms of the underbed drawers.

5. Glue bars **V**, **W**, **X**, and **Y** into their respective rails as shown in the large drawing; be sure the specified length of the bars is left exposed for each panel. Fasten rails **S** to posts **R** with

glue and countersunk 3-inch screws as shown. Add the hinges to the front rails where shown.

6. Set the nails and fill the holes. Sand and finish the bed and cabinet with sealer and two coats of nontoxic enamel. Use a clear nontoxic finish on the crib rail assembly and drawer pulls. Let the finish dry.

7. Remove the drawers and place the cabinet on the bed in the room where it goes. Drill counterbore holes in posts **R** for screws where shown; then screw —but don't glue—the end rail assembly to the front and back assemblies, using 2-inch screws as shown. Screw through cabinet base **L** into the ends of long rails **T**, using 2-inch screws as shown. Add the sliding bolts and their strike plates. Set in the crib mattress and put the drawers in their places.

Design: Don Vandervort.

BUY		TO MAKE		
Birch plywood (shop grade)				
2	¾-inch 4 by 8-foot sheets	Pieces **A–C**, **G**, **I–M**, and **Q** (see Detail 2)		
Fir plywood (grade AB)				
1	¾-inch 4 by 8-foot sheet	2	Bed cleats **D**:	¾″ by 1¼″ by 31½″
		2	Bed cleats **E**:	¾″ by 1¼″ by 76″
		2	Cleats **F**:	¾″ by 1¼″ by 9½″
		1	Mattress support **H**:	¾″ by 31½″ by 77½″
2	½-inch 4 by 8-foot sheets	Pieces **N–P** (see Detail 2)		
Clear fir, birch, or maple				
1	6-foot 2 by 2	2	Crib posts **R**:	1½″ by 1½″ by 32″
3	10-foot 2 by 2s	2	Crib rails **S**:	1½″ by 1½″ by 28½″
		2	Crib rails **T**:	1½″ by 1½″ by 54½″
		3	Crib rails **U**:	1½″ by 1½″ by 53¾″
Hardwood dowel				
53	⅝-inch by 36-inch lengths	21	Long front bars **V**:	⅝″ by 20½″
		21	Short front bars **W**:	⅝″ by 9″
		11	End bars **X**:	⅝″ by 28″
		21	Back bars **Y**:	⅝″ by 30″

MISCELLANEOUS

14′ of ¾″ by ¾″ clear fir, birch, or maple • 3d finishing nails • 1″ by #6 drywall screws 1½″ by #6 drywall screws • 2″ by #8 drywall screws • 3″ by #8 drywall screws 2 2″ brass butt hinges • 2 brass sliding bolts • 3 pairs of 22″ full-extension drawer glides 12 1¾″ plate-mounted casters with screws • Contact cement • Sealer 23¾″ by 31½″ sheet of plastic laminate • Wood glue • Wood putty • Clear nontoxic finish Nontoxic enamel • Crib-size mattress, 27¼″ by 52″, or bunk-size mattress, 30″ by 75″

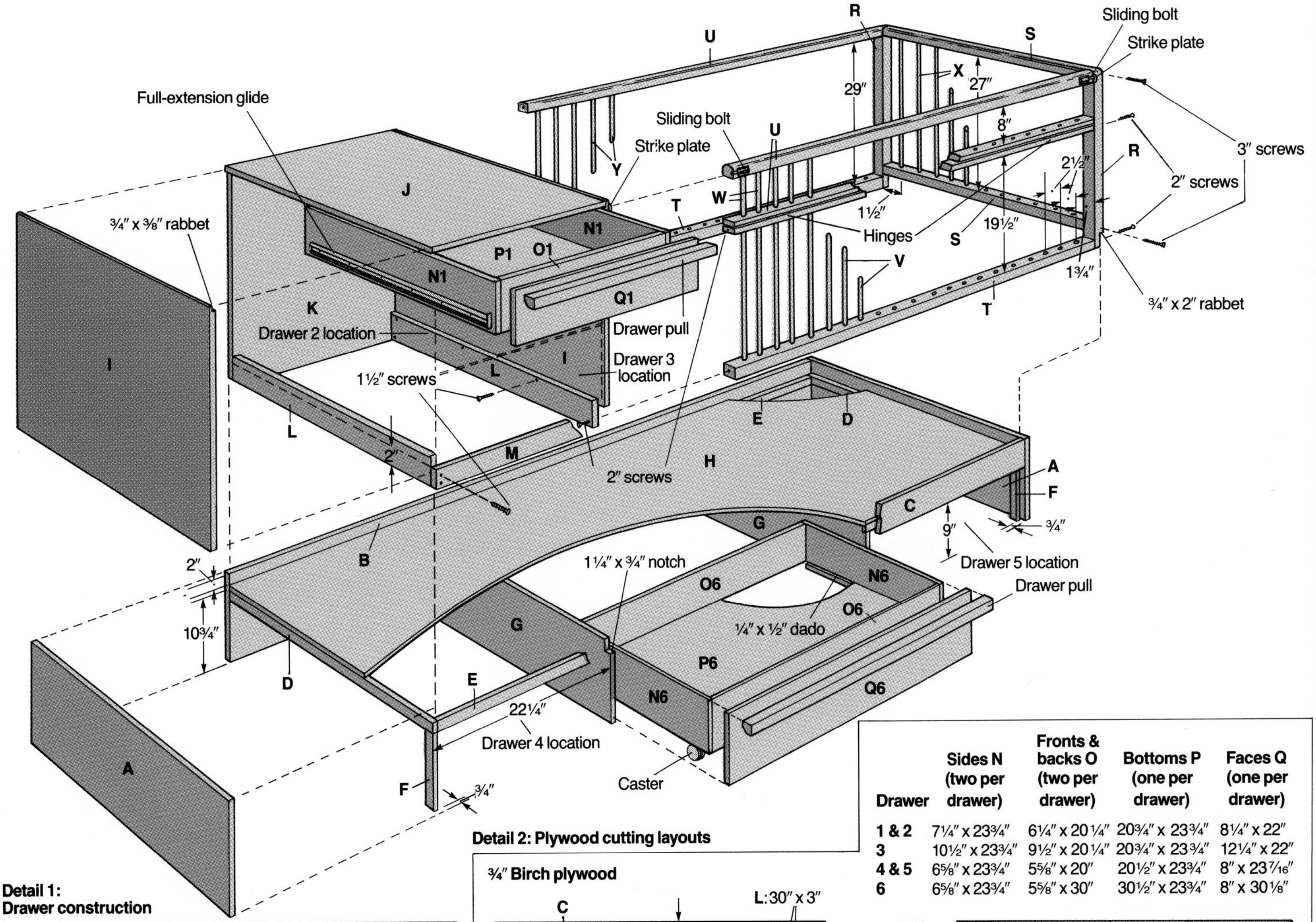

Full-extension glide
¾″ x ⅜″ rabbet
U
R
S
Sliding bolt
Strike plate
29″
X
27″
8″
Sliding bolt
Strike plate
U
3″ screws
2″ screws
R
2½″
W
T
1½″
Hinges
S
19½″
V
1¾″
T
¾″ x 2″ rabbet
J
N1
P1
O1
N1
Q1
K
Drawer pull
Drawer 2 location
I
Drawer 3 location
L
I
1½″ screws
L
E
D
M
2″
2″ screws
H
A
F
C
G
9″
¾″
Drawer 5 location
B
2″
1¼″ x ¾″ notch
O6
N6
Drawer pull
10¾″
G
¼″ x ½″ dado
O6
P6
D
E
N6
Q6
22¼″
Drawer 4 location
A
F
¾″
Caster

Drawer	Sides N (two per drawer)	Fronts & backs O (two per drawer)	Bottoms P (one per drawer)	Faces Q (one per drawer)
1 & 2	7¼″ x 23¾″	6¼″ x 20 ¼″	20¾″ x 23¾″	8¼″ x 22″
3	10½″ x 23¾″	9½″ x 20 ¼″	20¾″ x 23¾″	12¼″ x 22″
4 & 5	6⅝″ x 23¾″	5⅝″ x 20″	20½″ x 23¾″	8″ x 23 7/16″
6	6⅝″ x 23¾″	5⅝″ x 30″	30½″ x 23¾″	8″ x 30⅛″

Detail 1: Drawer construction

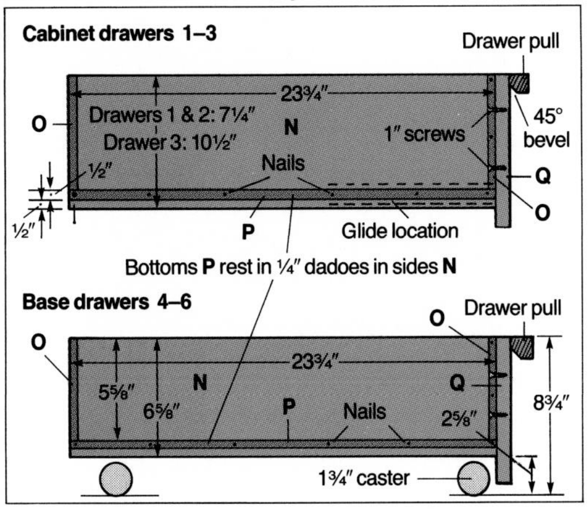

Cabinet drawers 1–3
Drawer pull
23¾″
O
Drawers 1 & 2: 7¼″
Drawer 3: 10½″
N
45° bevel
1″ screws
½″
Nails
Q
O
½″
P
Glide location
Bottoms P rest in ¼″ dadoes in sides N
Base drawers 4–6
O
Drawer pull
O
23¾″
5⅝″
N
6⅝″
Q
P
Nails
2⅝″
8¾″
1¾″ caster

Detail 2: Plywood cutting layouts

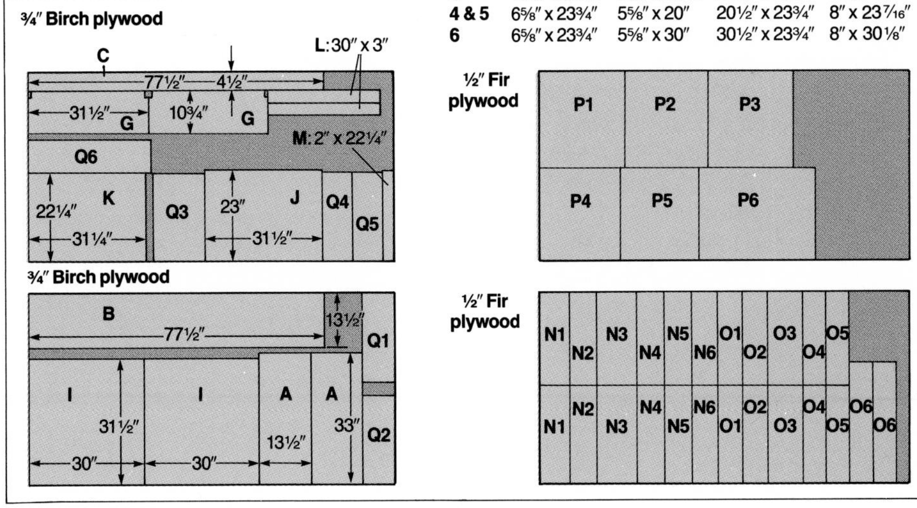

¾″ Birch plywood
C
L: 30″ x 3″
77½″
4½″
31½″
G
10¾″
G
M: 2″ x 22¼″
Q6
K
22¼″
Q3
23″
J
Q4
Q5
31¼″
31½″
¾″ Birch plywood
B
77½″
13½″
Q1
I
I
A
A
31½″
33″
Q2
13½″
30″
30″
½″ Fir plywood
P1
P2
P3
P4
P5
P6
½″ Fir plywood
N1
N2
N3
N4
N5
N6
O1
O2
O3
O4
O5
N1
N2
N3
N4
N5
N6
O1
O2
O3
O4
O5
O6
O6

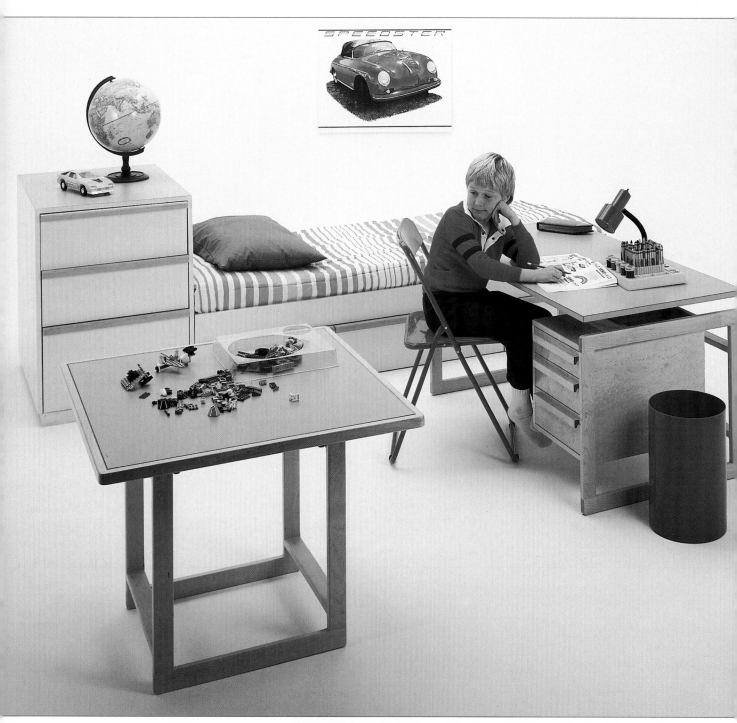

As the child grows, the furniture can be adjusted to fit. In a grade schooler's room, the three-position table is set in its highest configuration for model building (it changes quickly to its other positions as needed); the crib-to-youth bed has been separated into its dresser and bed components; and the adjustable desk (in its low position) is at a comfortable height for the young scholar.

Adjustable desk

To adjust this handy desk, simply rotate the two-way frame and reposition the cabinet and the top.

You'll need basic tools and a router, radial-arm saw, or table saw. Note: Our 1 by 2 maple measured ¾ inch by 1½ inches. If yours differs, just keep the overall dimensions accurate.

1. Cut pieces **A**–**J** to size (see the materials list and drawings). Cut 32 dowel pieces, each 1⅜ inches long. Bevel drawer pulls **J**. Cut dadoes and rabbets in the drawer and cabinet pieces (see the detail drawing). From the 1 by 4, cut positioning blocks; cut a stop block and drawer runners from scrap.

2. Glue and blind dowel (see page 45) frame pieces **A** to pieces **B**; glue and through dowel (see page 44) the **AB** assemblies to frame connectors **C**.

3. Glue and nail together pieces **D**, **E**, and **F**. Assemble pieces **G**, **H**, and **I** (see the detail drawing). Attach pulls **J**. With the cabinet on its back, position the drawers, leaving ¹⁄₁₆ inch around each one. Mark the location of each drawer-side dado on the cabinet. Glue and nail the runners on these marks.

4. From the particleboard, cut desk top **K** to size. Glue and nail the positioning blocks to **K**. From the laminate, cut one piece at 27 by 48 inches, two at 1 by 27 inches, and two at 1 by 48 inches. Apply to the top and edges of **K** with contact cement (see page 73).

5. Round or chamfer all wood edges, fill the holes, sand, and finish as desired. Turn the frame upside down in the "tall" position. Position the cabinet and drill two pilot holes through the top into each connector **C**. Repeat in the "short" position, using the holes as guides for drilling remaining connectors **C**. Mount the cabinet with 2-inch screws, set the top in place, and glue the stop block to the cabinet top.

Design: Helge Olsen.

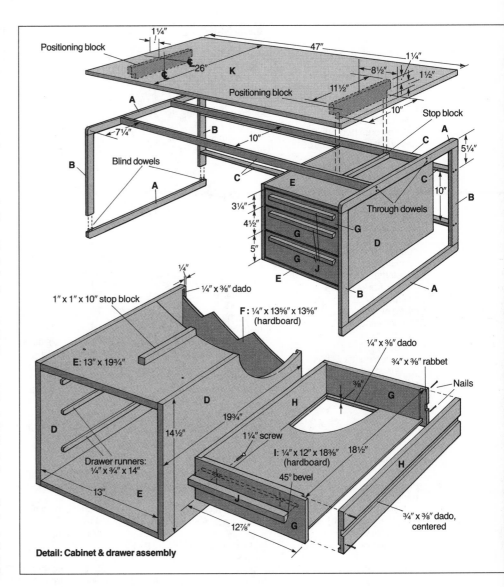

Detail: Cabinet & drawer assembly

BUY		TO MAKE		
Birch or maple				
Random-length 1 by 2s		4	Frame pieces **A**:	¾" by 1½" by 26"
		4	Frame pieces **B**:	¾" by 1½" by 19"
		4	Frame connectors **C**:	¾" by 1½" by 44½"
		3	Drawer pulls **J**:	¾" by 1" by 11"

MISCELLANEOUS

¾" Baltic birch plywood, 5' by 5' • ¼" hardboard, 4' by 4' • ¾" particleboard, 4' by 4'
48" by 48" sheet of plastic laminate • 2' of 1 by 4 pine or fir
#6 drywall screws: 6 at 1¼", 4 at 2" • 48" of ¼" hardwood dowel • 3d finishing nails
Wood glue • Contact cement • Wood putty • Clear nontoxic finish

INDEX

Sunset

Children's Rooms

& Play Yards

By the Editors of Sunset Books
and Sunset Magazine

Lane Publishing Co., Menlo Park, California

We gratefully acknowledge...

...the following individuals and companies for their encouragement and assistance in gathering the material for this book: Jeanne Clark, Gene Clements, The Cotton Works, Roy Davis, Gymnastics West, Sharon Owen Haven, House of Today, Kiyoko Ishimoto, Karen Loy, Tina Meyers, Minimal Space, Poppy Fabrics, Linda J. Selden, Anne Stewart, Antonio Torrice, and Joanne Woods. And a special thank-you goes to the designers whose names appear throughout the book.

Photographers

Richard Fish: 19 bottom left, 91 bottom, 94 top. **Frank Jensen:** 11 top. **Steve W. Marley:** 3, 11 bottom, 19 bottom right, 27 right, 28 top, 29 left, 54 top, 70 top left and right. **Ells Marugg:** 54 bottom right. **Don Normark:** 19 top, 30 bottom. **Norman A. Plate:** 22 bottom, 94 bottom. **Bill Ross:** 13 bottom. **Darrow M. Watt:** 4, 5, 6, 12, 13 top left and right, 14 20, 21, 22 top left and right, 27 top left and bottom left, 28 bottom, 29 right, 30 top and center, 35, 36, 37, 38, 43, 44, 45, 46, 51, 52, 53, 54 bottom left, 59, 60, 61, 62, 67, 68, 69, 70 bottom, 75, 76, 77, 78, 83, 84, 85, 86, 91 top left and right, 92, 93.

Supervising Editor:
Susan Warton

Staff Editors:
Kathryn L. Arthurs
Barbara G. Gibson

Special Consultants:
Peter O. Whiteley
Assistant Editor, Sunset Magazine
Diana Bunce
Staff Editor, Sunset Magazine

Design:
Timothy Bachman
JoAnn Masaoka Lewis

Artwork:
Sandra E. Popovich

Cover:
Circus-bright fabrics cover playful foam sculptures designed by Patricia Moser. You'll see their full potential on pages 44 and 45. The room on the cover was designed by James Caldwell and photographed by Darrow M. Watt.

Sunset Books
    Editor, David E. Clark
    Managing Editor, Elizabeth L. Hogan

Seventh printing October 1986

Contents

Children's Rooms 4-67

Sand frigate sails the high, leafy seas (see also page 70).

Play Yards 68-95

Index 96

Children's Rooms

Children's bedrooms mean so much more to them than places to sleep (usually the least popular use) that the physical space involved begs for a better name..."nursery" for the very young, or "lair" for boisterous types, or maybe "habitat" for just about any child.

So much goes on in this one corner of the world that is unquestionably a child's very own. In happiest circumstances, the surroundings serve as living room, kitchen, library, music room, budding artist's studio, mad scientist's lab — not to mention intergalactic space ship or junior discotheque.

No matter what we call them, the chunks of real estate that we allot to our offspring are hard-working and mercurial spaces. To design them wisely and ruggedly demands a fair amount of ingenuity, allowing for needs that will change from hour to hour as well as from year to year.

Naturally, we want to create a friendly, cozy, and safe environment — and, at the same time, we hope it will stay fairly shipshape over the years. Because kids' rooms are often undersized, compared to the clutter they must absorb, the furnishings we choose and the way we arrange them make a big difference.

If all of that sounds daunting enough to boggle a parent's brains, take heart. As you will see in this chapter, many families have come up with diverse and imaginative solutions to typical children's room problems. You'll notice that many different routes were taken to solve the problems, but all led to exciting results.

Mama's bedtime story draws a happy little girl's day to a cozy close.

If Baby so much as hiccups, the *angilhisaun* cradle bobs and sways gently on its ceiling-anchored spring. Directions for building this Eskimo cradle—which is transportable from living room to nursery to back garden —appear on page 8. Design adaptation: Douglas Stewart.

Baby gazes with wonder at his image (and Mama's, too) in the looking glass. His changing table sits inside an opened-up closet. Architect: James Caldwell.

Little "Moses in the bulrushes" takes the air on a summer afternoon, lying snug in a large, go-everywhere basket. (Next year, it can carry a picnic or firewood.)

Just a few nursery notions...

Ah, the bonny wee babe with its fist tightly clutching its blanket. In the first weeks at home, it may sleep most comfortably and conveniently in its parents' bedroom.

The requirements of a first nursery are simple: all you need are a cozy bed, a comfortable spot for feeding, a changing surface that is easy on your back, and plenty of fresh air and visual cheer.

Baby's bed

During your baby's first weeks, a bureau drawer or large wicker basket, equipped with a firm mattress and padded sides, makes an excellent, snug bed. As your baby grows, of course you'll need something bigger, like a crib.

Today's crib was originally designed in the late 19th century, when doctors feared that rocking a baby in a cradle might spoil it and might even foster brain damage. Cribs are still popular as an economical and practical first bed. But if you choose one, keep in mind that it makes an enormous bed for a newborn. Make it a smaller nest by filling one end in with firm cushions (the ticking of a wind-up clock tucked among them sometimes soothes babies just as it does puppies).

Despite the Victorians' qualms, there is really much to be said for the age-old cradle with its gently pacifying motion. A suspended version (such as the Alaskan baby bed shown on the facing page) can be moved from one room to another, or even outdoors —wherever you have a strong, safely secured hook for it (see "Anchor it safely," page 57). Directions for the cradle appear on the next page.

You might want to invest in a baby buggy, either new or previously occupied, to serve as a bed. Besides strolling with it in the park, you can wheel this lovely vehicle throughout the house, giving it a lulling jiggle if Baby whimpers as you cook or water the fern.

Serenity

For feeding and relaxing with your new son or daughter, provide yourself a comfortable place to sit or recline. Most mothers and babies love rocking chairs —but you may prefer a mattress with plenty of pillows, or even a wide hammock.

For Baby's sake (as well as your own, during night feedings), keep artificial lighting soft.

Visual stimulation

Very early, your baby will enjoy good things to look at. Bright colors and movement attract and delight the infant eye. They also create a mood of welcoming cheer in the nursery.

You might want to stitch a soft sculpture mobile like the one shown above. When Baby pulls on the ribbons, the satin "pillows" bounce on elastic cord.

Let your eye roam also to other sources of visual cheer: colorful cloth or paper kites to hang from the ceiling; a bit of stained glass or strips of bright featherweight cloth, hung to catch sunlight in the window; paper parasols, lanterns, or accordion-folded party decorations; even a few choice Christmas trimmings. Also, a bowl of swishing goldfish makes a baby coo with delight.

Eskimo cradle

You can hang the cradle shown on page 6 from a ceiling beam indoors or from a tree limb outside (to read how to anchor its hook securely, see page 57). Construction is quite simple.

You need four 1 by 4s (two 24 inches long, two 36 inches long), a 20 by 24-inch sheet of 1/4-inch tempered hardboard, two 18-inch-long 1 by 2s, and some 3/8-inch-diameter nylon rope (on the cradle we show, the rope is covered with decorative macramé). A 1-inch-diameter spring (garage-door type) can be added so that the bed will jiggle as the baby moves.

Glue and nail the 1 by 4s together to make the frame; bolt the 1 by 2s together in the middle to form a spreader, as shown in the drawing. Drill 7/16-inch holes for the rope in the corners of the hardboard, frame, and spreader, and assemble as shown above by knotting and threading the rope. Suspend the hardboard a few inches below the frame. For extra coziness, lap a small quilt over cradle sides and floor, stapling it underneath. Then lay bedding on top.

Garden-style safety gate

When shopping for a toddler's restraining gate, little Monique's parents felt that most of what they saw was unsightly, if not downright dangerous. Here's the alternative they designed to keep their daughter out of harm's way. It's charming enough that, even though Monique no longer needs it for her safety, she still loves to play with it.

The gate is built of 1 3/8-inch lattice glued to a square frame of 1 by 2s. It is hinged to the outside of the door jamb, and closes with a sliding lock on the outside.

Dresser-top changing table

By adding temporary roll bars to the top of a roomy chest of drawers, you can create a changing table that will continue its service through the years.

Matthew's father went one step further: he jigsawed a decorative top edge along the back roll bar. His son likes to trace its pastoral silhouettes with his hands while undergoing a diaper change.

The decorative back bar is made from 3/4-inch plywood; the sides are cut from 1 by 4-inch pine. Matthew's father cut the back bar following a pattern sketched on a long strip of paper. The sides were simply rounded down at the front to meet the top of an unfinished wood dresser. After careful sanding, the side bars were attached to the back bar with woodscrews and glue. Where the back bar joins the dresser, corner braces and screws are placed out of sight at the back. The sides fasten to the top of the dresser with two vertically countersunk screws near the front.

For preschool Picassos

Here is a low but expansive paper-dispensing table, designed by the mother of two young artists. Its surface is a 28 by 80-inch hollow-core door; supports and legs are clear fir. A large roll of paper (check with a newspaper plant or butcher supplier) revolves on a dowel at one end; plastic dish tubs, mounted on runners, slide out from underneath the table, like drawers.

Buy the paper roll first, then choose a dowel that will fit its opening and allow the roll to revolve freely. Positioning of the dowel on its upright supports will depend on the thickness of the paper roll.

Buy the plastic dish tubs before attaching the legs. Calculate the spacing of the legs by measuring the width of a tub just below its lip and adding the width of the runners on which the tub will slide.

Fasten all pieces with white glue and woodscrews, except for the dowel (which must be removeable from the holes in its supports). Sand and apply the finish of your choice.

Kitchen step-up box

Three-year-old William can carry his hollow cube from its low cupboard to the sink, to get a drink of water, or to the kitchen counter when he wants to help the cook (but only when his parents wish: the cupboard has a safety catch). Made from 5 feet of 1 by 10-inch pine, glued and nailed together with 2-inch finishing nails, the cube is wide enough for steady standing. For reinforcement, chamfer strips are glued to the inside corners. As an extra precaution, in case of a little spilled water, William's father added safety treads.

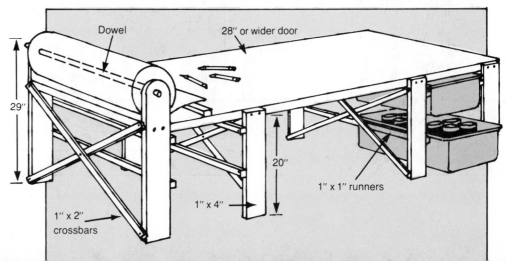

Dowel

28" or wider door

29"

20"

1" x 1" runners

1" x 4"

1" x 2" crossbars

Indoor romps for tiny Tarzans

Not long after a toddler's first steps comes every parent's favorite phase of childhood —the big Energy Explosion. This is the era in which most kids find it nearly impossible to slow down to a walk. Their seemingly constant motion — running, jumping, climbing, tumbling, wriggling —can be fun for everyone, but exhausting, too.

How can a run-ragged parent channel such boundless energy, especially when weather conditions keep everyone cloistered indoors? One way is to provide your small whirlwind with one of the good commercial indoor swings or kiddie gyms available today (for safety tips on hanging such play equipment, see page 57). Some further energy-dispensing ideas are shown here.

A new look at ladders

For children more than 3 or 4 years old, straight, wooden, round-runged ladders (such as you would find at a hardware store) provide all kinds of valuable coordination-improving experiences. More important: They're fun for your small monkeys to clamber on.

Try hanging a 6-foot ladder horizontally from the ceiling (see "Anchor it safely," page 57), using four heavy screw eyes and four doubled lengths of lightweight (but strong) chain. Position it so that it won't crash into the wall when swinging forward or back, or from side to side. The position of each screw eye should correspond to a corner of the ladder. Thread a chain through one screw eye. Slide one end of the chain under the corresponding end of the ladder's side; loop it back over the outermost rung and under the side. Connect the two chain ends with a padlock, adjusting length as necessary to give the ladder the right height. Repeat with the other three chains. Hang the ladder just out of reach—about 10 or 12 inches above your child's head height—so that Tarzan or Jane will have to take a little leap to catch one of the rungs.

On days when everyone is ready to climb the walls, why not let them do it? Bolt a ladder vertically to the wall studs—and suddenly you have an indoor mini-gym that takes practically no space at all.

First, measure the distance between your wall studs (usually about 14 inches; to locate the studs, consult page 57). You will need three crosspieces of 2 by 4 lumber, each long enough to extend over three wall studs. Drill each crosspiece in three places, to correspond to the spacing of the studs.

Next, center the ladder against the crosspieces and screw the ladder's sides securely to the crosspieces. Finally, screw the crosspieces tightly to the wall studs, through the previously drilled holes. In each case, use wood screws or lag bolts long enough to penetrate at least 2 inches.

Fold-up maze

This toy becomes, by turns, a labyrinth to explore, a playhouse, or just a freeform building toy.

To construct it, start with one or more 4 by 8-foot sheets of styrene foam board, sold at art supply stores. With a utility knife, slice the sheet into rectangles or into squares measuring 2 feet or larger (one 4 by 8-foot sheet can be cut into eight 2-foot squares). Cut large holes in some of the squares to make entrances and exits. Reinforce edges with wide masking tape, and with the same tape, join the squares on one side only, allowing them to hinge back on themselves. This way, they will fold up accordion-style. Let your kids paint them or cover them with contact paper (first "dust" the styrene foam with a cloth so the paint or paper will adhere).

Call it a "gymni-sleep." This cross between bunkbeds and a playground has everything that a boisterous little body could need on a cold, wet day: swing, slide, trapeze bar, and basketball net; innumerable places to climb; and a cozy mid-level pad for reading. You might want to add a sturdy ladder, and place thick carpeting underneath for extra safety. Design: Sheldon Smith.

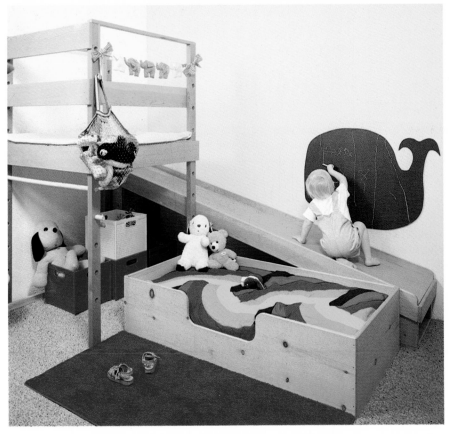

Neatly fitted to the scale of a city apartment, this sleeping-climbing-sliding-hiding play structure gives Gabriel all kinds of romping fun. His father built it when Gabriel outgrew his crib at age two. Extra climbing dowels will fit between the upright supports when he is a little older. Design: Donald W. Vandervort.

With traffic light excitement, two strong primary colors team up against a clean expanse of white. The more blazing red is kept in rein as a bright accent against the grass-green wall. Design: Karen Loy.

Color them a cheerful world

Sophisticated earth tones and tepid pastels may be favored by sophisticated adults. But children, as a rule, have a wider awake color sense: to them, often (but not always), the brighter it is, the better. As you decorate their rooms with paint, fabrics, carpeting, or all three, give them vivid, even loud colors. (Just take care not to go riotously overboard — too much color stimulus will overwhelm anyone.)

Of course, your child's age and personality will affect your color selection as well as other decorating considerations. Be sure you consult your son or daughter about preferences before you forge ahead. Go window shopping together. Bring home fabric swatches and paint sample cards for after-dinner selection games (such things make great materials for later art projects, too).

The chances are good that your own emotional responses to different colors will be similar to your children's, though they may favor a bolder and brighter personal environment. Grass green and sunny yellow generally evoke a fresh and cheerful feeling in people of all ages. Blue tends to pacify the spirit (used in excess, though, the deeper tones tend to be depressing). Children usually relish red (but, again, avoid an excess of this rousing color). And though primary colors are traditional favorites of the young, don't neglect to consider intermediates like orange or lavender, which can offer just as much warmth and good cheer. Any rainbow hue you choose will glow brightly against white.

Simple tricks with cotton prints lend cheer to a small boy's private world. Stretched fabric panels make up his picture gallery, and at naptime he likes to gaze at his "canopy"—simply a length of cloth draped from ceiling beams.
Design: Patricia C. Woerner.

A palette of warm colors, splashed casually against pale surroundings, infuses this nursery with a fresh and airy spirit.
Architect: James Caldwell.

Delicious as crayons to a child's eye are these primary-color walls, used to set a raised play platform apart from the more subdued sleeping portion of the bedroom.
Architect: Ronald Quigley.

Squeezing every last inch out of a tight space, built-in cabinets and a folding desk make it possible to sleep as many as three children in this room. When the desk hinges out of the way (see detail), you can pull out a trundle bed. Cabinetry: Norman Shaw.

Storage cubes, stacked and bolted together, free extra play space in this 10 by 11-foot room, shared by two energetic boys. Both bunks are elevated on the stacked cubes, which were purchased from an unfinished-furniture store.

Kids need elbow space & knee room

Coping with skimpy space is one of the most common problems faced by parents as they plan a child's bedroom. For adults, who really need little more than a place to put the bed and a few square yards for getting dressed, the small-scale bedroom typical of recently built homes may be adequate. But children have innate tendencies—as well as special needs—that make space planning more complicated. For a number of early years, they like to spread out on the floor to play. Often, too, they have to share the bedroom with a sibling. Even if they don't share, they need extra furniture because their room is a diverse activity center, not just a place to sleep. And finally, most kids accumulate a lot of cumbersome possessions that they don't often keep neatly stored out of sight.

You'll find ideas for freeing floorspace sprinkled throughout this chapter. For your family's needs, bunkbeds might be the answer—a variety of designs appear on the next few pages. If clutter and ease of cleanup are a special problem, look through the storage ideas on pages 24 to 27.

Opposite this page are photographs of small bedrooms where ingenuity with built-in furniture yielded maximum sprawl-out space. And below is a description of a very novel arrangement that offers not only extra floorspace, when desired, but also adaptability to a child's changing needs.

A room on ropes

Borrowing its style from the circus, one of the most imaginative small-space solutions we found is a trapezelike bedroom rigged up with bright yellow nylon ropes. The 8 by 12-foot room contains inexpensive, simple-to-make, and lightweight furnishings—all suspended from the ceiling. Ropes ($3/8$ inch in diameter) support shelves, a swing, and —for bedtime stories—an adult's swivel chair with its legs removed. (For an older child, you could add larger gymnastic challenges—a trapeze bar or a rope ladder.)

More yellow rope, threaded through pulleys, rigs a diaper-changing shelf that pulls up and out of the way when not in use.

For safety, each article of furniture hangs from four ropes and sturdy hooks screwed into ceiling joists (to read how to locate joists and secure hooks, see page 57). Just below the hooks, metal thimbles—available from boat supply stores—protect the swing-seat ropes from the wear of friction.

Ceiling joist hooks were placed in a grid pattern, 16 inches apart. (An electric drill made the work go quickly.) This enables the shelves, rocking swivel chair, and swing to be moved from one area of the room to another.

Swing seat, shelves, and underneath support for the chair were cut from 1-inch lumber. Lengths of rope were pushed through holes drilled in the four corners of each piece and knotted underneath.

Set up a room with moving parts... Fold-downs, roll-outs, raise-ups & pull-outs

Roller-skating storage

There is a subtle but sure psychological advantage to a toy bin that rolls on casters —it's a lot more fun than one that doesn't. When cleanup time arrives, it becomes a truck to drive back into its garage (under a desk or counter, under the bed, or in the closet). While it's out rolling, it can travel to various rooms with various kinds of cargo. It may bump into walls occasionally, but you can glue a strip of padding around its rim.

Make a simple open cube of plywood or particle board (a building plan appears on page 49). Or use the triple-layer cardboard discussed on page 50. If you don't want to make it yourself, you can purchase cubes from an unfinished furniture dealer. If round shapes delight you, look for a heavy fiber drum (suppliers are listed in the Yellow Pages under "Barrels and Drums"). Attach four large casters of good quality to the base of whichever bin you choose. Place a block of wood in the bottom of the bin for each caster screw to penetrate. For stability, fix the casters as close to the outside corners as you can manage.

The Murphy solution

Made famous as an escape route by Charlie Chaplin and other early slapstick film stars, the Murphy bed either folds up or slides into a closet, instantly emptying a room of disorderly linens and at least 18 square feet of useless bulk.

Today, you might have to move the family into an old-time boarding house to find an authentic "In-a-dor" bed. But here is an up-to-date adaptation of William L. Murphy's marvelous invention.

Our "Murphy" might be more accurately described as a folding chalkboard. Pivoting down from the wall, it sleeps either Junior or an overnight guest. In its "up" position, it becomes a surface for artistic expression of generous proportions.

Its base and sides are built like a shallow box of $3/4$-inch plywood. The good face of the base plywood is placed down to form the bed's underside, and painted with chalkboard paint. A 1 by 1, fastened (either nailed and glued, or screwed) to the sides, supports the base, and plywood triangles at the bottom corners add strength. The frame can be designed to hold either a cot-sized or a standard mattress.

The bed —which is actually an upper bunk — pivots down on a 6-foot piano hinge, screwed to a hardwood strip anchored to wall studs. A heavy chain, securely fastened at one end to a wall stud or ceiling joist (see page 57) and, at the other, to an end corner of the bunk, holds the bed level when it is folded down. At the head of the bunk, a 1 by 2 is screwed to the wall studs, further supporting the bed's weight. A short length of rope (also affixed to a wall stud) wraps around a boat cleat to hold the bunk in its raised position.

Disappearing desks

Whether supporting homework, chemistry experiments, or a jigsaw puzzle, a well-proportioned desk top is a very useful thing —as long as it is being used. At other times, it tends to block off space, get bumped against, and attract a confusion of clutter, since it is such a convenient spot to put things.

On the other hand, a desk that disappears when you don't need it is all the more appreciated when you do.

One such desk appears in the upper photograph on page 14. The ¾-inch birch-faced plywood top of this folding desk is attached to the cabinet behind it with hinges. The desk is supported by 2 by 2-inch legs that pivot on bolts through an apron made of 1 by 3s glued to the underside of the plywood top. Magnetic catches hold the desk closed when the legs are folded and the desk lowered.

Another disappearing desk, shown in the photograph on page 35, works like the slide-in breadboard commonly found in kitchens. Actually, it is a shallow, inverted drawer, surfaced on the top and sides with plastic laminate. Its front is a 1 by 3, and its sides and back are 1 by 2s. The sides and back are glued and nailed to the desk top, a piece of ½-inch plywood. To prevent it from tipping when extended, the desk slides into its cabinet base between 1 by 1 guides, which are glued to the inner sides of the cabinet. A stop fastened to the back prevents the desk from being pulled out too far.

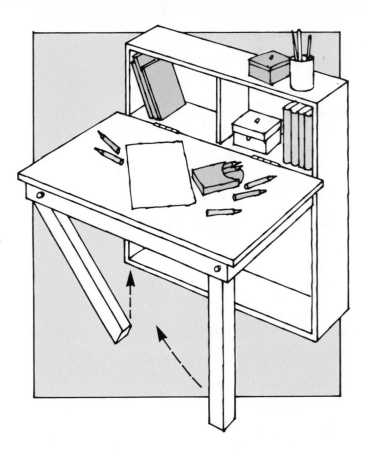

Elevating train board

A perennial Christmas favorite of many train-loving fathers (as well as quite a few sons and, doubtless, daughters too), a model railway takes up a lot of space after all of it has been set up. One father solves the problem by lifting the railway up to the ceiling when not in use.

Mounted on a heavy plywood board, the entire train layout is raised for storage, using a hand-cranked boat winch. Screws hold the winch to the studs of a wall corner so that the crank can turn freely. A single-wheel pulley and an eye bolt are attached within each corner of the board. Screw-in hooks hold four double-wheel pulleys to the ceiling beams.

Each of four ropes runs from the winch through one wheel of an overhead pulley, down through the corresponding board-mounted pulley, up through the second wheel of the ceiling pulley, then down again to attach to the eyebolt. The ropes can be removed, when desired, from the lowered board, which rests on sawhorses. Architect: Thomas Tomasi.

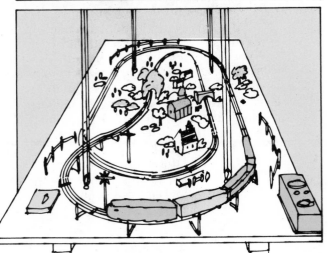

Sleeping high up... A favorite space-saver

For children and sailors, stacking beds have long been a solution to crowded sleeping quarters. As far as children are concerned, the system is generally sure to please. Forced by shortness of stature to look up at everyone except baby brothers and sisters, most children appreciate a spot from which they can look down at the world from time to time. An upper bunk, whether slept in by night or climbed into by day, provides just such a lofty—and relatively private—nook.

In planning, shopping for, or building bunks, safety should be your first consideration. You'll save yourself later anxiety, and possibly accidents as well.

The entire structure should be heavy and sturdy enough to accommodate several climbing kids at once. Make sure that the upper railing is strong, bearing in mind that children sometimes maneuver into odd locations during their sleep. Ladders or steps should be easily negotiable for the bunk owner (or owners). A base of wood slats, rather than wire, under the upper berth may prevent hair from becoming painfully caught in the "ceiling" of the lower bunk (check for adequate head-room, too). As a last precaution—in case someone does fall—try to provide thick carpeting around the base of the bunks.

While a stacking bed system abounds with virtues and remains a perennial favorite with kids, it sometimes does present problems. The worst, probably, is making the upper bed (especially for a not-very-agile parent). It helps to use a lightweight mattress, perhaps a slab of foam rubber, that you can lift off easily and cover with a fitted bottom sheet. Or you can sidestep the problem completely by giving your children washable sleeping bags that they can smooth down by themselves.

Another disadvantage to the upper bunk is likely to make itself felt if you live in a very warm climate or if the bedroom is poorly ventilated. In these conditions, sleeping on high sometimes becomes uncomfortable, because hot air rises to the ceiling.

Exploring new angles

Bunkbeds traditionally stack in two neat layers. However, if you are working out a design from scratch, you might survey other ways to orient the beds. Experiment with a floor plan of the bedroom and a paper card to simulate each bunk.

Create a right angle with the bunks in one corner, and you'll simultaneously create a little alcove-retreat or a nook where you can arrange desk and storage units. A right-angle plan also offers more head room for the occupant of the lower bunk.

Or, if you have a sufficiently long wall, put the bunks end-to-end. Each bed is quite separate this way (no more vexing kicks in the night for the upper occupant). And, again, you gain special play, work, or storage space under the elevated bed.

A very novel idea (shown in the lower right photograph on the facing page) is to raise both bunks. You may resolve a little rivalry at the same time.

From such a lofty vantage point, it's fun to look down on the world. And by raising the bed, you gain office space below. Design: Gerald Cichanski.

Headed for the kids-only zone, she climbs up to a comfortable corner retreat. Lacings of rope add to both safety and design of the raised bunks. Mural: Georgia LaRue. Bunk design: Tom Morrison.

These vinyl-sheathed cocoons —a bunk designer's response to the space age —are as cozy by night as they are sleek-looking by day. Design: Jim and Penny Hull.

Windows and portholes, for peeping through or puppetry, add to the appeal of these colorful sleep-and-play bunks. The lower one rests on purchased storage cubes, eliminating the need for a separate bureau. Design: Sharon Owen Haven.

As if inspired by a Calder sculpture, the clean lines and clear colors of this bunk system immediately wake up the imagination —in both kids and adults. Design: Maynard Hale Lyndon.

Upstairs-downstairs sleep & play systems

Besides bedding you down at night, these bunks offer daytime tunneling, hiding, fish-watching, mountaineering, confiding in a friend, or setting up a store or puppet show —not to mention such prosaic activities as finishing homework or putting away toys.

With a few added shelves, spacious cupboards, and sliced-out windows, a basic bunk or loft structure becomes a friendly miniature world, promising endless variations on the freeform theme of play. Most of the ones shown here were owner-invented and not difficult to build. They incorporate ready-made units and shelves from an unfinished-furniture supplier. Sheets of hardboard or plywood, painted in smashing colors and sculpted with a jigsaw, add the final, fanciful touch.

Fantasia in marigold colors calls to mind a fairy tale castle. Extra surprises are the aquarium, tucked beside a cozy reading nook, and a long, L-shaped tunnel that runs under the desk and lower berth, all the way into the closet. Design: Sharon Owen Haven.

Like an elevator, a yellow pail hoists toys upstairs to the sleeping loft that is transformed —by turns— into a stage, a balcony, an airship, or simply a quiet spot for a game of cards.

High in their crow's-nest, two sisters share a moment of conviviality. Curtains shelter the lower bunk to make it a cozy retreat for reading—or a theater for puppets.

Bunkbed framing offers opportunities to add extra features: here, a clothes pole, affixed within children's reach, finishes off a handsome wood structure with a row of colorful dresses. Architect: John Schmid.

Of childproof solidity and functional design, these bunks also unbolt to become separate single beds. If the room were tall enough, even a third could be stacked on top. Architect: George Cody.

Bunkbed extras... Accessories for more fun

Bunkbed systems are usually massive and labyrinthine enough to make it easy to incorporate extra features. The upright and horizontal members of the basic structure form a sort of skeleton for accessories, whether the accessories are built in at the start or added later. Bunkbed systems can be varied almost infinitely, with a little imagination; here are a few suggestions.

Extra storage to go with bunks

As all parents discover early on, children are born pack rats. Every nook, cranny, bin, or shelf soon fills up with their personal effects —bizarre treasures, new and worn-out toys, oceans of books, papers, and puzzle pieces, not to mention clothing. For this reason, the most useful accessory you can add to your bunkbed system may be one or more extra places to put things.

In an L-shaped bunk system, you can place shelves and even a desk surface between the upright members that support the upper bed. If you make the shelves wide enough and use sturdy wood, they can even double as a ladder to the top.

An especially helpful extra in a room shared by siblings is lockable personal storage. A cabinet built into—or hung near—the headboard of each bunk (as shown in the photograph on the opposite page), and equipped with a lock, will be much appreciated by the occupants. Even if it doesn't lock, such a cabinet lends a sense of private territory to each bunk.

Cozy curtains

Even the simplest, most inexpensive cotton curtains will transform a lower bunk into a cozy private "cabin" for reading or playing house.

If you want to curtain your child's bunk, the simplest approach is to string fabric panels on tension rods that fit tautly between the bunk's upright supports, as shown in the photograph on the facing page. The whole apparatus slips out easily when you need to wash the curtains.

You may want to curtain all four sides, or just one, two, or three—it will probably depend on how many sides of the bed are open to the room. For the side where the child climbs in and out, make two fabric panels of equal size, so that, when hung, they will open at the center. Along the top of each panel, sew an open hem through which you can thread the rod; allow ample hem width—at least twice the thickness of the rod—this way, the curtains will push apart easily.

Interesting ups and downs

Getting up and down is more fun if you provide something to scale in addition to a ladder (always be sure to provide the ladder, too). For example, you might rig a heavy cotton climbing rope, secured to a ceiling joist close to the side of the upper berth; consult "Anchor it safely," on page 57.

One family built in a cabinet below the upper berth, with clothing drawers that double as climbing steps. It is important to make such drawers as deep and tight-fitting as possible, to prevent them from falling out when someone steps on them. Metal foot strips were fastened to the drawer openings for further safety. The face of each step was attached securely to the drawer side pieces with glue and wood screws, as shown below.

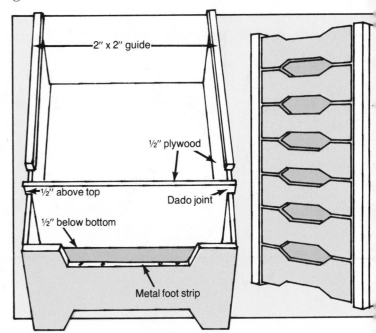

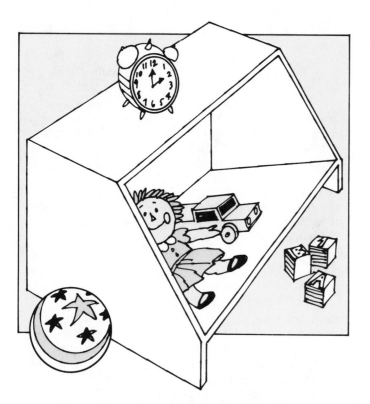

Order out of chaos... A place for everything

Curiosity-seekers' containers

If you and your kids favor an eclectic look, shop around for storage containers that, in themselves, provoke curiosity and offer play potential. Here are a few suggestions: The hollow, revolving portion of a barber's pole (found by parents in a used office supply warehouse); a brightly painted old-fashioned metal breadbox; a good-size mailbox; a sturdy small suitcase or briefcase; a fishing tackle box with its myriad compartments; a carpenter's plastic carry-around toolbox. Older children with younger siblings appreciate boxes that they can lock.

Before using any previously occupied container, no matter how beautiful, check to make sure it's perfectly safe. Avoid anything with sharp edges, and steer clear of old, painted things, in case the paint contains lead. Finally, make sure your containers never held anything toxic or irritating.

Preschooler's bedside table

The floor of this open cabinet slopes upward gently from back to front, preventing toys from tumbling out. A child can easily reach inside to take things out or put them away. Open to view, toys can be found at a glance. A roomy, tilted cabinet floor is an especially good idea for storing blocks, because they are so numerous and so inclined to topple.

Wall storage

Keeping lightweight toys, books, games, and other supplies on the wall frees extra floor space. For the very young, place shelves or other units within reach. An older child would probably enjoy a movable, safely locking ladder of the sort used in bookstores and libraries. Shelves with adjustable brackets allow flexibility as a child's size and needs change.

Painted or covered with wallpaper, circular containers cluster attractively on the wall in a colorful storage "collage." Large fiber drums (to find them, look in the Yellow Pages under "Barrels and Drums"), cut in slices, and with edges taped, make generous cabinets. Or at an art supply store, look for corrugated cardboard that you can roll into cylinders of various sizes; for sturdiness, allow two thicknesses for each cylinder, joining the layers with duct tape (a strong vinyl-backed tape available at hardware stores). Also tape on a cardboard base that you can nail to the wall for stability. Inexpensive but less rugged are heavy cardboard 3-gallon containers sold in some ice cream parlors.

Wooden fruit crates in sturdy and safe condition offer further alternatives. Wood soft drink boxes and—if you can find them—typesetters' drawers (castoffs from modernized printing plants) provide small compartments for miniatures and collections.

See-through organizers

When you can't find your purple crayon because it is hidden at the bottom of a coffee can, the usual solution is to dump the entire contents on the rug. But see-through storage alleviates many such searching problems.

One fun suspended container is the type of wire mesh basket sold in cookware departments for draining vegetables. A deluxe model comes in tiers of three. With a pulley system, these baskets become small elevators for delivering goods to upper bunks.

One mother made simple square bags of sturdy, fine-mesh netting, bound with bias tape and finished with heavy-duty zippers. Tape loops at the top make them easy to hang up. Each bag holds its own specialty, from small cars to cotton socks. (If your child is learning to read, you might want to add simple labels.)

String shopping bags have the same advantage of transparency (we show one in the lower photo on page 11). And as you rush out to the car with your toddler, grab one off the hook to take along for entertainment.

Baskets

From the wicker dish for Baby's cotton balls to the large straw hamper for dress-up clothes, well-constructed baskets are fairly indestructible, as well as versatile. Slide them under the bed for out-of-sight storage. Give a small child a picnic basket with a handle for carrying toys from room to room. An assortment of baskets on a desk top keeps art and school supplies in order. And, hung from one handle on the inside of the closet door, a small basket eases clothing storage. When it's hung low, its contents are easy to see and to reach.

Tidy solutions for clothes & other clutter

Some children, we've been told, are naturally neat and tidy. But most seem to be inclined the opposite way. One parent suggested wryly that kids should have tilting floors: at the push of a button, all the socks, blocks, and other debris would slide into a cavern hidden beneath.

Such a mechanism might prove a little too tricky for most parents to install. Fortunately, there are other ways to help clear up clutter and encourage tidiness. The first ingredient is some thoughtful planning—here are some ideas to help you with yours.

After-school catch-all

When kids come home from school laden with jackets, books, lunchboxes, and important mimeographed bulletins, what do they usually do as soon as they're inside the door? Pile everything in a heap on the first surface they find, whether it is an antique commode in the entryway or a crowded kitchen countertop.

To solve this problem, one family gave their children a network of individual nooks specifically designed to catch such clutter. It works well, because its location, just inside the back door, makes it instantly available to each arriving child.

As shown above, the labyrinth of shelves and alcoves was tucked neatly under a staircase. Adjustable metal brackets make it easy to rearrange shelves or to add more. Coat hooks are screwed to the backs and sides of the lower alcoves.
Architect: George Cody.

Redesign the closet

Children's closets nearly always have a lot of wasted space. You can probably rearrange this space with thoughtful planning to make it store both clothing and toys more efficiently. Given an organized storage space to start with, children are more likely to keep their paraphernalia in good order.

One good way to start is to lower and shorten the clothes pole to suit your child's small stature for several years. In the closet shown below, the shift of a clothes pole yielded room for innumerable shelves and even built-in drawers.

Rainbow graphic transforms the formerly uninspired appearance of plain closet doors. At left, a crowd of cuddly toys clusters on a doll pole — easy to take down, just as easy to put back; for more details, see page 34. Design: Anne Stewart.

Once their cargo was pop bottles and oranges, but today these crates lend their built-in niches to display treasured dolls and miniatures.

Numerous cubbyholes, shelves, and drawers built into the rear of a walk-in closet give a young lady many places to cache provisions like her doll's house and T-shirts.

The pride of ownership... They hung up their shingles

For children, as well as the rest of us, ownership is a source of pride and self-confidence. Usually, their biggest chunk of material wealth is real estate — their own rooms, or portions of rooms. On these two pages, eye-catching graphic designs name the owner of each bedroom with electric clarity.

Besides painted or printed graphics, there are a number of different ways you can give a room its own "monogram." Mount large wooden alphabet letters, such as you might find in a home building supply store, on a wall or door. Or, if you like to sew, stitch and stuff alphabet pillows to spell your child's name — patterns are available from major companies. Then arrange the pillows along your child's bed for both spelling and cuddling.

For a simple and pretty touch, you can decoratively paint, sketch, glue, or embroider the letters of your child's name on a suitable background, then frame your work and hang it in the bedroom.

Annie pours her day into her diary as she relaxes beneath a bold, Broadway-inspired graphic of her name. The screen to the right of her bed is fabric-covered; details appear on page 31. Design: Reo Haynes.

"N" gets a nuzzle for the nice noise it makes in the middle of a very nice name. Design: Reo Haynes.

Nine repeats of his face on the door let everyone know whose private world lies within (please knock). His crisp black and white banner is composed of photographic transfers of his face, block-printed on cotton.

Emphatic-looking on its high shelf, Eric's shingle names with authority the master of this bedroom. The spray-painted plastic letters were found at a hardware store. Design: Mary Martin.

In this apartment-scale bedroom, each bunk opens to its own half of the room (the floor is raised alongside the upper berth). An adjustable shelving system constructed against all four walls allows both storage and flexibility. Though it appears built in, the wall system is actually freestanding and can be disassembled and moved. A large mirror facing the foot of the beds (see detail) creates a feeling of extra space and extends the view of the ceiling mural. Architect: Joseph Kent.

Barn doors faced with redwood benderboard open for extra spaciousness —or close for privacy. Note the pull-out mattresses that hide under the kids' waterbeds, ready for overnight guests. Architect: William Bruder.

Sharing without crowding...Ways to promote peace

The social significance of sharing is a lesson children are taught early in life, first by Mother, then by Teacher. Worthy a lesson as it may be, the average child remains , at heart, as imperious and self-centered as the average 17th century French monarch —especially when it comes to sharing with a brother or sister.

If sharing is the only option, ingenuity in room planning can effectively ease matters. The two key problems are these: how to provide privacy (permanently or temporarily) without cramping, and how to clarify whose space belongs to whom in the jumble of the joint habitat. The following ideas offer some possible solutions.

Part-time room dividers

Siblings —as mercurial as the rest of us —tend to fluctuate between sweet harmony and guerrilla warfare, and sometimes need to be separated for a while. They also need occasional respites of solitude —no matter how they feel about their brothers or sisters.

For both these reasons, a room divider that you can open or close as desired helps to keep peace in a shared bedroom. If the dormitory dimensions are broad enough, you might suspend folding doors or shutters, a cloth or beaded curtain, or even one or more lengthy roller shades from the ceiling. Just make sure that the space doesn't convert into small vertical cells when divided in two, even if the division is only temporary. If that should happen, try instead to arrange the furniture —bookshelves, toy bins, even a bunkbed —to divide the room into territories.

Stretched fabric screen

Stretcher bars, usually used to make an artist's canvas taut, form the quickly assembled frame of a fabric privacy screen (shown in the upper photograph on page 28). When not being used to divide the children's bedroom or to form the walls of a playhouse, the screen folds flat for storage.

Stretcher bars are sold in art supply stores. You may also find them at decorative fabric shops, where they are used to hold fabric panels.

Plan a minimum of three panels for your screen, each no more than 6 feet tall by 2 feet wide.

Buy stretcher bars of the appropriate size, four for each panel, and lock them together at the corners to make each panel frame. Measure the outside dimensions of the frames and add 1 inch to both the length and width. Using tightly woven fabric, sew fabric pieces together into a "pillow slip" for each frame, making 1/4 inch seams, with the opening at the bottom; with the pillow slip wrong side out, box the top corners as shown below.

Fit the pillow slips over the frames, pull the fabric tightly together at the bottom of each frame, and neatly staple it to the frame's bottom. Join the panels, using three hinges —one each at the top, center, and base of each frame juncture.

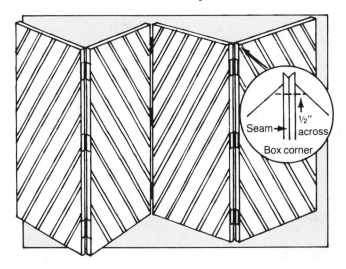

Personal corners

Young children love to rearrange their own environments to create cozy places —so why not encourage them? Give them lightweight plastic storage cubes (like those shown on page 11), carpet samples, pillows (perhaps one of those shown on pages 42 and 43), and squishy beanbag chairs. When they yearn for a place of their own, let them set up a personal parlor in a corner of their room. Finish off the private nook with a mirror and a bulletin board, if you like.

A paper perimeter

A simple approach to mural painting is to tack up a "stripe" of paper that runs horizontally all the way around the room, positioned so your child can draw comfortably while standing. When it becomes sufficiently embellished, replace it with a fresh strip. Use butcher, shelf, or wrapping paper; newsprint tears too easily. As an alternative perimeter, you might prefer a horizontal stripe of chalkboard paint (see next page).

An easel for two

Long a tradition in kindergarten, a two-sided easel is also very handy for use at home —especially when you have two small artists in the family. Usually, when you set up for poster painting, everyone wants to get into the act.

Here is an easel that you could make for the kids' bedroom or playroom, or for a corner of the kitchen or patio. Its frame is made of hardwood, its backboards are ⅝-inch plywood. The easel's two sides hinge along the top so that they fold together for storage when the wingnuts holding the stabilizing crosspieces are loosened. Two dowels attach each backboard to the frame by fitting into holes in the frame legs: four such holes, spaced at 2½-inch intervals along each leg, make height adjustments possible. The paint shelves are sized to hold square, lidded, plastic refrigerator jars. Design: W. W. Mayfield.

Big, broad paper

If you want to save your wallpaper, here's a wonderful way to deflect youthful artistic zeal to a better "canvas": simply provide an equally generous paper surface on which the children can draw or paint. An exciting size of paper will probably inspire the kids so much that they'll reward you with some very fine artwork.

What sort of paper makes the best substitute for bare wall? From newspaper companies, you can often buy inexpensive rolls of paper that come in widths of up to 55 inches. To sponsor an almost indefinite amount of mural painting, hang one of these rolls on a 2-inch-thick dowel or clothes pole from the pulley-rigged ceiling mount illustrated above. Just pull the artist's "canvas" down and slip it between wood strips that have been screwed to the wall. The strips serve both to keep the mural flat during the creative process and to help you tear the mural off neatly once it's completed.

If you haven't enough wall space to spare, but still want to provide a generous art surface, consider the paper-dispensing table design shown on page 9. Or, from a butcher's supplier, you can purchase a butcher-paper dispenser that bolts to a table or countertop.

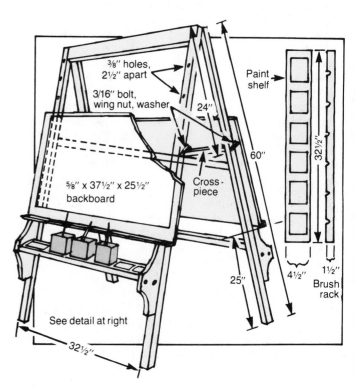

How to encourage a young artist's zeal

Before you buy any art supplies for your children's use, check the fine print on the labels for warnings about harmful ingredients. Unfortunately, some products sold for children have been known to contain toxic ingredients. Also, some stain more than others, and some have an unpleasant aroma. If in doubt about the safety of a product, follow the wisdom of kindergarten teachers: buy only water-base flowpens, genuine ceramic clay, and water-soluble powdered tempera paints (which you can thicken, after mixing them, with a little laundry starch).

Practical surfaces

For parental ease of mind, not to mention ease of elbow grease, a child's world should be surfaced with the most readily washable materials available. Naturally, such surfaces make especially good sense wherever kids indulge in arts and crafts, even if that spot is just one corner of the bedroom.

Vinyl wallpaper and floor coverings (the more rugged, the better) are ideal because they mop up with little scrubbing. If you paint the walls or furniture, use several coats of good high-gloss enamel to facilitate cleaning. Decorative plastic laminate, though expensive, holds up admirably atop counters and craft tables, and you can sponge it off with ease.

As an alternative to vinyl, rubber provides a heavy-duty and easy-to-wash floor surface. Janitorial suppliers, among other outlets, offer rubber matting that you could install near an art area. Or consider purchasing a thick plastic mat — the type used to prevent skids at entryways or under rolling chairs — from an office supplier. Lay it over carpeting (which should be a tough industrial or indoor/outdoor variety).

Chalkboards — anywhere, any size, any shape

Today's simple equivalent of the old schoolhouse slate is composed of nothing more than a hard surface well-coated with chalkboard paint (available at paint stores). What this means is that a chalking expanse can go on virtually any surface not needed for other purposes. Perhaps you could convert one side of a chest of drawers, one end of the bunkbeds (or the underside of a Murphy bed; see page 16), or one sliding door of the closet into a chalkboard. Or simply coat a sizable piece of hardboard with chalkboard paint and hang or lean it wherever the artist wishes. With a jigsaw, you can give the board a whimsical contour, like that of the whale shown on page 11. Remember, half the fun of scrawling with chalk is being able to loosen up and spread out, so provide as large a surface as possible.

Construction site

Blocks—those most satisfying and simple toys for builders of any age—deserve a corner of their own. Start a collection with traditional wood blocks from the toy store, adding to it with as wide a variety of safe knickknacks as you and your kids can find. Throw in a few oversize, lightweight blocks made from sturdy gift boxes and food cartons (perhaps covered with contact paper). A few large trucks or an indoor wagon are great for hauling and dumping.

Try to store each construction element—wood blocks, big blocks, and sundries—on its own shelf or in its own labeled bin. The best container is one wide enough so that Junior can easily reach for a few things at a time. For example, the open-front bin described on page 24 makes excellent housing for blocks. Or, if you use large plastic or hardboard cubes to store the blocks, the containers themselves may become part of a small-scale city.

Dolls & stuffed animals

Doll and stuffed animal lovers usually acquire an overflowing collection within the space of their first few birthdays. One mother took the trouble to sew a small plastic ring to the back of each soft friend so that the entire crowd could be hung on cup hooks when not needed for cuddling. She screwed the hooks to a floor-to-ceiling pole.

For children who feel cozier at night with favorite friends nearby, you might provide each doll with its own papoose pocket. Sew straps to each pocket and hang the pockets on a dowel; then suspend the dowel by a pretty ribbon from the wall alongside the bed.

Fooling around on the floor

Children spend so much time there that the bedroom floor deserves an open-minded second glance. While carpeting is definitely the coziest covering, it's best to leave at least a few square feet for vinyl or other smooth flooring where the kids can wheel trucks or set up a doll's house.

Another good idea is to collect a stack of carpet samples from discontinued stock (a very small investment—some shops offer them free of charge). With them, children can make their own patchwork carpet creations or steppingstones—or simply use the samples as comfortable, portable seating.

To the carpet collection, you might add a length of felt, accompanied by assorted felt and fabric shapes and stripes, so the kids can create floor collages.

We've seen designs painted on wood floors—for hopscotch, checkers, tic-tac-toe, and marble games. What about painting foot and paw prints in a path around the perimeter of the room? Or even across it?

Now you see it —now you don't. An inverted drawer slides in and out to give two brothers a smooth play surface for their miniature toys, which might topple on the carpeted floor. More details on their disappearing desk appear on page 17. Design: John E. Mason.

Tuck in a few inviting play places

A s we all know from our guidebooks for parents, child's play is a repertoire of important learning experiences. Both a source of relaxation and a very intense kind of work, it gives youth a chance to interpret our confusing world for themselves, in their own terms. If that sounds rather absurdly serious, take heart: play also happens to be fun.

On these two pages you'll find a few ideas for polishing up the play potential of bedrooms, play rooms, or any area in the house where kids can imaginatively create a world of their own.

Spic, span, and sunny, Amy's kitchen resides in one portion of her remodeled closet. Its daintily curtained "window," over the toy stove, is glued to a storybook picture of a formal English garden. Design: Sharon Owen Haven.

Low craft counter along one side of a laundry hall provides plenty of elbow room for finger painting. The blackboard (which the kids reach by climbing on the counter) slides up, disclosing a pass-through to the kitchen. A big laundry sink close at hand (but not shown) makes clean-up easy. Architect: Michael Moyer.

Blazing colors (some of them even glow in the dark) depict a world where skyscrapers dance and mountain roads meander right onto the bookcase top. Mural: Jeanne Clark.

Wrapping ribbonlike right around her nursery, Amanda's mural of cats and other furry creatures gives her friends she can talk to, first thing in the morning. Mural: Sidney MacDonald Russell.

Instead of wallpaper...Mural magic

The rich fantasy life of children sometimes kindles the same in their elders. Like shopping for shiny toys or reading Mother Goose aloud, imaginative play gives a grownup the chance to relive a bit of childhood.

One magic carpet to Never Never Land, discovered by a growing clientele of parents, is the superscale "canvas" of a fanciful mural artist. Shown here are a few examples of what can happen to children's walls and ceilings—and even furniture—when you employ one.

To find a muralist, you may have to do some searching. Ask decorators for references, or call art schools and galleries. The young artists whose work appears here include a sign painter, a theatrical set designer, and a high school student.

Dorothy and her mates from Oz parade on high across 5-year-old Jessica's wall, portrayed there by a talented 16-year-old friend. Mural: Nora Escalante.

Splashed across wall and ceiling, bright flowers appear to have taken flight from the print of the bedspread below. Mural: Jackson Art.

Canary-yellow bedsheet puts a bright face over a plain bulletin board wall. Simply thumbtacked in place, it comes down for washing as needed. Design: Sharon Owen Haven.

Waking up walls, dignifying doors

S ince every square inch of a child's room is at a premium, it's worthwhile to study all surfaces—walls and doorways, for example—for their potential environmental impact.

Wallpaper is fun, and so are murals—some of which you can buy in wallpaper form. Here on these two pages are a few more unusual treatments for walls and doors—to stir your imagination as you and your kids plan a bedroom face-lift.

Colorful paper patchwork wakes up the wall as it encourages early scholastic skills. Each "patch" was put together on a cardboard square, using contact paper and giftwrap scraps, then discreetly affixed to the wall with four tiny brass nails. Self-adhesive mirror tiles, set into the pattern just atop the storage cubes, add extra delight. Design: Joanne Bowen.

Graphics from one to ten

Big, bold, three-dimensional Arabic numerals, ordinarily used to identify street addresses, might look even more exciting on a child's bedroom wall. Look for them at home improvement centers. Or look in catalogs—we found some lovely rounded numerals in bright green glazed ceramic in a sophisticated home design catalog.

For a preschooler, you might affix the numerals one through ten to the wall in a horizontal row within the junior mathematician's reach. Here, they can be gazed upon, talked about, and even caressed with the fingertips. Perhaps they might bestow some good influence on future money management —or at least toward gold stars on first-grade schoolwork.

Pin-up mountain range

Bulletin boards generally look rather drab unless well papered with drawings, postcards, and other childish pin-ups. But we saw one that delights the eye—with or without window dressing. Wrapping around three walls, 4 feet high from floor to highest peak, this pin-up board takes the shape of a lengthy mountain chain. Besides the usual paper accumulation, the mountains' owners can pin up their own sketched and cut-out houses, roads, snowmen, trees, and forest creatures.

The mountain range was cut with a saber saw, in very freeform fashion, from 4 by 8-foot sheets of white bulletin board bought at a building supply store. Painted a rich shade of brown and capped with "snow," the peaks call to mind gingerbread with whipped cream as much as they do the Sierra Nevada, the Rockies... or even the Himalayas. Design: Jeanne Clark.

Supergraphic door decor

Bold, bright letters painted on the outside of Steve's and Kelly's doors let the whole world know at a glance whose room is whose.

If you want to try a similar graphic feat, first measure your child's door and then draw it to scale on graph paper. Design block letters within the door outlines on the paper. Short names like Steve or Kelly are easiest to work out in crisp, geometric lettering—but you might run a longer name diagonally.

Scale the letters up to their actual size on wrapping paper (a yardstick helps to keep lines straight). Cut out the enlargements.

Take the door off its hinges, sand it well, and paint it with an enamel undercoat. When dry, sand it again lightly and trace the letters onto the door. Paint both background and letters (maybe in the kids' favorite colors) with at least two more coats of enamel. For the neatest results, use the best brush you can buy.

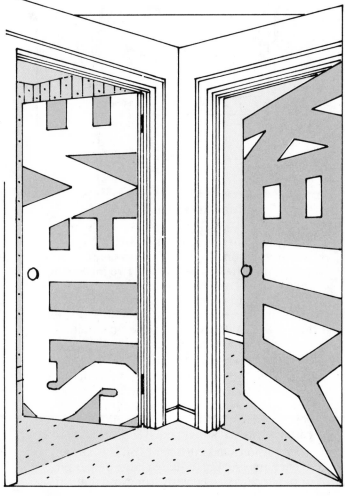

Measurement banner

Children love to see how quickly they're moving upward in life. And a measuring banner invites everyone to stand up and take a look. If you design the banner around two measuring tapes—one divided into traditional inches and the other into meters—you also offer lessons in the mysteries of metric conversion. Buy two tapes, each with meters on one side, inches on the other, at a fabric store.

Design a vertically shaped felt wall hanging and stitch the two tapes to opposing edges. A giraffe with its lofty neck readily lends its proportions to a measurement banner. But you might also choose a "tree trunk"—or a canary-colored "super pencil."

Handy for marking heights on the banner, at each measuring time, is a large diaper pin or paper clip, tagged with name and date.

Fabrications for future citizens

A bright new look with fabric paint

If you are already planning to make bedspreads and curtains for your child's room—had you thought of fabric-painting them? First wait for a department store linens sale; then buy enough full-size sheets to cover everything that needs covering. (Solid color cotton from the bolt is fine, too—but you'll need to sew more seams.) At an art supply store, look for jars of water-base fabric paint—the kind that bonds to cotton cloth as it tumbles at high heat in a dryer.

Whether you, your kids, or the whole family joins the painting fun, plan before you plunge ahead—things can get messy. On paper, sketch a scene you'd like to depict. Or, design and cut out stencils to paint through (large alphabet stencils from a stationer's might create a dictionary or monogram design). For stripes, plan to use guideline strips of masking tape to run your brush along; for polka dots, try a large thread spool, dipped in the paint. And for an interesting screened effect, try painting through a mesh fly swatter.

To begin painting, pin the sheets up on an outdoor wall, protecting the ground, if necessary, with a drop-cloth. Tape any stencils or stripe guidelines in place lightly, so that the sheets won't pucker when the tape is removed after painting. Offer hardware store brushes in assorted widths. Don't remove any taped stencils until the paint is completely dry.

Set the paint by tumbling the sheets in a dryer, on its hottest setting, for 45 minutes. (In later washings, to protect the paint, use cold water with mild soap or detergent.)

After drying, the painted sheets are ready to be made into bedspreads or curtains. (You might find the *Sunset* books *Slipcovers & Bedspreads* or *Curtains, Draperies & Shades* helpful here.)

Blue jeans jigsaw bedspread

John's casual coverlet, made with recycled jeans, doubles as a treasure chest and teaching toy. His mother's design includes pockets and belt loops to hold the boy's pint-size riches. Extra fun that came with the jeans are buttons, snaps, and zippers — for exercising preschool skills.

The top of the spread is a patchwork of cut-off jean legs. The entire single-bed-size creation required a dozen pairs of adult-scale jeans, both corduroy and denim.

Card table playhouse

Make a simple cotton duck slipcover for a card table (or any table of similar size), and you'll have the basic structure of a roomy little playhouse.

Seam the top to all four side pieces, but leave the sides detached from one another. Bind all raw edges with bias tape. Attach two 12-inch lengths of tape below each corner, so you can tie the sides together after slipping the "house" over the table.

Decorate the slipcover to please your own whims and those of your kids (unless this is a surprise, they're sure to want to help you). You might appliqué floral print rose bushes, or velveteen shutters, or even a few grazing sheep of fake fur — all with a zigzag stitch.

Doorway puppetry

To inspire spur-of-the-moment puppetry, all you need are a rectangle of cloth, a tension-mounted curtain rod, and a convenient doorway. Cut the cloth to fill the doorway from about half its height to the floor. Hem raw edges, leaving the top hem open at each end and making it wide enough to encase the rod. Ask your child to sit behind the curtain so you can mark the right position for a stage opening. Then cut out a window and bind its edges with wide bias tape. Add a simple curtain (the buttoned-on-type shown here is fun).

Thread the rod through the top hem, fit it between the door jambs—then pop some popcorn and settle back for showtime.

Pillows... For cuddling in the dark or in the day

Every bedroom needs at least one pillow. And for anyone in the family who can wield needle and thread, pillows are a snap to stitch. So pile in as many as you please —your kids will hug them, stack them, toss them, cherish them. Here are a few to get your collection off to a smooth and squishy start.

Children's own creations

Give your son or daughter a big pillow-size sheet of paper and ask for a big crayon drawing of a good pillow shape —maybe a favorite animal. Then look for fabric that will correspond to the artist's colors, and use the drawing as a sewing pattern. Transfer details to the pillow front with dressmaker's carbon, and zigzag-stitch them in place. Then seam pillow front to a backing piece, and fatten it with batting.

Tell the kids that drawings with simple contours (like the fluffy white cat shown on the facing page) are the easiest to translate into a pillow.

Kite & windsock pillows

In Japan, children get an annual chance to celebrate the joy of having been born a boy or a girl. On Boys' Day, May 5 (Girls' Day is March 3), one tradition is to fly giant cotton windsocks in the colorful shapes of creatures that live in the sea or in the air —fish, whales, hawks, and moths, for example.

Look for windsocks at Oriental import shops in March or April. The highly popular carp —filled with shredded foam, its mouth and tail stitched closed —becomes a beautiful bolster nearly as long as a child's bed or as wide as a love seat. Since washing will fade the delicate dyes, it's wise to spray the pillow with an aerosol soil repellent.

Boys' Day paper kites are more widely available than cotton the year around, in assorted sizes. Use these as patterns for a multi-colored pillow menagerie.

Funny-face pillow for busy fingers

You can sew a curious face on an 18-inch pillow— a face with a nose that laces, eyes that button, and a mouth that zips. The very young will love to toy with the cheerful gadgetry.

Cut out the pillow front and back, but don't sew them together until you've appliquéd the face. To make the mouth, cut out a pair of luscious red felt lips; join them with as heavy a metal 7-inch zipper as you can find. With zipper closed, appliqué the mouth to the pillow front.

The nose requires two felt strips, each 1 inch wide and 6 inches long; attach a row of three metal eyelets to each. Appliqué the strips to the pillow front, side by side, leaving their inside edges open and unattached. Thread a thick shoelace through the eyelets, and tie it at the top or bottom.

To make pupils for the eyes, sew on two large buttons. For eye variety, cut a number of pairs of felt shapes (such as circles, stars, or hearts in different colors) making a central buttonhole in each that a child can slip over one of the button-pupils. You might give the pillow variable cheeks, too —cutting these from felt in different shapes and colors. To attach them, sew big snaps to the pillow front and cheek undersides.

As a last, realistic touch, sew yarn fringe into the pillow seam on three (or even all four) sides, as you join the pillow front to its back. Then stuff the friend to make it properly plump.

Sleek, slick, and shiny satin surfaces look as delicious as they feel — especially in such soft sculpture shapes as candy bars and crayons.

Boy-size building blocks are actually foam rubber cushions. Joshua can also spread them out to sleep an overnight guest.

"Marshmallow" is a most appropriate name for Mary's humorous cat. Adapted from her own drawing, it is indeed a proud pillow (for details, see "Children's own creations" on facing page).

Jason's head, hands, and knees propel a caterpillar-like "tractor" across the floor.

The joys of piling up & tumbling down

Take a room full of foam cushions, add some small children—and you no longer have a room, but a blizzard of perpetual motion. Most of the motion is silly, and none of it is hazardous at all.

These crazy pillows come in two basic shapes that mesh delightfully when combined—one is a sort of performing seal's platform, the other a caterpillar mat that bends and ties to form a hollow hexagon.

Each shape acts very much like furniture but more closely resembles a squishy, elephantine toy. Stacked up, the shapes become instant soft sculpture to knock down—like a constantly collapsing circus.

What kids love is that the big foam cushions are colorful, lightweight, soft, and bouncy—with endless new uses for young inventors. Here are a few that Hilary, Jason and Xani discovered—in the space of maybe five minutes.   Design: Patricia Moser.

Five elephant footstools give Xani a palatial tunnel with guest seating upstairs.

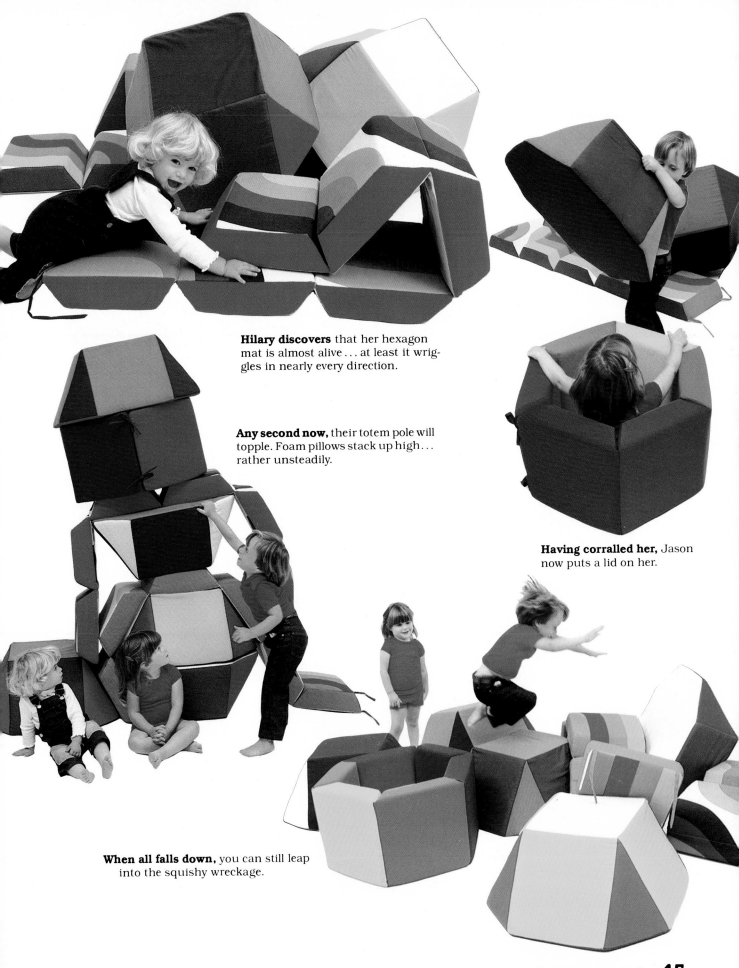

Hilary discovers that her hexagon mat is almost alive . . . at least it wriggles in nearly every direction.

Any second now, their totem pole will topple. Foam pillows stack up high . . . rather unsteadily.

Having corralled her, Jason now puts a lid on her.

When all falls down, you can still leap into the squishy wreckage.

Moonglow from an origami-trimmed lantern sets the mood for Gwynnie's woodwind magic. The young musician sits on a fully opened *shiki-buton,* a Japanese folding bed. (See facing page for more details.)

Sleeping sweet & simple

For reasons that still elude anthropologists, child psychologists, and school board officials, children love to sleep on the floor. They don't care if it's dusty, drafty, or hard on the back.

Maybe the elasticity of youth explains this predilection—after all, kids also wake up without kinky joints after nights passed in hammocks or on airplanes. Or maybe it's simply the refreshment of diversity. For in our portion of the globe at least, parents don't usually permit hammockry or floor-sleeping as a nightly routine.

In any case, it's wise to provide for occasional out-of-bed sleeping—whether for Junior alone on the night of an eclipse, or for a gaggle of slumber-partying 7-year-olds. Here are a few ways to do so.

Soft sculpture glamorizes the wall by day, then comes down at night to bed an overnight guest. The cool satin rainbow and lightning bolt make comfortable sleeping; the storm cloud proffers a pillow. Design: Heidi-Merry.

The *shiki-buton*

The Japanese, who have been sleeping down low for a long time, have devised some very cozy floor accommodations. One that is particularly elegant and versatile has become increasingly available here. Called a "shee-kee-boo-ton," it consists of three foam rubber pads, covered and linked with fabric. It is lightweight and foldable. Besides acting as bedding, it bends into a playhouse or an ottoman. And with one pad extended up the wall, it makes a very nice chair.

A luxurious accessory to a shiki-buton is a thick quilt that rolls up and fits into its own little drawstring duffle bag, to be used during the day as a bolster.

Sleeping on air... indoors or out

Partially inflated with air, a waterbed mattress makes a wonderful floor cushion for guest sleeping. One, two, or even three kids in sleeping bags can fit comfortably on its broad, squishy surface. It can take plenty of roughhousing, too — its hide is tough.

Outdoors, the versatile mattress offers further fun. For a stargazing sleep-out on the patio or lawn, it provides an oversized air mattress. In a swimming pool, it makes a slippery floating island.

With most canister vacuum cleaners, it's easy to fill a mattress with air. Shift the hose into the opening through which air flows out; then hold the nozzle against the mattress opening, turn on the vacuum cleaner, and watch the mattress balloon up (don't let it go too far, though).

A gurgly water filling delights kids, too. But a word of caution: indoors, there may be electrical hazard if you don't also use the frame and plastic liner that go with a complete waterbed. A water filling outdoors is safe, but insulate the mattress with a thick blanket, because the water will get chilly.

Hammocks

Every home with youthful inhabitants needs at least one hammock, if not half a dozen.

Install hooks for hammocks in your child's room (consult "Anchor it safely," page 57). Leave the hammock permanently in place—or roll it up until it's needed. Left in place, it makes a lounge on which to swing gently with a good book, or it's a place to store toys. Taken down and put away, it leaves the hooks free for other uses, like keeping jackets off the floor.

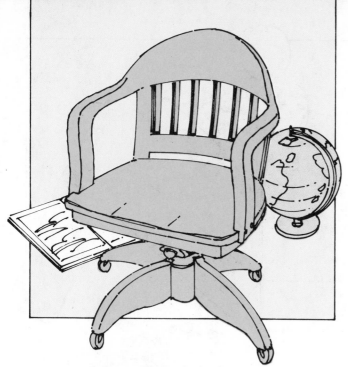

Swivel chair

Maybe the best feature of the classic swiveling office chair is its built-in capacity to whirl dervishly as well as to roller-skate across a bedroom floor. Most of these chairs also "grow" with a child (maybe all the way to Harvard).

Look for vintage oaken models at used office furniture stores (you may need to replace the casters). Or, if your taste leans more to sleek and contemporary designs, you can find up-to-the minute versions with molded plywood or plastic seats at Scandinavian furniture shops. Some of them are espeoially designed for kids.

Getting up high

It makes good sense to give your son or daughter something safe to stand on when reaching way up for things. Otherwise, the young explorer is bound to get there anyway—regardless of personal risks. At hardware stores, you can buy a tough little drum-shaped step stool whose casters retract under a child's weight, allowing a rubber suction device to grip the floor and steady the stool. Made by several different manufacturers, these are about 14 inches high and surfaced with skidproof rubber treads.

For an older child, you might look into ladders (dealers are listed in the Yellow Pages). Especially interesting is the rolling variety used in libraries, bookstores, and warehouses. Its spring-loaded casters operate exactly like those on the step stool, retracting under an older child's weight so that suction cups grip the floor.

Today's government regulations for ladders are strict, so ladders manufactured for commercial use should be quite safe at home. Remember, though, safety also depends on your child's age and skill.

No-nonsense, good-for-them furniture

Climb-up-to-the-table chair

When your butterball bouncer reaches the age of exploration, the highchair often becomes more interesting to climb into and out of than to sit in and sup in.

Especially if the highchair has become a bit wobbly, it might be a good idea to substitute this wonderful halfway-grownup version. Easily climbable and safely stable on its 24-inch base, its big bonus is holding Baby snug against the table — with the rest of the family.

The chair's curved backrest adjusts to cup a small child closely, and the armrests fit over the table top, to keep wriggly little bodies from sliding out during dinner. When it's time to get down, you loosen two butterfly nuts and slide the backrest away from the table, opening up a wider space through which your child can exit to freedom. You can also bolt the chair's seat at lower positions as the baby grows. Design: Sheldon Smith.

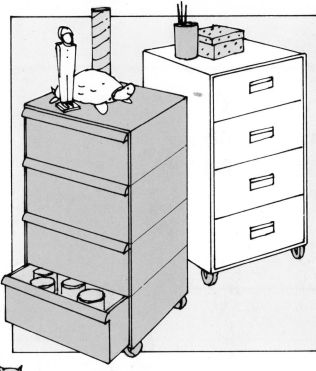

If you are the practical sort of parent who expects a piece of furniture to survive, fairly intact, the enthusiasms of a normally riotous childhood, then maybe you need an especially rugged chest. Or rather, maybe Junior does.

A metal or heavy plastic chest of drawers is likely to fare better than its traditional, often delicately crafted, wooden cousin. Metal tool chests, which sometimes come with heavy casters, will serve the family virtually forever. So will a metal file cabinet from an office supply store. You may want to improve either variety of chest with several coats of bright, high-gloss spray enamel.

A more versatile and less expensive unbreakable chest would be an expandable plastic drawer system which comes in units from shops that feature space-saving furniture.

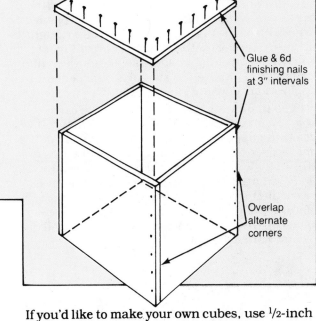

Glue & 6d finishing nails at 3" intervals

Overlap alternate corners

Versatility with solid geometry

Both the cube and its flattened-out cousin, the oblong, lend their shapes to modular furniture systems that are both flexible and fun.

You can buy both at unfinished furniture shops. Usually constructed in 16-inch-deep modules, they are solid enough to hold up for years, yet so inexpensive that you may want to collect a number of them. Paint them with a high-gloss enamel.

With an assortment of button-bright boxes, you and your kids can create (and re-create) an ever-changing environment. Stack them up to make a bookcase, the underpinnings of a desk, or even a condominium for dolls. Or spread them out into a train or a boat.

If you'd like to make your own cubes, use ½-inch plywood—one 4 by 8-foot sheet will furnish you with three 16-inch cubes. For each cube, cut four squares, each 15½ inches on a side, and one square 16 inches on a side. Glue and nail them together, as shown above, with the 16-inch-square piece on top. Sand them smooth and paint them with several coats of high-gloss enamel. (A cube arrangement appears in the lower photograph on page 38.)

Cardboard creations... Sturdy, good-looking & easy

As our tree population dwindles and our lumber prices soar, it becomes increasingly extravagant to supply children with pretty little wooden furnishings that they will soon outgrow. But riding to the rescue of the dollies' tea party comes thick cardboard—a low-cost plywood substitute that has been with us, scarcely noticed, for years. In slabs of three corrugated layers, it is virtually as sturdy as plywood and less than half the price.

Other virtues...& one curable vice

A joyful discovery for the parent who lacks physical strength or carpentry skill, making things with cardboard is much like making model airplanes. Triple-thick sheets of it, which are featherweight to lift, also cut easily with an ordinary breadknife. You can make perfectly adequate joints with interlocking slots, wedged-in supports, and generous applications of white glue and tape.

Keep in mind that, to take stress, the cardboard's corrugated "tunnels" should always run vertically in supporting members. And be wary of the one danger in the craft: cardboard's cut edges are surprisingly and sneakily sharp. Check assiduously to make sure that you've covered all edges left exposed after a piece is finished, using duct tape (or fabric or wallpaper, if you "upholster" your results as shown in the facing photographs). You can find duct tape at hardware stores.

Finding cardboard

It takes some searching by telephone to find industrial-strength, triple-thick cardboard. Look for sources under "Packaging Materials" in the Yellow Pages—some will stock sheets, usually in 4 by 6 or 4 by 8-foot sizes. Most suppliers can order the sheets for you if they don't have them on hand.

Large cartons that package refrigerators are also made of the same corrugated, triple-thick material. You can usually purchase these inexpensively from appliance dealers. Some will even give them away.

Simple table & chairs

A good starting project in cardboard carpentry might be the 20-inch-high table and its 14-inch chairs shown on the facing page.

The table's base is formed by two interlocking legs, joined by slots in the same fashion as many children's construction toys. As illustrated on the next page, one leg has a central slot cut halfway (plus 1/2 inch, for ease of joining) through its height, starting from the base; the other has an identical slot cut from the top. These slots are exactly the thickness of the cardboard—hold the cut edge of a cardboard sheet against the table leg and trace around it to make a pattern for the slot. After you cut the slots, slide the first leg down over the second, and the slots will interlock.

To sketch the table top's circular shape right on the 4 by 4-foot sheet from which you'll cut it, make a compass of scrap cardboard. The scrap should be as long as the radius you desire (ours is 20 inches, and yours can be no longer than 24). Poke a pencil through one end of the scrap and nail the other lightly to the center of the sheet. Swing the pencil end around to draw the circle; then cut the top out and lay it on the floor.

Position the base, its two members spread crosswise, on the table top. Trace the base's position, then glue the base in place. Reinforce it by gluing to the top, and then taping, four pie-shaped wedges, cut from scraps to fit tightly between each pair of legs.

The simplest stool design would be a miniature version of the table. Or you can make boxy chairs like those shown in the photograph. For the latter, you start by cutting and fitting together interlocking bases made of four 14-inch cardboard squares, each with slots on both sides. For strength, cut the slots at least 2 1/2 inches from each side edge (as shown on the next page).

Next, cut a square reinforcing wedge to fit tightly inside the open top of each base, and a seat just big enough to cover the base completely (14 to 16 inches square). Glue each wedge to the center of a seat's underside; then glue and fit the seats to the bases, pressing the reinforcing wedges tightly inside the bases. Reinforce all joints with duct tape.

Each set of chair back and arms was cut from a single strip of cardboard, then scored—cut through just the outside corrugated layer of the strip—where the arms form corners with the back. Joined to the chair seats with glue and tape, these strips are not absolutely essential. They may become wobbly after a few wild tea parties—but they should hold together at least until the chairs are outgrown.

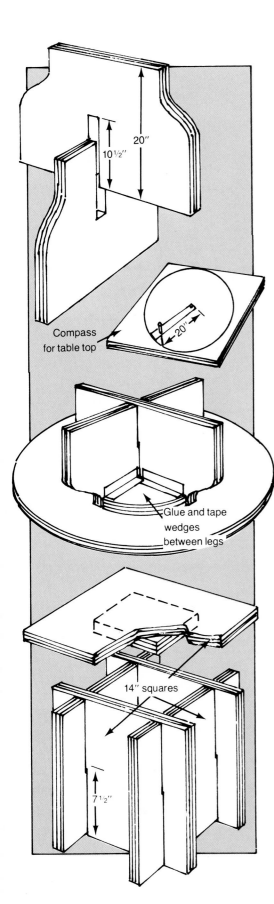

20″
10½″

Compass
for table top

20″

Glue and tape
wedges
between legs

14″ squares

7½″

Cardboard whimsy for tots or teddy bears fits together with glue, tape, and interlocking slots. Finish furniture (after taping cut edges) with enamel, glued-down fabric (vinyl is waterproof), or wallpaper. Design: Françoise Kirkman.

Puppet theater "hinges" with loops of heavy cord—you can fold it flat for storage. Its spongeable vinyl wallpaper surface makes an excellent overcoat for cardboard.
Design: Laura Ferguson.

Heirlooms...
Hand-me-downs
to treasure

As we scatter ourselves far afield,
quickening our pace from one roof
to the next, whatever will become
of heirlooms? It would be a shame to lose
every last bit of bric-a-brac in the shuffle.

While reverence for heirlooms may not
prevail today as widely as it once did,
many families still pass these treasures
along, even to youthful members. Parents
feel a special reassurance when their
baby sleeps in a cradle that has already
comforted generations of family young.
To a child, even a small silver trinket that
once sat on Great-grandmother's shelf
carries with it a sense of belonging and
self-worth. Heirlooms engender pride—
and a moderate dose of pride won't hurt
any of us.

If you have no readily available attic to
raid for family treasure, and the romance
of heirlooms stirs your fancy, you might
start a tradition with your own children.
Invest in a bit of history—a chest or a
rocker—that they can grow up with and
later hand down themselves.

Cradling her mother's (and grandmother's) favorite doll,
Zee-Zee reposes on her regally festooned Victorian bed.

Country antiques improve with a few nicks and scratches from service to children. These pieces also happen to blend delightfully with bold contemporary fabrics. Design: Judith Snable.

Little Megan's assorted wickerware has seen four generations' worth of comfortable nursery reclining.

A treasury of dolls fills her cabinet today, but tomorrow—who knows? Rare books, rare china...or maybe the very same dolls (a number of which are heirlooms themselves).

Fat hippo changing table was dreamed up by Timothy's carpenter father and painted by his mother. Storage crannies built into the animal's sides and between its jowls will serve for years, long after Tim has stopped wearing diapers. Design: Andy Andrews.

Fun furniture... For & from the young at heart

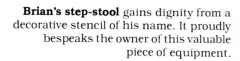

Daddy's darling dines in a very regal throne, indeed. Its painted fantasy tray is not only entertaining to look at, but fun to decorate with cooky crumbs. Design: Sidney MacDonald Russell.

While many of today's furniture designs for the young reflect, in miniature, the serious aspirations of adult "good taste," there is no particular reason why they should. Kids are very open-minded about matters of taste. They're also naturally zany —as are many of us parents, under our surface crust.

If strictly functional furniture reminds you more of a chilly boarding school than a happy home, the ideas on these two pages should cheer you up. Here are creations from parents who dared to scale the heights of whimsy as they furnished their kids with the otherwise humdrum necessities of life.

Brian's step-stool gains dignity from a decorative stencil of his name. It proudly bespeaks the owner of this valuable piece of equipment.

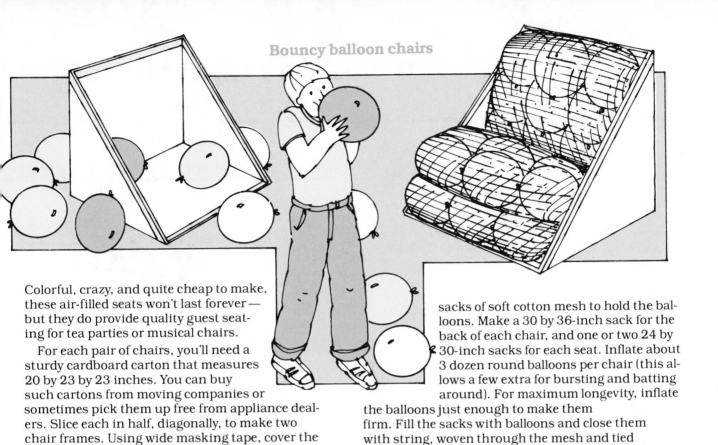

Bouncy balloon chairs

Colorful, crazy, and quite cheap to make, these air-filled seats won't last forever — but they do provide quality guest seating for tea parties or musical chairs.

For each pair of chairs, you'll need a sturdy cardboard carton that measures 20 by 23 by 23 inches. You can buy such cartons from moving companies or sometimes pick them up free from appliance dealers. Slice each in half, diagonally, to make two chair frames. Using wide masking tape, cover the cut edges, for they can be surprisingly sharp.

To make the air-filled cushions, you'll need to sew sacks of soft cotton mesh to hold the balloons. Make a 30 by 36-inch sack for the back of each chair, and one or two 24 by 30-inch sacks for each seat. Inflate about 3 dozen round balloons per chair (this allows a few extra for bursting and batting around). For maximum longevity, inflate the balloons just enough to make them firm. Fill the sacks with balloons and close them with string, woven through the mesh and tied loosely so you can free the balloons at the end of a party, or add new ones to replace popped ones.

Improvements with paint & découpage

From fancy showrooms to humble garage sales, our world is clogged with large, squarish articles of furniture that, while serviceable, are completely devoid of whimsy. It's up to parents and kids to improve their sad faces with jars or spray cans of high-gloss enamel in joyful colors. (In some cases, even a few swipes of fingernail polish make a great improvement).

Your decorating options are many. Consider stars, stripes, polka dots, or funny faces. Or follow the contours of the furniture, if they lead you in a fanciful direction... turn each drawer into a miniature mural, chair spindles into a rainbow medley.

If freehand painting alarms you, there are other approaches. Borrow motifs from children's books, giftwrap paper, or needlework patterns. Copy these or use them to make stencils (you can buy stencils, too, from a stationer) through which you can brush or spray the furniture. Or try découpage: affix a cutout paper collage, using white glue.

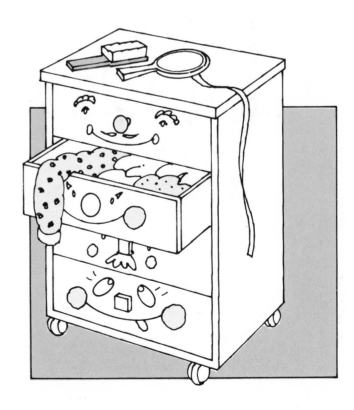

If you paint your furniture, let each color dry thoroughly—4 to 5 days—to avoid later chipping. When dry, coat either paint or découpage with clear polyurethane varnish for maximum protection. (You might find the *Sunset* book *Furniture Finishing & Refinishing* helpful here.)

Telephone booth

Teenagers are notoriously long-winded on the phone, but so, very often, are the rest of us — whether the teens are ahead of us or far behind.

While it's easy to appreciate the friendly appeal of Mr. Bell's miracle, in talkative familes the phone location sometimes becomes a rather noisy depot —especially at the busiest times of day.

One solution might be to unplug it and hide it in the linen closet, at least during dinnertime. On the other hand, if that closet —or any other —offers enough space for a lamp, a shelf, some big cushions, and a small bulletin board, you might transform it permanently into a home phone booth.

In such a nook, conversations can ramble on in privacy without your having to overhear every giggle and shriek. Here, too, telephone clutter — pinned-up messages and tattered books —will stay pleasantly out of sight.

Nooks, crannies & other clever little spaces

Flashy laundry chute

Shooting laundry down this big, shiny pipe is much more fun than bother. When not swallowing linens, it also makes an excellent echo chamber —for ghost voices in the basement.

One family's chute was pieced together from lengths of 18-inch-diameter galvanized heating duct that extend it from the owners' first floor to a laundry basket in the basement below. Its top is an 18-gauge adjustable elbow joint; it looks like a ship's funnel.

To find duct pipe, look in the Yellow Pages under "Furnaces" or "Sheet Metal Work" —or check with a plumbing contractor. Pipe lengths are crimped at one end, allowing one to fit snugly into another. The seams of both elbow and pipe sections should point downward, so that clothing won't catch as it tumbles through. Cover any rough spots with furnace tape. Architect: Daniel Solomon.

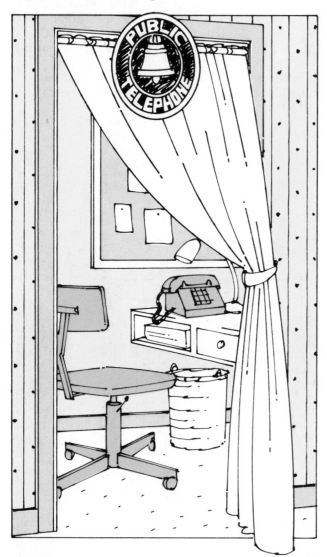

Alcove gymnastics

Even in a very small home, you're likely to find a few spare inches for a trapeze or chin-up bar.

Nellie's trapeze hangs in an open walk-through between the kitchen and dining room of her none-too-spacious city apartment. When the grownups are having a dinner party, it can be raised to the ceiling, out of the way. Hooks, placed just inside the eyebolts that anchor the trapeze to the doorway header, hold its chainlinks above head height. (See "Anchor it safely," below — Nellie's trapeze did come down when a grownup guest tried it once.)

Anchor it safely

How safely can you suspend chains or ropes from your ceiling to hold the ever-increasing weight of a child? Rugged hardware, deeply esconced in a joist or header, should be safe enough for all suspended delights, from cradle to swingseat. But there is no guarantee that whatever you hang up won't, with time and abuse, come tumbling down —perhaps under the stress of a mature and weighty guest. Also, keep in mind that nylon rope is just as strong as chain —and safer. Another safety precaution is to try your child's equipment under your own weight from time to time.

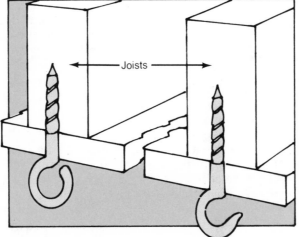

Joists

If you plan to hang anything, the first step is to find a ceiling joist or beam in which to anchor it solidly. Joists always run in the same direction, parallel to at least one wall of a room. Often hidden behind plaster or gypsum board, they are usually spaced 16 to 24 inches apart.

Locations will be easy to discover, and measurements to take, if you have access to an attic where these stocky timbers remain exposed. If you don't, knock firmly on the ceiling with the heel of your hand to find them. Starting from one corner of the room, working in both directions, space your soundings at the likely intervals mentioned above. A solid thud means you've found a joist; a hollow sound tells you to keep hunting.

No matter which method you choose, always doublecheck by drilling a tiny hole through the ceiling, or tapping in a tiny nail, to be sure of striking solid anchorage. If your ceiling is plaster, you may strike only $1/4$-inch lath at first, so penetrate a bit further to check for a joist. Use the same method to locate wall studs.

The simplest attachments for chains or ropes are large, heavy-duty eyebolts or ceiling hooks. The deeper and more tightly they penetrate the 6 to 8-inch joist, the longer they will stay put. Screw the hook or eyebolt far enough in so that its curve rests snugly against the ceiling.

Setting up for study

Sooner or later, homework makes inroads into the evenings of every school girl or boy. Tiresome a chore as it sometimes becomes for both parent and child, once homework starts, it generally doesn't let up for years. It's best to accommodate it as comfortably as possible. If you're lucky, you and the kids may even learn to enjoy it.

Many students do their homework on the living room sofa or spread out in front of the TV. But it may help to ease the task if you give them desks of their own — as well lighted, quiet, and spacious as possible. (Remember that littler kids, who breeze in after school blissfully free of such burdens, like to have their own desks or tables, too.)

Desk tops from doors

Available inexpensively in widths as narrow as 18 inches, hollow-core doors offer ample spread-out space when used as desk or counter tops.

If their standard 6-foot, 8-inch length is too much, doors can be cut down to smaller proportions. But this is a tricky job for anyone but an experienced woodworker with power tools. After slicing it, you must dig out a honeycomblike substance that fills its hollow, then replug the edge by gluing and inserting a cut-to-measure strip of wood.

On the other hand, a full-length door offers so much elbow room for on-going projects that it is well worth while to accept its bulk, if you possibly can.

Before choosing underpinnings for the desk, explore today's interesting array of modular storage units, with your child's size in mind. These units come in various sizes, made of wood or plastic. You can even buy drawer systems that stack — allowing the desk to "grow" with its owner. Young children need a height of about 20 inches. But around the age of 8 or 10, they'll feel more comfortable at a standard adult desk (29 inches high). At that time, you might buy a desk pedestal from an unfinished furniture store — or look for used, two-drawer office filing cabinets, possibly at an office supply warehouse sale.

Whatever supports you choose, it's safest to secure them to the desk top with molly bolts, even though the door is heavy and unlikely to wobble.

Desk lighting

Though Abe Lincoln grew up to become a most worthy President, renowned to every school boy and girl, he also grew up to be a very melancholy soul. It may have had something to do with reading books by candlelight in a murky cabin.

Eyes work hard when they focus on a printed page — and arithmetic problems sometimes take long staring. To ease things, try to arrange two light sources to illuminate your child's work, with shafts of light cast from either side. This usually means combining a good adjustable desk lamp with the overhead light. Tilt the lamp so that it casts neither shadows nor glare and doesn't shine in the young student's eyes. (Your child may or may not take all this seriously, but explain it anyway.)

Probably the best lamp to buy is the clamp-on type sold by art suppliers and stationers. From base to wide metal shade, it articulates in nearly every direction.

Also, don't neglect a reading lamp by the bed. It is particularly welcome near shadowy lower bunks. Clip-on types attach neatly to bed posts.

A raised, carpeted island — for comic books or floor games — separates individual desks, each assembled from Parsons tables and freestanding drawer units. Design: Sharon Owen Haven.

A pocket of tranquillity, brightly lighted by recessed lamps, makes it easier and more pleasurable for a serious student to concentrate.

On bouncy days, in boisterous weather...Three cheers for playrooms

With rainy days and weary winters, tempers sometimes start to fray from cabin fever. Kids wax fretful, wriggly, whiny. Parents' temples throb...

These are times when a playroom can magically transform misery into merrymaking. Even if nothing more than a carpeted chunk of attic space, a playroom is at times a heavenly haven for all concerned. Here, kids can explode as noisily as they please—and you don't have to hear every decibel of the din. Here, they can churn up a chaos of fun without cluttering everyone else's path—and without having, necessarily, to tidy everything up before bedtime.

While a playroom is perfectly well equipped with such thrifty toys as grocery cartons and inner tubes, you may want to add luxuries later, like a honky-tonk piano or computerized horse-racing.

Bold graphics in circus colors, brightly illuminated from above, transform a previously unused basement into a playroom. The expansive blackboard, cut from masonite, is bordered by bulletin board. Design: Don Merkt.

Wild and whimsical, this playroom features such wonders as a painted piano and a skyward-leaping horse. Behind the curved curtain, the floor was raised to make a stage. Design: Jeanne Clark.

Sled of vinyl flooring sample careens down the sloping floor of a rumpus room that appeared, as if by magic, when the roof line was raised during remodeling. Architect: George Cody.

Comfortably close by, Mama's little ones can call "Watch me!" through the open interior window between kitchen and playroom. She, in turn, can keep an eye on them while she cooks. Architect: James Caldwell.

A little imagination makes life a lot more fun

One of the sweetest charms of youth is its imagination. One of the bonuses of parenthood is getting cajoled into joining a few flights of youthful flamboyance. And one of the most resourceful laboratories for imaginative genius is the family dwelling.

Parents do vary in the degree of imaginative fervor that they find charming or tolerable. Some mothers will crochet a red Santa Claus suit for the TV to wear at Christmas; others will not. Some will allow rhubarb pizza for breakfast; others find eggs and oatmeal too sacred a routine to disturb.

But wherever we can fit a dose or two of imagination into our kids' bedrooms and play places, it's likely to add vigor and cheer to the average household atmosphere.

Hat rack occupies only a few inches of wall space in a small, shared bedroom. But in return, it offers these preschoolers a shape-matching puzzle board as well as all kinds of elegant head gear. Design: Anne Stewart.

Monkey limbs and a firepole give Kevin instant access — faster and funnier than stairs — to the kitchen. He and his brothers have the strongest muscles for miles around. Design: Jocelyn Baum.

Fanciful windows

The reasons for blocking out windows are generally of a practical nature. In cold weather, you probably want good, insulative coverings. If your child becomes frightened at night by inky glass or outdoor shadows, of course you'll want to shut out the goblins with curtains or a shade. And in some room situations, children need privacy — just as adults do.

But, if none of these conditions apply, you and your kids might enjoy a refreshing switch from traditional window coverings. One that delighted us consists of several horizontal rows of clothesline. Suspended by clothespins from the lines are an assortment of colorful children's knee socks — the odd socks that we all accumulate, either because the children outgrow them or, more often, because their mates get swallowed mysteriously by our automatic driers.

Another, rather romantic treatment is to suspend ribbons — matched, coordinated, or mixed up—from the window top. Sew a variety of objects to the ribbon ends to prevent runaway fluttering — a few bells, some shells, wood spools, brass washers…

Your kids can arrange a "stained glass" mosaic on the window if you supply them with white glue, colorful tissue paper, and thin, translucent vinyl from an upholstery or auto supply shop. Just scissor the vinyl into interesting shapes, each about 4 to 6 inches square, then glue the bright tissue paper to them. The vinyl mosaic "tiles" will adhere to clean glass when pressed in place (they don't stick very well if the window is damp); for later rearrangement, they simply peel off.

Photographic foolishness

Delight in one's own appearance is pandemic among youth (maybe among the rest of us, too, even when we pretend otherwise). And photographic wonders also seem to have a universal appeal.

Combine these two delicious truths, add a liberal helping of imagination — and you come up with "photographic foolishness," a zany kind of interior decor with numerous applications.

One source of this kind of fun is turning up with increasing rapidity at amusement parks: computer booths with machines that spew forth space-age camera likenesses for a moderate fee. These photos lend themselves beautifully to artistic improvement with colored pencils.

Kids also love superscale blowups of themselves. First, you need to take a memorable photograph — maybe an action glimpse of your child racing across a field, or a more formal pose in elaborate costume. Take the portrait's negative to a photographic laboratory for enlargement as a poster of exciting size. Any lab can make a black-and-white poster from black-and-white or color film; for color results, you may have to search through a photography magazine for a sophisticated mail-order supplier.

Affix the poster to a wall where it will have the most impact — or to the outside of the bedroom door, where it might startle the unsuspecting passerby right out of his shoes.

Waterworks

A long time ago, most well-appointed bedrooms had their own sinks. Today, the very idea may appall you at first — because of the expense, if not because of potential spills. But if you can install a sink in your son's or daughter's room, once either is old enough to avoid watery catastrophes, it is sure to be greatly appreciated.

People of any age are soothed and fascinated by water. An extra sink has practical value, too — it will save both commotion and soapy surfaces in the bathroom. As a versatile piece of play equipment, a handy sink encourages water colors and good grooming, sailing boats and mixing potions, bathing the dog or a rubber dolly, even brushing teeth and cleaning the goldfish bowl.

Choose a sink with an ample rim or, even better, counter space around it; install vinyl flooring below. For advice on home installation, consult the *Sunset* book *Basic Plumbing Illustrated.*

Keeping creatures

Parents' views on pet life in the bedroom vary as widely as do their views on everything else. But to children, pet appeal is nearly universal. Even if you already have family dogs and cats, sooner or later your kids will probably want to adopt something tiny and strange of their very own.

If you're squeamish about strange creatures, it won't stunt your kids' growth to forego keeping them indoors. And some pets should be banned for safety's sake: turtles sometimes carry an infectious disease called salmonella, and little friends captured in the garden may be tainted if you've used poisons outside.

Safer and more traditional are the creatures sold at pet stores. Easiest of all to care for, probably, are hardy fish such as goldfish and guppies. Infants and young children delight in them.

But older kids may find fish rather lacking in personality. In such a case, you might want to try either a guinea pig or hamster (they reproduce sometimes if you buy two), or mice or rats, if you can tolerate them. Assure yourself beforehand that Junior will handle all feeding and cleaning — rodents can be appallingly messy.

Wildlife in the bedroom— Pets & plants

Indoor gardens

If house plants lend cheer to the kitchen windowsill ...if we adults go a bit overboard in our adulation of a Boston fern...then imagine the wonder and delight that a little growing greenery will bring to a child.

The kind of plant that you and the kids select should depend on how far they have progressed toward the age of responsible garden-tending. It's best to stick to hardy plants that aren't likely to expire or droop disappointingly—aspidistra, devil's ivy, or sansevieria (also called "snake plant") are good choices.

Weird plants—cacti (provide gloves), succulents, the voracious Venus fly trap, or the sensitive plant, which curls its leaves when touched—have a special appeal to young gardeners. You may need to order these types from a plant catalog.

Small children appreciate the broader botanical adventure of starting their own greenery from fruit and vegetable scraps.Soak citrus seeds overnight, then tuck two or three into a container of potting soil; water every few days, and watch them sprout on a sunny windowsill. Or cut about 2 inches off the top of a carrot or beet; trim the leaves off, too. Place the top, cut side down, in a shallow dish containing about half an inch of water. Change the water every other day. When roots appear, plant the vegetable in a pot filled with moist sand; keep it well moistened on a sunny sill.

A child's house plant becomes an even greater source of pride when you also make a project of choosing and decorating its container. Spread white glue on a plain clay pot, let it dry out a little, and your child can create an elegant mosaic from an infinity of things that might stick onto it: macaroni, beans, shells, beads, bottle caps, old postage stamps, and on and on. Other interesting containers include decorated juice cans, cut-down milk cartons, outgrown tennis shoes, and discarded cowboy hats.

You can increase the pleasures of indoor gardening by arranging a fantasy landscape in a wide, shallow container. If it lacks drainage holes, line the base with a 1-inch layer of horticultural charcoal. Top that with potting soil to fill the pot to within 1 inch of its rim. Then plant an assortment of small-scale greenery with shallow root balls (young plants, sold in 2-inch pots, are about the right size). Add details to delight: miniature animals and buildings, tiny plastic people, perhaps a pocket mirror half buried in soil to simulate a pond (put ducks on it).

Room enrichment: Of endless possibilities, here are just a few

Whether your son or daughter is a reasonably good housekeeper or the more common sweet-but-untidy type, you're bound to find yourself poking around your child's room from time to time. Maybe you're there only to deliver clean T-shirts. Or maybe to hazard a peek under the bed for a lost rubber boot. Whatever your entry ticket, a quiet and solitary tour of the room can yield a bounty of good ideas for room enrichment.

Look around—soak up the atmosphere. It may give you clues to your child's phase of the moment, to needs and enthusiasms that fail to surface clearly in other ways. Start taking notes ... room enrichment can happen at Christmas, for a birthday, or any time in between.

Mechanical wonders

If we grownups rely on digital watches and pocket calculators to wend our way through an intricate world, our kids are bound to wish for a few fascinating devices of their own. And many of those sophisticated gadgets make fine room accessories for our young.

When the daily school routine starts, every child learns the down-to-earth meaning of clock time. Mornings may pick up their own smooth momentum if the young scholar possesses his or her personal alarm clock. A big wind-up type is least expensive, and there's something soothing and self-regulatory about winding it up every night at bedtime. On the other hand, many kids find the electrical, digital style of clock more exciting.

Christmases and birthdays offer opportunities to equip a child with items like a flashlight (with extra batteries) to keep at bedside; a mechanical pencil sharpener; and measuring devices, from metal compasses and rulers to room thermometers—especially those that uncloud the mysteries of metric conversion.

A good typewriter will delight a young reader and writer—even one who is still exploring the ABC's. One father found a decades-old model, made entirely of metal, at a thrift shop. Reconditioned for his son's fourth birthday, the typewriter came at a total cost below that of a less rugged (and less grown-up) plastic machine from the toy store.

Crazy day rescue box

Tuck this box out of sight and reach, on an upper closet shelf in a young child's room. It comes down only when you both need instant rescue from boredom or blues—during a sick day, a rainy day, or any garden-variety difficult day.

Stock it as you please with whatever you think will fascinate and delight. You might stash away a few books and toys right after a super-abundant Christmas if you can get away with it. It's a good place to stock interesting craft items, too—buttons, pipe cleaners, yarn, and fabric scraps, to name a few. And don't forget scissors, tape and white glue.

Gentle geography

For a school-age child (especially in the middle years), maps become fascinating to explore. Now is the time for a globe, if you don't already have one in the house.

Or you might provide a diverse collection of maps—a wall-size "atlas." Punch (and reinforce) holes in the upper corners of the maps and hang them on the wall, on cup hooks. They can be interchangeable, depending on the occasion for geographical exploration: before taking a plane trip to another state, when talking about forebears or foreign visitors, bringing to life a social studies assignment, learning the geography of one's own county, or exploring the topography of an upcoming mountain trip.

A little extra color, a little extra light make for brighter and jollier surroundings. Here are stimulating splashes: a plastic Mother Goose lamp (purchased at a toy store) and an ABC night light built with blocks by a fond and industrious mother; fluttery cloth and paper kites to float from the ceiling; an alphabet fabric panel, mounted on artists' stretcher bars; and a plastic-coated chart depicting various crusty characters who dwell in the sea.

Classic technology clusters around an intriguing—if still costly—newcomer: a home computer. Instruments shown here are (left to right) a globe, a barometer, a thermometer that dispenses weather information in both Celsius and Fahrenheit, and a battery-operated clock. The computer broadcasts math exercises via the family TV (it can also straighten out a parent's tax confusions).

Play Yards

The outdoor world exhilarates children immediately—and most of them leap at any chance they get to explore it. Even a vacant lot full of nothing but weeds and a few pieces of junk is, to them, full of interesting possibilities.

Children's outdoor play varies endlessly, and what we present in this chapter offers only a bare glimpse of the full panorama. For example, we haven't touched on some of the more delightful experiences that require no special equipment or adult involvement whatsoever: grinding dandelions for mud soup, discovering animals in cloud formations, making friends with a climbable tree, collecting creatures, chalking on sidewalks, throwing snowballs, or just standing under an umbrella to sniff the rain.

What we have gathered here, instead, are a few good ideas for beefing up the potential of backyard and playground fun—in ways that parents can manage better than can kids left to their own devices. Coincidentally, of course, this also means fostering their physical and mental development. But much as this may matter to us, it's good to remember that our kids are interested only in having a wonderful time.

We've included many safety tips throughout these next pages for minimizing the likelihood of play yard accidents. But risk-taking is a big part of children's outdoor fun, and some children seem to be insatiable daredevils. So safety outside the house is really something that we adults can only aim for, and then hope for. It's wise to be prepared with grounding in first-aid techniques.

Who could resist scrambling into the arms of an old, spreading oak tree— especially when one or two dip invitingly to the ground?

Sand...
One of life's earliest & sweetest pleasures

Why is sand so universally loved by children from the day they first discover it? Because it feels so good and does so much. Dry, it is tinglingly grainy to the touch, yet soft and soothing at the same time. Wet, it turns malleable and gooey, like its equally beloved cousins, mud and clay. Either way, sand is sheer delight to the fingers and toes—especially those of kids between ages two and six.

As the captain scans the horizon, the first mate casts a line into the leafy sea in hopes of catching some supper. Benderboard wrapped around six weatherproof posts forms the hull of their elegant craft, which includes a sandbox between fore and aft decks. Design: Scott Fitzgerrell.

Bright yellow striped canvas shelters kids from a hot summer sun. It also unsnaps to lie right over the sand as a screen against pets.

Sand gadgetry

Though hands and even feet are wonderful tools themselves, a collection of interesting implements will add immeasurable fun to sand play. Search garage sales and thrift shops for big spoons and ladles, fancy molds, strainers, colanders, funnels, coffee pots, and assorted pans. At home, you can make a generous sand scoop, cutting it out of a plastic jug container (thoroughly rinsed and its cut edge covered with plastic tape). Some large toy dump trucks and earth-moving equipment will add to the fun.

Sand without water is as short-changed as peanut butter without jelly. Be sure to provide at least a partially filled bucket or watering can—or, better yet, a quietly dribbling hose.

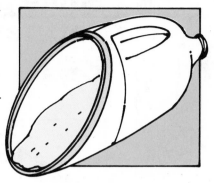

What kind, how much & where to find it

Ocean sand is said to be more hygienic than river sand, but the availability of either, of course, depends on where you live. Do ask for coarse washed sand, best for molding and least likely to be carried into the house on clothes and toes. Especially handy for adding to an already filled sandbox are sacks of about 100 pounds, containing about 1 cubic foot apiece. You can buy these from a lumber or garden supplier and from some toy stores.

A better plan, if you're filling a large sandbox for the first time, may be to buy in bulk and have the sand delivered. (Besides, it's fun to watch the dump truck.) To figure how many cubic feet you need, multiply the length and width of the sandbox by about two-thirds the sandbox depth. Be generous—for decent digging, the sand should be at least 12 inches deep.

Corralling the sand

A container for sand or pea gravel needn't be fancy. One big tractor tire, its opening widened with a saw, makes a wonderful corral. Kids can sit around its resilient rim, and they'll love to burrow in its recesses.

On the other hand, more elaborate sandboxes (like those shown on the facing page) are often as much fun for parents to build as they are for children to play in. And roominess invites socializing.

Modest or baroque, any sandbox needs adequate drainage, most easily achieved by putting a layer of gravel at its base, over the bare ground. Either place the box in partial shade or provide a canopy or beach umbrella. Screens to keep sand clean are discussed on the next page.

Cleaner & dirtier substitutes

Small children adore dirt and mud at least as much as sand, an affection that needn't cause too much alarm for parents. Mudpies are an early childhood enrichment well worth a few spatters on the corduroy.

At the other extreme, pea gravel is as pure and clean a sand substitute as the most fastidious parent could wish. The tiny river-polished stones don't squish as pleasingly as sand or mud, but neither do they cling to clothing or attract cats. Like sand, pea gravel comes either in small sacks containing 1 cubic foot each—or, more dramatically, in a dump truck.

Super sandboxes... Some parents' happy refinements

Slide-out sandbox cover

Even a small child can slide this cover into or out of its adjoining planter platform. The platform is framed at front and rear with redwood 2 by 12s, the sandbox cover with 2 by 6s. Tops of both are 1 by 2-inch redwood slats. Design: Jerome Gluck.

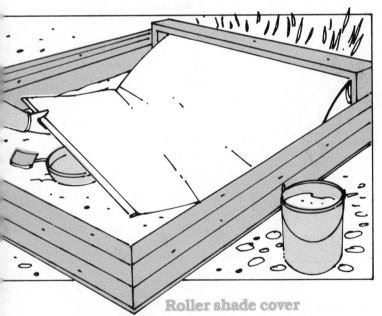

Roller shade cover

A vinyl-coated canvas roller shade shields the sandbox shown above from pets and leaves. (For tips on making your own roller shade, see the *Sunset* book *Curtains, Draperies & Shades.)*

The metal shade brackets, which are mounted at one short end of the sandbox, face inward so the slots that receive roller-points can face upward. A 2 by 6-inch board that hides the roller doubles as a bench. Design: H. Flint Ranney.

Sandbox doubles as play table

This neat little redwood sandbox has its own boxy lid that, when in place, forms a play table, garden seat, or plant stand.

When a big palm outgrew its bed in a paved patio, one family transformed the bed into a sandbox for their two small children. First they dug out about 6 inches of soil and lined the bottom of the bed with bricks for drainage. Concrete footings (about 6 inches deep) set at each of the four corners anchor 6-inch-long metal straps. The inside of the 32 by 36-inch sandbox frame—four redwood 2 by 12s butted at corners—fastens to the straps with woodscrews.

The 1 by 4s of the removable lid are nailed to a 2 by 2 lip on all sides and rimmed with mitered 2 by 3s.

To help keep splinters away, it's important to sand all surfaces thoroughly.

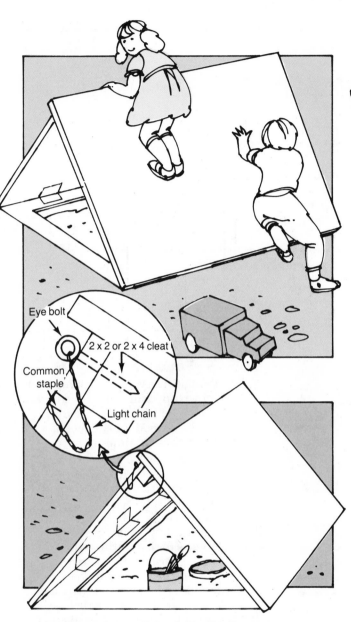

Wide rim makes bench

A good bench wrapping around all four sides adds to the fun of a sandbox. It offers comfortable seating or, when kids sit in the sand, a drag strip for toy cars.

The wide bench shown above is open underneath, making it easy to sweep spilled sand from the surrounding patio back into the recessed sandbox. After its young owner outgrows sand play, the box can become a planter for a tree.

Sand canopy supports swing

Since sand play is often most appealing in warm weather, a sun screen of some sort usually makes sense—unless the box is well shaded by trees. As shown below, the support for a sun canopy (made of lath or a bamboo shade) can carry a small child's swing at the same time—doubling the fun of the sandbox. Design: Thomas Gallup.

Climbable, slideable playhouse cover

Hinged panels of 3/4-inch exterior plywood give this super sandbox a peaked roof to shelter children from sun or rain. It's also a lot of fun to climb up and slide down the plywood "hill" between sand scenes. Several coats of exterior grade paint should prevent splinters.

To form the peak, one 3 by 6-foot panel butts against a 2 by 2 cleat on a 4 by 6-foot panel. The two are secured together as shown above. Heavy galvanized hinges affix each to the sandbox frame (fasten hinges with bolts and T-nuts, making sure ends of bolts do not protrude). When laid flat, the two panels provide a good surface for dumping loads of sand or baking sandcakes. Design: Rick Lambert.

Watery wonders, from patio wetcakes to lawn skidding

On a blazing summer afternoon, what could be more delicious than a backyard soak or splash? Kids turn into seals, wise enough to know that the best way to stay cool is to stay wet.

But even in cold weather, water never ceases to fascinate. Just washing their hands before dinner, little kids linger in blissful oblivion. Even when they're older and more sophisticated, few can resist the allure of a rain puddle or (if they're lucky enough to find one) a brook full of tadpoles.

As we grownups are very much aware, of course, water can also cause tragedy. Even a few inches is enough to drown a small child who trips and panics. Wading pools must *always* be emptied when no one is around to keep an eye on them.

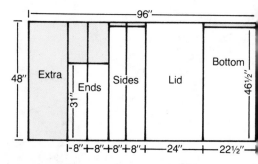

Water slide

Here's the only equipment needed for a riot of slippery glee: a large polyethylene sheet (commonly available as a dropcloth where paints are sold), a lawn, and a garden hose. First you wet the plastic thoroughly—if there's a dip in the lawn, it will become a wide, shallow lake. Then you simply run and skid across it, in any sliding posture that appeals, while your friend tries to zap you with the hose.

While there is little danger of drowning on a soppy polyethylene sheet, there is definite danger to the health of your lawn if you don't move the plastic to a fresh area after an hour's sliding.

Sand-water-clay table

To make the versatile rolling table shown opposite, you'll need a 4 by 8-foot sheet of 3/4-inch exterior grade plywood, plus 8 feet of 4 by 4 standard fir for legs.

Cut the plywood according to the diagram above; attach side and end pieces to the bottom with glue and woodscrews (end pieces will extend 3-1/2 inches at each side). Cut the 4 by 4 into four equal lengths for legs; attach these with carriage bolts, placing two through each 3-1/2-inch extension mentioned above and two more through each basin side into each leg. Countersink exposed ends of nuts and washers to prevent scratches. Drill a drain hole at least 3/4 inch wide in the basin bottom (which you plug tightly from the inside with a cork).

For clay play, cover the lid with canvas or oilcloth, stapling edges to the underside. The lid simply lifts on and off. For indoor-outdoor rolling, add heavy-duty casters.

Finish the table with several coats of exterior paint or polyurethane varnish; waterproof the basin with three coats of fiberglass resin.

Soothing sand at their fingertips, in the basin of this roll-everywhere table, absorbs their attention for hours. Adding water, they can make rivers and lakes—or sandy slush, the basic ingredient for patio wetcakes. Later, a canvas-covered lid turns the sand-water basin into a clay table (canvas removed, the table could further serve as a woodworker's bench). Building directions appear on the facing page. Design: Scott Fitzgerrell.

Simplest of climbers may look like nothing more than a boarded-up sawhorse, but, to kids, it's whatever they need at the moment—such as an Italian racing car or a galaxy cruiser. Design: Sam and Rita Eisenstat.

Tilted cube, with three links missing, makes an elegant climber for a crowd of clambering kids. Design: SunSeeker Cubes.

For scaling heights, here are backyard mountains

Quite early in life, the lure of getting up there beckons as irresistibly as Everest.

To small people, a challenging climb holds out tasty rewards: delicious muscle-stretching, proud mastery of scary situations, the heady thrill of towering above a world that normally towers above them. While they do all that purely for fun, climbing also significantly rewards their development—physical and mental, simultaneously.

Hazard, of course, is part of the experience—for daredevils, the best part. But you can scale down the actual risks when you build a backyard jungle gym. It needn't be taller than 6 or 8 feet to allow for triumphs. Cushion the ground with about a 12-inch layer of soft material (choices are listed on page 80).

To discourage scrapes and splinters, select lumber that has no cracks; sand it well and seal it against splitting from weather changes; round the corners and countersink all connective hardware. Unless spaced and braced for good stability, set upright members in at least 2 feet of concrete.

Almost a tree fort, three platforms plus cargo nets get you up into lofty and leafy places. A firepole (not shown) offers a quick way down again. Design: Walter Bliss.

Three ladders take you up to a bridge (a good place to play Three Billy Goats Gruff) with ample elbow room beneath for a tire swing. Design: Sam and Rita Eisenstat.

Gymsets: Play versatility in compact space

Not long ago, the rhythmic creak of a rusty swingset was a common note in the typical suburban cacophony. But in our times of consumer sophistication, the big metal backyard toy has fallen into some disfavor. One reason may be that fingers have been pinched after children grew bored with its routine motions and tried to expand the swingset's potential.

The great thing about a swingset, on the other hand, is that it steals very little space from other backyard enterprises, like vegetable gardening or patio picnics. Here are a few alternative structures —call them "gymsets"—that use up about the same minimal square footage (or very little more). But within their compact design are wide worlds of physical adventure.

Safe swingset alternative features a fat, soft inner tube swing; cotton climbing ropes; trapeze bar; rope ladder; and, at top, a horizontal ladder to crawl across. Design: Developlay.

She tightrope walks a smooth log affixed to a side yard "gymset." Notched log at left leads to a slide at far end.

A small world

Tucked into a garden corner, this small structure built of 4 by 4 posts and 2 by 6 railings offers immense diversity. On either side of a low platform are a 4-foot-wide slide and a ramp with climbing rope. Kids can also swing in a big inner tube, hang upside-down from a horizontal ladder, or do gymnastic tricks on a turning bar. When they've had enough for awhile, a private space under the platform offers retreat. Design: Playscapes.

Versatile sideyard structure

Built of hefty timbers, the climbing-swinging-karate structure shown below won't totter, even under a neighborhood onslaught.

Its three tall 8 by 8-inch pressure-treated Douglas fir posts (or substitute redwood) are set, 2 feet deep, in concrete cubes , shorter ones in 18-inch cubes. Beams are secured with countersunk bolts. Several lengths of galvanized pipe protrude from holes drilled through the posts; caps screwed on their threaded

ends safely finish them off to make climbing bars.

The long pair of cantilevered beams supports, interchangeably, a vertical tire swing or a karate bag. Either hooks onto a heavy eyebolt attached to a wide galvanized U that fits snugly between the beams.

Tops of the tallest posts are beveled and decorated with 2-inch-wide notches, and the entire structure is finished with a dark preservative. Redwood chips cushion the ground below it.

The structure was designed with versatility in mind, and each child in the family has a favorite use for it. Younger kids prefer climbing and swinging on the cantilevered tire. An older son needed to hang his karate bag where it could be kicked and chopped from all sides. And an older daughter favors gymnastic tricks on the galvanized-pipe bar linked between the central and furthermost posts. Landscape architects: Eriksson, Peters & Thoms.

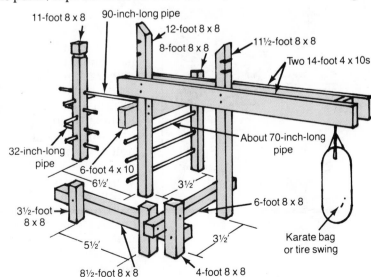

Ingredients for a first kiddie corral

A toddler's play space needn't be large—keep in mind that, like the sandbox or swing that occupies it, the play yard won't be used for more than a few years. But it should be generous enough to accommodate two or more kids happily.

For children younger than school age, the yard should be enclosed; it's also wise to carpet the ground with something soft, but kids need hard, smooth surfaces, too, for riding wheel toys. Keep in mind sun and shade patterns (you might want to plant a fast-growing tree in the play yard) and possible wind problems.

Keeping them off the street

Though it needn't be higher than about 3 feet, some sort of barricade is a must for keeping small children away from dangerous places, like busy streets.

The greatest security is provided by a metal fence of small chain links or welded wire, though these may look a bit barren without greenery. Some chain link fencing has spaces large enough for climbing, but wood slats inserted vertically will block off potential hand and foot holds. A fence of vertical boards is unclimbable by tots—but avoid splintery wood.

Play yard planning— For fun & practicality

Cushioning falls

Besides providing a good "drag strip" of smooth paving (for how-to details, consult the *Sunset* book *Walks, Walls & Patio Floors*), it's a good idea to provide the play area with a spongy ground cover—particularly where kids are most likely to take an occasional spill.

• Sand is undoubtedly the safest cushion for falls. And if you've ever taken a small girl or boy to the seashore, you know about the immediate appeal of sand, especially in vast expanses.

The more liberal the amount, the better. A depth of about 12 inches is not too much. Some public playgrounds feature "sand pools," scooped-out places with a thin layer of asphalt topped by 12 to 16 inches of sand. Each has several drainage holes filled with rock and topped with straw to keep sand out of them. (More details about sand appear on page 71.)

• Wood chips are a neater alter-

native. One cubic yard will cover 100 square feet to a depth of about 3 inches, providing a fairly good buffer for children's falls in most situations (but increase the depth to 5 or 6 inches under a swing). To keep the chips from blowing about in the wind, you'll need to dampen them from time to time. Use coarsely ground fir bark if you can. Pine bark is more likely to cause splinters.

• Smooth gravel (1/2 to 3/4-inch pebbles) makes a practical cushioning surface. Gravel is less expensive than wood chips, dries quickly, and requires virtually no upkeep. A 3-ton load will cover an area of 150 square feet to a depth of about 3 inches.

• Grass isn't quite as spongy a carpet as the materials listed above, but it still makes a good play surface. Most seed companies offer different mixtures of rugged, easy-to-grow varieties (but avoid mixtures that include clover, since it attracts bees). For maximum cushioning, keep the grass about 2 inches high.

A skateboard run

What sidewalk surfer wouldn't like a smooth, 4-foot-wide, concrete track complete with banked turns, sharp and gradual downhill drops, a small jump—and no cars in sight?

One grownup skateboarder built just such a track, with the help of his young nephews. First they contoured, soaked, and foot-packed a sandy slope; then they troweled concrete about 2 inches thick directly over the moist earth. The concrete was covered for a few days to help it cure without cracking (where soil is less stable, be sure to reinforce the concrete with wire mesh).

Children's play area

Hopscotch →

Garden

Pond

Bridge

A garden of children's delights

Rattle over a wooden plank bridge, skip down the hopscotch path shown at left, hop over the last square (if you hit it, a hidden doorbell will ring), and you're there —in the children's private play area. It doesn't look like much, but it has what makes kids happy: trees, dirt, water, secret hideaways, and room for imagination.

The play yard plan shown above started when one family had a flat back-of-the-house area bulldozed into irregular humps. Then they planted low-maintenance trees and shrubs to make a woodsy surrounding.

When the kids are feeling active, they can use standard play equipment set up in the center of the woods. On hot days they can soak their feet in a shallow 4 by 6-foot parent-built pond or in the stream into which the pond flows. Both are lined with plastic under pebbles, and edged with larger rocks. Perforations in the plastic allow some water to seep out, irrigating plants along the banks (leakage also prevents stagnation when the stream isn't running).

Guests beware: A valve hidden behind rocks adjusts a spray nozzle in the pond's center from dribble to geyser.

Swoops & squeals...
Swinging up
& sliding down

With its lulling-to-thrilling motion, a garden swing is a true classic of childhood—one of the few pleasures that our kids can experience in exactly the same fashion as their grandparents once did.

If there appears to be no practical purpose to swinging, it's because there actually isn't much, save a little muscle-flexing once you learn to pump and a certain amount of mother-bossing ("Push me! Higher!") before you do. However, for both woolgathering and simple gladness, swings are unbeatable.

Slides, on the other hand, challenge you (if you're very small) to earn your breathless thrill. First you must come to terms with getting up them, then with an instant of terror before you dare to let go and swoop downward. This is why gentle, not-too-lofty slides (like the wide one shown opposite) may be the friendliest choice for young children.

Swing seats & rigging

Tires and heavy inner tubes make good seats for either solitary or sociable swinging; some good tire ideas appear on pages 88 and 89. At toy shops you can find inexpensive plastic seats that cause no serious harm with an accidental thump. Or if you live near a boat supplier, try a boat fender (sketched above). Made of rubber and filled with either air or foam, it is 18 inches of lightweight length, with holes at either end for threading rope through.

Rope is probably a safer swing rigging than chain, simply because it is soft—but chains are good, too, and sometimes easier to link evenly to hardware. Use nylon rope for durability; cotton is just as strong, and easier on the hands when the swing doubles as a Tarzan-vine, but cotton is not weatherproof and will need more frequent replacement.

It isn't easy to find common hardware that will prevent friction from wearing through ropes or chains, in time. Metal nautical thimbles from a boat supplier ease friction. Or, if you rig a tire swing on a swivel or ball joint (used on the swing shown in the photograph opposite), friction will be lessened. And if you loop ropes or chains around a tree limb or fully accessible patio beam, encasing them in lengths of old garden hose will cut down on wear. See "Anchor it safely," page 57, for further safety tips.

For the very young, a wide slide

There are several advantages to a wide and not-too-high slide. Kids don't have to wait so long for their turns when two—or even three—can slip down together (besides, it's more sociable that way). And a generous width accommodates unusual antics more safely than do traditional playground types.

Construction details are given below for a simple 36-inch-wide plywood slide that bolts to the upright posts of a play platform.

If you face a slide toward the north, its metal surface will be less likely to become burning hot in the summer. Another trick is to use plastic laminate, in white or a pastel shade, instead of a metal surface. Just as slick, it won't heat up as much.

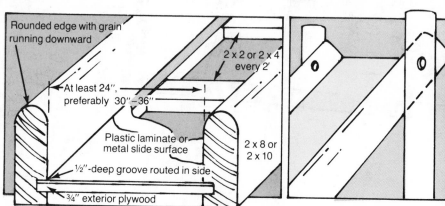

Rounded edge with grain running downward

2 x 2 or 2 x 4 every 2'

At least 24", preferably 30"–36"

Plastic laminate or metal slide surface

2 x 8 or 2 x 10

½"-deep groove routed in side

¾" exterior plywood

Slick but cool sliding surface is plastic laminate glued to plywood. (See drawing on facing page.) Design: Peter O. Whiteley.

Two, even three little kids can swing and twirl together on this swivel-mounted tire. Design: Peter O. Whiteley.

Thinking big...
Complex play rigs
invite the
neighbors in

The big, labyrinthine structures shown on these two pages can happily absorb a whole crowd of energetic kids at once. They offer enough variety that nobody ever gets bored—and there's ample scope for inventive games.

If you'd like to build a backyard structure on an ambitious scale, it will help to consult a playground designer—especially if you want to incorporate such hard-to-find materials as towering poles or a ship's cargo net.

Hefty beams jutting out from a two-story playhouse support a trapeze bar and swings— with room for extras later on. Design: Michael Moyer.

Visit schools, day-care centers, and parks where the outdoor equipment designs are exciting and versatile. Ask for references; parents and teachers may have done the building, but an architect who specializes in children's outdoor play is likely to have done the designing.

The softest surfacing underneath these structures is sand. Alternative materials and details on coverage are listed on page 80.

Rocking and revolving tire swing is suspended from a swivel affixed to the beams of the structure shown also in the other two photographs on this page.

Navigating a cargo net is fun, because it wiggles beneath you. This one, slightly spread out, also makes a fine, roomy hammock.

They zip down a sleek metal slide. Sand makes an agreeably soft landing pad. Design: Playscapes.

Balance, tone, stretch & strengthen... Ideas for junior gymnasts

Everyone in the family (maybe a few neighbors, as well) can enjoy backyard gymnastics with one of the easy-to-build exercise devices described here. You don't have to be Olympic material, necessarily—but if handstands or arm walking bring out the ham in you, all the better.

As you put this equipment together, keep safety in mind. Round all sharp edges and, to minimize splinters, sand the wood vigorously. Use the devices on level grassy ground, if you can.

To make them weather resistant, use resorcinal glue, and coat with a nonslippery exterior polyurethane or marine varnish.

A tumbling mat makes a soft landing pad for rolls, flips, and the occasional spill, yet it's also firm enough to give steady support when you traverse it on your hands.

It's hard work—but fun. Made of cotton, the rope won't hurt his hands; it's quite strong, but must be taken down in wet weather.

Less threatening than a fence top or tree limb, a balance beam offers the same off-the-ground experience. This unusual version also slopes gently from one end to the other. (Directions for a simpler balance beam appear on the facing page.) Design: Sam and Rita Eisenstat.

Low balance beam

Most of us more senior types had to grow up without the benefits to our physical and intellectual development of walking a balance beam. Some of us may have been lucky enough to "tightrope" walk a brick wall or sidewalk crack once in awhile, which amounts to almost the same thing.

At any rate, the balance beam (see drawing at right, and bottom photograph, opposite) has won much praise, over the last several decades, from educators who say that it bestows far-reaching benefits to small children who navigate it. Those benefits are said to range from gazelle-like grace to quicker absorption of reading skills. For older kids, the balance beam offers a place to do the splits or a handstand with a little more style than on ordinary lawn.

To make a simple balance beam, you glue and clamp together two 7-foot 2 by 4s (a single 4 x 4 would warp more easily). Cut notches 3-1/2 inches wide and 3 inches deep in both support blocks (8-inch-high 2 by 6s). Sand all edges smooth. Screw a metal joist hanger to the bottom of each notched block. Position and screw on bases of 2 by 6, as shown. To assemble, fit the two balance boards into the two supports (it should be a snug fit).

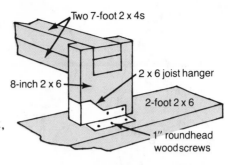

Handstand assists

These handy little wood grips, commonly used in gymnastics classes, further the pleasures of backbends, leg lifts, and hand or headstands.

Cut four trapezoid shapes from plywood; round top corners; drill 1-1/4-inch holes all the way through the top center of each. Apply glue inside holes and around ends of dowels; fit dowels in place. Sand thoroughly when dry.

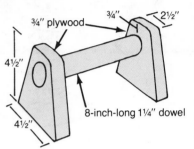

Shortened parallel bars

For arm walking, arm dips, leg lifts, leg swings—and other uses that kids will invent on their own—what your backyard may need is a set of these parallel bars.

Saw tapered tops on four 2 by 4-inch uprights, and drill holes 1-1/2 inches deep in their ends (as shown below) for dowel plugs. Cup the plywood base pieces and glue and nail or bolt these to the uprights. Drill an inch-deep hole 6-3/4 inches from the end of each banister rail; insert dowel plugs, then glue plugs in place in uprights. Sand all edges smooth; varnish to make weatherproof.

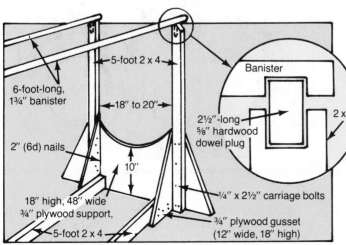

Armchair swing

The swingseat shown at left hangs from the steel-reinforced inner rings of a tire that has been turned inside out. Don't try to make it from a steel-belted tire—it's just about impossible to cut.

After scrubbing the tire, you slash it next to the inner ring, using a hacksaw. Cut away three-quarters of the tire's circumference.

Next, step on the tread and pull up hard on the rings to pop the tire inside out.

Rubbery tricks with tires & tubes

Easy to find and inexpensive

Toys made from tires have been hanging around backyards for generations. And for good reason: used tires are low in price or even free; they're easy to nail, bolt, or cut; and they're bouncy, soft, and virtually indestructible.

Finding old tires should be no problem. Service stations or tire shops are usually happy to donate a few rubber carcasses, especially those worn beyond the point of possible retreading. The same is true for inner tubes.

The first thing old tires usually need is a good scrub to wash away grime and black rubber dust. Then, to make most of the toys shown here—you need only a few easy-to-find supplies—rope, lag screws, and nuts and bolts (including U-bolts).

Six-tire totem pole for climbing

Six old tires and a pine pole make a durable vertical maze. Each tire is bolted to the pole with two 6-inch lag screws; they pass through a 2 by 4 by 8-inch block of wood inside the tire. Design: Ray Daykins.

Seven-tire super swing

Revered by its young riders, this seven-tire toy can swing, rock, and rotate—but you'll need a big tree to support it.

Five outer tires form seats, and each is joined to two inner tires of the same size, with 3/4-inch bolts, nuts, and washers (hacksaw off the end of each bolt, flush with the nut). One-inch ropes reach 45 inches from the tire seats to a swivel joint attached to a central hanging rope. If you can't find a swivel at the hardware store, look for one at a boat supply store. Design: William Potts.

A swing-around of tubes

Instead of tires (which would be too heavy for the ride), deflated inner tubes carry the passengers who ride this wonderful merry-go-round.

The tubes hang by ropes from an auto wheel assembly, bought at an auto wrecking yard. Its sturdy ball bearings allow the swing-around to rotate. The detail at left shows how the wheel assembly goes together.

The swing-around's 16-foot pole was set 4 feet deep in concrete.

Little domiciles, forts & retreats

If we remember that—to small children—many rooms must look and even feel like cavernous spaces, then it's easy to understand the instant appeal of a cozy little playhouse.

Most kids, at some point, invent their own shelters, which may be as simple and temporary as sheets draped over lawn furniture. Certainly they'll want to join the building activities, even when an adult designs the structure.

Presented here are two miniature dwellings that you and your chidren might like to set up. The photographs opposite will give you an idea of the wide range of styles possible in this Lilliputian field of architecture.

Versatile box house

Designed as an architectural course project, this simple playhouse consists of two plywood boxes, one of them small enough that even a young child can move it to various sides of its larger mate.

Increasing its play potential are circular openings to crawl through, a movable ramp to creep up or slide down, and notches and a chain ladder to climb.

Sheathing pieces for both units are cut from two 4 by 8-foot sheets of 5/8-inch exterior plywood (see cutting diagram below, right).

The big unit, which is 5 feet long, 4 feet high and 2 feet wide, has a frame of standard 2 by 2-inch lumber. Its 2-foot-square companion is built of 1 by 1-inch framing.

After cutting the plywood pieces, preassemble all the parts shown in the drawings (below, left) before gluing and nailing them to the frame (you may have to do some trimming).

The sides of the plywood ramp are base molding; plastic laminate makes its surface both slippery and splinter-free. A 1 by 1-inch lip at the top of the ramp locks inside any of the climbing holes.

After construction, be sure to round all corners and sand well. Finish with several coats of exterior paint or polyurethane varnish. Design: Cynthia Richardson and Merrilinn Zeppa.

Vegetable tepee

The framework for the tepee shown in the photograph, opposite, is very easy to erect—all you need are eight to ten long poles and a ball of heavy twine.

Lay three of the poles together in a neat row and, with twine, tie them securely near one end. Next, leaving the ball of twine uncut, stand the three poles up and spread them apart until they support each other—tripod fashion. Lay the remaining poles between the first three, spacing as equally as possible. Wrap the twine several times tightly around each as you lay it in place. When all are tied together, knot the twine and cut it from the ball, allowing at least 36 inches of extra length. Pull this length taut, and tie it toward the base of one pole, to help brace the tepee.

If you do all that in the spring, after danger of frost is past, and in a sunny corner of the garden, your child might like to raise some leafy coverage for the tepee base. Fast-growing and hardy, Kentucky Wonder beans (which can be harvested later for dinner) or scarlet runners make good tepee vines.

Charming little play cottage arrived as a hand-me-down from its site in an older friend's yard, then was painted to match the big house.

Scarlet runner beans—easy and quick to grow—drape Chelsea's beanpole tepee; its floor is carpeted with sand. See facing page for details.

Red, white, and blue graphic cube house makes a splashy addition to the backyard landscape.

This school has an everybody-built-it playground

Spooky to crawl through and great for chase games is this tunnel of welded steel barrels.

A quick slip down the slide rewards them after the joys of an arduous journey up, down, across, under, over, and through.

Look what can happen to an elementary school when parents, kids, and teachers team up with an architect to build the playground of their dreams. It took quite a few hardworking weekends, but when it was finished, everybody from kindergarteners to sixth graders (not to mention their elders) felt a glow of proud accomplishment.

Equipment choices were based on the kids' own suggestions. Funds were collected partly through their efforts in such imaginative projects as a "sundae social" and a silent auction of such services as babysitting, dog walking, and tutoring younger children.

Everybody banded together in small groups to put up the equipment, each major chunk assigned to a team. Each team included one or two experts who taught their skills to the less experienced. It all began as a project of a parent-teacher organization. Architect: Hugh Kennedy.

Free-wheeling monkey bars are hoops threaded on pipe; parallel bars in the background are chain encased in rubber hose.

Chain-linked tires knit together a swinging bridge that jiggles and jumps as kids work their way across.

Beyond the backyard... Playful & practical ideas for the whole family

We close this book with an eclectic assortment of outdoor ideas for the hale and hearty of virtually any age. Your kids can build the bike rack themselves, but chances are your own bike will be among the beneficiaries. And the ice-skating rink may inspire a wintry picnic party for the whole family, plus friends and neighbors.

The ideas shown in the photographs below offer not only playful appeal, but esthetic appeal as well. Basketball bouncing requires pavement, but pavement needn't look drab. Wading, instead of just walking, across a stone terrace is delicious fun—and the water refreshes the eye.

Soft colors painted on concrete glamorize a previously barren expanse. They also clarify zones for the players—the key, the free-throw line, and concentric lanes for games of Horse or Clock. Design: Art Ishida.

Cascading water spills down steps and into a wide, shallow pool—irresistible to barefoot kids, refreshing to their elders as well. Recirculated by a pump, the miniature waterfalls splash alongside railroad tie steps that lead from street level to an entry deck below. Landscape architects: Michael Painter and Associates.

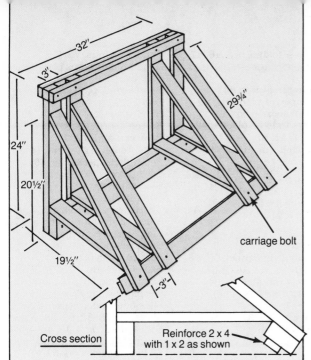

Cross section

Reinforce 2 x 4 with 1 x 2 as shown

Bike rack kids can build

The simple rack shown above is sturdy and portable, and has been tested by young carpenters in a Cub Scout troup. Made of 1 by 2s and 2 by 4s, it can be lengthened to hold three bikes if you increase its 32-inch dimension to 54 inches. But for more than three bikes, you'd best make a second rack.

Assemble the rack with twelve 1/4-inch-diameter carriage bolts and washers placed as indicated in the drawing; the other members are simply nailed in place.

Icy idea from Alaska

Three families from the freezing North have pioneered a simple way to make a skating rink from fresh snow.

They trample smooth the first snow to form a base rather like a gigantic pie shell. They then spray the "shell" with water to form a glaze, repeating gradually until the ice buildup is 2 to 3 inches thick. Once the ice gets this thick, it's only a matter of keeping snow and frost scraped off and smoothing the rink by adding more water. In very cold weather, when cracks appear, they simply fill them with slush, smoothing the seams with a mason's trowel.

One family put a base of polyethylene sheeting over the trampled snow; this method requires less water for good ice buildup, but prolonged use could damage grass underneath.

Beautiful basketball

Often the garage is the most practical place to mount a basketball net. Often, too, the results are somewhat unsightly. But with a little imaginative planning, home basketball can be as esthetic as it is athletic—note the graphic court shown on the facing page. Special paint for concrete is available in a variety of colors at most paint stores.

Another family painted a graphic decoration on the backboard itself. Going one step further, they flood the backboard (which has perforations in its design) with light at night, so that it also serves to illuminate the parking area. The backboard is a 58-inch disk made from two thicknesses of 3/4-inch plywood. Eight 1/2-inch-wide slits cut into the disk glow when the floodlight goes on. A 2 by 4's width behind the disk (see above) is an arc of the same plywood (one thickness only, 4 feet high by 7 feet wide) with an 18-inch-diameter hole cut in its center.

Bright yellow and orange against white, painted with sign-painter's enamels, turn the disk into a bold sunburst. Rainbow stripes decorate the arc. Architect: David Wright.

Index

Sunset

Children's Clothes & Toys

By the Editors of Sunset Books and Sunset Magazine

Lane Publishing Co. • Menlo Park, California

Book Editor:
Alice Rich Hallowell

Contributing Editor:
Holly Lyman Antolini

Design:
Lea Damiano Phelps

Illustrations:
Jacqueline Osborn

Photography:
Darrow M. Watt

Photo Editor:
JoAnn Masaoka

Acknowledgments

Our thanks to the many designers and home sewers who generously shared their time and talents with us. We are particularly grateful to Ellen H. Ahrbeck for her thoughtful critique of the manuscript, and to Cynthia Overbeck Bix, Karen Cummings, Phyllis Dunstan, and Heidi Merry for their editorial contributions. We also extend special thanks to Concord Fabrics, Lynne B. Morrall, Sara Robb, and Myrna Wacknov.

Cover: A bright beanbag chicken makes a whimsical steed for this little girl and her child-size doll. You'll find instructions for the chicken on page 90, for the doll on page 80. Other projects shown include the doll's quilted jacket (page 62), our model's appliquéd bears and heart pin (page 43), and a pair of sock dolls (page 72).

Sunset Books
    Editor, David E. Clark
    Managing Editor, Elizabeth L. Hogan

Second printing October 1986

Contents

Children's Clothes

Techniques, embellishments, projects

Countless are the ways you can enhance a child's garment to make it special. This chapter is chock-full of ideas to use on the next garment you make, buy, or rejuvenate.

Consult "Techniques," pages 5–23, for valuable hints on the basics, such as how to make clothes that grow with your child. And look to "Embellishments" on pages 24–57 for ways to dress up fabric—appliqué, Seminole patchwork, painting, and more. Step-by-step projects on pages 58–63 tell you how to make some extra special clothing items, from first snip to last stitch.

Techniques

Here's an abundance of ideas—both practical and pleasing—on how to handle the basic ins and outs of sewing clothes for children. It seems formidable at first to deal with all the little bits of fabric, tiny corners, and tinier fasteners. But with the following tips and instructions at your fingertips, you'll soon discover that children's clothes can be amazingly easy to sew.

On the following pages, you'll find sewing techniques to use as you make a garment from a pattern. You'll also find suggestions, whenever possible, for using the same techniques on completed garments that need some work.

The following information will take you from the basics of measuring your child and determining the correct pattern size (see "Measuring up," page 7), to such helpful techniques as simplifying seams (see "Seams," page 16). Especially important for children's clothes are techniques for adding room to grow (see "Making clothes that grow," pages 10–13), as are ideas on how to cover seam lines once growth tucks and hems are released (see "Operation coverup," page 13, and "Ruffles & strips," page 11), and many more.

With all this information at your fingertips, you'll find "Techniques" a good reference section to consult whenever you start a new project or rejuvenate an old one.

The emphasis in this book is on the needs and tastes of children ranging from infants to preschoolers.

INFANT: newborn to 6 months
TODDLER: 6 months to 2½ years
PRESCHOOLER: 2½ years to 6 years

Pattern selection

It's difficult to keep up with children's sizes—during their first few years, children seem to grow faster than you can blink an eye, and staying one step ahead of their clothing needs isn't easy.

Cut the challenge down to size by choosing patterns with simple lines and easy directions. Then decorate these garments with lots of trims or colorful embellishments to make them special and fun (see "Embellishments," starting on page 24).

Below are some pattern-selection hints that apply to all children's clothes. You'll also find some special features to look for, corresponding to your child's stage of development and needs. Keep these ideas in mind when you shop for garment patterns.

Basic guidelines

Children's wear is ideal for the sewing novice—most designs are simple, little fitting is required, and youngsters won't notice any mistakes you may make while mastering a technique.

Whatever your level of expertise, remembering these hints will help you get the most from each pattern you purchase.

● There must be plenty of room throughout a garment for ease of movement, without its being droopy or baggy. For example, drop shoulder or kimono sleeves are comfortable and unrestrictive, and accommodate lots of growth (**Ill. 1**).

Ill. 1

Roomy pants legs with elasticized hems allow room for running without the hazard of tripping (**Ill. 2**).

Ill. 2

● Details are important to consider. For example, shoulder straps should crisscross in the back of a garment so they won't fall off the shoulder. For further support, an epaulet or strap at the shirt shoulder will moor the strap in place.

Avoid using bows to tie garments at the shoulders. They may look pretty at first, but they untie all too quickly and are difficult for the young to manipulate.

● To allow for rapid growth, look for patterns that already (or can be easily altered to) include growth tucks, adjustable straps, and elasticized waistbands.

● Look for patterns with options for variety, such as blouses with several variations, or pants with short and long legs or various hem treatments. Also keep in mind the variety you can get by embellishing a simple garment. The plainest dress comes to life with the addition of some ribbons, buttons, or appliqués.

You can use one pattern over and over again, with no one the wiser, if each version has its own personality (**Ill. 3**). A big fringe benefit is that you become familiar with a pattern as you reuse it, and you can make each garment a little faster than the time before. Or you can make several

For little treasures

This simple purse can win any little girl's heart, and it's small enough to make with leftover fabric scraps.

You'll need: Scrap fabric, interfacing, ¼"-wide double fold bias tape, 1 yard narrow ribbon, 3 appliqués, 1 snap or 1" strip of nylon self-gripping fastener.

● Step 1. Enlarge pattern; cut two A and one B from fabric. Cut one A from interfacing. Sandwiching interfacing between fabric layers, baste A pieces, *wrong* sides together.

● Step 2. Stitch bias tape over straight edge of piece B. Then baste B, *right* side up, to bottom half of A to make pocket of purse. Pin bias tape around outer edge of purse; turn under ends of tape and overlap them ¼"; stitch in place. Fold purse along foldline; press.

● Step 3. Use ribbon for shoulder strap; stitch ends at dots on back of purse. Stitch appliqués over ends of straps.

● Step 4. Fasten purse flap with the snap or self-gripping fastener. Cover fastener stitching with third appliqué.

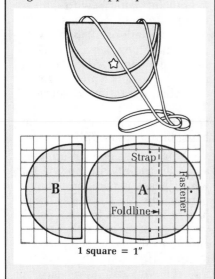

1 square = 1"

. . . Pattern selection

versions at once, assembly-line fashion, for the ultimate in efficiency.

Ill. 3

● Look for patterns that transcend seasons. Can you make the garment in different weights of fabric? Are there long sleeves and short sleeves? Are there pieces to add for layers of warmth? Though kids grow quickly, you can use one pattern to cover two seasons if the garment is adaptable.

Playclothes should be easy to make and tough to wear out, but there's always a need for a special party outfit. Since dressy clothes aren't worn frequently, they're the place for intricate details and pretty fabrics. By incorporating growth tucks (see "Making clothes that grow," starting on page 10), you can afford the time to make an exquisite garment, knowing that it can last for several years, or several children.

Changing needs

As children grow and develop from infants to toddlers to preschoolers, their abilities and their resulting clothing needs change dramatically. Awareness of these needs will help you provide a wardrobe that's attractive and functional.

Infants. Infants are pretty restricted in movement for the first few months of their lives. Warmth and comfort are the most important clothing considerations at this time.

Sleepers with feet or closable bottoms are the most in demand, since they keep babies warm when the covers are kicked off.

Choose front-opening garments with easy access to the baby's diaper. Make sure slip-over garments fit easily over the head. Don't let fasteners get too small or too numerous—it's hard to button lots of tiny buttons on a squirming baby.

Toddlers. Still in diapers, toddlers require clothes that are easy to change. Look for snaps at the crotch and legs of pants, or elasticized waists in pants and skirts.

Coveralls are a good choice for toddlers who are crawling and learning to walk; they protect the legs and don't ride up while the toddler's in motion.

Older toddlers and preschoolers. Playclothes are necessities for these age groups. Choose patterns that encourage physical activity; avoid designs that restrict movement. Even dressy clothes should be comfortable.

As toddlers learn to manipulate small objects and coordinate their movements, they'll want to dress themselves (though undressing is their forte!). By the middle of the preschooler years, children are able to dress themselves independently.

To help children in this learning process, choose patterns for pull-on clothes or clothes with front openings that are easily seen and reached. Keep the number of fasteners to a minimum. (See "Fasteners" on pages 20–21 for further details.)

Measuring up

Children come in all shapes and sizes, just as adults do. Body measurements—rather than age—are the best indicators of the correct pattern size needed for a child. Update these measurements each time you shop for patterns, since children grow quickly.

When you're looking for children's patterns, you'll notice that many designs are interchangeable for boys and girls. Boys' bodies are at the same stage of development as girls' from infancy through preschool.

Size ranges

Each pattern company has its own sizing system; look for size and measurement charts at the back of each pattern catalog. Though sizes are fairly standard among pattern manufacturers, they do vary in the Infant or Baby sizing categories; check the charts carefully before you buy a pattern.

Infants. Baby or Infant pattern sizes are designed for babies not yet able to walk. Since movement is limited for a young child, fitting clothing to exact body dimensions isn't necessary. Use height and weight measurements to determine pattern sizes at this stage.

Toddlers. Toddler pattern sizes are designed for a figure between a baby's and a child's.

Some Toddler sizes seem to overlap into the Children's size range. The important difference between the two is the diaper allowance provided in Toddler sizes. In addition, the Toddler dresses are shorter than a similar Child's dress.

In this size range, the chest, waist, and height measurements are the most important. If there's a disparity between your child's measurements and those on the manufacturer's chart, use the child's chest measurement instead of height as a guideline for shirts, jackets, or dresses. Likewise, use the waist measurement for pants and skirts; it's easier to alter the length of a garment than the width (see "Altering" on page 8).

Preschoolers. Preschoolers move from Toddler sizes into Children's sizes. Children's pattern sizes reflect a widening back and shoulder dimension. They're narrower than Toddler patterns through the waist and hips because they no longer provide room for diapers.

In addition to waist, chest, and height measurements, you'll need to record your child's back waist length, hip, and crotch measurements.

Taking measurements

As you take each measurement, hold the measuring tape snug, but not tight. Take children's measurements over their underwear, including diapers (**Ill. 1**).

Getting a child to hold still long enough for you to take accurate measurements can be a challenge—but you can try making a game of it.

Because a child's waistline is hard to locate, tie a string around the child's middle and have the child bend or twist from side to side as if doing calisthenics (**Ill. 2**). This movement shifts the string to the natural waistline.

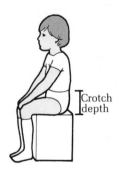

Ill. 2

To take an accurate crotch depth measurement, sit the child on a flat surface and measure the distance from the child's waistline to the surface (**Ill. 3**).

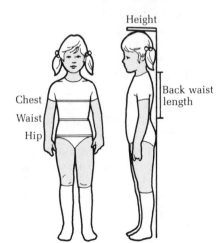

Ill. 3

Ill. 1

Altering

It's hard to imagine how quickly a child can grow. But right before your very eyes, those plump round bodies stretch out long and lanky. During their first six years, children grow up much more rapidly than they grow out, so alterations for height are more common than those for width.

Lengthen or shorten

If your child's back waist or height measurements differ from the pattern size, adjust the pattern at the pattern adjustment lines, or at the hem.

If your child's measurements differ from your pattern only in the back waist, alter the pattern in the bodice on any garment with a waistline, such as a dress, a jumpsuit, or overalls. If height is the problem, adjust the hemline or the pattern adjustment lines below the waist. Instructions follow.

Remember to repeat any alterations on the *back* of the garment as well as the front. If you've altered the length of a garment in an area with buttons, carefully respace the button and buttonhole markings so the spaces between buttons are equidistant.

The bottom line. If the pattern's hemline is relatively straight, shorten the garment's length by carefully redrawing the cutting line. To lengthen, tape tissue paper to the hem edge and redraw the cutting line to the desired length.

Inside lines. When the pattern's hemline curves, or you want to alter the length in another specific area of the garment, find the pattern's lengthen/shorten adjustment lines—they run perpendicular to the grainline.

Shorten the pattern piece by measuring up the desired amount from the adjustment line; draw a line across the pattern piece. Make a fold on the adjustment line and bring the fold up to the drawn line; tape in place. Carefully redraw the pattern cutting lines (**Ill. 1**).

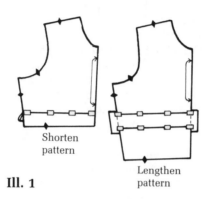

Shorten pattern

Lengthen pattern

Ill. 1

Lengthen pattern pieces by cutting across the adjustment line and spreading the two pieces evenly over tissue paper. Tape both pattern pieces in place on the tissue paper; carefully redraw the cutting lines (**Ill. 1**).

Widening seam allowances

This is a good technique to use on clothes without waistline seams. It adds extra fabric to the side seams to allow you to widen the garment later, prolonging the garment's life.

Increase the pattern side seams, sleeve facings, or underarm seams by ¼ inch. These measurements add 1 inch to the total garment width.

Construct the garment according to the all-in-one side seam method on page 19. Stitch a ⅞-inch-wide seam.

When it's time to widen the garment, restitch the seams ⅝ inch or ½ inch from the edge; remove the original stitching.

Glossary

Here you'll find definitions and illustrations of sewing terms used throughout this book.

Bias
The diagonal line formed by folding the fabric so the crosswise threads run parallel to the selvage.

Fabric cut along the bias is very stretchy—helpful when you want fabrics to follow a curve.

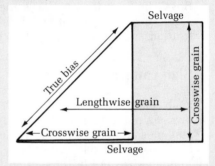

Double-stitched seam
An all-in-one seam and seam finish used on sheer fabrics, lace, and fabrics that tend to curl at the edges, such as knits.

Sew a plain seam. Then stitch another row within the seam allowance, ¼ inch from the first row, using either a straight or zigzag stitch. Trim seam allowance.

Ease stitch
A type of gathering stitch that eases a longer fabric edge so it fits against a shorter one to make a seam without showing gathers. This allows extra room for movement in areas such as shoulder and elbow seams.

Stitch ⅛ inch outside the seamline on the longer piece, between the ease marks using long machine stitches. Pin the garment pieces together; pull the thread to distribute the gathers evenly. Stitch the seam without catching gathers.

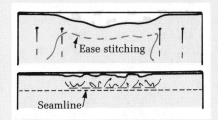

Edgestitch

A straight line of functional or decorative stitching, close to the edge of the fabric. Stitch the fabric, *right* side up, ⅛ inch to 1/16 inch from the edge of the fabric.

Graded seam

Seam allowances trimmed to different widths to minimize bulk. Use in areas such as facings, where both seam allowances are pressed to one side.

Trim the seam allowance that will lie against the fabric to ⅜ inch. Trim the remaining seam allowance to ¼ inch.

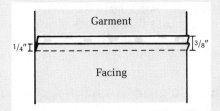

Narrow hem

To sew a narrow hem, turn the raw edge under ¼ inch; press. Turn under ¼ inch again; press. Machine stitch close to the edge.

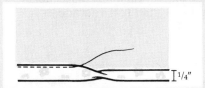

Slipstitch

An invisible hand stitch used to join two pieces of fabric in a seam, or to stitch a flat hem on the wrong side of the garment.

On seams, pick up one fabric thread with your needle. Do the same on the opposite fabric, about ¼ inch forward. Pull the thread taut.

On hems, pick up one fabric thread alongside the hem edge. Then take a stitch through the top of the folded hem edge.

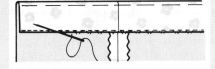

Stab stitch

A stitch technique used primarily for embroidery.

Inserting the needle perpendicular to the fabric, pull the thread completely to the *wrong* side before bringing the needle back up to the surface.

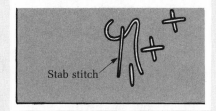

Staystitch

To prevent garment pieces from stretching out of shape during garment construction.

Before sewing the garment, stitch all the curved or bias-cut edges of each garment piece in the seam allowance, ¼ inch from the seamline, using the stitch length you'll use for seams.

Stitch-in-the-ditch

Stitching through a seam so that no stitches are visible on the right side of the fabric. This technique is used when you turn a cuff, waistband, collar, or facing and stitch its underside to the garment's *wrong* side at the seamline.

To do so, stitch through the seam from the *right* side of the fabric, spreading the fabric on either side of the seamline as much as possible so as to place each stitch in the seam itself.

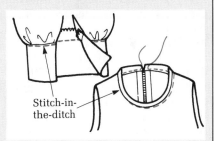

Understitching

A row of stitching to prevent seams from rolling to the outside of the garment edge, especially on facings and collars.

Press the seam allowances and facing or undercollar away from the garment; pin in place. With the *right* side up, stitch close to the seamline through the facing and seam allowances.

To understitch a collar, stitch only along the outer edge of the collar. Start and finish the stitching about 1 inch from the collar points; it's impossible to get the presser foot any closer to the point.

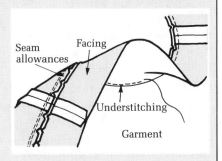

Making clothes that grow

Children are notorious for growing quickly—seemingly before your eyes. Clothes that fit them one day seem to have shrunk the next. To get the most wear out of the children's clothes you make, either add growth features as you make them, or plan attractive ways to lengthen the garments later.

Before adding any growth features to a garment you're making, assess the value of the effort. Consider the life expectancy of a particular garment with respect to your child's rate of growth and activity level. Crawling toddlers and climbing preschoolers often wear out their playclothes before they outgrow them. The most likely candidates for growth features are dressy clothes and sturdy, long-wearing garments such as overalls.

Fabrics best suited to growth features are light to medium-weight ones that wear well, are colorfast, and won't show scars where stitches are removed. Avoid napped fabrics, which may become crushed and marked by stitching and wear.

To make the release of growth features as simple as possible, use a long machine stitch when you sew the growth tuck. On inside tucks, use a slightly different color of thread that clearly contrasts with construction seams inside the garment.

Here are some simple ideas for prolonging a garment's usefulness:

● Plan to increase length eventually by adding a ruffle or a patchwork strip to a hem edge.

● Make slightly deeper hem and wider side seam allowances than usual, then let them out later.

● Make shoulder straps longer, and reposition the strap buttons as length is needed.

Inside growth tuck

Hidden behind a hem, an inside growth tuck can add as much as 2 inches of length to a garment. And by using the technique below, you can let out the tuck without removing the hem stitching.

Plan to make the finished tuck ½ inch to 2 inches deep and at least ½ inch shorter than the hem allowance so it won't peek out beneath the garment's edge. For example, **Ill. 1** shows a common 3-inch hem allowance accommodating a 2-inch tuck. Releasing the tuck increases the garment length by the depth of the finished tuck.

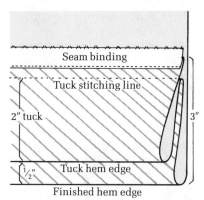

Seam binding

Tuck stitching line

2″ tuck

3″

½″ Tuck hem edge

Finished hem edge

Ill. 1

Begin by modifying your front and back pattern pieces to accommodate the tuck: tape tissue paper to the bottom edge of each piece.

Determine the finished hem length and mark it on the pattern tissue. Add the depth of the hem allowance plus twice the finished tuck depth (the additional length needed to make the tuck). Use the total to determine the bottom edge of the unhemmed garment, measuring down from the finished-length mark; then mark the bottom edge on the tissue. Extend the pattern side edges to the new bottom edge.

Cut the fabric garment pieces and mark tuck foldlines on the *right* side of the fabric as shown in **Ill. 2**, measuring up from the bottom of each piece.

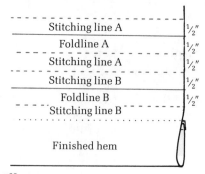

Stitching line A ½″
Foldline A ½″
Stitching line A ½″
Stitching line B ½″
Foldline B ½″
Stitching line B

Finished hem

Ill. 2

After constructing the garment, turn under the finished hem edge; press. Make the growth tuck by folding the hem allowance along the tuck foldline, *wrong* sides together; press.

Align the tuck foldline with the appropriate throat plate guideline for the desired finished tuck depth; stitch the tuck. Press the tuck toward the hemline; proceed with the hem.

Outside growth tuck

You can decorate a garment as well as create extra room for growth by adding outside growth tucks (**Ill. 3**). Place one to three rows of these horizontal outside tucks just above the hem, waistline, or sleeve hem. The tucks can be ⅛ inch to 1 inch deep.

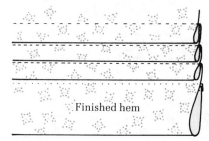

Finished hem

Ill. 3

A ½-inch tuck will add 1 inch to a garment's length when it's released. You can release each tuck separately as needed without removing the hem.

Begin by lengthening your front and back pattern pieces with tissue paper and marking the bottom edge as explained under "Inside growth tucks," allowing twice the finished depth of each tuck you intend to add along with the hem allowance.

For tucks on sleeves, cut across the sleeve pattern 1 inch above the bottom edge and insert a piece of tissue paper as described under "Bodice tuck." Keep the tucks very narrow (⅛ inch to ¼ inch).

For tucks above the waist, add extra length to the body of the bodice pattern and keep the tucks ¼ inch to ¾ inch deep.

After cutting the fabric garment pieces, mark tuck foldlines on the *right* side of the fabric as shown in **Ill. 4**, measuring up from the bottom of each piece and making sure the bottom tuck is positioned high enough not to interfere with a hem or seam. **Ill. 3** shows three ½-inch tucks.

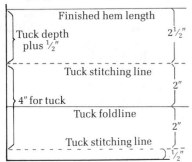

Finished hem length	
Tuck depth plus ½"	2½"
Tuck stitching line	
4" for tuck	2"
Tuck foldline	
	2"
Tuck stitching line	
	½"

Ill. 4

Construct the garment and proceed with the hem. Fold, press, and stitch the tucks, as described for "Inside growth tuck." Press the tucks toward the hem.

(Continued on page 12)

Ruffles & strips

Suddenly there's a lot of leg showing beneath the edges of clothes that are practically new. If there's no more hem to let down, help clothes keep up with the child by adding some ruffles, or a fabric insert. Whichever device you use, repeat it elsewhere on the garment to lend credibility to the ruse.

First aid station

Tattered knees and flapping pockets; vexing rips and defiant stains—sound familiar? Maybe too familiar? Despair no longer. Here are some suggestions for reinforcing and repairing children's clothes.

Reinforcements. For the major areas of concern—knees, elbows, and pockets—take action to avoid problems before they occur. Reinforce stress points as the garment is being made or when it's fresh from the store.

If your child is especially hard on pockets, see "Pick a pocket" on page 18 for reinforcing hints. Or baste folded pieces of seam binding under pocket corners on the *wrong* side of the garment to prolong pocket life.

Reinforce knee and elbow areas by making a patch of lightweight fabric interfacing for extra durability. To cover a knee, make it large enough to stretch from the inseam to the outside seam of a pants leg; stitch it into the garment seams against the fabric's *wrong* side. For an elbow, sew a patch to the *wrong* side of the garment in the vulnerable area (or use fusible interfacing and fuse it in place, if you don't want stitches to show).

Patches. Outside patches are a fun, bright way to perk up clothing while repairing or reinforcing worn-out spots. Be adventurous and creative: play with colors and fabric types and shapes—patches don't have to be square to be functional.

Whatever the style and location of a decorative patch, make sure it coordinates with the garment in some way. Use patches of fabric from coordinating garments or accessories, or carry your cover-up technique to other parts of the garment for a pulled-together look. On the knees, use a fabric that matches the shirt; cover a tear with an appliqué that's repeated around the skirt or up on the sleeve. Hand or machine embroider a design over a small patch, and continue the needlework in a pattern on the garment. Then the clothes are not only repaired—they take on a whole new personality.

For added protection and dimension, quilt the patch fabric or pad the patch with a layer of polyester fleece. For durability and extra strength, zigzag stitch around the outside edge of the patch through the garment fabric, and stitch again inside the first row of stitching.

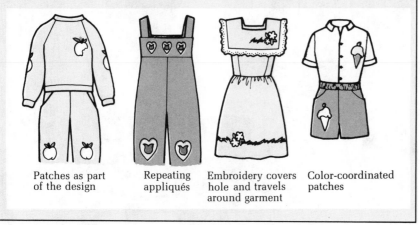

Patches as part of the design

Repeating appliqués

Embroidery covers hole and travels around garment

Color-coordinated patches

Bodice tucks

An inside or outside tuck at the waist of a garment allows room to grow between the shoulder and the waist (**Ill. 5**). A finished bodice tuck can be up to ¾ inch deep, adding twice its depth or up to 1½ inches of length when released. You can add this tuck on the inside or outside of a garment at the natural waistline.

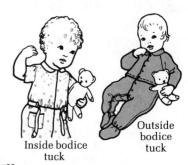

Inside bodice tuck

Outside bodice tuck

Ill. 5

To place a growth tuck in a bodice, first modify your front and back pattern pieces. Draw a line across the pattern piece, perpendicular to the center front or back line, 1 inch above the waist seamline. Cut along the drawn line and insert a piece of tissue paper. Keeping the original waist size, redraw the side seams.

After cutting the fabric garment pieces, mark tuck foldlines as shown in **Ill. 6,** measuring up from the waistline seam. Mark the lines on the *right* side of the fabric for an *outside* tuck, and on the *wrong* side for an *inside* tuck.

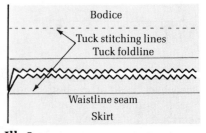

Bodice

Tuck stitching lines
Tuck foldline

Waistline seam

Skirt

Ill. 6

After stitching the waistline seam and before installing the zipper or other fasteners, fold and press the fabric along the tuck foldline, *right* sides together if the tuck is *inside, wrong* sides together if the tuck is *outside.* With the waistline seam allowances held out of the way, stitch the tuck just above the original waistline seam, as described for "Inside growth tuck," above (**Ill. 7**). Press the seam and tuck toward the bodice; insert the zipper.

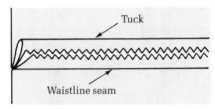

Tuck

Waistline seam

Ill. 7

When you release this tuck you'll have to release and re-stitch the bottom of the zipper.

Shoulder tucks

You can create two or three ⅛-inch to ¼-inch-deep vertical tucks on each shoulder of a garment. These tucks are *release tucks:* rather than running the full length of a garment piece, the stitching stops so that the tuck opens at the bottom, releasing fullness. They will add ½ to 1½ inches of fullness in the chest area and allow an increase in breadth across the shoulders later. The tucks can be stitched on the inside or the outside of the garment (**Ill. 8**).

Inside tucks   Outside tucks

Ill. 8

Alter the front and back bodice pattern pieces by drawing a line down from the center of the shoulder on each piece, perpendicular to the shoulder seam and stopping even with the center of the armhole (**Ill. 9**). Next, draw a second line at a right angle from the bottom of the first line to the armhole edge. Cut along the drawn lines and spread the two pieces on tissue paper as shown in **Ill. 9**, until the shoulder seam line is opened the distance needed to accommodate the shoulder tucks: twice the total depth of all the finished tucks. (For example, two ¼-inch tucks will require a 1-inch spread.) Redraw the shoulder seam.

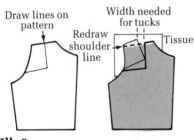

Draw lines on pattern

Width needed for tucks

Redraw shoulder line

Tissue

Ill. 9

Perpendicular to the shoulder seam, draw 2-inch-long tuck foldlines on the front and back pattern pieces. For tucks stitched on the *inside* of the garment, mark the tuck foldlines on the *wrong* side of the fabric. For tucks on the *outside,* mark the foldlines on the *right* side. Fold-lines should be equidistant from the center of the shoulder. All foldlines should be spaced so that the stitching of adjoining tucks will not overlap.

Stitch the shoulder seams; press open. For inside tucks, fold and press the garment, *right* sides together, on the tuck fold-line; stitch the tucks, as directed for "Inside growth tuck," above. For outside tucks, fold and press the garment, *wrong* sides together, and stitch.

Operation cover-up

When hemlines are lowered and growth tucks released, wear marks, stitch marks, and crease lines may be evident. If so, it's time for creative cover-ups.

Don't approach this task as simply a patching mission. To make your camouflage effective, expand your thinking to include more than just a one-line cover-up. Instead of one row of rickrack to cover a crease line, use three or more rows, experiment with different sizes or colors, and even mix in some other trims. Laces, braid, ruching, or strips of patchwork are all great solutions.

Divert attention to other parts of the garment as well as the portion you're covering, to make the design look well planned and balanced. For example, after covering hem or shoulder tuck lines, carry the theme—or a hint of it—to other areas, such as pockets, sleeves, yokes, or waistbands. A little planning like this can result in a great rejuvenation.

The final touch

The next time you give a handmade gift, delight child and parent by attaching a personalized gift tag. It adds an extra touch of *you*, making a gift very special.

Ideas abound, both functional and fun. For example, a garment tag that provides care instructions and includes an extra button or two is a most appreciated gesture.

A toy takes on its own personality when you add a card that provides the name and "biography" of this new friend. A short, whimsical story is sure to capture the fancy of its receiver and make the gift endearing.

Let the design of the tag reflect the personality of the gift or the event being celebrated—try a birthday-present tag shaped like a birthday cake or a clutch of balloons.

Imitate the shape of the gift itself, or something you'd associate with it. For example, tag a teddy bear with a honey pot or a paw print. A shirt with a stenciled design can have a similarly stenciled tag, or a tag cut in the stencil shape.

If handmade gifts become a habit, you might want to design a standard tag that represents you and your craft. A sewing machine, spool of thread, or pair of scissors will clue everyone in.

Tucks

To lend a touch of crisp neatness to a garment, take some tucks. Tucks are small folds of fabric, stitched in place. Some patterns feature them as part of the garment design; if not, you can add them yourself for a new look.

Vertical tucks can be stitched the full length of garment pieces such as those for a bodice or sleeve. Or they can be stitched a short way and left open at the bottom, releasing fullness and allowing room for future growth. The latter type—known as a release tuck—is discussed under "Shoulder tucks" on page 13.

There are three types of tucks: *blind tucks, spaced tucks,* and *pin tucks* (**Ill. 1**). Blind tucks overlap each other, each concealing the stitching of the next. Spaced tucks are separated by spaces of fabric. Pin tucks are very narrow—usually ⅛ inch deep or less; they may be either blind or spaced.

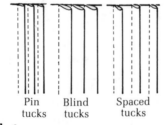

Pin   Blind   Spaced
tucks tucks   tucks

Ill. 1

To introduce vertical tucks to a flat pattern, stitch the tucks into the fabric before cutting the pattern pieces. Begin by estimating how much yardage you'll need: multiply the number of tucks by twice the finished tuck depth and add this measurement to the pattern width.

When you're ready to stitch the tucks, mark their foldlines on the *right* side of the fabric along the fabric grainline. Fold the fabric, *wrong* sides together, along the foldlines; press. Align each tuck foldline with the appropriate throat plate guideline for the desired finished tuck depth (or if the tuck is deeper than the available guidelines, place a piece of masking tape to use as a guideline); stitch the tuck.

Position the pattern pieces over the tucked fabric with the pattern grainline arrow parallel to the tuck lines (**Ill. 2**). Proceed as the pattern directs.

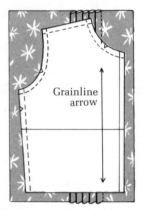

Grainline arrow

Ill. 2

Scalloped tucks. To impart a delicate and old-fashioned air to a party outfit or to embellish a christening gown, you might add some *scalloped tucks*.

To construct a scalloped tuck, stitch a ¼-inch-deep tuck. Mark ½-inch intervals and make scallops by taking two overhand stitches in each spot and pulling each taut (**Ill. 3**). Conceal the thread between the scallops by drawing it through the inside of the tuck.

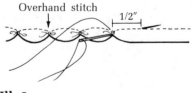

Overhand stitch   1/2"

Ill. 3

Ruffles

Ruffles are one of the most feminine touches you can add to a child's outfit. Rows upon rows of them make any little girl feel like a princess. Even a pair of corduroy overalls becomes dainty when a simple ruffle is added.

A ruffle is a strip of fabric, cut two to three times longer than the finished ruffle's length and then gathered to fit the garment. The fabric weight and the size of the ruffle determine the amount of fullness you'll need. Sheers and lightweight fabrics need extra fullness for body; heavy fabrics are gathered with less fullness, to avoid bulk and weight. Deep ruffles need more gathering than shallow ones to look full.

There are two basic types of ruffles: ruffles stitched into a garment seam or onto a raw edge, and freestanding ruffles with headings, stitched to a garment surface.

Ruffles can appear at any seam or raw edge. Try adding them at necklines, cuffs, or hems, down the front edge of a blouse, or in a yoke seam. Ruffles also add a pleasing touch to the side seam of pants, on the outside edge of shoulder straps, around the edges of a vest, or in tiers on a skirt.

Ruffle in a seam

Once you've decided to add a ruffle to a seam or edge of a garment, you can choose to finish its bottom edge with a narrow hem or a self-faced hem. The finish you select determines the amount of fabric you'll need.

Narrow-hemmed ruffle. A narrow hem requires the least fabric and is best suited to light to medium-weight fabrics. To determine the dimensions of the strip of fabric for a ruffle with this finish, measure the length of the seam or edge to which the ruffle will be attached and multiply it 2 to 3 times, depending on the desired fullness of the ruffle. If you wish to use bias fabric for a softer look, see "Cutting bias strips" on page 32. Then determine the depth of the ruffle by adding 1⅛ inch for the hem and seam allowance to the desired finished depth.

Stitch a narrow hem at the bottom edge of the ruffle; continue with "Gathering and stitching," below.

Self-faced ruffle. To make a self-faced ruffle, follow the directions for the "Narrow-hemmed ruffle," doubling the desired finished depth and adding two seam allowances to obtain the ruffle's depth dimension. Fold the fabric in half lengthwise with *wrong* sides together; pin in place. Gather both layers as one.

Gathering and stitching. Make two rows of long machine stitching—gathering threads—within the seam allowance (½ inch and ⅜ inch from the raw edge of a ⅝ inch seam); don't backstitch. With *right* sides together, pin the ruffle to the garment in equal increments, leaving the ruffle fabric loose between pins.

Secure the gathering threads at one end. At the other, pull the bobbin threads until the ruffle fits snugly against the garment, adjusting the gathers until they are even. Then secure the loose ends of the gathering threads.

Pin the ruffle in place at frequent intervals to maintain the adjustment (**Ill. 1**). Stitch the seam, if the ruffle is attached to a raw edge. If the ruffle is inserted in a seam, stitch the garment according to pattern directions.

Ill. 1

Ruffle with a heading

A ruffle with a heading is a decorative ruffle stitched directly to the *right* side of a garment, forming two ruffles in one.

Cut or piece together a strip of fabric the desired finished depth of the ruffle, including the upper and lower ruffles, plus ½ inch for hemming. To determine the length, follow the directions under "Narrow-hemmed ruffle," above. Turn both raw edges under and stitch a narrow hem in each; then stitch two rows of long machine stitching, ½ inch apart, at your chosen line of division between the two ruffles (see "Gathering and stitching," above).

To attach the ruffle to the garment, mark a line on the garment to use as a placement guideline. Pin the *wrong* side of the ruffle in equal increments to the *right* side of the garment, matching the guideline to the ruffle division line. Adjust the gathers as directed in "Gathering and stitching," above. With the ruffle facing up, topstitch just outside each gathering line. Carefully remove the gathering stitches (**Ill. 2**).

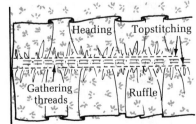

Ill. 2

Seams

When your child shows off the marvelous new garment you've made, the seams aren't likely to be the center of admiration. Yet that wonderful new outfit could be very short-lived without a careful choice of seam type. The finished seam in a child's garment must be smooth and pliable for comfort, but sturdy enough to withstand hard wear and frequent washing.

If you sew a plain seam in a garment, it is wise to add some reinforcement to ensure its durability.

- Strengthen the seam by topstitching: press both seam allowances to one side and topstitch through all layers, ¼ inch from the seamline.

- On knit fabrics, prevent seam allowances from curling by stitching a second seam in the seam allowance, ⅛ inch from the seamline. Trim the seam allowance close to the stitching.

Below, you'll find some less familiar seam techniques that are excellent choices for children's clothes, though they might not be described in your pattern guidesheet.

Flat-fell seam

The flat-fell seam creates a sturdy finish that will withstand hard wear and frequent washing, making it the perfect choice for your youngster's hard-working playclothes and sleepwear. It adapts well to straight or slightly curved seams and suits all but the heaviest of fabrics.

To make a flat-fell seam, stitch the seam with the *wrong* sides of the fabric together; press the seam open and then to one side. Trim the bottom seam allowance ⅛ inch from the stitch-ing (**Ill. 1**). Fold the top seam allowance in half as shown. Pin it in place over the bottom seam allowance; edgestitch it to the underlying fabric.

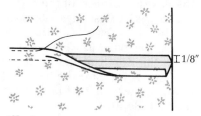

Ill. 1

French seam

The French seam is strong and easy to stitch, and leaves no raw edges to ravel or to irritate delicate skin. It's especially good for sheer fabrics, on which seams are visible. The French seam works well on straight seams, but it's not recommended for curves or sharp corners.

To construct a French seam (**Ill. 2**), stitch a ⅜-inch seam with the fabric's *wrong* sides together. Trim the seam allowances to ⅛ inch from the stitching; press the seam open. Now turn the fabric and fold it so the *right* sides are together, using the seam you just completed as the foldline. Stitch ¼ inch away from the fold, enclosing the raw edges. Press the seam to one side.

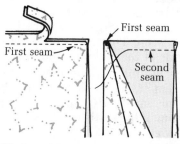

First seam

First seam

Second seam

Ill. 2

Taped seam

For a decorative finish, you can encase seam allowances in bias tape to make a taped seam. Reverse the garment, and you see the seamline centered between two rows of topstitching. It's a great way to take care of bulky, raveling, or quilted fabrics, as well as reversible or unlined garments. Choose bias tape in matching or contrasting colors or patterns (or see page 32 to make your own).

Inside taped seam. Construct the garment according to pattern directions. Trim the seam allowances to ¼ inch; press open. If your fabric is quilted, reduce its bulk by cutting out exposed batting.

Fold the bias tape in half and press a crease down the center. Align the bias tape over the open seam, centering the crease over the stitching (**Ill. 3**). Baste the tape in place to ensure that the stitching which will show on the reverse side of the garment will be even. Then edgestitch (see page 9) down each side of the bias tape. Remove the basting threads.

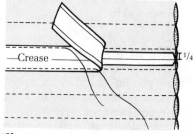

Crease

Ill. 3

Outside taped seam. Construct the garment with the seam allowances exposed on the *right* side by stitching the pieces with the *wrong* sides together; continue as described above.

Facings

Little clothes have little facings—and you may find them more than a little difficult to handle. When the neck and armhole facings in your pattern are too small to manipulate, replace them with either a combination facing or a self-bias casing.

No matter what type of facing you use, select the fabric carefully and use the tips under "Facing finishes" to ensure successful results.

Fabric selection. Since facings should be flat and invisible from the *right* side of the garment, the weight of the fabric used for the facing is of prime importance. With light to medium-weight fabrics, use the same fabric or fabric weight for the facing as for the garment. With heavier fabrics or pile fabrics, reduce bulk by choosing a facing fabric of lighter weight and tight weave.

Though only your child will know, it can be fun to make the hidden facings in a contrasting color or print, to add a very special secret touch to a garment.

Combination facing

You can easily combine your pattern's separate neck and armhole facings into one piece, called a *combination facing*. The combination facing eliminates the exasperation of handling many small pieces in a small area, and also reduces bulk. The bit of effort you spend making a new pattern piece is a small price to pay for the ease of handling it provides.

Make a pattern for a combination facing by placing tissue paper over the garment pattern and tracing the existing armhole, shoulder, and neck lines (**Ill. 1**). Then, following each side seam allowance edge, draw a 2-inch

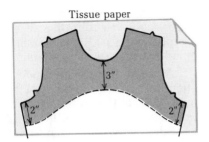

Tissue paper

Ill. 1

line down from the armhole.

Mark a point 3 inches down from the center of the neckline. Connect the center point with the two side lines, using a curved line as shown. The curve must arc in this manner to ensure freedom of movement in the chest and shoulder areas. Make a pattern for both the front and back of the garment.

Join the front and back facings at the shoulder seam and finish the lower facing edge according to pattern directions. With *right* sides together, stitch the facing to the bodice at the neck and armhole seamlines.

Turn the garment *right* side out by reaching through the space between the facing and garment shoulder and pulling the garment back through the space (**Ill. 2**). Lift the facing away from the garment and stitch the side seam in one continuous seam; press open. Proceed as the pattern directs.

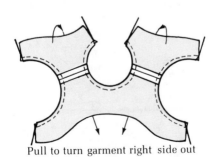

Pull to turn garment right side out

Ill. 2

Facing finishes

Whether you use the facings supplied with your pattern or decide to make the combination facing, it helps to take some precautionary measures to prevent unsightly rolling or bulging at the facing edges. Follow these hints for professional results.

● Trim $1/16$ inch from the neck and armhole edges of facing pieces before attaching them to the garment. Because the facing is now slightly smaller than the garment, the garment fabric will roll in slightly rather than the facing rolling out.

● Avoid the bulk problem posed by heavy fabrics: simply finish the facing edges by overcast stitching or by binding them with bias tape (see page 32).

● After sewing facings to a garment, remember not only to trim, but also to grade the seams, leaving the widest seam allowance against the garment.

● Finish facing seams with understitching to prevent the facing from rolling to the outside of the garment.

Self-bias casing

You can eliminate facings altogether by binding raw edges with bias tape. This makes a simple, attractive finish for necklines and armholes as well as cuffs and hems, and is an ideal way to reduce the bulk of heavy or quilted fabrics.

First, trim the garment seam allowance of the area to be bound $1/4$ inch from the seamline. Cut a length of bias tape 2 inches longer than the area to be bound. To install it, follow the instructions in "Encasing a raw edge" on page 33.

Pick a pocket

Pockets are places for tucking treasures or parking hands, and sometimes just for looking pretty.

For extra strength and durability, line or interface pockets. In addition, reinforce pocket edges by stitching a small triangle or square or zigzag stitching a ½-inch-long bar tack at each upper corner. Double stitching the pocket in place adds strength, too.

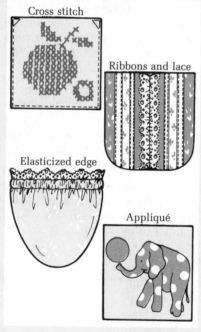

Cross stitch

Ribbons and lace

Elasticized edge

Appliqué

Possibilities for enhancing a patch pocket are limitless: change a basic U or square shape into a heart, half-circle, or pleated cargo pocket shape. Add a flap or an elasticized opening. Trim the pocket with buttons or tucks. Cut the pocket fabric on the bias, quilt it, add a trapunto or appliqué design, or embroider it.

Decorative trims add special touches to pockets. Add ribbon, rickrack, eyelet ruffle, piping, or colorful topstitching across the top or around the edges of pockets.

Collars

You can perk up a seemingly ordinary collar in countless ways. Simply using a different fabric color or texture is a good start.

A touch of trim calls special attention to any collar. At the outer edge of the collar, use piping, lace, or a fabric ruffle to add appeal. Follow the collar shape with a line of rickrack, soutache braid, or narrow ribbon. Add spice with rows of decorative stitchery.

Eliminating the collar altogether is another option. Try a simple bias-bound neckline instead (see page 33) or attach a ready-made lace collar. Knit collars and cuffs can be purchased in kits to add to a knit shirt.

Collar construction tricks

Here are some helpful ideas to use when you're making a collar.

- Keep an undercollar invisible and help the collar maintain its roll by trimming 1/16 inch from the outer edges of the undercollar before stitching the collar pieces together. Understitching is another way to guarantee a perfect collar edge.

- Reinforce collar points by using small stitches—at least 12 stitches to the inch—near the points (**Ill. 1**). Instead of pivoting at the points, take 2 or 3 stitches diagonally across each point, as shown. You'll discover that the points are much easier to turn and they won't open up.

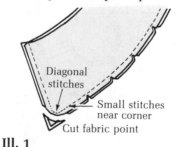

Diagonal stitches

Small stitches near corner

Cut fabric point

Ill. 1

Knit neck

A few inches of knit ribbing are all you need to convert a knit shirt pattern into a turtleneck or crewneck style. It makes an easy pull-on shirt for youngsters who like to dress all by themselves.

To determine the dimensions of the ribbing you'll need for a collar, double the desired finished collar height and add 1¼ inches for seam allowances. This will be the width of your ribbing piece, measured parallel to the ribs of the knit. Next, determine the length you'll need by folding the ribbing in half lengthwise—perpendicular to the ribs of the knit—and stretching it around your child's head, making sure it isn't too snug. To this measurement, add 1 inch for seams; then cut the ribbing.

With right sides together, stitch the narrow ends of the ribbing together ½ inch from the edge. Fold the band in half lengthwise, *wrong* sides together. Divide its circumference into four equal sections with the seam as one division; mark the divisions with pins. Divide the neckline in the same manner.

Pin the band to the garment neckline with right sides together, matching quarter marks and aligning the ribbing seam with a shoulder seam (**Ill. 2**). With the collar on top, stitch the collar and garment together ⅝ inch from the edge, stretching the collar to match the neckline as you go. Trim close to the stitching, then proceed with the pattern as directed.

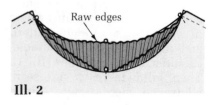

Raw edges

Ill. 2

Sleeves

Children's sleeves present problems from top to bottom. At the top is the arduous task of stitching tiny armhole seams. A simple bypass method will make the job easier. At the bottom is the challenge of providing hem variety. That's easily met with one of the elasticized cuffs below. Or try binding sleeve edges with bias tape for soft appeal (see page 33) or adding knit cuffs to knit sleeves (see "Knit neck" on the facing page).

Flat seam sleeve attachment

Do you wince at the thought of stitching tiny sleeves into tinier armholes? Try this technique: stitch the sleeve cap to the armhole before stitching the side seams or sleeve seams. It's remarkably manageable.

Finish the garment shoulder seams and neck edge according to pattern directions; don't stitch the side seams. Gather the sleeve cap if directed by your pattern, but don't stitch the underarm seam. With wrong sides together, stitch the sleeve cap to the armhole; stitch a second row ¼ inch away from the first, in the seam allowance (**Ill. 1**).

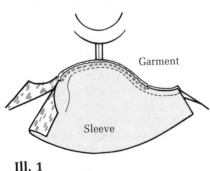

Ill. 1

Pin the side seam and underarm seam and stitch this edge in a continuous seam from the garment's bottom edge to the sleeve's bottom edge (**Ill. 2**). To make a smoother and stronger curve as you round the armhole seam, make a small diagonal stitching line instead of pivoting the fabric.

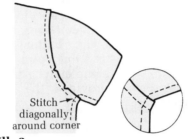

Stitch diagonally around corner

Ill. 2

Elasticized sleeve hems

You can add elastic to the hem of a full sleeve or substitute it for a cuff on a gathered sleeve. Or position the elastic slightly higher so it leaves a ruffle at the edge.

Hem with self-casing. To make a self-casing, re-mark the pattern by measuring ¾ inch below the sleeve's finished hemline (if your hem allowance is only ½ inch, you'll need to add tissue paper to the bottom of the sleeve pattern). Draw a line and use it as your new cutting line.

Wrap ¼-inch elastic around the child's arm at the point the cuff will touch. Make sure the elastic fits comfortably without pinching; add an extra ½ inch for overlap, and cut the elastic.

Stitch the sleeve's underarm seam. Tack down any seam allowances within the casing area to make it easier to pull the elastic through the casing. Turn the sleeve's bottom edge under ¼ inch; press. Turn it under again, ½ inch; pin in place. Stitch the upturned hem edge to the sleeve, leaving a 1-inch opening for the elastic. Edgestitch along the bottom edge (**Ill. 3**).

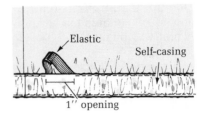

Elastic
Self-casing
1″ opening

Ill. 3

Insert the elastic through the opening. Overlap the elastic ends ½ inch and stitch them together; stitch the casing opening closed.

Ruffled hem with self-facing. To add a simple ruffle at the wrist, follow the directions above for "Hem with self-casing," adding twice the desired ruffle depth to the ¾ inch you allow below the finished hemline. (For example, to make a 1-inch ruffle, you'll add 2¾ inches below the pattern's hemline.) It's best to make the finished ruffle at least ½ inch deep.

Cut the elastic and stitch the underarm seam as directed under "Hem with self-casing." Turn the sleeve's bottom edge under ¼ inch; press. Turn it under again, the depth of the ruffle plus ½ inch (1½ inches for a 1-inch ruffle); pin in place.

Stitch the upturned hem edge to the sleeve, leaving a 1-inch opening for the elastic (**Ill. 4**). Stitch again ½ inch below the upturned edge. Insert the elastic and close the casing as directed under "Hem with self-casing."

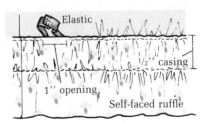

Elastic
½″ casing
1″ opening
Self-faced ruffle

Ill. 4

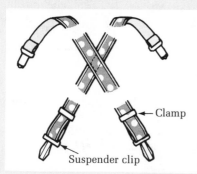
Fasteners

Dress infants with ease and encourage youngsters to dress themselves by simplifying the task with handy fasteners. Look for patterns with fasteners on the front of the garment, where they can be easily seen and reached.

Toddlers 2 to 3 years old are eager to dress themselves and can manipulate large buttons. By the time they're 3 to 4 years old, they can completely dress themselves—provided the fasteners are in front.

Buttons

Buttons are a source of endless fascination for little children. There's a limitless assortment of decorative buttons to choose from (see "Buttons for fun" on the facing page).

The two basic types of buttons are those with shanks and those without. If you're using a flat, shankless button, make a thread shank to prevent strain on the fabric. When the fabric is sheer or the buttons purely decorative, no shank is needed.

To make a thread shank, choose a pin, toothpick, or matchstick equivalent to the desired shank thickness (the thickness of the garment plus ⅛ inch) to use as a spacer. Place the spacer on top of the button as you sew the button to the fabric, stitching through the button and over the spacer (**Ill. 1**).

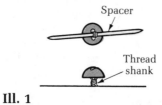

Spacer

Thread shank

Ill. 1

When the button's secured, remove the spacer. Pull the button away from the garment until the stitches are taut. Wrap the thread end several times tightly around the stitches under the button to make the shank; secure the thread end (**Ill. 1**).

You can also make a thread shank on your sewing machine, using the spacer technique outlined above and following your machine manual's instructions on button stitching.

Zippers

Zip—it's open! Zip—it's closed! What could be more mesmerizing than a zipper? Those with large pull tabs are especially easy to manage, and encourage children to dress themselves.

Choose a zipper with the weight and flexibility to match your garment fabric. If a zipper will lie against the skin, use a nylon type rather than a metal one.

Shorten zippers by whipstitching across the zipper teeth at the determined length and cutting off any excess zipper tape ½ inch below the stitches.

Nylon self-gripping fasteners

As you make your child's garment, nylon self-gripping fasteners—also known as hook and loop tape—may be practical substitutes for buttons and snaps. They're simple to stitch in place, and they open and close quickly—a boon in dressing babies. They're also easy for little fingers to operate. This type of fastener tends to be stiff; it isn't suitable for use with sheer fabrics or in long strips.

Hook and loop fasteners are available by the yard in strips of various widths, or in precut geometric shapes. Some have an adhesive backing for self-basting.

To install hook and loop tape, position the tape along the garment center front lines, or the center of the marking where the original fastener was to appear (**Ill. 2**). Place the loop half of the tape on the upper side of the underlap and stitch around the outer edges through all layers. Place the hook half on the underside of the overlap and stitch as you did the first half.

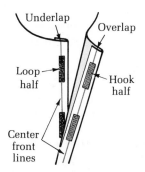

Ill. 2

Snaps

Snaps are especially good closures for infants' and toddlers' sleepers, T-shirts, and rompers. They're available individually or on cloth tape you can purchase by the yard (**Ill. 3**).

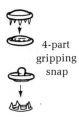

4-part gripping snap

Ill. 3

A decorative four-part snap is simple to install without special equipment. Follow the manufacturer's instructions, adding interfacing as directed to reinforce any areas of lightweight fabric that need it.

Buttons for fun

Buttons do more than hold a garment closed: they decorate! So many imaginative buttons are available—bright red hearts, cheerful ducks, gingerbread men, even alligators. Why not put them on your children's clothes just for fun?

Try new and surprising places for buttons: on a waistband, down the front of a T-shirt, on a sleeve, or on a pocket.

Hems

The home stretch: when the hem is done, the outfit is ready to wear! Whether you're creating a new garment, adapting a hand-me-down, or taking up a gift that's a bit too long, the same principles of hemming apply.

The tendency is to make a child's hem as deep as possible to allow for growth. But the depth of a hem should be determined by the style of the garment and the weight of the fabric, so keep these guidelines in mind:

Make plain, straight hems as deep as 3 inches. Make flared hems with fullness in the hem allowance no deeper than 2 inches. For a garment such as a circular skirt, make the hem only 1 inch deep. Use narrow, machine-stitched hems for blouses and shirts. Avoid wide hems if the fabric is heavy or bulky.

To hem quilted fabrics, trim the batting from the hem allowance (you'll have to remove some quilting stitches to do this) and stitch the hem by hand or machine. Or cut the hem allowance away and encase the raw edge with bias binding (see page 33).

Machine-stitched hems

Machine-stitched hems are the best choice for children's clothes because of their strength and durability, not to mention the fact that they're done in a jiffy. Machine stitching is suitable for all fabrics except those that are heavy or napped.

Topstitched hem. Topstitching finishes a hemming job quickly and adds a decorative touch to the garment's edge. Use a long straight stitch or try one of your machine's decorative stitches for an irresistible accent (see pages 24–25). (Remember, though, that decorative stitches are difficult

to remove if you want to let the hem down later.)

Turn the raw edge of woven fabrics under ¼ to ½ inch before turning the hem edge, to prevent raveling (this isn't necessary for knits). Turn the hem edge under and pin or baste it in place. Stitch on the right side of the garment, securing the hem and the turned edge with one or more evenly spaced rows of stitches. On knit garments, cut away any excess fabric above the topstitching to within ¼ inch of the top row of stitching (**Ill. 1**).

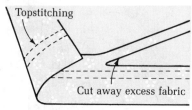

Ill. 1

Repeat the rows of stitching elsewhere (on the sleeve hem, at the neck, or at the waistline) to unify the garment's design (**Ill. 2**).

Ill. 2

Blind hem. The machine blind-stitch is a strong finish that's barely visible on the outside of the garment. Most zigzag machines are programmed to stitch a blind hem (**Ill. 3**). Check your

machine's manual for specific instructions.

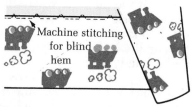

Ill. 3

Hand-stitched hems

Hand-stitched hems are usually reserved for special-occasion clothes on which a soft, invisible hem is desired. They also provide a smooth finish for heavy or napped fabric. Here are some tips to keep in mind as you hand stitch hems for your children's clothes.

If the garment shape flares at the hem, you'll need to reduce the fullness in the hem allowance. First, ease stitch (see page 8) with a long machine stitch ¼ inch from the raw edge; adjust the fullness at frequent intervals. Then place a press cloth between the hem and the garment to prevent a hem imprint on the front of the garment. With an iron, steam the hem to shrink out any excess fullness.

To stitch the hem on a lightweight or sheer fabric, precede the hand stitching by folding the raw edge under ¼ inch and machine stitching close to the fold. Pin the hem in place and secure it with a blindstitch.

Before hand stitching, prepare a fabric that tends to ravel: machine stitch ¼ inch from the raw edge. Pink close to the stitching. Pin the hem in place and secure it with a blindstitch.

Another way to prepare loosely woven fabrics for hand

stitching is to finish the edge with seam binding (on a straight hem) or bias tape (on a flared one). If the fabric is heavy, fold the taped edge forward and blindstitch the inside hem edge to the garment (**Ill. 4**), to avoid creating a crease on the garment's right side.

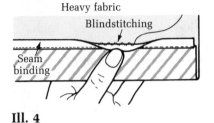

Ill. 4

Removing a hem

Once you've removed stitches to let down a hem, you may find a telltale sign of the original hem in the form of a soil line, persistent crease, or wear line.

If the hemline is creased, sponge it with a solution made of equal parts of white vinegar and water. If the crease stubbornly refuses to disappear, steam it by sandwiching the hemline between two damp press cloths lined with aluminum foil on the outside, and pressing it with a hot, dry iron.

If a line persists, you can disguise it in any of several imaginative ways—see page 13 for ideas. Whatever decorative finish you decide to add, make it compatible with the garment style and fabric and, if possible, repeat it elsewhere on the garment for harmony and symmetry.

Away with stains

Along with a child comes the inevitable problem of stains. It's amazing the number of messy things a child can get into! Below is a chart that deals with the most bothersome stains, giving quick and easy ways to remove them. (Except where otherwise specified, the treatments are for washable fabrics. If yours is nonwashable and no technique is given, have the stain removed by the dry cleaner.)

There are two basic rules for stain removal: First, be sure to treat a stain promptly. Then launder or dry clean the item immediately after treatment.

Most common stains respond to pretreatment with a commercial enzyme presoak, followed by laundering.

Here are definitions of some cleaning terms:

● Freezing: Hardening the staining substance by pressing an ice cube on it.

● Presoaking: Placing the stained fabric in water or a solution containing a stain-removal agent for a specific time. Follow by laundering.

● Pretreating: Rubbing an enzyme presoak or a liquid detergent into the stain.

● Scraping: Gently using a dull knife or spatula to remove the staining substance.

STAINS	TREATMENT
Blood	Sponge or soak stain immediately in cold water. If stain remains, pretreat it with an enzyme presoak. Sponge nonwashable items with a mild solution of detergent and water.
Chocolate	Sponge promptly with cold water (for tougher stains, soak in cold water at least 30 minutes). Rub with a detergent; rinse. If stain persists, sponge remaining stain with a cleaning fluid.
Crayon/Cosmetics	Sponge liquid detergent over stain, rubbing until suds are produced. When stain is no longer visible, rinse thoroughly. Repeat until stain is gone. For nonwashable items, sponge repeatedly with a cleaning fluid.
Egg	Scrape off as much as possible and sponge with cold water. Avoid hot water at all costs; it will set the stain permanently.
Fruit & juice	Soak immediately in cool water. (If stain is old, soak in hot water.)
Grass (foliage, flowers)	Sponge with rubbing alcohol to remove the stain from washable and nonwashable items; test colors first, and dilute if necessary. (Don't use on acrylic.) If stain persists, rub with detergent.
Gum	Freeze until gum is hard, then scrape it from fabric. If stain remains, sponge with a cleaning fluid.

Embellishments

Turn a simple garment into a prized possession: just add a touch of trim or stitchery. Boys and girls are thrilled to have their clothes decorated with their favorite objects or scenes.

From machine stitchery to fabric paint, you'll find in this section a treasure chest full of ideas to make your projects one of a kind. Whether you've just dabbled in the fabric arts, or have logged many years with a needle and thread, these instructions will help you create magical effects with the clothing you make.

Though the following embellishments are easier to execute on the flat fabric before you construct a garment, all of them—except smocking—are transferable to completed clothes.

As you browse through this section, let your imagination inspire you to develop ideas for design, color, and technique. Large illustrations throughout the chapter present these fabric crafts, translated into clothing for boys and girls—adapt their ideas to your child's personal preferences. "How to transfer a design," page 38, offers several ways to move your design from paper to fabric.

Decorative machine stitching

Your sewing machine is the key to a treasure trove of decorative stitching ideas. All you need are some brightly colored threads— the machine will transform them into marvelous decorations.

You can use programmed stitches or freehand embroidery to decorate garments you're making or clothes you've bought. Machine-stitched decorations are also ideal for touching up worn clothes; hiding hemline marks, stains, and small tears; or just giving a face lift.

Programmed stitching

Most sewing machines have at least one or two stitches that can be used decoratively. Such decorative stitches are either built into a machine's functions or programmed with the addition of a cam or cassette. Use them in single or multiple rows, mixing stitch designs and thread colors.

Decorative stitching is very becoming in any number of spots: around the edge of a collar or on the narrow bib of a pair of overalls or a pinafore, for example (**Ill. 1**).

Ill. 1

Use it to sew a machine-stitched hem, creating instant enhancement. You can also work your way up from the hem of a skirt, pants, or sleeves with many horizontal rows of stitches (**Ill. 2**).

Ill. 2

Machine preparation. Consult your sewing machine manual for specific instructions regarding the features on your machine and any preparation needed for the stitch you've chosen.

Try different thread varieties for your upper thread, to create special effects. Lightweight thread makes a small stitch very delicate; machine buttonhole twist adds a bold appearance; and metallic thread makes a dazzling accent (**Ill. 3**).

Intricate stitch with fine thread

Open stitch with heavy thread

Ill. 3

Freehand machine embroidery

Master the technique of moving an embroidery hoop under your sewing machine needle, and you can create a limitless variety of freehand embroidered designs, including monograms. Adding the same delightful personal touch as hand embroidery, machine-embroidered designs are faster to complete and more durable.

This technique requires practice and familiarity with the handling of your machine. Experiment with several test samples to get used to hoop movements and a fast machine speed, and to become accomplished at making smooth, even stitches.

Fabric preparation. Create your design on paper first. Begin with simple shapes and move to more complex ones as you become more proficient at your embroidering technique. Transfer your design to the *right* side of the fabric (see "How to transfer a design," page 38).

For napped fabrics, such as terrycloth or velveteen, transfer the design to tissue paper or organdy and pin it onto the fabric. This prevents the stitches from getting lost in the pile.

If you wish to machine embroider a knit, use only a moderate stretch knit. Hand baste organdy or interfacing to the *wrong* side of the knit fabric beneath the design, to prevent shifting or stretching while you machine stitch.

Use an embroidery hoop with an adjustable screw to keep your fabric taut as you stitch. Insert the fabric into the hoop as shown in **Ill. 4**; it's the reverse of the way fabric is inserted for hand embroidery.

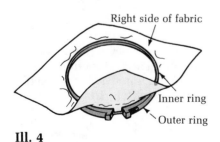

Right side of fabric

Inner ring

Outer ring

Ill. 4

Machine preparation. Remove the presser foot and ankle and lower the feed dogs. Consult your sewing machine manual for specific directions.

To make stitches that are smooth on the surface, use thread that is strong but not heavyweight for the upper thread. An extra-fine or a basting thread in the bobbin reduces fabric puckering.

Stitching. Place the hoop under the machine needle. Then *lower the presser foot lever;* though it can be hard to remember, this is a very important step. Take one stitch and bring the bobbin thread up to the surface (**Ill. 5**). Secure the thread by taking several stitches in place; then clip the thread ends. Continue stitching, following the line of your design and keeping your hands on the rim of the hoop rather than on the fabric as you direct it.

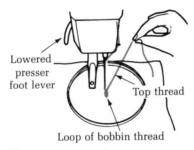

Lowered presser foot lever

Top thread

Loop of bobbin thread

Ill. 5

On the first test sample, check thread tensions. If the bobbin thread appears on the surface, loosen the upper thread tension. If that doesn't solve the problem, consult your sewing machine manual.

By setting the machine on a straight stitch, you can create line drawings similar to a pencil line, with greater flexibility than with a programmed stitch.

For satin stitch monograms or outlined designs, set the machine on a zigzag stitch. Keep one edge of the zigzag stitch along the design's lines to ensure smooth, straight edges (**Ill. 6**). Keep all stitches horizontal by moving the hoop straight toward you and away from you, working gradually from the left side of the design to the right as you would write with a pencil. Never move the hoop diagonally or rotate it.

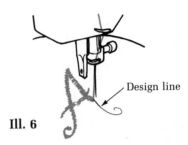

Design line

Ill. 6

To fill in embroidery designs, move the hoop rapidly back and forth horizontally to create a hand satin stitch effect. You'll be blending the stitches as if coloring with a crayon (**Ill. 7**).

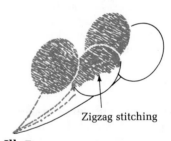

Zigzag stitching

Ill. 7

When one area of color in your design is complete, take a few stitches in place to secure the thread; clip the thread ends close to the fabric. Begin a fresh area of color as described above. When the design is done, bring the presser foot lever up and remove the hoop from the machine bed. If you used tissue paper or reinforcing fabric, cut away any that remains.

Embroidery

A trail of flower buds, a locomotive and boxcars, hearts, ducks, or even dinosaurs can find their way onto a garment and into young hearts with the help of some embroidered stitches. Though you usually embroider garment pieces before they're assembled, you can also embroider a completed or purchased garment. Many pattern transfer and embroidery design books are available at needlework shops. Or you can create your own designs (see "How to transfer a design," page 38).

Materials & supplies

First, choose your fabric and thread. Then, with some needles and a hoop, you're ready to get your embroidery project underway.

Fabric. The fabric of most children's clothes is sturdy and firmly woven—just right for embroidery. But all kinds of fabric—even knee socks—can be embroidered.

Whatever fabric you embellish, preshrink it before you embroider it. If you plan to make a counted cross stitch design on a fabric with an uneven weave, a napped fabric, or a knit, use waste canvas to guide your stitches (see "Stitchery magic," facing page).

Thread. Six-strand embroidery floss is the most common embroidery thread. Separate it into two-strand pieces for stitching. Pearl cotton, another favorite, is available in two thicknesses, size 3 and size 5. For an accent that sparkles, try a metallic or rayon thread.

Choose your thread according to the desired effect of the design. Pearl cotton, for example, is thicker and therefore more prominent and less delicate than embroidery floss.

Needles. The needle you use must have an eye large enough to allow your choice of thread to pass through easily.

Sharps and crewels are the needles recommended for embroidery. For most stitches, a sharply pointed needle is best. Try a chenille needle if you prefer a particularly large eye and a sharp point for your stitching. A blunt point is necessary for counted cross stitch, to avoid piercing the fabric's threads.

Hoop. The tautness of the fabric in an embroidery hoop prevents puckered, uneven stitching. Insert the fabric, *right* side up, across the top edge of the hoop's inner ring. As you tighten the outer ring's tension, make sure the fabric is held taut, with straight grain.

If you've already cut out a garment pattern piece and the fabric isn't large enough to fit into an embroidery hoop, baste scrap fabric pieces to its sides to increase the surface area.

Basic stitches

You can make exciting needlework designs using only a few simple stitches. The basic instructions below apply to all types of thread.

Cut the thread in lengths of 18 to 24 inches. Longer threads may begin to untwist or fray at the ends from being pulled through the fabric.

To embroider clothing or quilts that will receive hard wear and lots of laundering, attach the first thread to your fabric by taking several tiny backstitches in an area you'll cover later with stitches. (Avoid knots—they can slip and come untied; use them only on a project that won't be worn or handled regularly, such as a sampler or wall hanging.)

To finish a thread, weave it through several stitches on the *wrong* side of the fabric; cut the thread close to the fabric's surface. Start new threads by weaving them in the same manner.

Straight stitch. For details such as facial features or flower stamens, use stitches in a row, radiating from one point, or randomly (**Ill. 1**).

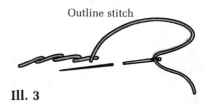

Straight stitch

Ill. 1

Running stitch. Use to designate lines. Keep stitches and spaces uniform in length (**Ill. 2**).

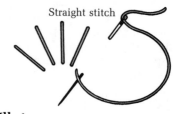

Running stitch

Ill. 2

Outline or stem stitch. Names describe stitch function. Keep thread on same side of needle with each stitch (**Ill. 3**).

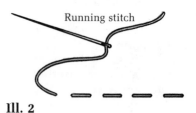

Outline stitch

Ill. 3

Satin stitch. Align stitches side by side, with no gaps, to fill in an area of color. Start in center of area to be filled and stitch to one end; return to center and continue to opposite end (**Ill. 4**).

Satin stitch

Ill. 4

Backstitch. Work from right to left with uniform stitch lengths, with beginning of one stitch touching end of another. Use for outlining or lettering (**Ill. 5**).

Backstitch

Ill. 5

Cross stitch. Work a row of half cross stitches from left to right; work back, stitching the other half. Upper half-cross of all stitches must slant in same direction to prevent a haphazard shading effect (**Ill. 6**). *Counted cross stitch* is worked on even-weave fabric, using a graph as a reference for stitch placement.

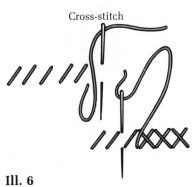

Cross-stitch

Ill. 6

Blanket stitch. This makes a good border. Hold thread loop until needle and thread are pulled through fabric so that each stitch secures previous loop (**Ill. 7**).

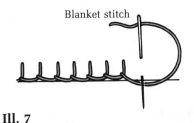

Blanket stitch

Ill. 7

Chain stitch. Hold thread loop until needle reemerges. Anchor last chain by inserting needle on other side of loop (**Ill. 8**).

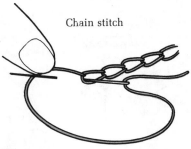

Chain stitch

Ill. 8

French knot. This stitch adds dimension to designs. Twist thread clockwise around needle; hold thread taut as needle is pulled through fabric (**Ill. 9**). To make a *bullion stitch*, continue twisting the thread 5 or 6 times around the needle.

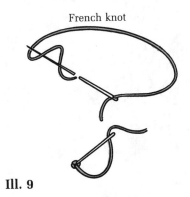

French knot

Ill. 9

Stitchery magic

You have just the perfect counted cross stitch pattern to decorate a baby's socks or a boy's denims, a turtleneck, T-shirt, or terrycloth robe. But how can you cross stitch on fabric with an uneven weave? Your problem is solved: now there's a starched cotton canvas called *waste canvas*. Use it as directed below to provide an even-weave surface wherever necessary.

Baste a piece of waste canvas on the fabric's right side, over the area to be cross stitched. Use a blunt needle for loose-weave fabrics and a sharp one for dense fabrics such as denim. Stab stitch your cross stitch design through both layers, using the even weave canvas as a guide for your pattern. A hoop isn't necessary, since the canvas is stiff enough to provide a firm surface.

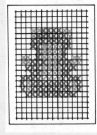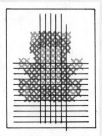

When the pattern is complete, pull out the basting threads and dampen the canvas to remove the sizing (on satin or velvet, use only steam). Carefully pull the canvas threads, one by one, out of the stitching. Pull all the vertical ones first, then all the horizontal ones. Tweezers make the job easier. The cross stitching remains on the surface of the fabric.

Waste canvas is available in many sizes, and is purchased by the yard.

Smocking

Smocking sweethearts

A classic decorative treatment, smocking never goes out of style. Its attractive stitches and soft gathers transform the plainest of garments into a delight to behold. Smocking gathers in fullness at a yoke, a bodice, or cuffs; a smocked panel insert livens up a garment. Both techniques add splendor to boys' and girls' clothing.

Does the sight of a little smocked garment make you sigh in memory of your own childhood favorite? The timeless craft of smocking—working embroidery stitches over gathers of fabric—is still popular today, transforming the simplest garments into heirloom treasures.

Don't let the complicated look of smocking deceive you. Once you've mastered a few basic stitches, it's surprisingly simple to make beautiful patterns.

There are two distinct methods of smocking: American and English. In American smocking, you gather the pleats as you work the decorative stitches. English smocking has two separate steps: you gather the fabric first, then work decorative stitches over the gathers. The English technique, described below, ensures more consistent results.

You can work English smocking into a garment in two ways. In its traditional role, smocking gathers in the fullness of the fabric at such spots as sleeves, waist, and yoke. But it can also be a smocked panel, inserted into a garment for a purely decorative effect.

Materials & supplies

Whether you plan to use smocking as an integral part of the garment or as a decorative insert, complete the smocking before constructing the garment. Since the garment is likely to be a special outfit, use the best materials possible to ensure long-lasting results.

Fabric. Use light to medium-weight fabrics for smocked garments. Natural fibers are recommended since they hold the shape of pleats well; synthetics are difficult to shape.

If you're inexperienced with smocking, it's best to begin with a garment pattern designed for smocking. If you choose an unsmocked pattern, cut the fabric pieces for the area to be smocked 2½ to 3 times as wide as the desired finished width of the area. The amount you increase depends on the fabric you use; heavier fabrics should have less fullness.

Thread & needle. Six-strand embroidery floss and pearl cotton are used for smocking stitches. The embroidery floss—separated into three-strand pieces—provides a delicate look on lightweight fabrics, and is especially good for intricate, close stitches. Use additional strands with heavier fabrics. Size 5 pearl cotton is bolder and more durable, suitable for heavy fabrics and playclothes. It works well with open patterns of stitches.

An embroidery (crewel) needle works best for smocking.

Pleating

The fabric area to be smocked must first be gathered into many pleats. You can save much time and effort by pleating with a gathering machine. Though the machine is expensive, many fabric and needlework stores have them and offer a pleating service; try to find a store that does. Otherwise, mark and gather the fabric by hand.

Marking the fabric. Evenly spaced dots are used to mark the placement of gathering stitches and to determine the width of the fabric pleats. Iron-on transfer dots are available in various sizes (also referred to as gauges)—use a size with wider dot spacing for heavier fabrics. Or

draw your own dots with a transfer pencil.

Before you begin marking the fabric, make sure the grainline is straight. Working on the fabric's *wrong* side, position dots parallel with the grainline, covering the entire area to be smocked. To draw your own dots, space them from edge to edge, ⅛ inch to ⅜ inch apart both vertically and horizontally (farther apart on heavier fabrics).

Gathering the fabric. For the gathering thread, use a double strand of regular sewing thread, or a single strand of button and carpet thread, in a color that contrasts with the fabric and smocking threads (it will be removed later). Run the thread through beeswax to help prevent knotting and breaking.

Work from right to left on the *wrong* side of the fabric, using a new thread for each row. Complete each row with one continuous thread.

Start each row by knotting the thread end and taking a stitch in place at the farthest right-hand dot. Take running stitches across the entire area to be smocked, picking up a dot per stitch (**Ill. 1**). It will be easier to take the stitches if you roll the fabric over the 'index finger of the hand holding the fabric.

Pick up dot with each running stitch

Ill. 1

Let the thread end hang down from the end of each row. When all the rows are stitched,

pull the gathering threads to form tight pleats in the fabric. Gather the fabric until it's about 1 inch narrower than the desired finished width, to allow for slight expansion when the gathering threads are removed.

Holding the fabric at the top and bottom edges, snap it firmly to make the pleats fall into place. Use an iron to steam the pleats; don't press.

Tie the ends of adjacent gathering threads together to keep them from pulling out while you're smocking. The gathering threads will serve as guidelines for the smocking stitches.

Designing stitch patterns

You can purchase garment patterns that include smocking designs, or buy separate smocking designs known as plates. Or you can design your own pattern of stitches. Carefully plan the use of color and stitch types so the pattern maintains vertical balance—with the rows neither too close together nor too far apart.

The elasticity of the smocking is an important consideration if your smocking is controlling the garment's fullness. Certain stitches—such as the wave and the trellis—are elastic and allow the fabric to stretch. Others—such as the cable and the outline—have very little give and hold the fabric firmly. Choose a balanced combination of elastic and controlled stitches to get the best performance from your smocking. If too many elastic stitches are used, the smocking will be limp. With too much control, the smocking won't have elasticity. Use controlled stitches where the most control is needed: at neckline and cuff edges, for example.

(Continued on page 30)

Basic stitches

Though there are many different smocking stitches, they all stem from a few basic stitches that are easy to learn. Just space, repeat, or combine these basic stitches for unlimited variations.

As you work each stitch across the fabric, refer to these pointers for the best results.

• Stitches are worked from left to right, using the gathering threads as guidelines to keep the smocking straight and evenly spaced.

• Start each row with a knot on the *wrong* side of the fabric; take one stitch in place at the first pleat on the left. To finish a row, bring the thread back to the *wrong* side of the fabric after the stitch at the last pleat to the right. Secure the thread with a knot; cut the thread end.

• Hold the needle horizontally as you work; pick up only the top third of a pleat with each stitch. If you pick up more fabric, you'll decrease the elasticity of the smocking.

• Work with an even tension, pulling each stitch so it's snug, but not too tight.

• If a new thread is needed in the middle of a row, bring the working thread to the *wrong* side of the fabric between two pleats. Secure it with a knot and cut it. Start the new thread at the same place by knotting it and bringing it up in the space where you want the stitch to continue.

Outline and stem stitch. These stitches are identical except for the direction they slant. Because rows of outline and stem stitches have little stretch, they're often used to control gathers at the top and bottom of the smocked area.

To make a row of outline stitches, start the thread at the first pleat on the left. Take a stitch from right to left through the second pleat, keeping the thread *above* the needle; pull the stitch snugly. Repeat the stitch in the next pleat, keeping the thread above the needle and stitching parallel to the gathering-thread line (**Ill. 2**). Finish with the last stitch in the last pleat to the right.

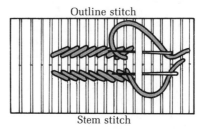

Outline stitch

Stem stitch

Ill. 2

The stem stitch is worked the same way, except that you keep the thread *below* the needle as you make each stitch.

Cable stitch. This stitch is quite inelastic; use it as you would the outline stitch, to control gathers. Use it also for *back-smocking* in areas where no stitches appear on the right side. Worked on the *wrong* side of the fabric, back-smocking prevents the pleats from puffing out of shape.

Work this stitch as you would the outline stitch, but alternate the position of the thread: above the needle for one stitch, below the needle for the next (**Ill. 3**).

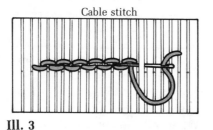

Cable stitch

Ill. 3

Wave or chevron stitch. A variation of the cable stitch, the wave stitch is very elastic and exercises little fabric control.

Begin at the first pleat on the left, at a gathering-thread line. Make sure there's another gathering-thread line above the one you're using as a guide. Work a cable stitch with the thread below the needle. Move up half a row and, inserting the needle in the right-hand side, pick up the next pleat, keeping the thread below the needle; pull it snug. Complete a cable stitch by picking up the fourth pleat, keeping the thread above the needle.

Move down to the gathering-thread line and pick up the next free pleat, inserting the needle from the right and keeping the thread above the needle. Repeat the above procedure to the right-hand end of the pleats (**Ill. 4**).

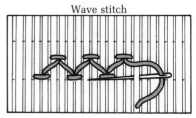

Wave stitch

Ill. 4

Surface honeycomb stitch. Another cable stitch variation, the surface honeycomb stitch has little control, permitting a lot of elasticity in the smocking.

With the thread below the needle, make a cable stitch in the first two pleats along the gathering-thread line. Move up half a row and take the next stitch as you would for the wave stitch (above), but pick up the *second* and *third*, rather than the third and fourth, pleats in the cable stitch. Continue as for the wave stitch, but overlap each upper and lower cable stitch one pleat instead of proceeding to the next free pleat. Repeat the procedure to the end of the pleats (**Ill. 5**).

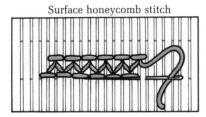

Surface honeycomb stitch

Ill. 5

Trellis stitch. This is an elastic stitch with a lot of stretch. It's versatile: layer it to make chevrons; invert alternate rows to make diamonds. The stitch begins at one gathering-thread line, works diagonally up to the next gathering-thread line, turns, and works back down.

Start at the first pleat on the left with a stem stitch. Then work four stem stitches, each one moving up one quarter of the space between the gathering threads. Make an outline stitch along the upper gathering thread. Then work down with four outline stitches. Repeat the procedure across the fabric (**Ill. 6**).

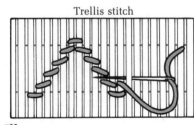

Trellis stitch

Ill. 6

Finishing

Carefully remove the gathering threads and shape the smocking to its finished size. With an iron, steam it to set the pleats (don't press or you'll flatten the smocking). Continue with the garment construction as your pattern directs.

Hearts aplenty

Use a clever combination of simple stitches and—voila!—rows of smocked hearts adorn a special garment. This smocking is designed to fit into a garment as a decorative insert. Repeat the 3½-inch-high design to fit the width you need.

Cut lightweight fabric to the desired height plus 2 seam allowances; cut it three times as wide as the desired finished width, plus two seam allowances. Use three strands of embroidery floss in each of three different colors for decorative stitches. Use directions under "Smocking," beginning on page 28. Mark pleating dots ¼ inch apart, spacing rows ½ inch apart. Gather and secure the pleats.

● First gathering-thread line: Using color A, cable stitch.

● Second line: Using color B, wave stitch, extending stitch halfway down to next gathering-thread line.

● Third line: Using color B, alternate trellis stitch and wave stitch. Exaggerate each trellis so that it extends from bottom of wave stitch at second gathering-thread line to ¾ the depth between lines 3 and 4. Needle should enter pleat at a 45° angle with each stitch in the trellis. Wave stitch should extend halfway down to next gathering-thread line.

● Fourth line: Using color C, trellis stitch with needle at 45° angle for each stitch. Start at bottom of wave stitch in third gathering-thread line; end halfway between lines 4 and 5.

Repeat the above rows of stitches in reverse order to create a mirror image.

Design: Nan Turner.

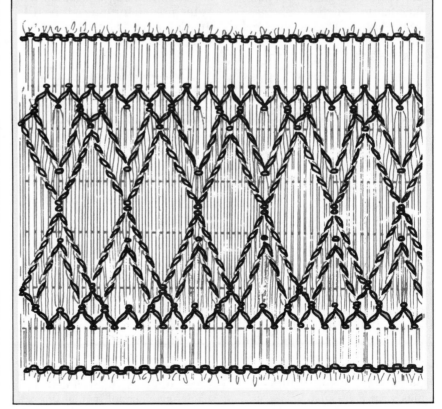

Tapes & trims

Piping, braid, and bias tape can add bursts of color to any youngster's outfit. Laces, ribbons, and ruching give a garment a feminine aura that little girls love. Combined tapes and trims can create sensational garments for both girls and boys, from infants to preschoolers—and beyond.

Cutting bias strips

Strips of fabric, cut on the bias, are a staple item used in making such trims as bias tape (see below) and piping (see page 34). They can also form the basis of other decorative elements, such as ruffles (see page 15). Below are two methods of cutting fabric for bias strips.

In the first method, used primarily to cut strips for short lengths of trim, straighten the fabric and trim it evenly along the crosswise grain. Then fold the fabric so the selvage is aligned with the crosswise grain (**Ill. 1**).

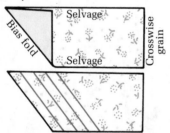

Ill. 1

Press or mark along the bias fold. Open the fabric and measure, mark, and cut bias strips of the appropriate width, using the bias foldline as your guideline.

Continuous bias strips. For projects requiring extensive lengths of bias tape, this method is the fastest and most efficient. For example, ½ yard of 45-inch-wide fabric yields about 12 continuous yards of 1½-inch-wide bias strip.

Fold a fabric square diagonally and cut along the crease line (**Ill. 2**). Positioning triangles as shown, stitch a ¼-inch seam; press the seam open. Use a diagonal edge as a guideline to measure and mark strips of the correct width, parallel to the edge.

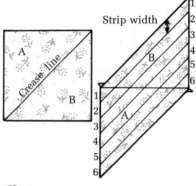

Ill. 2

With edges mismatched as shown, stitch edges together in a ¼-inch seam, forming a tube (**Ill. 3**). Cut along marked lines to form a spiral strip.

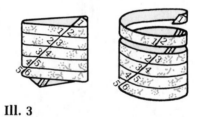

Ill. 3

Bias tape

Bias tape is a wonderfully useful and versatile trim. It's the perfect finish for either straight or curved fabric edges because of its stretch and flexibility.

Use bias tape on garments you make yourself to replace facings, encase raw edges, or make garments reversible (see "Taped seam" on page 16). You can also use it as an accent trim at pocket or hem edges on ready-made clothes or ones you make yourself.

Make your own bias tape from your garment fabric or contrasting fabrics, using the directions that follow. Or use pre-packaged tapes. Several widths and styles are available, the most common being ½-inch-wide single-fold bias tape. Its edges are folded under to meet at the middle.

Double-fold bias tape goes one step further than the single fold tape: it has an extra fold slightly off the center line. This extra fold makes the tape ready to use to encase raw edges.

Making bias tape. Make your own bias tape any width you desire, depending on the degree of boldness you want. Use your garment fabric if it's light to medium weight, or use light to medium-weight cotton or cotton/polyester blend. Avoid loosely woven or crease-resistant fabrics that won't hold a press.

Though ½ inch is the most common finished width for bias tape, wrap a piece of scrap fabric over the edge of the garment to be trimmed, to decide if you need more or less width. To determine the necessary length, measure from edge to edge all the garment seams that will require bias tape; add 1 inch per seam for seam allowances. Choose the appropriate cutting method from "Cutting bias strips," above. Cut the bias strips the desired width plus ½ inch.

Fold the raw edges of the bias tape under ¼ inch, *wrong sides together*; press. This step will be much less time consuming if you use a bias tape maker; it will automatically fold the edges.

If you wish to make your single-fold tape into double-fold

tape, fold it in half lengthwise, *wrong* sides together, and press. Make the fold slightly off-center, so one side of the tape is approximately 1/16 inch wider than the other.

If the bias tape will be used on a curved surface, steam it to fit the curve before applying it to the garment.

Encasing a raw edge. You can apply bias tape to a raw edge in one of two ways. A combination of hand and machine stitching gives a polished look; machine stitching alone provides a quick, sporty, topstitched finish.

To encase an edge with a combination of hand and machine stitching, begin by trimming the garment seam allowances to a width slightly narrower than the finished bias tape. On an edge that was originally designed to be sewn into a seam, such as an armhole or neckline, you'll need to cut away the entire garment seam allowance before applying bias tape.

Cut the tape to the length of the edge to be covered, plus 1 inch. When the tape will make a continuous band around the opening, such as at an armhole or a hem edge, fold one narrow end of the tape under 1/2 inch; pin in place in an inconspicuous area. The unfolded end of the tape should overlap the folded end 1/2 inch (**Ill. 4**).

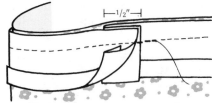

├─1/2"─┤

Ill. 4

If the garment edge has an opening or is part of a separate piece, such as a neckline or a
(Continued on page 34)

The winning edge

Bias tape along the edge of a hem, armhole, or neckline can bring a garment to life, and a surprise touch of piping in a seam or along an edge makes any garment an instant success. Use contrasting colors or prints for dramatic emphasis. Try a metallic piping for a little dazzle, satin piping in velour garments for sheen, or velveteen in wool for softness.

Glow in the dark

All parents worry that their children won't be visible when playing outside. Adding reflective tape to outdoor clothing and gear can help lessen these worries. Two types of reflective tape—reflective and fluorescent—are available in fabric strips or patches. (Bicycle stores are the most likely place to find both these products.)

Reflective material is made up of tiny beads that reflect light beams, such as those from headlights of approaching cars, back to their source. It's more effective than fluorescent material at night, but it doesn't glow in daylight.

Fluorescent material both emits and reflects light, so it seems to glow on its own. It's more effective in the daytime than at night.

Apply these tapes to anything your child might wear or carry in the evening. Don't forget umbrellas, boots, and Halloween costumes. Several colors are available; you can choose one that coordinates with the garment's colors.

Use strips of tape to make stripes or chevrons on sleeves and pants, or rows around a hem. Cut patches into shapes and add them like appliqués for a whimsical touch. How about reflective tape clouds on a vinyl slicker or a row of stars around the hem of a parka?

patch pocket, turn both narrow ends under ½ inch to create a finished edge.

After pinning the tape to the garment, stitch along the tape foldline; clip any curves.

Fold the tape over to encase the seam. On the wrong side of the garment, pin the long folded edge of the tape to the garment near the stitching line, and slipstitch by hand (**Ill. 5**). These stitches shouldn't show on the front of the garment. Slipstitch the ends closed.

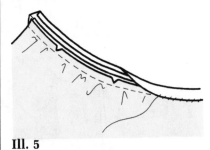

Ill. 5

For the topstitched application, use double-fold bias tape, cutting it and the garment edge as described above. With the wider side of the tape on the inside of the garment, slip the folded tape over the raw edge to encase it. Fold and overlap the ends of the tape as described above; pin the tape in place. Machine stitch close to the free edge of the tape, taking care to catch both the outside and the inside layers of the tape. Slipstitch the ends closed.

Piping

Piping—fabric-covered cord—is a purely decorative trim, but—wow!—can it make a difference in a garment's appearance! You can use it to define seam lines, accent unusual features, provide a special edge finish, or add a spark of color to any garment you make yourself.

Finished piping is available in fabric stores, but you can make your own in any size or color. Use light to medium-weight fabrics to cover the cord; try satin, metallic, or velveteen fabrics for dynamic effects.

Cable cord is used as the filler in piping. The ⅛-inch width is usually recommended for children's wear, but use a thicker cord for heavy fabrics or a special effect.

Making piping. Measure from edge to edge the length of each seam where you plan to add piping. Use this measurement to determine the lengths of bias fabric and cord you'll need. Cut bias strips, using the appropriate method under "Cutting bias strips" on page 32. Make the strips wide enough to fit comfortably around your choice of cord, adding two ½-inch seam allowances.

Wrap a strip, *right* side out, around a cord, keeping the raw edges even. Using a zipper foot, baste close to the cord without crowding it; later, you'll stitch the garment seam between the basting and the cord.

Piping a seam. Pin the piping to the *right* side of one of the garment pieces along the seamline, with the cording extending over the seamline on the inside, matching the piping stitching line to the garment seamline. If the seam curves, clip the piping seam allowance as needed (**Ill. 6**).

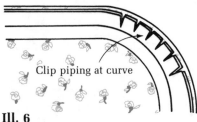

Clip piping at curve

Ill. 6

At an outside corner, clip the piping seam allowance to allow it to make a 90-degree turn (**Ill. 7**).

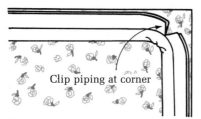

Clip piping at corner

Ill. 7

Using a zipper foot, baste the piping to the garment, stitching on the piping stitching line.

Pin the garment pieces, *right* sides together, with the piped garment piece on top. Using a zipper foot, sew the seam, stitching slightly to the garment side of the visible row of basting.

Piping an edge. When piping an edge, such as that of a vest or sleeve cuff, you must start and finish the piping in an inconspicuous spot, such as under the arm or at the shoulder seam. Make the piping 1½ inches longer than the length needed (see "Making piping" for the method of calculating dimensions). Pull the cord out of the piping fabric and snip off ¾ inch from each end. Install the piping in the seam between the garment and its facing, using the directions in "Piping a seam" (see facing page) for basting and sewing. Overlap the empty ends of the piping, as shown, curving the piping ends down below the seamline for a smooth, finished edge (**Ill. 8**).

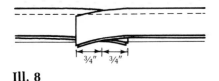

¾"   ¾"

Ill. 8

Covered cording. Covered cording is similar to piping, but the seam is finished; the seam allowances aren't visible. Your pattern may call for it for making button loops, straps, and various trims that aren't stitched into a seamline.

To make cording, cut a length of ⅛-inch cord twice the desired finished length suggested by your pattern. Using the directions under "Cutting bias strips" on page 32, cut a bias strip of fabric the desired finished length plus ½ inch. Make the strip wide enough to fit around the cord, adding two ½-inch seam allowances.

Starting at one end of the cord, wrap the bias strip around the cord with the *wrong* side of the fabric facing out and the raw edges even. The fabric will cover only half the length of the cord.

Using a zipper foot, stitch along the length of the fabric, close to the cording. Stitch from the end of the cord that is enclosed in fabric to the other end of the fabric. Then stitch across the end of the fabric, through the cord, leaving the same seam allowance as you did along the lengthwise seam. Trim the lengthwise seam close to the stitching (**Ill. 9**)

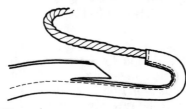

Ill. 9

Turn the fabric right side out, pulling it over the uncovered end of the cord. Cut off the newly exposed end of the cord as close as possible to the fabric end. Install the cording as your pattern directs.

Ruching

Have you ever heard of ruching? Borrowed from Victorian dress, ruching is a pretty way to turn a garment into a treasure. It can liven up a ready-made garment or be the crowning touch on one you make yourself.

Ruching is a pleated strip of fabric, stitched to a garment's surface. Use a single row of ruching to outline a neck edge or front placket, or to echo the line of a hem. Add vertical rows to create frills on the front of a bodice or christening gown.

Preparing the fabric. Use a light to medium-weight fabric for ruching, or substitute ½-inch-wide ribbon or galloon lace (a lace finished decoratively along both sides).

If you're using fabric, cut it into 2½-inch-wide bias strips, using the directions in "Cutting bias strips" on page 32. Whether you're using fabric, ribbon, or lace, make the length of the strip 2½ times the desired finished length, measuring the pattern pieces to determine the finished length needed.

If the strip is fabric, fold it in half lengthwise, *right* sides together; add thread, following the instructions below for ease in reversing a fabric tube. Pin the strip's sides together. Stitch along the length of the strip, ¼ inch from the raw edge. Press the seam open and turn the fabric tube *right* side out to make the ruching strip. Press the ruching strip so the seam lies down the middle of the back. (Ribbon and lace are already the appropriate width and require no preparatory folding or stitching.)

NOTE: To facilitate turning long tubes of fabric inside out, place a piece of heavy thread or

(Continued on page 36)

narrow cording inside the fabric near the fold before stitching the tube. Let the thread extend out both ends. Stitch it to one end of the fabric, to secure it; then stitch the fabric tube's seam without letting the thread get caught in it.

Pull the free end of the thread, which in turn will pull the fabric tube *right* side out. Cut the thread from the fabric.

Making box pleat ruching. Mark the ruching strip alternately at ½-inch and ¼-inch intervals. Form pleats by folding along the markings, alternately folding toward the right and left as shown (**Ill. 10**). The upper and lower pleats will be ½ inch wide. Pin the pleats as you fold them. Baste down the center of the ruching strip.

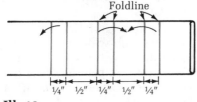

Ill. 10

Mark a line on the garment to use as a ruching placement guideline. Starting at a side seam, pin the ruching to the *right* side of the garment. Stitch down the center of the ruching strip to attach the ruching to the garment; remove basting (**Ill. 11**).

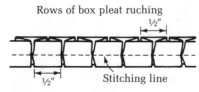

Ill. 11

Making rose ruching. Make the box pleat ruching described above and attach it to the garment. Gather the center of each upper pleat by whipstitching it

in the center with a double strand of thread, anchoring each whipstitch at the stitching line (**Ill. 12**).

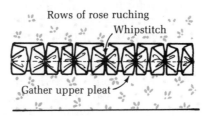

Ill. 12

Ribbons for trim

There are ribbons to suit all situations. Take a trip to the fabric store to contemplate all the possibilities. Some ribbons are soft velvet; some have pretty filigree work on the sides. Dots, stripes, delicate flowers, or lines of trains, whales, or boats ornament the surface of satin and grosgrain ribbons. Deciding where to put such ribbons is fun—don't be afraid to mix and match. Use them to touch up a hand-me-down or to add a spark of color to a garment you make yourself.

Ribbon is available either packaged or by the yard. Check to be sure the fiber content is compatible with your garment. Pretreat ribbons as you would your fabric; most are preshrunk and washable.

Simplify sewing by securing the ribbon to the fabric with a fabric glue stick. If the ribbon ends won't be sewn into a seam, turn the raw edges under to prevent raveling.

Attach ⅛-inch-wide ribbon by stitching down the middle. For wider ribbon, edgestitch along each side (**Ill. 13**). Try attaching solid colored ribbon with programmed stitching for an interesting effect.

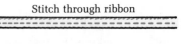

Stitch through ribbon

Ill. 13

You can hand sew ribbon in place, using embroidery floss; incorporate a variety of embroidery stitches (**Ill. 14**).

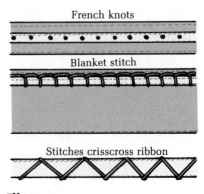

Ill. 14

A touch of lace

Lace is a bit of detail that never goes out of style. Just a touch of lace at a collar or cuff alters the look of any garment you've made or bought. Add more, and you'll transform a simple garment into a treasured party dress.

Lace is available in a number of different fiber contents. For children's clothes, washability is a must. Remember to preshrink lace before using it.

Gathered lace. Some laces are available preruffled, or you can gather lace into ruffles yourself (follow the directions on page 15, making only one row of gathering stitches close to the lace's edge). The seams of collars, cuffs, and yokes beg to be embellished with ruffled lace trim. Stitch it into the seams like piping (see page 34).

Flat lace. Many types of flat lace are available. Single-edged lace, such as eyelet, is used in the same manner as gathered lace. It's also used like piping along garment edges. Double-edged flat lace—for example, the type called *beading*, with slits through which you can weave ribbon—is sewn directly to a fabric surface, not into a seam. For a particularly delicate, airy application, try the insertion method below, adding the lace before the garment is completed.

Lace insertion. Pin flat lace in place on the *right* side of the garment piece; zigzag stitch along each edge, using thread the color of the garment fabric. Turn the garment to the *wrong* side and cut the fabric lengthwise behind the lace, midway between the stitched lines. Trim the fabric to within ¼ inch of each stitched edge and hand sew a rolled hem on each side (**Ill. 15**).

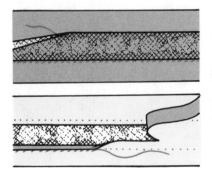

Ill. 15

Places for laces, ribbons & bows

Use ribbons and lace to decorate all kinds of garments, from playwear to fancy dresses. Line them up row after row for a new yoke look; let them peek out of unexpected places. Trim pockets or cuffs, cover seams, or highlight fabric inserts. Add a surprise touch of lacy color to a dark outfit, or a line of ducks on a ribbon to the bib of coveralls.

How to transfer a design

Delight a child by adding a personalized touch to clothing, toys, or any fabric project with designs appliquéd, embroidered, or even painted onto fabric.

Before you begin to sew, stitch, or paint, you have to get the pattern onto your fabric. Below you'll find several methods for enlarging or reducing patterns to the size you need, and for transferring that pattern to your fabric.

Reducing & enlarging a pattern

You've found the perfect elephant shape to appliqué onto a pair of jeans, but it's in a book and it's not quite the right size. What do you do? Use one of the techniques below to enlarge or reduce the design.

Photocopying. For fast, accurate results, take your pattern to a photocopy service. For a small fee, you can have the pattern enlarged or reduced on paper or transparent vellum. Better quality reproductions are available at a higher cost, and some photocopy services can reproduce in color.

Overhead projector. To resize a number of patterns, overhead projectors are available for rent at audio-visual equipment stores. A projector is the best solution when you want to make a substantial enlargement.

Making a grid. You can use a grid to size a pattern without mechanical aids. To do so, you'll need a supply of vellum graph paper.

Place the graph paper over the pattern and trace the design. Identify each vertical and horizontal row with numbers and letters. Determine by measuring the design how much it must be enlarged or reduced to become the proper size. Then choose a grid that much larger or smaller than the original grid. For example, if you've traced a design onto graph paper with ¼-inch grid squares and the design must double in size, choose a grid with ½-inch squares.

To make the new grid, either use another graph paper or draw your own grid, scaled to the proper size. Mark the new grid with the same numbering system you used for the original grid. Transfer the pattern lines carefully from grid box to equivalent grid box (see below).

Original design

Enlarged design

Transferring a pattern

Now you're ready to transfer your design to your fabric, using one of the transfer methods below. Preshrink and press your fabric before transferring a pattern to it.

Light table. Most of us don't have access to an electric light table, but on a sunny day, it's easy to create your own. Light to medium-weight fabrics that are light in color are easiest to work with.

Trace your pattern onto tracing paper. Tape the paper, *right* side up, onto a window. Center your fabric, *right* side up, over the paper and tape it in place. Trace the pattern outlines onto the fabric (see "Other marking tools," below).

Dressmaker's carbon. Washable dressmaker's carbon paper is ideal for use on most fabrics, except those with a nap.

Tape your fabric, *right* side up, to a hard, flat surface. Center and pin the pattern to the fabric, leaving the bottom edge free. Slip the carbon paper, shiny side down, between the fabric and the pattern.

With an empty ballpoint pen or blunt pencil, trace the pattern outlines. Press firmly but carefully to avoid tearing the pattern paper.

Heat-transfer pencil. Use this method for smooth-textured fabrics from light to heavy in weight. You'll find transfer pencils in fabric stores.

Trace your pattern onto tracing paper with a felt-tipped pen. Flip the tracing paper to the *wrong* side and retrace the design lines with the transfer pencil.

Center and pin the paper, *right* side up, to the *right* side of the fabric so the transfer pencil marks are against the fabric. Press the paper-and-fabric sandwich according to the pencil manufacturer's instructions.

Other marking tools. Use dressmaker's chalk or a pencil to mark pattern symbols and placement lines onto your fabric.

Appliqué

Add an appliqué to a garment and watch the owner's smile grow! Playful and practical, appliqués are always a welcome addition.

Appliqué consists of shapes cut from one piece of fabric and applied to another. Use appliqués to add color and pattern, hide a stain or tear, or even name names. The shapes, sizes, and colors you choose make an appliquéd garment a personalized possession.

Traditionally, appliqué is stitched by hand, but the zigzag stitch on your sewing machine permits a contemporary version of the art. Machine appliqué is recommended for most children's clothes and toys because it's a faster and more durable technique than hand stitching.

Appliqué techniques are the same whether you're in the process of making a garment or are enhancing a completed one. Below are the techniques of fabric preparation and stitching that will help you achieve the most pleasing results.

Getting ready

Before you begin stitching your appliqué, make a few preparations: consider the suitability of the garment you want to appliqué, choose fabric and thread, make a pattern, and cut out the fabric pieces.

Which garment? You can add an appliqué to a garment made of just about any fabric, from lightweight cotton to velveteen.

As long as you don't use a very detailed or large pattern, you can machine appliqué even on a knit fabric. To prevent the knit from stretching, hand baste a nonwoven, nonfusible interfacing to the *wrong* side of the fabric, underlying the area you plan to appliqué. Stitch the appliqué through both the fabric and the interfacing. When the appliqué has been stitched, cut the interfacing away as close to the stitching as possible.

Appliqué fabric. You can use just about any fabric for an appliqué; it needn't be the same type of fabric as the garment it will adorn. Tightly woven plain-weave fabrics are always good choices for appliqué, but also consider corduroy, satin, or velveteen for tactile and visual pizzazz. When you combine different fabrics, make sure they have similar care requirements.

If you're going to machine appliqué a design made of lightweight or knit fabric, add stability to the appliqué fabric by applying fusible interfacing to the *wrong* side of it *before* cutting the appliqué pieces; fuse it according to the manufacturer's directions.

Thread. Whether stitching by hand or machine, use a thread color the same as or slightly darker than the appliqué fabric color. Use a contrasting color only for dramatic effect.

Regular sewing thread is suited to both hand and machine stitching. Size 5 pearl cotton or three strands of six-strand embroidery floss add a bold, decorative look when hand-worked in an embroidery stitch.

Pattern. Your design may be as small as a flower on a collar or as large as a landscape across the back of a jacket. Whatever the size, a pattern is important for the cutting and placement of the appliqué fabric.

Begin by enlarging or reducing your appliqué design until it is the size it will be on the garment (see "Reducing and enlarging a pattern" on the facing page). If your design contains a lot of pieces, consider making two patterns: one to cut into individual pattern pieces, and one to keep as a master to guide you in placing the pieces on the garment.

Cut the pattern into separate pattern pieces, one for each separate piece of appliqué fabric. Lay these pieces on the *right* side of the appliqué fabric for machine appliqué, or on the *wrong* side for hand appliqué. Make sure the fabric grainline runs the same direction on all of the pieces. Trace each pattern piece on the fabric.

If an appliqué piece will be overlapped by another piece, extend the side that will be hidden about ½ inch beyond the pattern piece's edge to eliminate any chance that a gap will appear between appliqué pieces when you sew them down.

If you plan to machine appliqué, cut along the traced lines of each appliqué piece. If you plan to hand appliqué, add ¼ inch for the seam allowance around the perimeter of each appliqué piece before cutting.

Basting

Baste your appliqué pieces in place—using thread, glue stick, or fusible web—before stitching them, to prevent puckering and slipping.

Before you start basting, decide on the sequence in which you will add the pieces. Think of the pattern three-dimensionally; work from background to foreground. For example, to make up a scene, you would lay down first the sky, then the mountains, and finally the trees. You would lay down an ice cream cone before the ice cream.

(Continued on page 40)

Vested interests

One basic vest pattern can satisfy a child's fascination for anything from sailboats to teddy bears. Transform each vest you make with a different decorative technique. Embroidery, appliqué, or fabric paint, alone or combined, can add a colorful and whimsical touch. Add rickrack, buttons, or ribbons to personalize a vest, or enhance it with quilting to add texture.

Once you've decided on your sequence, baste and stitch each piece in the appropriate order.

Thread baste, glue, or fuse the appliqué fabric to the garment, using one of the techniques below. If you are going to appliqué by hand, keep the basting ½ inch or more from the fabric edge so that you can still turn the seam allowance under before stitching.

Thread basting. Hand baste the appliqué to the garment by taking long running stitches through both layers of fabric, using cotton basting or sewing thread. Don't stitch too close to the edge of the appliqué or the basting stitches will get caught in the appliqué stitches.

Fabric glue stick. This is handy for basting, especially to hold down corners and points. Once you've glued your appliqué in place, you can easily lift and reposition it, if necessary. The glue dissolves in the wash, leaving no stain or stiffness.

Fusible web. Cut a piece of fusible web the same size and shape as each appliqué piece. Fuse the appliqué to the garment fabric, following the manufacturer's directions.

Machine stitching

Any zigzag sewing machine can create a satin stitch to use when appliquéing. A satin stitch is a zigzag stitch with the stitches so close together that they appear to form a thick, solid line—very attractive as it outlines each appliqué piece. A bit of practice is required before you can stitch smooth lines, but once you feel confident, you'll be surprised at how quickly you can finish your appliqué project.

The first step. Slightly loosen the upper thread tension on your machine until you can see the upper thread on the underside of the fabric when you stitch a sample scrap. The bobbin thread will always be out of sight, so don't bother to change the bobbin thread when you change the upper thread color to match a new piece of appliqué fabric.

The width of the stitching depends on the weight of the appliqué fabric and the overall size of the appliqué. The more lightweight, small, or delicate the design, the narrower the satin stitch should be.

Stitching. Take a few stitches in place before starting to satin stitch. Then, for the greatest durability, stitch so that the outer edge of the satin stitch falls just outside the outer edge of the appliqué piece.

Work slowly at first to prevent thread build-up or open spaces in your stitching. Always keep the stitches perpendicular to the edge of the appliqué piece.

If your garment fabric puckers or shifts when you begin stitching, try pinning a patch of tear-away stabilizing fabric, slightly larger than your whole appliqué design, underneath your garment fabric. Stitch through the stabilizing fabric; tear away from the stitching line when the appliqué is completed.

Cornering. Try a few practice maneuvers and you'll have corners under control. Stitch all the way down one side to the very corner of the appliqué and leave the needle in the fabric on the outside swing of the zigzag stitch (**Ill. 1**). Pivot the fabric and continue stitching down the other side. Pull the fabric slightly from behind to keep it from getting

stuck and to prevent the stitches from piling on top of each other.

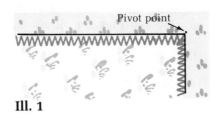

Ill. 1

Curves. Curved edges present the same problem as corners; pivoting is essential to success. When you reach a curve, insert the needle into the fabric on the curve's outside edge—into the appliqué fabric if the curve is concave; into the background fabric if the curve is convex—and pivot slightly (**Ill. 2**).

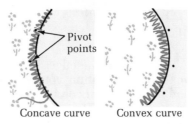

Ill. 2

Once you pivot, your next few stitches will overlap the previous stitches; pull the fabric slightly from behind to keep the stitches from piling up. Continue pivoting as necessary to work smoothly around the curve.

Points. As you approach a point while stitching, tailor the stitching to the point's configuration by gradually reducing the width of the zigzag stitch (**Ill. 3**). At the very point, insert the needle on the outside edge of the appliqué—the side not yet stitched. Pivot and stitch down the other side, gradually increasing the width of the zigzag until the stitch reaches its original size.

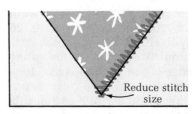

Ill. 3

Finishing. Take several stitches in place to end your stitching, whether to finish the project or just to change thread colors.

Cut the thread ends close to the fabric. Remove any stabilizer you may have used.

Hand appliqué

The whipstitch, running stitch, and blanket stitch are the most popular stitches to use in securing appliqués by hand. In all cases, the ¼-inch seam allowance is turned under along the appliqué edge as you go. Hand stitching finishes an appliqué beautifully, but it's time-consuming and not as durable as machine stitching.

The first step. Baste the first appliqué piece in place (see "Basting," on facing page), leaving the seam allowance flat.

Working 2 to 3 inches at a time along the edge of the appliqué piece, turn the seam allowance under. (A seam ripper makes the job easier—**Ill. 4.**) Insert pins perpendicular to the edge, 1 to 1½ inches apart.

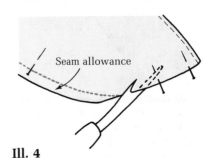

Seam allowance

Ill. 4

(Continued on page 42)

Start a thread as you would for embroidery (see page 26). With either the whipstitch or the running stitch, sew the pinned edge of the appliqué piece to the garment, using regular sewing thread and a size 8 or 9 quilting (betweens) needle. Or use the running stitch or the blanket stitch, sewing with embroidery floss or pearl cotton, and using a size 7 or 8 embroidery needle. Remove the pins as you sew.

Continue turning, pinning, and sewing the piece's edge in 2 to 3-inch sections. Tips on handling curves, corners, and points are included below. When you come to the end of a thread or a line of stitching, finish it as you would an embroidery thread (see page 26).

Stitching. Use any of the following stitches to secure your appliqué pieces to the garment.

● Whipstitch. This is a very secure stitch. Insert the needle in the garment fabric at the very edge of the appliqué piece and bring it up through the appliqué fabric, no more than ⅛ inch from the edge, taking a small diagonal stitch (**Ill. 5**). Reinsert it into the garment fabric a little farther along, and continue stitching.

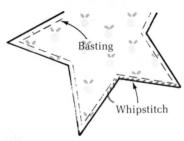

Basting

Whipstitch

Ill. 5

● Running stitch. When worked in embroidery thread, this stitch is very decorative. See "Basic stitches" on page 26 for directions; take tiny stitches (¹⁄₁₆ to ⅛ inch long), no more than ⅛ inch from the edge of the appliqué.

● Blanket stitch. This stitch effectively outlines the appliqué shapes. See "Basic stitches" on pages 26–27 for directions.

Handling curves. Clip the seam allowance of a concave curve every ¼ to ½ inch before folding it, to ensure a smooth, flat edge (**Ill. 6**). Clip less than ¼ inch into the fabric. Strengthen the seam in a clipped area by placing the stitches very close together.

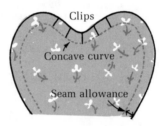

Clips

Concave curve

Seam allowance

Ill. 6

To smooth the edges of convex curves, position your index and middle fingers on the folded edge and press down. Run the needle under the allowance, gently prodding excess fabric into evenly distributed folds (**Ill. 7**). Pin and then stitch the edge.

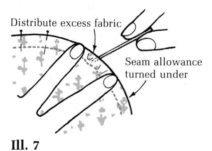

Distribute excess fabric

Seam allowance turned under

Ill. 7

Points & corners. To stitch a point, turn the seam allowance under along one side of the appliqué piece; stitch to within ½ inch of the end. Trim off the triangle protruding from under the appliqué piece (**Ill. 8**).

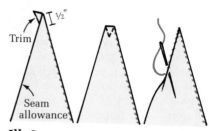

Trim

½"

Seam allowance

Ill. 8

Turn under ¼ inch of the piece's point as shown; stitch to the end of the first seam. Turn under the adjacent seam allowance and continue stitching, taking a few additional stitches as you round the folded point to help smooth the edges.

Use the same technique to stitch corners smoothly.

Appliqué variations

Enhance your appliqué work with some embroidery, quilting, or three-dimensional effects. The dramatic results will reap lots of applause.

Quilting. Outline-quilt your project around the appliqué to highlight the shape of the design. To emphasize design features, pad the shape using the trapunto technique. See "Trapunto" on page 50 for directions.

Embroidery. Add French knots to give dimension and texture. Use other embroidery stitches to add detail. See "Embroidery" on page 26 for directions.

Three-dimensional appliqué. By only partly attaching a shape to the garment fabric, you can give your appliqué a touch of whimsy. For example, make an apron for a doll appliqué by gathering a piece of fabric and stitching it to the doll's waistline. Or whipstitch an elephant ear so it flops as your toddler walks.

Your pick of patterns

There are countless places to find a design that's just perfect for your newest appliqué project. Don't feel restricted to using a design pattern only on the project on which it appears. For example, you can adjust the size of the appliqué designs for the "Animals-on-parade quilt" on page 70 and add them to a jacket, crib bumpers, or the knees of overalls. Other places to find designs suitable for children's clothes are coloring books, magazines, and greeting cards.

On this page, we've included the designs you see appliquéd on the jackets shown in the index (page 96) and on the overalls on the cover. The enlarging key under the appliqué grid enables you to make the designs the size they appear on the garments. You can make them larger or smaller to suit the needs of your project (see "How to transfer a design," page 38).

If you prefer to hand stitch the appliqués rather than using a machine satin stitch, add ¼-inch seam allowances to all of the designs.

The heart at the bottom corner of the page is an actual-size pattern for the heart pin shown on the cover. To use the heart as a stuffed pin or as a hand-stitched appliqué, add a ¼-inch seam allowance around the edge. Use the shape exactly as it appears for a machine appliqué project.

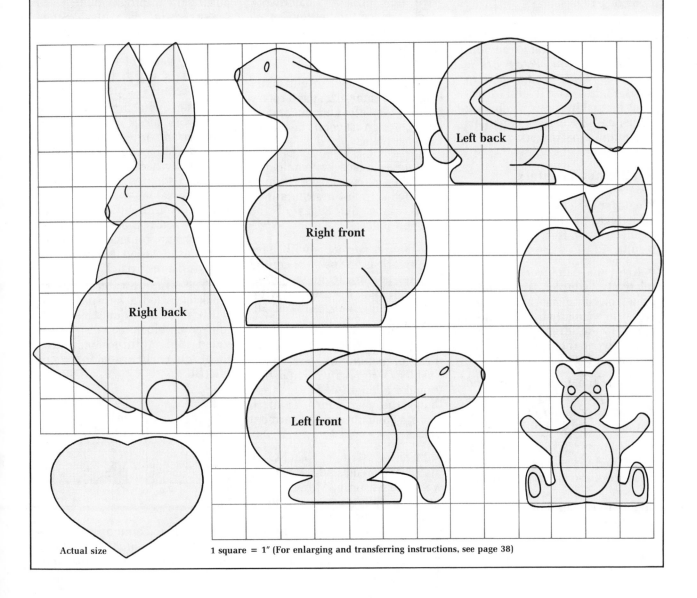

Left back

Right front

Right back

Left front

Actual size

1 square = 1″ (For enlarging and transferring instructions, see page 38)

Patchwork

Patchwork is the art of joining small pieces of fabric, such as rectangles, triangles, and squares, to form a geometric pattern within a block shape. Usually, blocks are then sewn together to form a continuous fabric with a repeating pattern.

Because of its nature, patchwork adapts easily to many different shapes and sizes. It works equally well as a narrow strip for borders or inserts, a full piece of fabric for an entire garment, or even as a single block for medallions or patches.

You can adapt many of the available patchwork patterns to children's wear. Refer to the Sunset book *Quilting, Patchwork & Appliqué* for specific pattern ideas. Below you'll find directions for making basic patchwork strips, and for the fundamentals of Seminole patchwork.

Patchwork pointers

Whatever type of patchwork you undertake, the hints below will assure trouble-free, professional results.

● Keep the patchwork patterns relatively simple, since children's clothing has fairly small areas to embellish. The basic piece in children's patchwork should be no more than 2 inches square.

● Match the fiber content and fabric weight of the patchwork as closely as possible to the fabric of the garment it will decorate.

● Combine fabrics in various light, medium, and dark colors. The colors you choose will evoke a mood—from lively crayon brights to romantic pastels.

● Select fabrics with varying scales of print. A combination of small, medium, and large prints will be much more interesting and pleasing than three polka dot fabrics in three colors. Key the prints to the size of the child, avoiding extremely large designs.

● Wash the fabrics before using them. Cut off both selvages before cutting the patchwork pieces.

● Accurate marking and cutting are essential to successful patchwork. A clear plastic ruler and triangle are excellent tools to have on hand for patchwork piecing, since they allow you to draw lines using previous markings and the fabric print as guidelines.

● When you need to cut many shapes the same size, use a rotary cutter. It neatly and accurately cuts through several layers of fabric at once.

● When a piece of patchwork will be used as an insert, be sure to allow ⅝ inch for seam allowances along the edges of the finished piece.

● When a garment will have patchwork as an insert or central feature, be sure to fit the insert accurately into the garment without changing any garment dimensions.

● When making an entire garment of patchwork, first piece the blocks of patchwork together to make a length of fabric larger than the garment's pattern pieces. Then cut out the garment pieces.

● Machine stitch patchwork pieces for greatest durability in wear and washing. Allow ¼-inch seams on all pieces; sew them using a medium-short stitch length (10 to 12 stitches per inch). When you're stitching strips to use in such techniques as the four-patch or Seminole, use a short stitch length (16 stitches per inch).

● Line patchwork garments to protect the seam allowances from fraying and pulling apart.

Patchwork in strips

Piecing patchwork patterns can become very time consuming. When the design allows, you can expedite the process by sewing long fabric strips together and cutting them into segments to be reworked into the pattern. Since children seem to grow faster than the time it takes to finish a demanding garment for them, any shortcut is worth looking into. All it takes is a little planning.

When you first look at a patchwork block, you may not perceive any order to the pattern, but closer inspection may reveal that it's divided into a number of smaller squares or triangles. These divisions make up a *grid pattern*. A grid pattern is easy to reproduce by piecing together, cutting, and repiecing strips of fabric as detailed below under "Making a four-patch."

The simplest grid-pattern block is called a *four-patch*—it is divided into four squares. A four-patch block may also be divided into multiples of four—eight squares to a side, for example (**Ill. 1**).

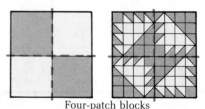

Four-patch blocks

Ill. 1

Another common block is called a *nine-patch:* it contains nine squares—three across and three down. In another version, each of the three squares is divided in quarters, creating six across and six down.

You can create any number of combinations by varying the size of the squares or by alternating the four-patch blocks with solid blocks of fabric.

Making a four-patch. Decide on the finished size of the squares in a block and add ¼ inch to each edge for seam allowances. A 2-inch finished square would be cut as a 2½-inch square.

Following the lengthwise grain, measure and cut each of two different fabrics into strips of your chosen width (2½ inches, to make 2-inch finished squares).

Sew two strips—one of each fabric—along one long edge, *right* sides together. Press the seam allowances to one side (toward the darker of the two fabrics, if they contrast greatly). Cut this strip into segments of your chosen length (2½ inches for a 2-inch finished square).

Invert one segment and pin it to another, *right* sides together, carefully aligning the center seams. Sew one edge and press the seams to one side to complete your four-patch block (**Ill. 2**). If the finished squares are 2 inches, the unfinished block will be 4½ inches square—4 inches when its edges are joined to other blocks.

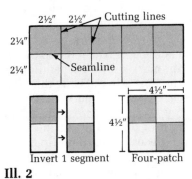

Ill. 2

(Continued on page 46)

A penchant for patchwork

Patchwork can liven anything—the edge of a vest, a hem, a cuff. Use it as an insert on a dress, bonnet, or overalls. Work it into fabric for a quilt, jacket, bib, baby bunting, or shirt yoke. A single patchwork block can appear as a medallion on the back of a shirt, and a single strip of patches can adorn each side front of a jacket.

You can make more blocks and join them together into larger blocks to create a large piece of fabric, or join them side by side to make a strip of fabric for borders and edges.

Making triangles. For variety, piece strips to make triangle shapes. Then piece the triangles into squares to use in the four-patch blocks, or into a single triangle row for a border design.

● *Triangle rows.* To make a single row of triangles, begin by stitching together strips of two different colors of fabric as described in "Making a four-patch," sewing at least four fabric strips together. Cut across the strips in segments and stitch the segments into a length of squares of alternating colors, like a checkerboard fabric (**Ill. 3**).

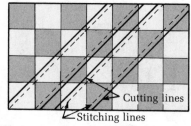

Ill. 3

Align your ruler so that it bisects a line of squares on the diagonal: mark this diagonal for one strip stitching line. Move to the next line of squares and mark the other seamline on the diagonal. Add ¼ inch outside each line for seam allowances, and mark the cutting lines (**Ill. 3**). Continue until the whole fabric is marked into strips of triangles; cut the strips.

● *Triangle squares.* Use the strip method to produce squares containing two different-colored triangles; it simplifies the process of piecing together a complex four or nine-patch block design.

To make the triangle squares, begin by measuring the diagonal of one of the finished squares in the block. (A 2-inch square, for example, has a 2⅞-inch diagonal.) Stitch a checkerboard of fabric strips as directed above for "Triangle rows," making the finished edge of each square equal to the diagonal of the squares in the finished block.

Mark and cut strips of triangles as directed above. Mark a line down the center of each triangle at right angles to the strip edge (**Ill. 4**). Cut along these lines; each segment will form a square of the correct size for use in your four or nine-patch block.

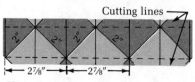

Ill. 4

Seminole patchwork

Seminole patchwork originated with the Florida Indians. It's a colorful variety of patchwork that looks terribly complex, yet is surprisingly simple (**Ill. 5**). It is best adapted for use as a strip insert in a garment.

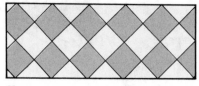

Ill. 5

The basic technique is much the same as the strip-piecing method for the four-patch, described above. Fabric strips are sewn together to make a piece of striped fabric, which is then cut into narrow striped segments. The narrow segments are sewn

together in a stair-step configuration to make a new design. The results are truly dramatic and intriguing.

Though books full of Seminole designs are available, we've provided one of the basic patterns to get you started. Once you've mastered the technique, you can invent variations by adding more strips of fabric, changing fabric widths, substituting different colors or cutting pieces diagonally, or adding mirror images. It's fun to experiment with endless permutations.

Whatever design you use, mark and cut the fabric strips along the grainline, making them ½ inch wider than the desired finished width. Make the strips as long as your fabric width. Bias tapes are particularly easy fabrics to use, since their edges are already folded to make ¼-inch seam allowances; the crease makes a handy guideline for stitching.

Always keep in mind that accurate and careful measurements are essential to the success of this technique. Follow the "Patchwork pointers" on page 44 for general directions.

Diamond Jubilee. This is a basic Seminole pattern—a good one to learn on. Cut three strips of fabric, each in a different color. Make the two outer strips 1½ inches wide and the center strip 1¼ inches wide. Stitch them together with ¼-inch seams; press the seams to one side.

Spread the fabric strip on a flat surface. At the left end of the strip, mark a line perpendicular to the long edges. Using this line as a guideline, mark divisions every 1¼ inches across the entire length of the strip. Cut the strip into pieces along these lines.

Pin the pieces together, aligning the lower edge of the

center color in each left-hand piece with the upper edge of the center color in each right-hand piece. Stitch the pieces together as you pin them, using ¼-inch seam allowances (**Ill. 6**). Each succeeding piece will form a stair-step with the previous one.

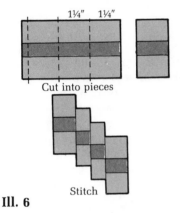

Ill. 6

When you have completed a strip of fabric, turn it on its side so the pointed edges become the top and bottom. The center color will now appear in diamond shapes. To add a border to the Seminole strip or to stitch it to a garment, use the top and bottom points of the center-color diamonds as the markers for your final stitching lines (**Ill. 7**). When stitched in place, the patchwork strip is 1¼ inches deep and about 36 inches long. Trim the ends of the strip to straighten it.

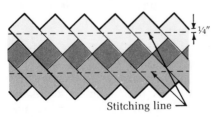

Ill. 7

Try variations of this design by adding more rows of color. Each new row adds at least ½ inch to the height of the strip, but won't have a noticeable effect on the length. Vary the width of the strips—enlarge them all or alternate narrow ones with wide ones.

● *Adding a border.* A border of contrasting fabric helps finish the edges of a Seminole patchwork strip and provides a frame for the work by separating it from the garment fabric. The border can be as wide as you wish, but should be no less than ¼ inch wide, plus ½ inch for seam allowances. (Remember to add the depth of these two borders to the finished depth of the patchwork when calculating the total dimension, especially if you're adding the piece to a garment.)

After cutting two border strips, mark lines ¼ inch outside the final stitching lines of the patchwork strip, on the upper and lower edges. Align the raw edge of a border strip with one of the drawn lines, *right* sides together; stitch a ¼-inch seam. The seam should run along the final stitching line of the patchwork piece. Repeat with the other border strip. Trim the edges of the patchwork piece even with the edges of the border seam allowances.

● *A new slant.* To vary the Diamond Jubilee pattern for a more exaggerated diamond effect, sew the three original strips of fabric together as directed above. Then use the following directions to cut the striped fabric diagonally, making slanted pieces of fabric.

Use a clear triangle to mark slanted lines at a 45-degree angle, marking the first line twice the width of the pieces to be cut. Make this mark along the top edge of the fabric for pieces that slant up to the right, along the bottom edge for pieces that slant up to the left.

Draw a line from the top or bottom of the guideline along the short edge (depending on your choice of right or left slant for the pieces) through the mark (**Ill. 8**). Continue to measure and mark pieces, using this line as your guideline. Then cut and sew these pieces as directed for Diamond Jubilee.

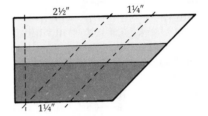

Ill. 8

● *Mirror image.* To make a dramatic chevronlike variation of the Diamond Jubilee pattern, using the slant-cut technique above, sew the three original strips of fabric together as directed for the Diamond Jubilee. Then fold the resulting strip in half and pin it, *wrong* sides together (**Ill. 9**). Mark the pieces off with diagonal lines as directed under "A new slant," above, and cut through both layers. When you turn all the pieces *right* side up, half of them will be mirror images of the other half. Sew them together, alternating slants and aligning the center color, using the directions for the Diamond Jubilee pattern, above.

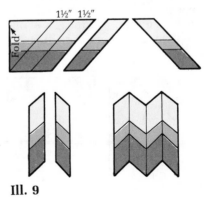

Ill. 9

Quilting

Does the word "quilt" conjure up cozy images of padded, handsomely stitched layers of fabric? Whether you prefer to quilt bed covers, buntings, overalls, or jackets, there's no limit to the stitching patterns you can use.

Quilting is the process of joining three layers of fabric: the top or *face*, the filling or *batting*, and the bottom or *backing*. The pattern of stitching you use to quilt the layers can stand alone as a design element or embellish the face fabric's print or design.

There are several ways to quilt fabric: the standard method of stitching the two fabric layers and the batting all at once like a sandwich; a variation called *trapunto*—stitching the fabric layers first and then stuffing batting only in specific areas; and tying—knotting the layers instead of stitching them.

Quilting designs

Before you start your standard quilting or trapunto project, give careful thought to your quilting design. Below are some options, ranging from simple to more complex. (See "Tied quilts," on page 51 for information on designing for that method.)

Background quilting. Background quilting designs fill an entire piece of fabric with simple repeating patterns of stitching, such as a grid, channels, a stairstep zigzag, or scallops (**Ill. 1**).

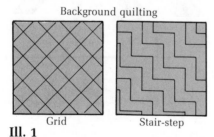

Background quilting

Grid   Stair-step

Ill. 1

Motif quilting. In motif quilting (also called ornamental quilting) the stitched design becomes a prominent feature. Designs—traditional, contemporary, or abstract—appear in medallion shapes or as running borders (**Ill. 2**). For children's clothes, choose relatively simple designs.

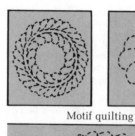

Motif quilting

Ill. 2

Outline quilting. One or more lines of quilting stitches just outside the contours of a fabric print emphasize the print's shape (**Ill. 3**). This technique can also effectively highlight appliqué or patchwork on the face fabric.

Outline quilting

Ill. 3

Preparing to quilt

More is involved in preparing to quilt than just picking a pretty fabric.

Once you've chosen a face fabric, you'll need backing fabric and batting. Marking the stitching lines and basting the layers together are required work before you actually begin to quilt. The steps may seem lengthy, but they ensure successful results.

Fabric selection. Choose light to medium-weight, firmly woven fabrics, such as cottons or cotton blends, for clothing and quilts. Napped fabrics, such as velour or velveteen, are suitable if you use a simple quilting design.

Avoid oversize prints on the face fabric; they can overpower tiny bodies. The exception to this rule is certain large graphic prints that fit perfectly onto the back of a vest or around a bunting. You can create your own appliquéd, painted, printed, or patchwork face fabrics and use quilting to highlight their designs.

Select a lightweight, tightly woven fabric for the backing. Its care requirements should be similar to those of the face fabric.

Preshrink all fabrics before you quilt them.

Batting. For warmth and durability, use polyester batting instead of cotton batting as a quilt filler. Polyester batting is easy to stitch, and you can space your stitched quilting lines up to 4 inches apart without running the risk that the batting will shift over time.

Batting suitable for quilting ranges from a thin fleece to a high-loft variety. The higher the batting's loft, the more shrinkage you'll see in the quilt size when you stitch the layers together. A common choice for clothes and quilts is ¼-inch batting. It's available by the yard or in precut packages.

Marking. In most cases, the quilting lines must be marked on the face fabric before you begin to baste, to indicate your design. To transfer your design lines to the fabric, see "How to transfer a design" on page 38. Unless your design must be centered on a garment (see below), mark, baste, and quilt your entire yardage before cutting the garment fabric pieces.

Marking isn't necessary on patchwork fabric; you usually use the seamlines of the patchwork pieces as quilting lines. Likewise, when outline-quilting a fabric print or appliqué, follow the design contour instead of drawing lines.

If you're machine quilting a repeating pattern with parallel lines, or a grid, and you have a quilting guide attachment, you need to mark only the first line. Set the guide equal to the distance between the rows. When you stitch, you'll use the quilting guide to follow the contours of the previous stitching line (**Ill. 4**).

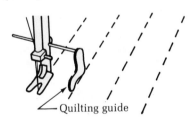
Quilting guide

Ill. 4

If your quilting design must be centered on parts of the garment, as in outline or motif quilting, you'll need to mark each garment fabric piece separately. Begin by positioning and pinning each pattern piece to your fabric; baste around the pattern edges to mark them.

Then remove the pattern and cut the fabric at least 2 inches outside the basted outline. Cen-

ter and mark the quilting design inside this area with a transfer pencil. After you quilt each fabric piece, reposition the pattern piece over it, centering the pattern over the quilted design, and cut the fabric to the pattern size. You'll find that the original basted outlines will seem to have shrunk, drawn in by the quilting stitches.

Basting. Basting the three fabric layers together before quilting is essential to the success of your project. If you don't baste, puckering and shifting will run rampant when you quilt.

On a smooth, flat surface, layer first the backing, right side *down*; then the batting; and finally the face fabric, right side *up*. Make sure they're all flat and smooth—wrinkles that get basted in will live forever. Pin the layers to hold them in place.

Use basting thread or a thread in a pale contrasting color to hand baste the layers in long running stitches.

Baste in straight lines, creating a radiating pattern, rather than following your marked quilting lines. Begin each line of basting at the center of the fabric; work toward the edges (**Ill. 5**). First complete a horizontal line, next a vertical line, and then the diagonals. The finished basting lines shouldn't be more than 4 inches apart to ensure smooth quilting.

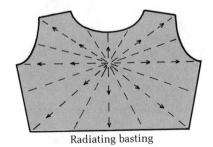
Radiating basting

Ill. 5

Quilting stitches

Standard quilting can be done by hand or machine. Since children's clothes and crib quilts will be washed frequently and worn hard, machine quilting is the better choice—it's quicker and more durable.

Machine quilting. Practice machine quilting on a basted sample of your face, batting, and backing fabric. Keep your practice stitching patterns open and not very intricate.

To stitch repeating lines and simple outlines, adjust the stitch length on your sewing machine to 8 to 10 stitches per inch. Loosen the thread tension and presser foot pressure slightly. Use a small-hole throat plate and a clear presser foot, if your machine has them.

To prevent puckers, always stitch in one direction, working from center to edges of fabric.

To machine quilt a motif or intricate pattern outline, use freehand machine embroidery techniques (see page 24); they'll let you maneuver the fabric layers easily (**Ill. 6**).

Freehand quilting

Ill. 6

To start and stop stitching, take a few stitches in place, then clip the thread ends close to the fabric.

(Continued on page 50)

Three-dimensional fabric

Quilting—here and there, or everywhere on a garment—adds dimension and warmth and an extra touch of texture. Use it to outline an appliqué, patchwork, or large graphic print. Use quilting alone to add a pattern to solid-color fabric. Try tied quilting to make a winsome, puffy jacket. Or let a touch of trapunto turn an ordinary garment into one that's simply smashing.

Hand quilting. To hand quilt, stretch the face, batting, and backing in a hoop and stitch through all three layers.

Always work from the center of the fabric toward the edges, to prevent puckers or shifting. Use an 18-inch length of quilting thread, knotted at one end. Pull the knot into the batting to conceal it.

To stitch, rock your hand in a slight up-and-down movement, taking three or four short running stitches at a time through all the layers.

To end the thread, make a single looped knot about ¼ inch from the quilt face. Insert the needle into the face close to where the thread last emerged, and slip the needle horizontally through the batting and up through the face again. Tug gently on the thread until the knot pops into the batting; cut the thread close to the quilt face.

Trapunto

Trapunto is the technique of outlining motifs with stitches and then stuffing them for a padded, sculptural effect. You stitch only the two layers of fabric together, without batting between. Then you pad the stitched areas with loose batting or yarn.

For the face, use a light to medium-weight, firmly woven fabric. A lightweight fabric such as muslin or voile is best for the backing. You'll need to line a trapunto garment to protect the stitched openings in the backing fabric.

Stuffed trapunto. This technique is great for highlighting part of a fabric print or appliqué, or for adding dimension and texture to a motif without using batting throughout the whole garment.

Transfer your quilting design to the face fabric and mark, cut, and baste the garment pieces as directed on pages 48–49 for outline and motif quilting, under "Preparing to quilt."

Stitch the design by hand or machine, following the instructions in "Quilting stitches," pages 49–50. You can stitch just the design's outline, or add more stitching to shape details. For example, you might only outline-stitch a duckling, but for a swan, you'd add stitching to define the head, wing, and feathers (**Ill. 7**).

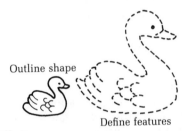

Outline shape

Define features

Ill. 7

When the design is completely stitched, cut a small slit in the backing, within each design area enclosed by stitching. Be sure to cut *only* the backing fabric, not the face. Using a blunt needle or crochet hook, insert a small amount of batting between the layers (**Ill. 8**).

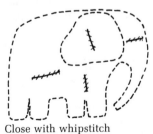

Close with whipstitch

Ill. 8

Continue adding stuffing to each stitched part of the design until the motif is smooth and puffy. Don't overstuff—it creates puckers and distortion.

Corded trapunto. Traditionally used to highlight a motif, corded trapunto makes a beautiful play of shadow and light through the subtlety of raised outlines. These raised lines can also delineate a repeating pattern or stripes.

To prepare for corded trapunto, mark, cut, and baste your fabric pieces as in "Stuffed trapunto" on facing page. When you stitch the design, using the directions under "Quilting stitches" (pages 49–50), stitch two parallel lines, 1/8 to 3/8 inch apart, instead of one line (**Ill. 9**). The two lines create a channel into which you'll insert cording.

Trapunto channels

Ill. 9

Thread a blunt tapestry needle with a single or double length of washable yarn or cotton cording. Working through the backing, carefully insert the needle between the two layers at the beginning of the design (**Ill. 10**).

Yarn

Ill. 10

Run the needle through the stitched channel, bringing it out where the design curves or turns a corner. Insert the needle again and continue, leaving a little extra yarn out at each turn to prevent puckering. Be careful not to catch any face fabric in your nee-

dle. At the start and finish, trim the yarn ends close to the fabric, and work them into the holes.

Tied quilts

Tying is a quick and easy technique for holding a sandwich of fabric and batting layers. It maintains a billowy loft because, unlike stitching, the widely spaced knots don't compress the batting.

Prepare your fabric layers as described in "Preparing to quilt," above. Decide where the knots will work best in the overall scheme of the quilting. For example, if your face fabric is patchwork, tie the corner of each block along the seamlines, or tie through the center of each block.

Space the knots no more than 6 inches apart. On small garments, maintain proportion by spacing knots no farther than 3 to 4 inches apart.

Tying knots. Use a long needle with a double length of durable yarn, pearl cotton, or crochet thread to knot the quilt layers.

Always start from the center of the basted layers and work toward the edges. Insert the needle from the face through to the backing, drawing the yarn through and leaving a 2-inch tail on the face.

Bring the needle back up to the face and cut the yarn, leaving another 2-inch tail. Tie the two tails in a square knot, left tail over right, then right tail over left (**Ill. 11**). Trim the ends evenly.

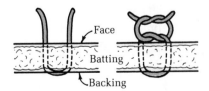

Face

Batting

Backing

Ill. 11

Painting

Use fabric as your canvas and paint directly on it to create exciting designs on your children's clothes, toys, or room decorations. It's surprisingly simple to master the technique, and there's no need to worry that your artwork will fade in the wash—it's permanent.

Sewing skill isn't a prerequisite for fabric painting. You can paint designs on finished garments almost as easily as on uncut fabric yardage.

Choose your medium: fabric pigment paints and dyes, fabric pigment crayons, or indelible ink markers. Apply them in freehand designs or stenciled patterns, or stamp them on—directions follow.

Whatever method of painting you choose, keep the design simple. Coloring books or posters with simple shapes are a good source of design ideas. Think big: paint a design up the leg of a pair of overalls and carry it right onto the bib (**Ill. 1**), or cover an entire wall banner.

Use fabric as a paint canvas

Ill. 1

Small is beautiful, too—paint some little shapes across the yoke of a jumper, on a pocket, or around a baby's bib (**Ill. 2**). The smaller your paintbrush, the more detail you can add to your design.

Use delicate art in tiny places

Ill. 2

Setting up to paint

Prepare a work area, gathering all the necessary tools and supplies so they're at your fingertips before you start to paint. Fabric paints are water soluble until heat set, so soapy water is all you need to clean brushes and equipment, as well as your skin. But cover your work surface and your clothes to protect them from splatters, especially if your children are going to join you in this creative adventure.

Work surface. Cover a piece of cardboard with plastic or acetate and place it under the fabric you're going to paint. If you're working on a finished garment, such as a T-shirt or a jacket, slide the plastic-covered board between the fabric layers. Pin the garment to the cardboard to keep the fabric smooth and taut while you work.

Paint, stamp, or stencil your fabric according to the directions below. Leave the fabric on the board while the paint dries; the board will help set the paint.

Fabric. You can paint a length of fabric before cutting and sewing it into a project, or paint directly onto a ready-made garment. Wash any fabric you purchase before you paint it.

A woven or knit fabric of cotton or cotton/polyester blend, of any weight, will give the best color resolution from the paint. A 65 percent cotton/35 percent polyester blend is best, but you can use a fabric with as much as 50 percent polyester. Avoid other synthetic fabrics; they won't retain the high color intensity that these fibers will.

Choose white or a pale pastel fabric if you don't want the fabric color to interfere with your paint colors.

If you want to paint within specific design lines, transfer the design to the fabric before you start painting, using the directions under "How to transfer a design" on page 38.

Paint. Fabric paints are made of pigments that actually dye the fabric when and where they're applied. Once the paint is set with heat, it permanently impregnates the fabric and won't wash out or wear off.

All types of fabric paint come with manufacturer's directions for application and cleanup.

Artist's acrylic paints aren't recommended for children's clothes. Once dry, they form a crust on fabric that can flake off; in addition, they require dry cleaning. But acrylics are useful for painting shoes or other accessories—to carry a particular color or design to all parts of a child's wardrobe.

Direct painting

Painting is the easiest and quickest way to enhance fabric. Using motifs ranging from simple abstract paint strokes and repeating patterns to elaborate murals, you can make your own patterned fabric for any purpose.

Use artist's brushes to apply fabric paint. If you want a bold stroke, use a large brush.

Place a small amount of each paint color in a white plastic bubble tray—the type used for water colors (**Ill. 3**). If you expose large amounts of paint or work directly from an open paint jar, your paint will dry out.

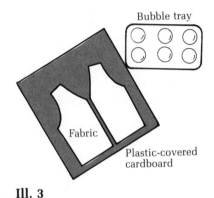

Ill. 3

Mix paints to create any color or intensity you want. Add extender or water for a paler, water-color look.

If your design calls for clean, sharp lines at the edges of each painted area, place masking tape along those edges before you begin to paint. The tape will prevent the paint from seeping through, and there'll be a sharp edge when it's removed (**Ill. 4**).

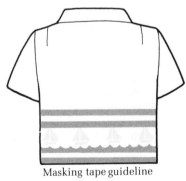

Masking tape guideline

Ill. 4

Use the masking tape technique to keep the edges between adjoining colors sharp, but don't apply the tape to a painted area until the paint is completely dry.

Hesitant to put the first line of paint on your fabric? Loosen up by trying your hand on some scrap fabric—you'll soon be eager to get to your project, and then to another, and another.

Once you've finished painting a project, let the paint dry thoroughly before lifting the fabric from the plastic-covered surface. Then heat-set the painted surface to fix the colors permanently: with a dry iron, press the fabric, using the paint manufacturer's directions for temperature and time.

Stamping

Stamps can be made from practically anything you have on hand. They're easy to use, so let your preschoolers join in the fun.

Repeating shapes in single file can add a final touch around a garment's hem, yoke, cuffs, or bib. Or watch a bigger and bigger design grow as you stamp large areas of fabric.

Below, you'll find a variety of common stamp-making materials to choose from—and you may want to invent your own.

When you make stamps, remember that the pattern you cut will appear as a mirror image when stamped onto fabric. If you have a one-way design, such as one using letters and numbers, be sure to cut it backwards (**Ill. 5**).

Potato stamp

Ill. 5

To prepare for stamping, spread fabric paint on a piece of aluminum foil or a cooky sheet. Use a plastic-covered piece of cardboard underneath the fabric, as described on the facing page in "Setting up to paint." Stamp the paint over the fabric, pressing firmly to ensure adequate paint transfer. Let it dry before moving the fabric. Heat-set the painted surface as described in "Direct painting," at left.

Potato stamps. These are age-old stamping tools. To make one, cut a potato crosswise and mark your design in pencil on the cut surface. With an art knife or narrow kitchen knife, cut away any part of the potato that isn't within the design lines, making a raised surface for your print.

Foam. The foam you use to fill mats or cushions makes a good stamping surface. Cut the foam into shapes with scissors, and glue each shape to a piece of heavy cardboard or acrylic to make a backing and handle (**Ill. 6**).

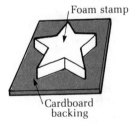

Foam stamp

Cardboard backing

Ill. 6

Rubber stamps. Those wonderful stamps you see in stationery stores make good fabric-paint stamps. Just spread fabric paint onto an uninked stamp pad and press the stamp into the pad to pick up paint. Use a piece of rubber foam as a pad if you can't locate an uninked stamp pad.

(Continued on page 54)

Stenciling

Stencils make repeating patterns that are quick and easy to complete. Whether the motif is galloping horses or entwined flowering vines, professional-looking results are yours with very little effort when you use stencils. Make your own designs (see below), or purchase ready-made stencils in fabric, craft, or art supply stores.

To prepare for stenciling, follow the guidelines in "Setting up to paint," page 52. Stretch your fabric over the plastic-covered cardboard; tape it in place with masking tape to prevent it from slipping. Also tape your stencil in place on the fabric.

Handling the paint. A special stencil fabric paint is available—it's like fabric paint, but thicker. Its thickness prevents it from running or smearing under the stencil cutout and from drying out if you use it directly from the jar.

The thickness also keeps the paint from permeating the wrong side of the fabric. This is quite a plus when you want to paint on finished garments, especially those with linings.

You'll need only a small amount of paint at a time. Don't be tempted to use too much; it will bleed through the fabric. To apply the paint, use a stencil brush with a thick set of bristles, cut bluntly across the bottom. Apply paint either by pouncing the brush (tapping it directly against the fabric) or by using a circular motion, working from the outer edge of each shape toward the center.

Work with one stencil and one paint color at a time. After you've filled in all the spaces on one stencil, let the paint set for a

few minutes before removing the stencil. Then align and tape the next stencil, using the registration marks for accurate placement. Be careful not to smudge the paint; it's thick and may take some time to dry.

Once the paint is dry, heat-set the stenciled fabric, using the method described in "Direct painting," page 52.

Making a stencil. You can create or adapt any design you want to make your own stencil.

Stencil paper is inexpensive and will withstand repeated use. But you might consider using acetate instead—its transparency makes it easy to position on the fabric, and it's especially useful when you have multiple layers of stencils.

Trace your design onto stencil paper, using the techniques in "How to transfer a design" on page 38, or trace it on acetate, using a felt-tip pen. Use a different stencil layer for each color in the design.

Cut the stencil with an art knife, working over a heavy cardboard or glass surface.

Use registration marks to line up each repeating design or different-color stencil (**Ill. 7**).

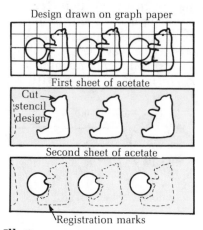

Design drawn on graph paper

First sheet of acetate

Cut stencil design

Second sheet of acetate

Registration marks

Ill. 7

Adhesive stencils. Letter and numeral stencils on adhesive paper are available in various sizes. They can be used in either of the two ways described below.

In the first method, cut the background adhesive evenly between letters to make rectangles with a letter in the center of each; pull a background rectangle away from its backing and apply it to the fabric. Mark a guideline on the fabric for straight placement of each letter. Use the spacing dots on the stencils or space each letter evenly according to your own specifications.

Fill the letter space with paint. After the paint has set for a few minutes, remove the adhesive. You'll have a clearly defined letter painted onto your fabric (**Ill. 8**).

Adhesive background

Ill. 8

To use the second method, apply the adhesive letters themselves to the fabric along marked guidelines (see above). Affix all the letters before you begin to paint. Draw a design around them and apply masking tape to the design edges as directed under "Direct painting," page 52, to keep the edges sharp when painted. Paint over the letters, filling in the design. After the paint has set for a few minutes, lift the letters. You'll have letters the color of your fabric, surrounded by a paint color (**Ill. 9**).

Adhesive letter

Ill. 9

Alternatives to paint

Besides fabric paint, there are several other ways to color designs on fabric. Fabric-marking crayons and indelible-ink markers are two examples.

Fabric crayons. Children especially enjoy using fabric crayons—they look just like wax ones. Look for iron-on crayons or pastel dye sticks in art supply stores, hobby shops, or fabric stores.

Follow the manufacturer's directions for coloring and heat-setting the crayon or pastel designs.

Felt markers. Use indelible felt-tipped markers to add highlights or details—such as whiskers on a cat's face or rosy cheeks on a stuffed doll—to painted or appliquéd designs.

Also use markers to draw on small areas of fabric, such as socks, tights, collars, and cuffs.

Heat-setting isn't necessary to make indelible ink permanent. Once you've marked your fabric, the line is there to stay. These markers are best kept out of reach of children.

Paint a pretty picture

Kids love color, and with fabric paints you can add it with abandon. Whether you brush it, stamp it, or stencil it, fabric paint adds glorious colors with amazing ease. From head to toe, hair ribbons to sneakers, on bibs, buntings, overalls, shirts, skirts, and jackets—everything becomes a canvas for fabric paints.

Children's Clothes   55

Dyeing fabric

Plain knit shirts and socks, or even canvas coveralls take on a whole new life when they're dyed in vibrant colors. Hand-me-downs that look faded and sad turn bright and exciting after a dyebath in your child's favorite color.

Clothes made of natural fibers, such as cotton and wool, absorb and retain color intensity better than synthetics. Fiber blends are also suitable, but 100 percent synthetics may not hold a color satisfactorily.

Dyeing techniques

Though several types of fabric dye are available, they're basically either hot-water or cold-water dye. Check the package to be sure the dye you choose provides the best color absorption and is safest for your fabric.

Whatever dye you choose, follow the manufacturer's directions carefully, and let the hints below lead you to successful results.

● If possible, use a fabric scrap to test the fabric's ability to retain the dye. To see how the color sets, let the scrap dry; it will be a lighter shade dry than it was wet.

● Wash new fabrics before dyeing them, to remove any finishes that might inhibit the dyeing process. Also wash used garments to remove spots or soil.

● Protect yourself with rubber gloves and a smock.

● To create different colors, mix dye solutions according to package directions. Also take your fabric color into account: any color already on the garment will combine with the dye to produce a third color. For example, a light yellow shirt dyed in blue dye will turn green.

More dyeing ideas

It isn't necessary to dye an entire garment uniformly in order to change its color. You can paint with dye, using as many colors as you like; you can inhibit color absorption with wax; or you can dip the garment repeatedly into the dye for graded shades of color.

Painting. Paint dye solution directly onto fabric just as you would fabric paints (see "Direct painting" on page 52). Though the technique is the same, the results may be slightly different.

Dye solution is thinner than fabric paint; when it penetrates the fabric, it migrates slightly into the neighboring fibers. The edges of a line painted with dye will be soft and fuzzy, rather than sharp.

Use this softness to your advantage when designing your dye-painted pattern. Neighboring colors will blend with each other, creating a third color.

When it's dry, heat-set the dyed fabric to make the dye permanent. Follow the directions under "Direct painting," page 52.

Resist dyeing. The *resist method* is a batik variation, involving the application of wax to create a design (**Ill. 1**). Any area of fabric you cover with wax before dyeing will remain uncolored after the dye is applied and the wax is removed.

Melt paraffin and apply it to the fabric, covering the areas you don't want dyed. Use an inexpensive natural-bristle paintbrush; you'll discard it when your project is complete.

Once the wax dries, paint your design on the fabric with dye, following the directions in "Direct painting" on page 52. The waxed areas will repel any dye applied to them.

Let the dye dry thoroughly. To remove the wax, sandwich the fabric between layers of newsprint and press with a hot, dry iron for about 20 seconds to melt the wax out of the fabric. The newsprint will absorb almost all the melted wax. Wash the fabric to remove any wax residue.

Ombré colors. A subtle flow from a light to a dark shade of color—the French call it *ombré*—is easily obtained by repeatedly dipping fabric in dye. Rubber gloves are particularly important for this technique.

Submerge the entire garment or length of fabric in the dyebath for just a few minutes. Remove and rinse the fabric according to the dye manufacturer's directions. Repeat the dyeing process several times, each time dipping less of the garment into the dyebath (**Ill. 2**).

Ill. 1

Ill. 2

Young artists' gallery

As soon as they can hold a marker, children are fascinated with the art they create. Their early random lines and shapes progress into primitive figures.

Through their artwork, you can see the amazing development of children's muscle control and coordination and their perception of the surrounding world.

Keep those treasured dabblings permanently on display—preserve them on fabric, using such thread or fabric techniques as embroidery or appliqué. Or let your budding artists create directly on fabric with fabric paints or markers.

You can make aprons, jackets, book bags, pillows, or even quilt squares with your new "designer" fabric (**Ill. 1**). Or you can use it to adorn finished garments, sheets, or curtains—adding new life to simple backgrounds.

Ill. 1

Art in a new medium

Your children hurry home from nursery school or day care and proudly present their artwork of the day. But—horrors—you've run out of space on the refrigerator gallery. What to do? Try immortalizing the art by transferring it to a garment or piece of fabric via hand or machine embroidery, appliqué, or fabric paint.

Follow the instructions in "How to transfer a design," on page 38, to enlarge or reduce the drawing to fit the intended project, and to transfer the basic lines of the art onto the fabric. Then follow this book's instructions dealing with the medium of your choice.

Whatever your medium, be sure your rendition captures the whimsy and color of the original drawing. Let your young artist have some influence in the fabric makeover by choosing the thread or fabric colors.

Use further techniques to embellish the new fabric art. For example, add dimension to an appliqué with quilting, or enhance it with embroidered details (**Ill. 2**).

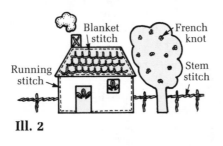

Ill. 2

Painting on a fabric canvas

It's a rainy day and the children are quickly losing interest in their crayon-and-paper drawings. Replace the paper with fabric and the crayons with fabric paint or fabric crayons. Along with gleeful children, absorbed in their work, you'll be rewarded with some very special custom-designed fabric.

Rarely is inspiration an obstacle, but a child's ability may be. Understand your child's artistic capabilities and tailor your project to them.

Toddlers may not draw specific shapes, but they're masters of the squiggly lines that soon become wonderful abstract patterns, full of color and movement. They can also manipulate stamps made of potato, foam, or rubber. Preschoolers can handle paintbrushes and fabric crayons, as well as simple stencil designs.

The "Painting" instructions on pages 52–55 will give you ideas and information on fabric paints and how to handle them on fabric.

Carefully cover any surface in the work area that you don't want painted, including the children's clothing. Secure a stretched length of fabric to a covered floor, table, or wall.

For painting or stenciling, place a small amount of each paint color in a saucer, and supply large-handled brushes to work with. Children can dip their paintbrushes into assorted colors and splatter the fabric with dots and splashes.

For even freer forms, spread the paint onto a cooky sheet, so toddlers can dip their hands into it and fingerpaint or fingerprint.

Let children design their own potato stamps, and help them cut out the shapes. Then let them freely experiment, stamping designs in different colors all over the fabric.

Stencils are another way for children to manipulate paint into a neatly defined design. Make the stencil shapes simple and relatively large (at least 4 inches in diameter).

Children can place the stencils where they please and spread the paint over the design. Once the paint is dry and the stencils removed, they can decorate any remaining spaces.

Projects

A bounty of bibs

Making clothes for children can be more fun than you ever imagined. Their garment designs have simple lines that make for fast and simple sewing and allow lots of room for personalizing.

Then there's the bonus of whimsy: you can let your imagination run wild when you sew children's clothes. Who but a child would dare to dance in a pair of bear paws (page 60)? And bibs (at right) are a good place to free your decorative fancy.

Since boys and girls up to age six have the same body types, their clothing patterns are interchangeable. The colors, patterns, embellishments, or trims you use will personalize each item you make. For example, the jacket or vest on page 62 gains its character from the trims you use to decorate it. Let your child help choose the fabric and trims; it'll be a rewarding experience for both of you.

Choose machine washable and dryable fabrics for all children's clothes. Preshrink all fabrics before you begin a garment.

For each project that follows, a reduced pattern appears on a grid. Enlarge the pattern, following the instructions in "How to transfer a design" on page 38.

Here are three easy bib patterns you can personalize with trims from rickrack to ribbons, or with enhancements from cross stitch to patchwork; see pages 24–57 for embellishment ideas.

Just about any firmly woven fabric can be used for a bib, as long as it's machine washable. For double mileage, make the bibs reversible by using a backing fabric with a texture or print that contrasts with the front fabric.

You'll need . . .

Circular bib—11½″ diameter:
- ⅓ yard fabric
- ⅓ yard medium-weight interfacing (optional)
- ¾ yard piping
- ¾ yard wide single-fold bias tape

Rectangular bib—10 by 15″:
- ½ yard fabric
- ½ yard medium-weight interfacing (optional)
- 2 yards wide single-fold bias tape

Bib with pocket—12″ long:
- ½ yard vinyl fabric
- 2¼ yards double-fold bias tape

Note: The yardage listed will accommodate several bib pieces; depending on the width of your fabric, you'll be able to make from two to four complete bibs.

Circular bib

1 Enlarge pattern pieces A (bib) and B (ruffle) to full size, using grid scale. Cut fabric pieces as directed on grid (cut one of the A pieces in a contrasting fabric, if desired); add any embellishments.

2 Cut two A pieces from interfacing, if desired. Baste interfacing to wrong side of each bib piece.

3 Pin piping to right side of bib front, ½ inch from outer edge. Using a zipper presser foot, baste along piping stitching line (see page 34).

4 Stitch ruffle strips together along short end, ¼ inch from raw edge; press seam allowances open. Fold strip in half lengthwise, wrong sides together. With a long machine stitch, stitch ⅜ inch from raw edges; pull bobbin thread to gather fabric.

5 With raw edges matching, pin ruffle to right side of bib front along outer edge, spacing gathers to fit; baste ⅜ inch from edge.

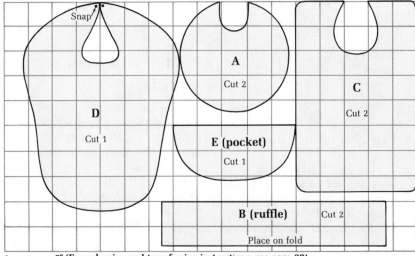

1 square = 2″ (For enlarging and transferring instructions, see page 38)
Seam allowances included

6 Pin bib back piece to front, right sides together. With bib front on top, stitch around outer edge, just inside piping basting stitches. Turn bib right side out; press. Baste opening closed.

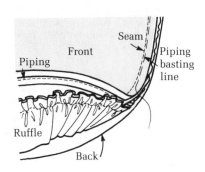

7 Press short ends of bias tape ¼ inch to wrong side. Matching center of neck to center of bias tape, encase neck edge of bib with bias tape, as described in "Encasing a raw edge," page 33. Stitch from one end of bias tape to the other, creating ties at the same time you finish neck edge.

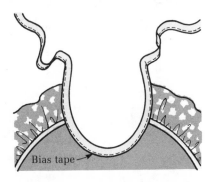

Bias tape

Rectangular bib

1 Enlarge pattern piece C to full size, using grid scale. Cut two fabric pieces, one in a contrasting fabric, if desired; add any embellishments.

2 Cut two C pieces from interfacing, if desired. Baste interfacing to wrong side of each fabric piece.

3 Pin front and back bib pieces, right sides together; stitch ½ inch from edge, leaving neck edge open. Turn right side out; press.

4 Cut a 44-inch piece of bias tape to encase neck edge of bib, following Circular Bib Step 7.

Optional: Encase outer edges of bib, as described in "Encasing a raw edge," page 33.

Bib with pocket

1 Enlarge pattern pieces D (bib) and E (pocket) to full size, using grid scale. Cut fabric pieces.

2 Using the topstitched application described in "Encasing a raw edge," page 33, encase straight edge of pocket with bias tape. Pin *wrong* side of pocket to *right* side of bib; stitch ¼ inch from edge, leaving top edge of pocket open.

3 Using the same topstitched application as in Step 2, encase outer edges of bib and neck edge with bias tape.

4 Sew snap to bib neck at marks.

Design: Tricia Bourdakis.

Animal slippers

Usually slippers are quickly forgotten and banished to the back of the closet. Not so with these friendly faces! One basic pattern helps you create a pair of lambs, cats, frogs, or bear paws that are sure to please the most discerning little feet.

You'll need . . .

To make one pair of slippers:

½ yard fabric (Use machine washable fake fur for cats and bear paws, fake fleece for lambs, corduroy for frogs.)

10 by 45-inch lightweight lining fabric

¼-inch-thick batting

1 package grip-fabric (sold for pajama bottoms)

4 black ball buttons* *(for lamb, cat, or frog eyes)*

White satin scrap *(for frog eyes)*

Synthetic suede scrap *(for bear claws or lamb ears)*

White fur scrap *(for cat ears)*

2 small pompons *(for cat noses)*

Dental floss *(for cat whiskers)*

*For infants and young toddlers, you may prefer to make embroidered eyes (using black satin stitches) instead of sewing on buttons. This is a safety precaution for children who are still trying to pull or chew on anything tuggable.

Stitching the slippers

Note: Stitch ¼-inch seams throughout.

1 Outline child's foot on paper. Measure length of foot and add 1 inch. Divide number of inches by 6 to determine size of your pattern grid squares. (Example: Child's foot is 4¼ inches long. Adding 1 inch equals 5¼ inches; dividing by 6 equals 0.875 [or ⅞] inch.) Make grid squares ⅞ inch for all pattern pieces, or round up to 1 inch if your child is growing quickly. Draw grid and transfer each pattern piece from grid below.

2 Cut fabric pieces, as follows: Cut 2 Tops from fake fur or fabric, and 2 Tops from lining. (*To make frog, also cut 2 Tops from batting.*) To cut fake fur, pin pattern pieces to wrong side of fabric; cut backing only, avoiding cutting into the pile.

Cut 2 Soles each from grip-fabric, batting, and Top fabric, reversing pattern for right and left foot.

For frog eyes, lamb ears, and cat ears, cut 2 of the 4 pieces from a contrasting fabric (see materials list above for suggestions).

3 For each slipper, pin Top fabric and lining, right sides together. Stitch around inside curve; clip seam. If using fake fur, carefully pull hair ends from seam to avoid flattened ridge at seamline.

For frog Top, baste batting to wrong side of fabric and work with fabric and batting as one piece. Trim batting seam allowance close to seam.

4 Press seam allowances open. With lining pulled away from fabric, stitch back seam as shown in illustration below.

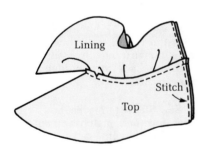

5 Baste the 3 Sole layers together—grip-fabric, right side down; then batting; then slipper fabric, right side up.

6 With slipper inside out, pin Sole to Top, holding edge of Top lining away from seam; stitch around outside edge. Slipstitch lining to Sole, enclosing seam allowance.

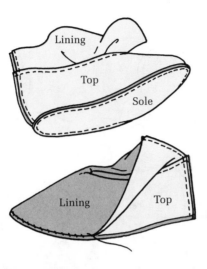

7 Turn slippers right side out. Stitch-in-the-ditch (see Glossary, page 9) at back seam to prevent lining from slipping.

8 *For frog eyes, cat ears, and lamb forehead,* stitch pieces, right sides together, leaving bottom edges open. *For bear claws,* fold each piece with right side inside; stitch along straight edge.

Turn pieces right side out and stuff with batting. Turn raw edges ¼ inch to inside and slipstitch pieces to slippers.

For lamb ears, blanket stitch suede and fleece pieces, wrong sides together. Slipstitch to slippers.

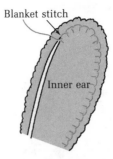

9 *Sew button eyes (and cat noses)* in place with heavy-duty thread. (Or embroider eyes, using a satin stitch with 3 strands black embroidery floss.)

Make cat whiskers by threading a 4-inch piece of dental floss through Top; tie ends in a square knot. Do this twice on each side of nose. Trim whiskers to desired length.

Design: Françoise Kirkman.

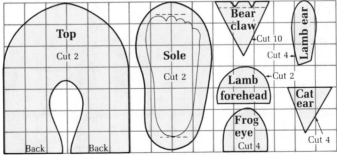

1 square = length of foot + 1″ ÷ 6   ¼″ seam allowance included
(For enlarging and transferring instructions, see page 38)

Children's Clothes   61

Wardrobe toppers: Jackets & vests

From one simple pattern, you can make a wardrobe of jackets and vests for boys and girls. Add sleeves for a jacket; leave them off for a vest. Use a center or asymmetric opening, with ties or buttons to lock in warmth.

You'll need . . .

  1 yard quilted fabric or medium to heavyweight nonquilted fabric

  1½ yards wide bias tape

  ¼ yard fabric for front band

  1 yard lining fabric (optional)

Making the pattern

1 Determine the appropriate size pattern by measuring around the child's chest when he or she is fully dressed; add 2 inches to this measurement. Pattern sizes are shown at the top of the next column; if your child's measurement is in between two sizes, use the larger size.

Size 1: 23″ chest   Size 4: 27″ chest
Size 2: 25″ chest   Size 6: 29″ chest

2 Enlarge the pattern using the grid scale (see page 38); then make any necessary adjustments for size on the full-size pattern (see chart on facing page).

Optional: To make an asymmetric closing, first cut the back and front Jacket patterns apart at the shoulder line, and add ½-inch seam allowances to all shoulder edges. Then redraw *one* front closing by moving front edge 2 inches past original line. Extend diagonal neck edge to intersect new front edge.

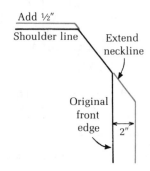

Add ½″
Shoulder line
Extend neckline
Original front edge
2″

Making the jacket

Note: If you don't line the jacket, stitch flat-fell seams (page 16).

1 Cut fabric pieces as directed on grid, and add any embellishments (see pages 24–57 for ideas). If you cut pattern at shoulder line to make an asymmetric closing, stitch front pieces to back at shoulders, right sides together.

2 Sew Sleeves to Jacket body, right sides together, matching center of Sleeve edge with Jacket shoulder line.

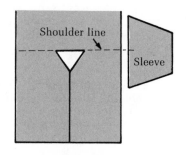

Shoulder line
Sleeve

3 Fold garment in half at shoulder line, wrong sides together. On both sides, sew side seam and underarm seam as one.

Optional: Sew lining pieces, following steps 1–3. Baste to jacket, wrong sides together.

4 Stitch Neckband and Front band pieces together with a ¼-inch seam; press seam allowances open. Turn one long edge of band ¼ inch to wrong side; press.

5 Pin unfolded edge of band to jacket front edge with *right* side of band on *wrong* side of jacket; match neckband markings with shoulder lines. Stitch ¼ inch from edge. Press band and seam allowances away from jacket.

6 Fold band over onto right side of jacket and pin to jacket front just beyond stitching line; edgestitch.

7 Finish sleeve and hem edges with bias tape, following directions in "Encasing a raw edge" on page 33.

8 Make closing ties by cutting 4 strips of bias tape 8 inches long. Turn short ends ¼ inch to wrong side. Fold strip in half lengthwise with wrong sides together. Topstitch ⅛ inch from all edges. Evenly space ties at front closing and stitch just inside front band, as shown, above right.

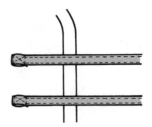

Optional: Buttons can be used instead of ties, but garment will fit a little more snugly. Position them at seamline of jacket and front band.

Making the vest

Note: If you don't line the vest, stitch flat fell seams (page 16).

1 Cut Vest as directed in Jacket Step 1, omitting Sleeves.

Optional: Cut lining piece; base to Vest, wrong sides together.

2 Cut 2 strips of bias tape—each 13 inches long for Size 1, 14 inches for Size 2, 15 inches for Size 4, 16 inches for Size 6. Matching center of bias tape to shoulder line, stitch bias tape to each Vest armhole. Follow techniques described in "Encasing a raw edge" on page 33.

3 Finish vest, following Jacket Steps 3–8.

Design: Stephanie Thompson of Mousefeathers.

(diagram: Front band Cut 2; Neckband Cut 1; Jacket back Cut 1; Shoulder; Jacket front; Sleeve Cut 2)

1 square = 2" (For enlarging and transferring instructions, see page 38)

½" seam allowance included

Pattern Size	Adjustment in Length	Width	Sleeve	Front Band
1	Subtract 1" from both front and back lower edges	Subtract ½" from each side edge (2" decrease overall)	Subtract 1" from upper sleeve edge	Subtract 1" from band length
2	No change	No change	No change	No change
4	Add 1" to both front and back lower edges	Add ½" to each side edge (2" increase overall)	Add 1" to upper sleeve edge	Add 1" to band length
6	Add 2" to both front and back lower edges	Add 1" to each side edge (4" increase overall)	Add 2" to upper sleeve edge	Add 2" to band length

Toys & Accessories

Playthings, quilts, room decorations

The dolls, toys, quilts, and decorations in this chapter are designed especially for infants, toddlers, and preschoolers. The skill level required for making each project varies from novice (banners or hobby horses) to advanced (stenciled quilt or playhouse), but with a little time and patience, even the toughest can be tackled.

For most of the following projects, a reduced pattern appears on a grid. Enlarge the pattern, following the instructions in "How to transfer a design," page 38.

Stuffed accessories

Either pinned to clothes or worn as pendants, these easy-to-make shapes are sure to please.

You'll need . . .

Scraps of felt (*For star, use metallic fabric*)

Loose batting

Safety pin (*For lamb necklace, use ⅛-inch-wide ribbon*)

Sequins (*for fish, elephant, and cowboy boot*)

Pearl cotton (*for elephant, cowboy boot, and lamb*)

Glass beads (*for elephant and lamb eyes*)

2 buttons (*for race car*)

Pipe cleaner (*for lamb*)

Ribbon, 1½ inches wide (*for star*)

General directions

Refer to specific project instructions below before proceeding.

1 Transfer pattern to stiff paper (see page 38); cut along outlines.

2 Outline pattern pieces on fabric; *don't* cut out shapes. Place 2 pieces of fabric together, marked side up; stitch short stitches along marked outline, leaving an opening.

3 Trim fabric close to stitching. Stuff main shape with batting, and stitch closed.

4 Add features to front of shape. Whipstitch safety pin to back.

Fish. Before stuffing, complete decorative stitching on tail and fins; stuff body only. Whipstitch fin in place. Sew rows of sequins, working from tail to head. Use 1 sequin for eye.

Elephant. Glue decorations on saddle; outline hoofs with felt-tipped pen. For tail, cut three 1-inch pieces of pearl cotton; fold them in half and wrap at top with thread. Thread pearl cotton through tail top and insert ends (½ inch long) into opening in body; stitch opening closed. Complete decorative stitching around ear, and whipstitch ear in place. Sew on glass bead eye.

Race car. Complete decorative stitching on "exhaust," and shade as shown in photo, using a black felt-tipped pen; insert tab of exhaust into opening, and stitch opening closed. Glue on fabric number and stripes, and sew on button wheels.

Cowboy boot. Stitch contrasting-color stripe on front before stitching boot together. Fold narrow strip at top so that edge is caught in seam, forming a loop. With double strand of pearl cotton, attach sequin for spur, wrapping cotton around boot. Blanket stitch over cotton on instep.

Lamb. Using pearl cotton, sew bullion stitches (see page 27) on front before stitching lamb together. Use zipper foot to stitch around edge of shape. Before stuffing lamb, cut pipe cleaner in half; fold both pieces in half and insert them together into openings (as shown on grid) to form 4 legs and a double loop at the top. Stitch ears in place. Sew on beads for eyes. Add a stitch of thread for each nostril. Tack small bow to forehead. Thread 2 strands of ⅛-inch-wide ribbon through loop for necklace.

Star. Draw star on wrong side of metallic fabric. Place 2 pieces of fabric right sides together, and stitch around outline. Trim close to stitching, turn right side out, and stuff. Decorate with felt and ribbon.

Design: Phyllis Dunstan.

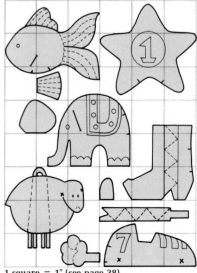

1 square = 1" (see page 38)
Cut 2 of each piece
Leave opening between notches

Fold & carry crib

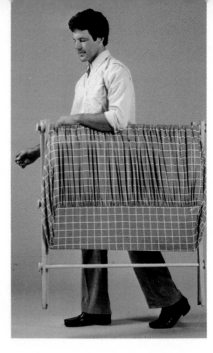

Portable and lightweight, this 36-inch crib allows you and baby to pick up and go—whether you're off to the beach or just to the back yard. Fabric handles make the crib easy to carry; a folding frame makes it easy to store in car trunk or closet.

You'll need . . .

4 1 by 2s, 4 feet long

5 ¾-inch hardwood dowels, each 36 inches long

10 2-inch wooden drawer pulls

10 2-inch #12 woodscrews

24 by 35-inch piece of ¼-inch plywood or tempered hardboard

Wood glue

4 yards medium-weight, firmly woven fabric, 45 inches wide

3½ yards ¼-inch nylon cord

24 by 35-inch foam mattress, 3 inches thick

1½ yards fabric (for mattress cover)

22-inch zipper

First the frame . . .

1 For each leg, make a 45 degree cut across one end of each 1 by 2. Measure from pointed end and cut boards 41 inches long. Starting at square end, mark each 1 by 2 at 2, 18½, and 32 inches. At each point, drill 3/4-inch holes for dowels. Sand to round off *square* ends only.

2 On each end of 4 dowels, place a drawer pull. Mark center, then drill hole through pull and dowel end for screw.

3 Connect two legs by running a dowel through bottom holes in 1 by 2s (angled ends of legs point same direction). Glue dowels into position; screw pulls to dowels. Repeat for other two legs.

4 Place frame halves together so legs cross at center holes, and angled ends of legs point outward. Cut two 1½-inch pieces of dowel. Glue one piece into *inner* 1 by 2 of each intersection, positioning dowel so one

end is flush with inside frame surface and other end projects toward other 1 by 2. Sand exposed dowel end to allow frame to pivot; don't glue outer 1 by 2s. Drill hole in pull and dowel, as in Step 2. Insert exposed dowel ends into outer 1 by 2s, and screw pull to dowel ends (see insert at right).

. . . Now the crib

1 Cut fabric pieces according to pattern and mark points for A, B, C, D, and E. Join Side pieces by matching A to A and D to D. Stitch right sides together ½ inch from edge.

2 Pin Slot Facing pieces along top edge at B, E, and C, right sides together. Mark slot; stitch along both sides of marking (see pattern). Cut slot. Turn Facing to inside; press and topstitch slot.

3 Turn under top edge of Side piece ½ inch, then 2½ inches, to make a casing. Stitch close to casing edge.

4 Gather bottom edge of Side piece (see "Gathering & stitching" on page 15) until markings on Side piece match Bottom piece. Pin and stitch Side to Bottom ½ inch from edge; stitch again ¼ inch from edge.

5 Stitch narrow ends of each Handle, right sides together, to make a loop. Press long edges under ¼ inch. Then fold Handle lengthwise, wrong sides together, so folded edges meet;

edgestitch. Stitch 1½ inches from bottom seam to make a loop for the dowel.

6 Insert dowels through casings from B to C, slipping Handle loop onto dowel at midpoints E.

7 Cut nylon cord in half. With each half make a 48-inch circumference circle; tie knot and trim excess. Feed cord loops through short ends of casing and slip loops over dowel ends.

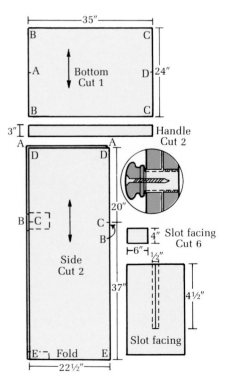

Fit dowels into frame; don't glue. Add pulls and screws, as in Frame Step 2.

8 Cut 2 pieces of mattress cover fabric, each 28¼ inches wide and 38 inches long. Placing right sides of fabric together, install zipper in one short side; open zipper a few inches. Keeping right sides together, stitch ½ inch from remaining edges. Open each corner and stitch across seam. Turn right side out through open zipper.

9 Mattress and board lie flat on bottom of bed. To close bed, turn mattress and board on their sides; fold bed frame and carry.

Design: Françoise Kirkman.

Alphabet quilt

Set aside several evenings to complete this project—you paint the stencils as you put the quilt together, and you must allow time for the paint to dry before continuing. This is a project for people with some sewing expertise.

You'll need . . .

For a 38½ by 48½-inch quilt:

4 yards neutral fabric (for quilt and backing)

⅝ yard rose fabric

¾ yard green fabric

2 yards polyester quilt batting

Thread to match neutral fabric

1 jar *each* of red, green, white, yellow, violet, and black fabric paint

#2 and #6 stencil brushes

Stencils: 1 package *each* 3, 2½, and 1-inch letters; 1 package 2½-inch numbers

Note: Our quilt was made with polished cotton. If you use this fabric, don't prewash—and don't machine launder the finished quilt. Dry cleaning is recommended to retain the fabric's polished appearance. If you're using plain cotton or cotton blends, do prewash all fabrics before starting your quilt.

Assembling the quilt

Note: Stitch all seams ⅜ inch from edge.

1 Mix all paint colors. For each, start with 1 teaspoon white, then add a little color. Seal with aluminum foil; store in refrigerator until ready to use. (For painting preparation and stenciling technique, see "Painting fabric," pages 52–55.)

Green = white, green, dash of red
Peach = white, red, yellow
Rose = white, red, dash of black
Lavender = white, violet

2 Cut rose fabric into 2½-inch-wide strips, green fabric into 5-inch-wide strips, from selvage to selvage.

3 Cut a 9 by 11-inch rectangle from neutral fabric. Mark guidelines on rectangle (see Diagram 2). Mark parallel lines 1½ inches from each guideline to create 1½-inch squares.

Stencil 1-inch letters in squares, alternating rose and peach colors. Let dry thoroughly; then heat-set (page 53).

4 From one green strip, cut four 5-inch squares; set aside. Using the rest of the strip, cut 1-inch-wide strips along crosswise grain. Fold 2 strips lengthwise, wrong sides together, and pin to short sides of rectangle; trim ends to fit. Baste ¼ inch from edge. These strips create a trimming, similar to piping but without a filler cord, between the center rectangle and rose strips.

5 Cut rose strips 1 and 2 (see Diagram 1) to fit short sides of rectangle. Pin to rectangle over green strips, right sides together; stitch. Turn rose strips right side up; press.

6 Trim two of the 1-inch-wide green strips to the length of remaining sides of the rectangle (not including rose fabric) plus ½ inch. Turn narrow edges of strips ¼ inch to wrong side; press. Fold strips lengthwise; center on remaining sides of rectangle (the strips won't extend to rose fabric). Baste to side of rectangle as in Step 4.

7 Cut rose strips 3 and 4 to fit long sides of rectangle; attach as in Step 5.

8 Cut batting and backing to fit rectangle; baste layers together. Machine quilt grid pattern in stenciled area; quilt rose strips in rows 1 inch apart. Refer to "Quilting," pages 48–51, for specific directions.

9 Cut 4½-inch-wide neutral strips 5–8, measuring length against rectangle. Cut out four 4½-inch squares and stitch to ends of strips 7 and 8. On strips, draw a guideline 1 inch from bottom edge; align bottom edge of letter on guideline. Using 2½-inch letters and green paint, begin and end stenciling ¾ inch from narrow edges. On each square, position a 2½-inch letter (see Diagram 3); stencil with rose paint. Let dry thoroughly; then heat-set.

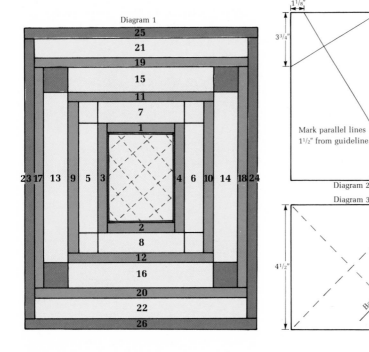

Diagram 1

Diagram 2

Mark parallel lines 1½" from guideline.

Diagram 3

Base for letter

10 Cut and pin strip 5 to quilted piece, right sides together. Cut and add a backing strip, the same size as strip 5, right side against *wrong* side of quilted piece; stitch through all layers. Press strip 5 and backing away from quilt. Cut batting to fit between backing and quilt; baste layers together. Quilt ¼ inch from seamline. Repeat for strips 6–8.

11 Cut and stitch rose strips 9–12 (and their backing) to rectangle. Quilt in rows 2 inches apart. Quilt ¼ inch from seam on stenciled strips.

12 For strips 13–16, cut 5-inch-wide strips of neutral fabric the length of rectangle. Placing 3-inch letters on fabric as in Step 9, stencil

with lavender paint. Let dry thoroughly; then heat-set.

13 Stitch 5-inch green squares to both ends of 15 and 16. Add strips 13–16 as in Step 10. Add rose strips 17–20 as in Step 11.

14 For strips 21 and 22, cut 4½-inch-wide strips from neutral fabric the width of rectangle. Begin and end stenciling ⅞ inch from narrow edges. Use 2½-inch number stencils and alternate rose and peach. Let dry thoroughly; then heat-set. Add to quilt as in Step 10.

15 Use green strips for strips 23–26. Stitch right sides of strips 23 and 24 to wrong side of quilt; press

strips away from seam. Turn remaining edge of strips ¼ inch to wrong side; press. Cut batting 4½ inches wide and the length of strips; whipstitch one edge to seam allowance.

16 Fold strip and batting to right side of quilt, overlapping seam ⅛ inch; stitch strip close to edge.

17 Cut strips 25 and 26 two inches longer than quilt edges. Stitch strips to quilt with 1 inch extending at sides. Fold fabric edge and add batting as in Step 15. Fold 1-inch extensions to inside, then repeat Step 16. Blindstitch edges closed.

Design: Phyllis Dunstan.

Animals-on-parade quilt

Appliquéd animal figures march across a vividly colored patchwork quilt, charming any child and brightening any room. Fabric loops transform this quilt from crib cover to wall hanging.

You'll need . . .

For quilt 36 by 45 inches:

1½ yards red fabric, 45 inches wide

2 yards yellow fabric, 45 inches wide

⅔ yard turquoise fabric

½ yard *each* purple and green fabric

1 yard quilt batting, 45 inches wide

Thread to match each fabric color

⅔ yard fusible web, or glue stick (optional)

Making appliqué strips

Note: Preshrink and press all fabrics.

1 Enlarge pattern pieces according to grid scale (see page 38). Cut four of each figure, reversing one figure for elephant and hippo. Use yellow fabric for hippos, green for camels, purple for cows, and turquoise for elephants.

2 Cut four crosswise strips, each 7½ by 37 inches, from red fabric.

Space animals evenly on each strip, positioning reversed hippo and elephant as shown in photograph. Baste in place with fusible web or glue stick, or thread baste (see "Basting," pages 39–40).

3 With same color thread as animal, machine appliqué animals to fabric, following directions on pages 40–41.

Making patchwork strips

Note: Use ½-inch seams throughout.

1 Cut nine lengthwise strips, each 3 by 20 inches, from both the turquoise and the red fabric; cut nine lengthwise strips, each 3 by 15 inches, from both the green and the purple fabric.

2 Alternating colors, sew turquoise and red strips, right sides together, along long edges. Press all seams in same direction. Repeat for green and purple strips.

3 To make checkerboard strips, mark lines 3 inches apart across turquoise and red striped fabric. Cut on marked lines to make six 3-inch-wide strips. Reassemble strips in sets of two, reversing strips so colors and seam allowance directions are opposite; stitch. You now have 3 strips of fabric 18 squares long and 2 squares wide. Set aside.

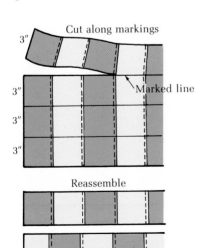

Cut along markings

3″

3″ Marked line

3″

3″

Reassemble

4 To make triangle strips, mark and cut across green and purple striped fabric, making four 3-inch-wide strips. Sew all four strips, right sides together, to make a checkerboard pattern. Cut out triangle strips, including ½-inch seam allowances, following directions for "Triangle rows" on page 46.

Assembling the quilt

1 Cut 8 crosswise strips, 1½ by 37 inches each, of yellow fabric. Stitch patchwork and appliqué strips together in the order shown in photograph, stitching a yellow strip between each two patterned strips.

2 Cut batting same size as quilt face. Cut yellow backing 3 inches wider and 3 inches longer than quilt face.

3 Lay backing on flat surface with wrong side up. Center batting over backing; then place quilt face over batting, right side up. Baste layers together (see "Basting," page 49).

4 Machine quilt through seamlines that join appliquéd and yellow strips (see "Machine quilting," page 49).

5 Trim backing to extend 1 inch beyond each side of quilt face. Fold side edges of backing ½ inch to inside; press. Bring folded edge over quilt face, pinning it to quilt ½ inch from edge. Stitch through all layers close to pinned edge. Repeat with top and bottom edges. Stitch a square at corners, as shown.

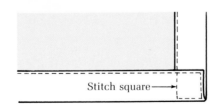

Stitch square →

6 Make dowel loops for wall hanging by cutting a strip of yellow fabric 2 by 16 inches. Fold strip in half lengthwise, right side out; press.

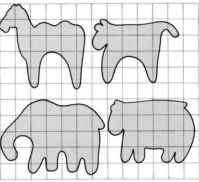

1 square = 1″ (see page)

Open strip and fold long edges to wrong side, meeting at crease; then fold again along crease and press. Stitch close to edges. Cut strip into 4 equal pieces.

7 Stitch together short ends of one piece, ¼ inch from edge. Turn loop so seam is on inside at bottom of loop. Stitch across loop ¼ inch from edge with seam. Repeat for remaining strips. Space loops evenly across top of quilt; hand stitch in place.

Design: Karen Cummings.

Snuggly sock dolls

These soft, huggable dolls will spend many a night tucked in bed alongside your child.

You'll need . . .

For one dressed doll:

1 pair athletic tube socks with stripes (men's socks *for Big Sister*, boys' socks *for Baby Brother*)

12 ounces loose polyester filling

1 skein of 2-ply yarn

2 black ¼-inch shank buttons; 1 white ½-inch flat button

1 package red and white extra-wide double-fold bias tape

Fabric crayons in red, pink, and brown

8-inch length of twill tape

1 package cocoa brown liquid dye

Heavy-duty thread

For Big Sister's clothes:

½ yard red and white calico fabric

½ yard blue and white calico fabric

½ yard elastic cord

For Baby Brother's clothes:

¼ yard blue and white calico fabric

Scrap of white flannel fabric

Making the doll

Note: Stitch all seams in dolls with narrow zigzag stitch, close to edge.

1 Cut stripes off socks; set aside for *Big Sister's shoes*. Mix dye with water, according to manufacturer's directions. Dye socks a shade darker than desired skin tone.

Enlarge pattern pieces according to grid scale (see page 38). Transfer body piece outlines to socks and cut out.

2 Stuff Head. To shape face, insert balls of batting under cheeks and chin. To form nose, cover ½-inch flat button with sock fabric by taking small running stitches around edge of fabric, and pulling up thread to gather fabric, enclosing button; then place button inside head and press into batting, between cheeks. To make nostrils, bring threaded needle up inside head, through one hole in fabric-covered button, and out through face at nostril point. Catching a few sock threads with needle, push needle back into face, through button, and through head to back; secure thread at back of head. Repeat for other nostril.

3 Mark locations for eyes; color cheeks, mouth, and eyebrows with fabric crayons. Bringing threaded needle up through head, shape mouth by taking a tiny stitch at each end, pulling thread tightly to depress fabric; repeat at center, if de-

sired. Secure thread at back of head. Sew on button eyes in same manner, using heavy-duty thread.

4 Pin Arm seams, right sides together, and stitch, leaving top open. (Avoid overstretching material.) Turn Arms right side out. To make Legs, first cut, fold, and stitch slashes in Leg pieces, forming feet. Then stitch and turn, as for Arms. Stuff Arms and Legs, molding knees with balls of batting.

Turn Body inside out; pin Legs and Arms between Body front and back, and stitch. Turn Body right side out, stuff, and slipstitch shoulders closed. Turning raw edges under, slipstitch head to body.

5 *To make Big Sister's hair*, cut a 4 by 9-inch piece of cardboard; wrap yarn lengthwise around it 100 times, and cut yarn along one edge of cardboard. Measure back of head from forehead to neck, and cut twill tape that length. Center yarn over tape, spreading to cover length of tape. Press transparent tape over yarn and twill tape; stitch through all layers. Peel off transparent tape. Cut bangs at one edge, if desired; hand stitch hair through twill tape to center of top and back of head, using heavy-duty thread. Tie pigtails with bias tape, and tack bias tape to head.

For Baby Brother's hair, follow same procedure but use 4 by 4-inch cardboard. Pull random strands forward and tack in small bunches around face; trim short.

---

1 square = 2" (For enlarging and transferring instructions, see page 38)   ¼" seam allowances included

Making the doll clothes

1 Enlarge pattern pieces and cut out fabric. Also cut an 8 by 26-inch rectangle for Skirt of *Big Sister's dress*.

2 For *Big Sister's dress*, make narrow hems (see page 9) at center back edges of Bodice. Stitch Bodice front to back at shoulders. Make narrow hems at lower Sleeve edges. Measure and cut elastic for wrist, and tie a knot at each end. Zigzag stitch over elastic on wrong side of Sleeve, ¾ inch from edge. Gather Sleeve caps; stitch to armholes. Stitch side and underarm seams in one continuous seam.

Leaving a 2-inch opening at top, stitch Skirt back seam. Gather Skirt top and stitch to Bodice. Make a narrow hem at bottom of Skirt. Topstitch bias tape to neck edge (see page 34). Make a buttonhole and sew button at dress neck. Center and tack a 24-inch length of bias tape over seam between Bodice and Skirt, for sash.

For *bloomers*, turn bottom edges of legs under ¼ inch; turn again and stitch. Measure and tie one end of elastic; thread elastic through casings. Stitch leg seams, then stitch crotch seam. Repeat casing procedure for waist.

For *Shoes*, zigzag seams; turn right side out.

3 For *Baby Brother's Top*, stitch side seams. Topstitch bias tape to neck, hem, and armhole edges, extending tape 2 inches on each side at top of armholes to make ties.

For *Diaper*, turn fabric edges under ¼ inch; zigzag hem.

Design: Philippa K. Mars and Babs Kavanaugh.

Furry friends

How can you resist the beguiling character and soft, cuddly features of these two woodland friends? Both make wonderful companions for the young and young-at-heart.

You'll need . . .

For one stuffed animal:

½ yard fake fur (*for raccoon, gray; for bear, brown*)

1½ pounds loose polyester filling

2 round ½-inch-diameter buttons for eyes

Scraps of synthetic suede (*beige for bear snout, inner ears, paw pads, and soles; brown for bear nose; gray for raccoon inner ears; black for raccoon nose and mouth*)

10 by 10-inch piece of black fake fur (*for raccoon tail and mask*)

¼ yard firmly woven black fabric (*for raccoon hands and feet*)

Note: To cut fake fur, pin pattern pieces to wrong side of fabric; cut backing only, avoiding cutting into the pile. When stitching seams, push pile away from seamlines.

Making the bear

1 Enlarge bear pattern (solid-line pieces) according to grid scale (see page 38). Cut fabric pieces as directed on grid, adding ½-inch seam allowances. Reverse pattern pieces for Body Side, Head Side, and Snout Side to make left and right sides. Cut Snout Top, Snout Sides, Chin, Paw Pads, Soles, and 2 of 4 Ear pieces from beige suede. Cut a 2-inch circle for Nose from brown suede. Cut all other pieces from brown fake fur.

2 Stitch curved darts in Body Front; press toward center. Appliqué Paw Pads to arms on Body Front.

3 Pin and stitch Body Side pieces to Body Front, right sides together, leaving feet open at bottom edge. Stitch again to reinforce curves; clip curves. Stitch Soles to bottoms of feet, right sides together; clip curves.

1 square = 2″ (see page 38)   Arrows indicate grainlines

Add ½″ seam allowances to all edges

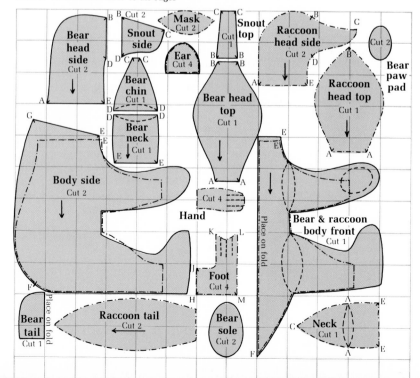

4 Stitch Body Side pieces, right sides together, along back seam.

5 To make head, stitch Snout Side pieces to corresponding Head Side pieces, and Snout Top to Head Top, right sides together, matching symbols. Stitch Chin and Neck together, then stitch curved dart in combined piece. With right sides facing, pin one Snout/Head Side piece to Chin/Neck piece, matching symbols; stitch. Repeat for other side. Then pin and stitch top Snout/Head piece in place. Clip curves and point; turn head right side out. Stitch darts in Nose; glue in place at tip of Snout.

6 With body wrong side out and head right side out, pin head to body, right sides together. Stitch, leaving back of neck open.

7 Turn bear right side out. Stuff body and head; slipstitch neck opening closed. Hand stitch button eyes in place.

8 Stitch inner and outer Ear pieces, right sides together, leaving bottom edge open. Clip curves and turn right side out. Turn raw edges under ½ inch; slipstitch Ears to head.

9 Fold Tail piece, right sides together; stitch curved side, leaving end open. Clip curves and trim seam. Turn right side out and stuff. Turn raw edges under ½ inch; slipstitch Tail to body at F.

Making the raccoon

1 Enlarge raccoon pattern (dotted-line pieces) according to grid scale (see page 38). Cut all fabric pieces *except Tail* as directed on grid, adding ½-inch seam allowances. Reverse pattern pieces for Body Side and Head Side to make left and right sides; reverse Hand and Foot patterns for 2 of the 4 pieces. Cut Hand and Foot pieces from black woven fabric; cut Mask from black fake fur. Cut 2 of the 4 Ear pieces from gray synthetic suede; cut Nose from black synthetic suede. All other pieces are cut from gray fake fur.

2 Stitch darts in Body Front; press toward center. With right sides together, stitch one Hand or Foot piece to each arm and leg on Body Front; repeat for limbs on Body Side pieces.

3 Pin and stitch Body Side pieces to Body Front, right sides together, leaving feet open between points K and L. Stitch again to reinforce curves; clip curves. To close each foot, bring raw edges together, matching seams in center; stitch across end.

4 Stitch Body Side pieces, right sides together, along back seam.

5 To assemble head, stitch Head Top to one Head Side piece, right sides together, matching symbols. Repeat for other Head Side. Stitch Head Sides together from B to C. Stitch curved dart in Neck, and then stitch to Head Side pieces, matching symbols. Clip curves and points; turn head right side out.

6 Follow Bear Step 6.

7 Turn raccoon right side out and stuff. Fill hands and feet first, then stitch fingers and toes along markings. Continue stuffing body and head; slipstitch neck opening closed.

8 Trim fur on snout close to backing; also trim Mask pieces. Machine zigzag along edge of Mask pieces; hand stitch them in place on face. Cut 2 by ¼-inch mouth from black synthetic suede. Hand stitch Nose, mouth, and button eyes to face.

9 Follow Bear Step 8.

10 To make Tail, cut five 9 by 2½-inch strips *each* of gray and black fur. Alternating colors, stitch them together with ¼-inch seams to make a 10 by 9-inch rectangle. Cut Tail pieces from rectangle. Stitch pieces, right sides together, matching fabric stripes. Clip point; turn Tail right side out and stuff. Turn raw edges under ½ inch; slipstitch Tail to body at F.

Design: Françoise Kirkman.

Learning toy: Lesson in a shoe

While playing with the Old Woman and her shoe, children can practice such skills as lacing, zipping, buttoning, tying, and snapping. Dolls of Mom and kids double as finger puppets for hours of absorbing imaginative play.

You'll need . . .

For one shoe house:

¾ yard blue felt

¼ yard gray felt

2 pieces black felt, 9½ by 11 inches

1 9 by 9-inch square *each* white, pink, red, brown, bright green, and dark green felt

⅜ yard polyester fleece

¾ yard craft-weight interfacing

1 package small appliqués of cherries

1 plastic separating zipper, 9 inches long

18 ¾-inch circles of nylon self-gripping fastener

2 red buttons, ¾ inch wide

1 large (coat-size) hook and eye

5 large sew-on snaps

10 hammer-on eyelets, ½-inch diameter

1 1½-inch buckle form

1 pair 38 to 40-inch shoelaces

Blue embroidery floss

Fabric glue or glue stick

Lightweight cardboard

For old woman and 6 children:

4 9 by 9-inch squares pink felt

Colored felt scraps

Yarn scraps

Black embroidery floss

Making the shoe house

1 Enlarge pattern pieces (see page 38). Transfer and cut as directed in steps below.

2 Cut 4 Side pieces from blue felt, 2 from fleece, and 2 from interfacing. Mark windows and door on one felt Side piece; transfer all other markings to same and one reversed felt piece.

3 With marked sides together, baste marked Side pieces, ½ inch from edge A; press seam open. Starting 1½ inches above bottom edge, install zipper in seam; stitch across top and bottom of zipper to secure to felt.

4 Spread zippered pieces on a flat surface, unmarked side up. Layer fleece, interfacing, then unmarked felt pieces on top (edges will overlap at center, over zipper); baste layers together.

5 On marked side, stitch just outside zipper stitching lines. On inside, cut the overlapping layers away from zipper area, close to stitching.

6 Topstitch sides through all layers, ⅜ inch from edges; trim fleece and interfacing from seam allowance between felt layers. Topstitch again, ⅛ inch from edges.

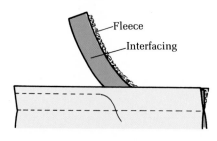
Fleece
Interfacing

7 Stitch along window and door markings. Stitch again ⅛ inch inside door markings. Cut out windows just inside stitching lines. Cut door between stitching lines along top, bottom, and right sides.

8 Cut two strips of red felt, ½ by 2 inches, for window boxes. Glue at bottoms of windows; stitch close to edges and across middle of each. Cut ¼-inch-wide strips of white felt for door trim; glue in place as marked; stitch close to edges of felt. Sew hook to door, eye to shoe, as door-fastening.

9 Cut tree and grass patterns from brown, dark green, and light green felt. Glue to plain Side; stitch in place. Glue and stitch cherry appliqués to tree.

10 Attach eyelets, as marked, to both front edges of Sides. Stitch red buttons and the loop halves of self-gripping fasteners to top edges, as marked.

11 Cut 2 Toe pieces from blue felt, 1 from fleece, and 1 from interfacing; transfer markings to one felt piece. Place marked felt piece on a flat surface, marked side down. Layer fleece, interfacing, then unmarked felt piece on top. Stitch as described in Step 6.

Stitch along window markings; cut out windows just inside stitching lines. Cut a red felt strip, ½ by 2¼ inches, for window box; stitch in place close to edges and across middle.

12 Cut two strips, 1 by 8½ inches, from blue felt; edgestitch strips together on long sides to make buckle strap. Pin strap to Toe at window, cutting edge at angle to fit; stitch in place. Cover buckle form with red felt. Cut a 1 by 6-inch strip of blue felt; fold in half and slip over buckle prong and center bar. Using a zipper foot, stitch across strip close to center bar. Attach free ends to Toe edge, as marked.

13 Transfer 3 long and 2 short Shutters onto white felt. Stitch along outlines through two layers of felt. Stitch horizontal lines with black thread, to make slats. Cut out shutters just outside stitching. Sew one snap half to back of each shutter and remaining half to shoe. Snap shutters in place.

14 Cut felt hearts, leaves, and numbers; glue to shutters and door.

15 Cut one Tongue from pink and one from blue felt; stitch together, ⅛ inch from edge. Sew tongue to toe at C, with edge of toe overlapping blue side of tongue ¼ inch.

16 Cut 2 Soles from blue felt, 1 from fleece, and 1 from interfacing; transfer markings to one felt piece. Place marked felt piece on a flat surface, marked side down. Layer fleece, interfacing, then unmarked felt piece. Stitch as described in Step 6. Then stitch marked lines across sole.

17 Place toe edges B over Sides, overlapping ¼ inch; stitch through all layers close to edge of toe. Pin top of shoe to sole, wrong sides together, matching center backs and center

toes. Blanket stitch pieces together, using 6 strands of embroidery floss.

18 Cut one end off each shoelace; overlapping cut edges, stitch laces together. Lace shoe, starting from bottom. Tie at top.

19 Cut 2 Roof pieces from black felt. On one piece stitch the hook sides of 12 self-gripping fasteners, as marked. On the other piece, stitch the hook sides of 4 fasteners, as marked. Stitch Roof pieces together, with fasteners facing out, along short

edges only. On roof inside (side with 4 fasteners), draw a line parallel to each short end, 1¾ inches from edge (you'll use these lines to position the roof ends). Fold Roof in half lengthwise, insides together, and press the crease.

20 Cut 4 Roof Ends from blue felt, omitting tabs from 2 pieces, for front gable. Cut 2 Roof Ends from interfacing ⅛ inch narrower on all edges; omit tabs on one of the interfacing pieces. Stitch layers together close to edges. Cut slits for buttonholes in tabs, as marked. Bind slit edges

(Continued on page 78)

. . . Learning toy

with a small blanket stitch, using 3 strands of embroidery floss.

21 Press roof-end flaps to inside. Pin *outside* of one flap to *inside* of roof, matching flap seamlines to marked line on roof, as shown; stitch through all layers. Repeat for remaining roof end.

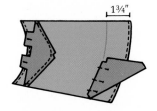

1¾"

22 Cut two pieces of cardboard, 4½ by 7½ inches. Slip into roof openings between layers of felt. Stitch close to lower edges of Roof.

23 Transfer Shingle outlines 6 times onto gray felt. Stitch along lines through two layers of felt, using small stitches; cut out just out-

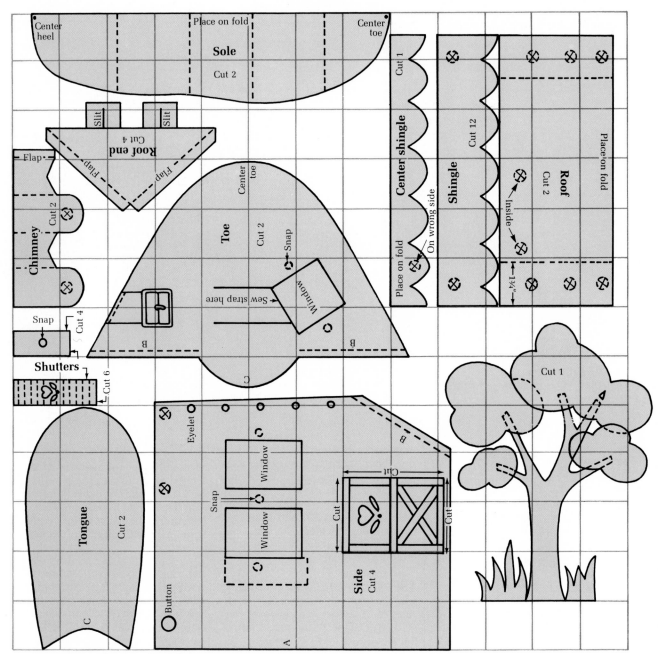

1 square = 2" (For enlarging and transferring instructions, see page 38)
Seam allowances included where necessary.

78   Toys & Accessories

side stitching. Stitch the loop side of a self-gripping fastener to each Shingle end, as marked.

24 Transfer Center Shingle strip onto gray felt; stitch along lines. Cut just outside stitching lines. At one end, stitch the hook sides of 2 self-gripping fasteners to outside, as marked. Glue center of underside to peak of roof.

25 Transfer Chimney onto red felt. Stitch along lines through two layers of felt. Then, with contrasting thread, stitch horizontal and vertical lines to make ¼-inch bricks above tabs. Cut out close to outline stitching. Stitch the loop sides of 2 self-gripping fasteners to inside of chimney tabs, as marked. Fold chimney on dotted lines; glue narrow flap to inside.

Making finger puppets

1 Enlarge patterns for Child and Old Woman. Trace patterns onto pink felt. Stitch on traced lines through two layers of felt, using small stitches; cut just outside stitching.

2 Cut eyes and cheeks from felt. (Optional: Use a paper or leather punch for perfect circles every time.) Embroider mouth with single strand of black floss. Glue eyes and cheeks in place.

3 Transfer clothing patterns onto felt scraps. Through two layers of felt, sew sides of dresses and sides and inside legs of overalls, on drawn lines. Cut out clothes just outside stitching and along lines; turn right side out. Dress each figure; slipstitch overall shoulders closed. Cut pockets and trims from felt scraps; glue in place.

4 In color to match each set of overalls, cut a 1 by 2-inch strip of felt; bring narrow edges together and stitch along raw edge. Tack to back of overalls for finger loop. Slip finger between girls' backs and dresses instead of making a loop.

5 To make each boy's hair, wrap yarn lengthwise around a 1¾ by 3½-inch piece of cardboard; don't overlap yarn when wrapping. Press tape over middle of yarn on one side of cardboard; slip yarn off cardboard. Keeping yarn flat, machine stitch down center of yarn, through tape and bottom layer of yarn; peel tape away. Sewing over first stitching, hand stitch yarn to center back of head, starting at forehead and ending at nape of neck. Cut yarn loops and trim to desired length. Apply glue to head to hold yarn ends in place.

6 To make each girl's hair, use a 1¾ by 5-inch piece of cardboard, and proceed as described above. Tie loose hair with ribbon, or braid hair.

7 For old woman's hair, use a bit of loose batting; glue in place.

Design: Phyllis Dunstan.

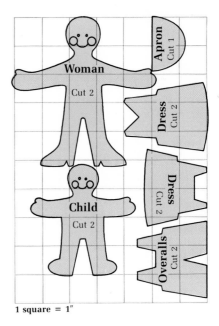

1 square = 1"

Child-size dolls

Lovably lifelike, these cuddly girl and boy dolls stand tall enough to wear toddlers' size 2 clothing—maybe their owners' hand-me-downs. Elastic foot loops link around a child's feet for dancing.

You'll need . . .

For one doll, 33 inches high:

1½ yards heavy unbleached muslin, 45 inches wide

1 package ½-inch elastic

2 white buttons, ½ inch in diameter

Felt scraps, black and white, for eyes

Felt-tipped pens or fabric crayons, for face

3 pounds loose polyester filling

Heavy-duty off-white thread

Cardboard

7½ ounces thick rug yarn (for girl's hair)

5½ ounces curly (bouclé) yarn (for boy's hair)

Making the doll

Note: Stitch ⅜-inch seams.

1 Enlarge and transfer patterns, including markings (see page 38). Fold muslin in half, selvage to selvage; cut out Doll pieces as indicated on grid.

2 With right sides together, making ¼-inch seams, stitch darts in Doll front and back. (Center dart in back of head joins 2 sides of Doll back.) Press all darts flat.

3 Stitch 2 Doll back pieces at center back seam, right sides together, leaving seam open between markings. With right sides together, stitch 2 pieces for each Arm, leaving upper end open. To reinforce, stitch again where thumb joins fingers. Clip seam allowance at wrist. Repeat for Legs, leaving seams open at toes (A-B-A) and at top of Leg. Stitch again to reinforce curve at ankle; clip seam allowances at ankle and back of knee.

4 With wrong side out, flatten toe area of each foot, folding at B and matching A's at center. Stitch across, B to A to B, to shape toe area.

Flatten each heel. Stitch across corner, as shown, to shape flat bottom of each foot.

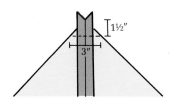

5 Turn Arms and Legs right side out. With filling, firmly stuff feet and calves of Legs; stuff thighs loosely. Stuff Arms firmly to within 1 inch of tops. Baste across tops of Arms and Legs to enclose filling.

6 With right sides together and raw edges even, place Legs between bottom edges of Doll front and back, making sure feet face forward. Stitch across bottom edge. Poke legs out through Doll back opening.

7 Baste Doll front to Doll back along sides and head; machine stitch as basted. Stitch again to reinforce curves at neck and waist; clip seam allowances. Cut slot in each shoulder, as marked. With thumbs facing up, insert Arms into slots, having right sides together and raw edges even. Check arm positions, then baste; machine stitch, using a zipper foot.

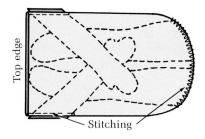

Stitching

8 Turn Doll right side out. Stuff with filling as firmly as possible. Hand stitch back opening closed with heavy-duty thread. Using same thread, hand stitch to shape fingers and toes. Wrap elastic to fit loosely around each foot. Stitch ends firmly to top of foot; then sew on small button, to cover ends.

9 For nose, cut a 2-inch (or smaller, if desired) circle of muslin. With heavy-duty thread, sew a running stitch ¼ inch from edge, to gather; stuff with tuft of batting, and pull stitches tight to shape nose. Slip-stitch to center of face. From felt scraps, cut 1-inch white circles for eyes and ½-inch black circles for pupils; appliqué or glue in place. Draw lips and brows, and tint cheeks, with felt-tipped pen or fabric crayon.

10 *To make hair for girl Doll:* Wrap rug yarn from top to bottom around 8¼ by 10¾-inch book or heavy cardboard until covered. Fasten yarn end, then hand stitch along one end of book to secure strands; cut yarn at opposite end, and remove book. Place stitched yarn on Doll's head with stitching line over center of head. Hand stitch over first stitching to hold in place. Fold yarn to one side, over stitching. Repeat procedure for other side of head. To

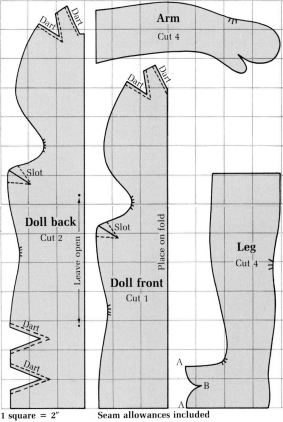

Arm
Cut 4

Doll back
Cut 2

Leave open

Slot

Slot

Place on fold

Doll front
Cut 1

Leg
Cut 4

Dart

A

B

A

1 square = 2"   Seam allowances included
(For enlarging and transferring instructions, see page 38)

make bangs, repeat process, wrapping yarn around 3 by 5-inch cardboard and stitching along 5-inch side. Stitch bangs across forehead of Doll. Tie hair into 2 ponytails; tack to head.

11 *To make hair for boy Doll:* Wrap bouclé yarn around 3 by 10-inch cardboard, and hand stitch along one 10-inch side, as in Step 10. *Don't cut yarn;* slip looped fringe off cardboard. Stitch to head from side to side across forehead. Repeat the process, stitching overlapping rows of yarn fringe to head, from front to back, until head is covered.

Design: Françoise Kirkman.

Banners that blaze with color

Bold and brilliant, these banners brighten a child's room or wave from a window to announce a birthday. This grand-scale project is so simple that children can do it themselves.

Make the springtime or birthday banners shown on these pages, or dream up your own design for a special occasion—perhaps one like the summertime tree banner pictured on page 95.

You'll need . . .

For either painted banner:

1 jar *each* of violet, green, blue, red, yellow, and orange fabric paint

1 square foot of ½-inch-thick foam

Cardboard

#8 stencil brush

Small-blade art knife

Transfer pencil or dressmaker's chalk

For one birthday banner:

White, loosely woven cotton or cotton blend fabric, 38 by 72 inches

½ yard of wide ribbon

1 roll *each* of 4 or 5 colors of crepe paper streamers

Masking tape

Cardboard tubing, bamboo rod, or dowel, 42 inches long

For one springtime banner:

White twin-size flat sheet

Cardboard tubing, bamboo rod, or dowel, 56 inches long

Making the birthday banner

1 Turn all fabric edges under ¼ inch; press. Turn under again ½ inch, on sides and bottom; press. Machine stitch close to hem edges.

2 Enlarge star and heart designs, using grid scale (see page 38). Trace design outlines onto foam square;

cut out with art knife. Glue forms to cardboard backing to make stamps.

3 Outline freehand ribbon designs and lettering on fabric with transfer pencil (see photo at left). Use stencil brush to paint ribbons and lettering. (For preparation and painting instructions, see "Direct painting," page 52.)

Dip foam stamps into paint and press carefully onto fabric (see "Stamping," page 53). Allow to dry, and heat-set according to paint manufacturer's directions.

4 Turn under folded top edge 3½ inches and machine stitch close to hem edge, leaving side edges open. Insert tubing, bamboo, or dowel through hem opening.

5 Cut crepe paper streamers twice the banner's length. Fold in half and divide into two bundles, wrapping folded tops of each bundle with masking tape. Stuff taped ends into open ends of tubing, or tape to bamboo or dowel. Wrap ribbon around protruding ends of tubing, bamboo, or dowel.

Making the springtime banner

1 Trim sheet to 52 by 86 inches, making one hemmed edge the bottom edge of the banner. Turn unhemmed edges under ¼ inch; press. Turn under again 1½ inches on sides and press; machine stitch close to hem edges.

2 Enlarge butterfly and tulip designs, using grid scale (see page 38). Cut and mount foam forms as in Birthday Banner Step 2. Cut out separate forms for butterfly wings and body, so you can use contrasting paint colors for each.

3 Following Birthday Banner Steps 3 and 4, outline tulip stems, blue blocks, and border design with transfer pencil. Then paint and assemble banner.

Design: Julie Salles Haas.

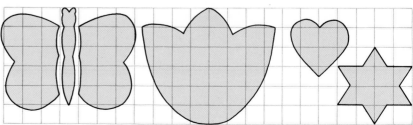

1 square = 1″ (For enlarging and transferring instructions, see page 38)

Inching upward chart

What happier way to celebrate a child's growth than with this colorful measurement chart? Besides marking off inches, it displays favorite photographs, from babyhood to the present.

As the child grows, change the pictures. Or use the frames to display locks of hair, report cards, or other memorabilia.

You'll need . . .

For one growth chart:

1¼ yards double-faced quilted fabric, 45 inches wide

¼ yard firmly woven fabric, for name and birth date

¼ yard firmly woven, heavyweight, white fabric, 45 inches wide, for chart center

1½-inch-high letter stencils, for child's name

1-inch-high letter and number stencils, for birth date

1 measuring tape

Assorted pieces of fabric (6 inches square to 7 by 8 inches), for picture frames

Snapshots of child

Assorted trimmings (such as bias tape, braid, eyelet, lace, piping, ribbon, rickrack) for frames

1 yard heavy acetate, for windows

1 package wide bias tape, for hanging

1 dowel, 18 inches long, 1 inch in diameter

1 metal curtain rod or wooden slat, 18 inches long

Making the chart

1 From quilted fabric, cut a 21 by 45-inch rectangle. Cut a 1 by 2-inch rectangle out of each corner, as shown at top of facing page.

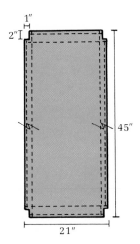

2 Mark front and back faces of quilted fabric (back folds over front to make border). Turn long edges of rectangle ½ inch to *front*; topstitch close to edge. Fold again 1 inch to *front*; topstitch ¼ inch from hem edge.

3 Turn top and bottom edges ½ inch to *front*; topstitch close to edge. Mark a parallel line across fabric *back* 2 inches from top and bottom folded edges.

4 Using 1½-inch-high letter stencils, cut child's name from fabric.

5 Place quilted fabric so that *back* is facing up and *top* edge is closest to you. Center letters of child's name between folded edge and marked line, with *base* of letters positioned *toward* folded edge. Machine appliqué letters in place (see page 40).

6 Using 1-inch-high letter and number stencils, cut child's birth date from fabric. Repeat procedure in Step 5, placing letters and numbers between bottom fold and marked line. Place *tops* of letters and numbers just below topstitching.

7 Cut a 9 by 38-inch strip from white fabric. Fold strip in half lengthwise, right sides together. Stitch long sides together, ½ inch from edge. Turn right side out; press flat, with seam at one edge. Center white strip on chart front; edgestitch in place.

8 Pin measuring tape 1 inch from left edge of white strip. Position tape so 20-inch line is at bottom edge of strip, and numbers increase going up the chart. Edgestitch along both sides of tape. Cut off excess tape at top and bottom.

9 Arrange pictures and assorted fabric squares and rectangles in vertical rows down chart sides. When arrangement is pleasing, mark position of each fabric piece on chart; make markings ½ inch narrower all around than fabric, to allow for hems in frames.

10 After deciding how much of each photograph you want to be visible, cut paper patterns to make a window for each frame. Cut a piece of acetate ½ inch larger on all sides than each window pattern.

11 Centering window patterns on right sides of fabric pieces, trace window openings. Stitch along traced lines; cut out window openings ¼ inch inside stitched lines. Clip corners to stitching, then press window edge under ¼ inch all around, along stitched lines.

12 Lay each frame on marked position on chart. On chart front, beneath frame pieces, mark openings to insert pictures, ½ inch above top edge of each window opening and ¼ inch wider than picture to be inserted. Stitch marked openings with buttonhole or zigzag stitching, as if making giant buttonholes, and slash.

13 Turn outer edge of frame ¼ inch to wrong side; topstitch. Embellish each frame as desired with ribbons or trims (see photo above).

14 Stitch acetate windows to backs of frames, close to window edge, catching the ¼ inch turned under in Step 11. Place frames on chart, making sure that each covers its slot. Topstitch frames to chart along all outside edges.

15 Cut 1½ yards of bias tape. Fold in half lengthwise; topstitch close to long edges; press.

16 Fold chart's top and bottom edges to front along marked line made in Step 3, forming 2-inch hems. Leaving side edges open, topstitch hems in place over ends of white center strip. In top hem, make tiny holes through all thicknesses, 2 inches from each end and ½ inch from top.

17 Slip pictures into their frames. Insert dowel through top hem, curtain rod through bottom hem. Thread bias tape through holes made in Step 16; stitch or tie ends together. Pull tape up from both front and back, to form doubled hanging loop. Hang chart so its lowest tape measurement reflects actual inch measurement from floor. With indelible ink, mark child's height on white center strip, next to measuring tape.

Design: Pamela Seifert.

Tooth fairy pillow

Deposit baby teeth in the Tooth Fairy's little moiré purse, then settle her down for the night. The next morning, peek inside—there should be a glint of silver in place of last night's ivory.

You'll need . . .

For one tooth fairy, 17 inches tall:

½ yard firmly woven ecru cotton or cotton-polyester blend fabric

¼ yard ecru moiré fabric

¼ yard heavy interfacing

Assorted ecru eyelet ruffle:
⅛ yard, 1 inch wide
½ yard, 2 inches wide
⅓ yard, 2½ inches wide
1 yard, 3 inches wide
⅔ yard, 4½ inches wide

Satin ribbon:
1 yard peach, ¼ inch wide
1 yard peach, ⅛ inch wide
1 yard tangerine, ⅛ inch wide

1 package ecru double-fold bias tape

1 pound loose polyester filling

1 skein bronze heavy rug yarn

Thread to match rug yarn

1 package each of brown, blue, and rose 6-strand embroidery floss

2 small circles of nylon self-gripping tape (optional)

Making the doll

Note: Use ½-inch seams unless otherwise indicated.

1 Enlarge and transfer pattern pieces (see page 38). With right sides together, fold cotton fabric in half, selvage to selvage; cut out Doll, Base, and two of four Purse pieces for lining. Cut two Wings and two Purse pieces from moiré fabric. Cut two Wings from interfacing. Transfer pattern markings to right side of fabric for Doll face, arm joints, and wing placement on Doll back.

2 Following markings, embroider brows and eye outlines in stem stitch with 3 strands of brown embroidery floss; use brown straight stitches for lashes, blue satin stitches for irises of eyes, and rose satin stitches for lips (see "Embroidery," page 26).

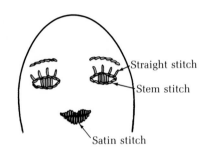

3 Sew Doll front to back, right sides together, leaving bottom edge open; clip curves. Turn right side out.

4 Stuff arms with filling, from hands to elbow markings. Using zipper foot, machine stitch elbow joints as marked. Stuff remainder of arms to shoulder markings; stitch as marked to make shoulder joints. Turn doll wrong side out.

5 Sew Base panel to open end of Doll, right sides together, leaving a 4-inch opening in back for stuffing.

6 Turn Doll right side out. Stuff firmly with filling. Slipstitch opening closed.

7 For hair, cut 27 strands of bronze yarn, each 24 inches long. Attaching one strand with each stitch, use matching thread to hand sew centers of strands to center of head, forming a "part" from forehead to back.

8 Starting 2 inches from stitching at top of head, braid yarn hair on each side. Tack braids to side of head at neckline, then coil into a bun at back, following direction of arrows (following). Tuck braid ends under; tack braids and ends securely to head. Tack on small bows of ⅛-inch peach and tangerine ribbons.

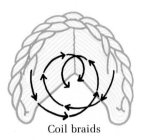

Coil braids

9 Place moiré Wing pieces right sides together. With both interfacing Wing pieces against wrong side of one moiré piece, pin together all 4 layers. Machine stitch layers together, ¼ inch from edge, leaving a 3-inch opening in one side.

10 Trim interfacing close to stitching; clip curves. Turn Wings right side out. Press, turning under raw edges of opening. Slipstitch opening closed. Topstitch close to outer edge of Wings. Stitch again ¼ inch inside first stitching. Whipstitch center of Wings to center back of Doll at marking.

11 Doll skirt is 5 overlapping rows of eyelet ruffle, each attached to Doll body. Measure distance around Doll, 4½ inches above base; add 1 inch for seam allowances. Cut 4½-inch-wide eyelet this length. With right sides together, join eyelet ends in diagonal seam, as shown, to form circular band. Slip band over Doll, then whipstitch in place.

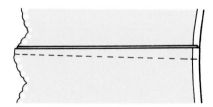

12 Repeat Step 11 with 4 remaining graduated widths of eyelet ruffle, each row overlapping the one below. (The second row overlaps the first by 2 inches; remaining rows overlap preceding rows by 1 inch.) For rows 2 and 3, use 3-inch-wide eyelet; for row 4, 2½-inch-wide eyelet; for row

5, 2-inch-wide eyelet. Leaving long ends free at center front, slipstitch ¼-inch peach ribbon over waistline edge of uppermost ruffle. Tie ends into a bow.

13 For collar ruffle, wrap 2-inch-wide eyelet around neck, folding top edge of eyelet at center front to make a V-shape. Fold under raw edges and whipstitch to center back, along Wing seam. Slipstitch ¼-inch-wide peach ribbon over top edge of ruffle. At center front, tack on bow of tangerine ribbon.

14 To keep hands joined, sew self-gripping tape circles to fingertips (pile circle on *outside* of one hand, hook circle on *inside* of other hand). Or simply stitch hands together permanently, *after* completing Purse.

15 To make Purse, match top edges of moiré and cotton Purse

pieces, right sides together. Place 1-inch-wide eyelet between layers, with straight edges even. Machine stitch ¼ inch from top edge. Turn right side out; press.

16 Pin Purse with moiré sides together; sew side and bottom edge, ¼ inch from edge, including eyelet ends in seam. Secure seam ends with backstitching (for strength). Turn right side out.

17 Cut a 4-inch length of bias tape for Purse handle. Machine stitch long edges together. Hand sew ends of tape inside Purse at center front and back. (If doll hands are to be permanently joined, slip handle over arm before stitching hands together.) Decorate Purse center front with small bow of tangerine ribbon.

Design: Karen Cummings.

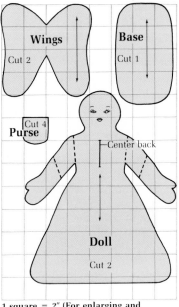

1 square = 2″ (For enlarging and transferring instructions, see page 38)

Arrow indicates lengthwise grain

Puppet menagerie

Stitch up this winsome quartet of furred and feathered characters, and then watch them come alive in the hands of delighted young puppeteers.

You'll need . . .

For one skunk or beaver:

⅜ yard medium-pile fake fur (*for skunk*, black; *for beaver*, brown)

Loose polyester filling

3 black dome-shaped buttons, ½ inch in diameter

5 by 36-inch strip of white, high-pile fake fur (*for skunk gusset, tail, and stripe*)

Scrap of red print fabric (*for skunk's scarf*)

Scrap of brown synthetic suede (*for beaver tail*)

Scrap of polyester batting (*for beaver tail*)

⅜ yard orange rib knit fabric (*for beaver's cap*)

1 white yarn pompon (*for beaver's cap*)

Scrap of white felt (*for beaver teeth*)

Scrap of corduroy fabric (*for beaver ears*)

For one chicken or parrot:

½ yard felt (*for chicken*, yellow; *for parrot*, red)

Loose polyester filling

2 black dome-shaped buttons, ⅜ inch in diameter

Fusible web

2 squares *each* of lavender, blue, turquoise, orange, and hot pink felt (*for parrot*)

1 square *each* of orange and rust felt (*for chicken head*)

Scrap of green calico fabric (*for chicken's collar*)

¾ yard green ribbon, ¼ inch wide (*for chicken's collar*)

Skunk or beaver

Note: When stitching seams, push pile away from seamlines.

1 Enlarge and transfer pattern pieces (see page 38), and cut fabric pieces following instructions on grid. *For beaver*, cut Body, Head, Gusset, and 2 of 4 Ear pieces from medium-pile fur; cut other 2 Ear pieces from corduroy. Cut Tail pieces from synthetic suede, and Cap from rib knit fabric. *For skunk*, cut Body, Head, and Ear pieces from

medium-pile fur; cut Gusset, Tail, and Stripe pieces from high-pile fur; cut Scarf from red fabric.

2 Stitch Body pieces, right sides together, leaving bottom open. Clip curves; turn right side out. Turn hem under ¾ inch; topstitch. (*For skunk*, first sew Stripe to Body back with zigzag stitch along edges.)

3 Pin one Head piece to Gusset, right sides together, matching symbols; stitch from A to B. Repeat for other Head piece; stitch front head seam from A down to neck opening. Clip curves; turn and stuff.

4 Stitch Ears, right sides together, leaving bottom open. (*For beaver*, use 1 fur and 1 corduroy piece for each Ear.) Clip curves and turn. Turn edges under ¼ inch; slipstitch to head.

5 Pin Tail pieces, right sides together; stitch, leaving end open. Clip curves; turn. (*For beaver tail*, cut additional Tail piece from batting. Pin synthetic suede Tail pieces, right sides together; then pin batting piece against one suede piece and stitch through all 3 layers; trim, clip, and turn. Make bar tacks, as marked.) Stitch tail to back body at lower edge.

6 Turn lower edges of head under ¼ inch, and slipstitch to body with heavy-duty thread. Sew buttons in place for eyes and nose with heavy-duty thread. (*For beaver teeth*, transfer pattern to white felt; don't cut. Stitch on lines through 2 pieces of felt; cut Teeth out close to stitching, cutting halfway up between teeth at center. Slipstitch teeth to head.

7 *For skunk's Scarf*, turn edges under ¼ inch, turn again ¼ inch, and topstitch. *For beaver's Cap*, cut ear slits; fold Cap right sides together and zigzag stitch close to side edge. Fold bottom edge under ⅛ inch, and zigzag stitch hem.

Parrot

1 Enlarge and transfer pattern pieces (see page 38), and cut fabric

pieces following instructions on grid. Cut Body and Head from red felt; cut Wing, Chest, and Tail pieces from blue, orange, turquoise, lavender, and pink felt. Also cut corresponding Wing and Chest pieces from fusible web (cut web for Wing pieces A and B along dotted lines).

2 Arrange Chest pieces in order of descending size. Bond pieces to each other with fusible web; then bond chest to Body front along placement lines.

3 Pin Body pieces, *right sides together*, and stitch, leaving bottom open. Clip curves and turn. Stitch through both layers on wings following marked lines.

4 Arrange 3 large Wing pieces in order of descending size, matching edges at F; bond to each other and to wing backs on body with fusible web. Center smallest Wing piece D over edge F. Pin Tail pieces together in order of descending size, adding small Tail pieces E; machine stitch tail to bottom edge of body back through all layers.

5 Outline Beak pieces on orange felt; don't cut. Leaving straight sides open, stitch just inside lines through 2 layers of felt; cut out just outside stitching. Stuff beak loosely.

6 Pin beak to one Head piece at B-C. Pin Head pieces, right sides together, and stitch, leaving bottom open. Clip, turn, and stuff. With heavy-duty thread, slipstitch head to body, then sew on buttons for eyes.

Chicken

1 Enlarge and transfer pattern pieces (see page 38), and cut fabric pieces following instructions on grid. Cut Body and Head from yellow felt; cut Face pieces from rust felt. Also cut 2 Face pieces from fusible web.

2 Follow Parrot Step 3.

3 Follow Parrot Step 5, but do not stuff beak. Repeat process for Comb and Wattle pieces, outlining Wattle twice on felt.

4 Bond Face pieces onto Head pieces, as marked, using fusible web. Fold Beak pieces lengthwise, with upper beak overlapping lower beak, and folded edges facing away from each other. Pin folded *Beak*, plus *Comb* and *Wattle*, at marked locations on one Head piece, as shown. Then follow Parrot Step 6.

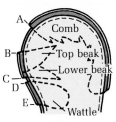

Chicken

5 To make Collar, cut a 14 by 5-inch rectangle of green calico. Turn short ends under ¼ inch, turn again ¼ inch, and topstitch. Fold fabric in half lengthwise, right sides together; stitch ¼ inch from raw edges. Turn and press; stitch ½ inch from seamed edge to form casing. Thread ribbon through casing; gather Collar around chicken's neck and tie ribbon in a bow.

Design: Philippa K. Mars & Babs Kavanaugh.

1 square = 2″ (For enlarging and transferring instructions, see page 38)   ¼″ seam allowances included

[Pattern grid with pieces labeled: Skunk or beaver body, Skunk or beaver gusset, Chicken or parrot body, Skunk tail, Beaver tail, Parrot wing, Skunk head, Beaver head, Parrot tail, Chicken or parrot head, Ear, Parrot wing, Teeth, Parrot tail, Chicken face, wattle, Parrot chest A, Chicken top beak, lower beak, Beaver cap, Chicken comb, Parrot tail, Skunk scarf, Skunk stripe, Parrot wing, Parrot beak]

Beanbag buddies

Comfy to curl up in, sturdy enough for a bouncy ride, our ring-necked mallard and bright red hen quickly become favorite friends.

You'll need . . .

Note: Use firmly woven cottons or cotton blends, 45 inches wide.

For one beanbag hen:

4½ yards red and white print fabric

¼ yard red fabric

Scraps of white fabric

5 pounds loose polyester filling

7 cubic feet (2½ bags) styrene foam pellets

Heavy-duty thread

For one beanbag duck:

1 yard dark green fabric

¾ yard white fabric

½ yard each yellow and black fabric

1¾ yards red and white print fabric

1½ yards red fabric

Scraps of white fabric

6 pounds loose polyester filling

7 cubic feet (2½ bags) styrene foam pellets

Making the hen

Note: Stitch ½-inch seams.

1 Enlarge and transfer appropriate pattern pieces (see page 38) and markings (ignore dashed lines on Body Top, Body Side, and Underbody). Cut Head, Beak Gusset, Neck Circle, and Body pieces from print fabric; Comb and eye pupils from red fabric; and eyes from white scrap.

2 Machine appliqué eye and pupil in place on each Head piece. With right sides together, stitch 3 Comb pieces in place on each Head piece; press seams open.

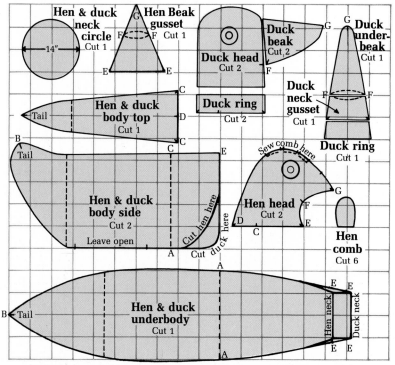

Hen & duck neck circle — Cut 1 — 14"

Hen Beak gusset — Cut 1 — G F F E E

Duck head — Cut 2

Duck beak — Cut 2 — G F

Duck under-beak — Cut 1 — G

Hen & duck body top — Cut 1 — Tail C D C

Duck ring — Cut 2

Duck neck gusset — Cut 1 — F F

Duck ring — Cut 1

Tail B — Tail

Hen & duck body side — Cut 2 — Leave open — Cut hen here — Cut duck here — A A

Sew comb here

Hen head — Cut 2 — D C G F E

Hen comb — Cut 6

Hen & duck underbody — Cut 1 — B Tail — A A

Hen neck — E E — Duck neck — E E

1 square = 5" (For enlarging and transferring instructions, see page 38)

½" seam allowances included

3 Folding right sides together, stitch curved dart F in Beak Gusset. Matching E, F, and G, stitch one edge of Gusset to each Head piece, right sides together. Clip curve. Matching Comb pieces, right sides together, stitch 2 Head pieces along top curved edge, leaving straight edge (neck) open. Clip curve and corners; turn right side out.

4 Firmly stuff Head with filling, poking in small amounts at a time. When Head is packed full, place Neck Circle over neck opening, wrong sides together, matching edges. Use zipper foot to stitch neckline seam, enclosing stuffing.

5 Stitch Body Top to each Body Side, right sides together, matching B and C; clip curve. With right sides together, matching E, A, and B, stitch Underbody to remaining edges of Body Sides, leaving 10 inches open in one straight side. Clip curves. In-

sert Head (upside down, beak forward) into neck opening. Match D and E; use zipper foot to stitch over Neck Circle. Turn hen right side out.

6 Have someone hold hen open. Fill with pellets, using funnel of heavy paper to fill completely. Carefully pin closed. Hand stitch closed with heavy-duty thread.

Making the duck

Note: Stitch ½-inch seams.

1 Enlarge and transfer appropriate pattern pieces (see page 38). Separate body pieces as indicated by dashed lines, adding ½ inch to these edges for seam allowances. Cut Tail portions of Body from black fabric; Center Body from print; Front Body from red; Head, Neck Circle, Neck Gusset, and eye pupils from green; Ring from white; and Beak, Under-beak, and eyes from yellow.

2 Stitch Under-beak to Neck Gusset, right sides together, making curved seam F as marked. Stitch remaining long Gusset edge to matching edge of Neck Ring piece, as positioned on grid. Press seam open. Stitch Beak and Ring pieces to Head pieces, as positioned on pattern. Clip seam allowance of head at F. Press seams open. Appliqué eyes and pupils as in Hen Step 2.

3 Stitch Head/Beak pieces, right sides together, along curved edge of Head and out across top of Beak. Stitch Under-beak/Gusset to Head/Beak, right sides together, easing Beak to fit. Clip curves and corners; turn right side out. Finish head as in Hen Step 4. With right sides together, making ½-inch seams, piece patchwork sections of Body Top, Sides, and Underbody. Press seams open. Finish duck as in Hen Steps 5 and 6.

Design: Françoise Kirkman.

Tender-hearted bear quilt

Loving hearts float upward from baby's bear. A charming wall hanging, it's also a cozy crib-size quilt.

You'll need . . .

For 1 quilt, 35½ by 44½ inches:

1⅔ yards firmly woven cotton or cotton blend print fabric, 45 inches wide

1 yard navy fabric, 45 inches wide

¾ yard green fabric, 45 inches wide

½ yard brown fabric, 45 inches wide

¼ yard beige dotted fabric

¼ yard mauve dotted fabric

1 yard quilt batting, 45 inches wide

Size 5 pearl cotton: 1 skein *each* in black, yellow, and each fabric color

Assembling the quilt

1 Enlarge pattern pieces according to grid scale (see page 38), adding ¼-inch seam allowances, and trace on wrong sides of brown, beige, and mauve fabric, following photograph for color placement; cut out pieces.

2 From print fabric, cut a 20½-inch square for quilt center. Curve corners, using pattern. Arrange bear pieces and 2 smaller hearts on square; baste in place (see page 39). Hand appliqué with matching pearl cotton (see page 41). Satin stitch bear's eyes with yellow pearl cotton, and nose with black. For mouth, use a running stitch and black pearl cotton (see page 26).

3 From green fabric, cut a 26½-inch square; curve corners, as in Step 2. Center print square over green square; appliqué in place. Turn piece face down. Carefully cut away green fabric, stopping ½ inch from appliqué stitching. On right side, appliqué remaining heart in place.

4 From navy fabric, cut a 45 by 36-inch rectangle. Center appliquéd square over it. Appliqué green fabric edge to navy fabric. Carefully cut away navy fabric, as in Step 3. Press.

5 Mark diagonal quilting lines 4 inches apart on navy border (see "Quilting," pages 48–51). Cut print fabric backing piece and batting the same size as finished quilt face.

6 Assemble and baste quilt layers (see page 49). Quilt along diagonal lines and all appliquéd edges.

7 Following directions in "Cutting bias strips," page 32, make 1½-inch-wide bias tape from print fabric. Bind quilt edge with bias (see page 33).

Design: Sonya Barrington.

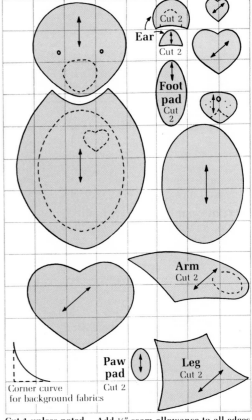

Corner curve for background fabrics

Ear Cut 2

Foot pad Cut 2

Arm Cut 2

Paw pad Cut 2

Leg Cut 2

Cut 1 unless noted   Add ¼" seam allowance to all edges
1 square = 2" (see page 38)

Hop-along hobby horses

Either of these horses, or your own variation, is sure to "whinny" its way into your child's heart.

You'll need . . .

For one horse:

⅓ yard low to medium-pile fake fur

20 by 4-inch strip high-pile fake fur

½ pound loose polyester filling

2 large and 2 small half-dome buttons

Heavy-duty thread

White glue

3-foot dowel, ⅜ inch or ½ inch in diameter

Scrap of corduroy (for horse ears)

⅛ yard gold lamé (for unicorn horn)

Assembling the horse

Note: When stitching fake fur, push pile *away* from seams.

1 Enlarge and transfer pattern pieces (see page 38). Cut Head, Gusset, and Ears from low-pile fabric.

(*For horse,* cut 2 of 4 Ears from corduroy.) Cut Mane from high-pile fabric. (*For unicorn,* cut Horn from gold lamé.)

2 Stitch Head pieces, right sides together, from A down to neck edge. Pin and stitch Mane to Gusset at B. Pin Gusset/Mane to one Head piece; stitch from A to C. Repeat for other Head piece. Turn right side out and stuff head above neck.

3 Slipstitch one seam joining Mane to head below C. Stuff neck except for bottom 2 inches. Insert dowel in neck; spread glue inside neck. Bring remaining seam edges together. Wrap heavy-duty thread around neck to secure it to dowel; let dry. Slipstitch remaining seam closed.

4 Stitch each pair of Ears, right sides together, leaving lower edge open. (*For horse,* use 1 fur and 1 corduroy piece for each ear.) Turn right side out; slipstitch to head.

For unicorn, stitch Horn pieces, right sides together; turn and stuff. Slipstitch Horn to head.

5 Sew large buttons in place for eyes; use small buttons for nostrils. If desired, add bridle of ½-inch-wide ribbon, neck scarf, or fake flowers.

Design: Philippa K. Mars and Babs Kavanaugh.

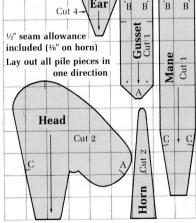

1 square = 2" (For enlarging and transferring instructions, see page 38)

Miniature dream cottage

Transform an ordinary card table into this charming playhouse, complete with see-through windows and cheery appliquéd garden. This project is recommended for those with sewing experience.

You'll need . . .

- 1 card table, 34 by 34 inches
- 2 sheets corrugated cardboard, 36 by 72 inches
- 2 yards quilted blue fabric, 45 inches wide, for roof
- 4½ yards heavy blue corduroy, 45 inches wide, for walls
- 1½ yards white corduroy
- 1½ yards red corduroy
- ½ yard purple corduroy
- ¼ yard *each* light green and dark green corduroy
- 12 yards red extra-wide double-fold bias tape
- 1½ yards heavyweight acetate
- 1 spool thread for each fabric color
- ½ yard nylon self-gripping fastener tape

Making the house

1 To make cardboard roof, measure, mark, and cut one Gable and one Roof from *each* sheet of cardboard, following layout above right. (Also cut Gable pattern [minus tabs and flaps] from paper, to use later). Using metal straightedge and utility knife, score cardboard along dotted lines; fold. Matching center X's on Roof, securely tape Gable tabs and flaps to underside of one Roof. Tape second Roof to underside of first.

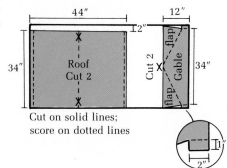

Cut on solid lines; score on dotted lines

2 Cut Roof fabric 40 by 45 inches. Lay wrong side up over Roof form, leaving a 3-inch overhang over each Gable. Pin darts to fit fabric snugly at 4 corners and 2 Gable peaks. Remove from form; stitch darts as pinned. Turn all outer edges under ½ inch; topstitch ¼ inch from edge.

3 To cut out Front Wall from blue corduroy, center paper Gable pattern across width of fabric. Extend slanted roof lines to selvages with chalk or pencil. Measuring 24½ inches from bottom edge of Gable pattern, mark bottom line across fabric. Cut out piece on roof and bottom lines. Turn bottom edge under ½ inch, turn again 1 inch and pin; turn side edges under 5 inches. Topstitch close to all hem edges. Center and cut 12 by 21-inch opening for Door.

4 To trim Door opening, cut 5-inch-wide strips from white corduroy; piece into a 2⅛-yard length. Fold long edges under ½ inch; press. Fold strip lengthwise, wrong sides together, aligning folded edges; press. To attach trim, start at bottom edge of opening, turning narrow edge of strip under ½ inch; pin strip over raw edge of Door opening with inside of fold against edge of opening. To turn corners, make a mitered corner on front and back sides of trim. Stitch trim to wall through all layers, ¼ inch from trim edge.

5 Cut tulip shapes from purple corduroy, stems and leaves from dark and light green corduroy, and numbers from white corduroy; appliqué to wall (see page 39). If desired, stitch mailbox of blue corduroy.

6 For Front Door, cut red corduroy 19 by 26 inches. Turn bottom and sides under ½ inch; turn again 1½ inches, and topstitch close to hem edge. Mark a 10-inch-radius semicircle for window, cut out opening, and bind edges with bias tape (see "Bias tape," page 32). Cut acetate slightly larger than opening; stitch folded bias tape "spokes" to acetate. Center acetate on wrong side of window opening and stitch to Door, close to window edge.

7 Cut cat and doorknob shapes from dark green corduroy; appliqué to Front Door. With all bottom hems even, pin and stitch finished Door across top of Front Door opening, against *inside* of trim.

8 To make Back Wall, mark, cut, and hem blue corduroy (see Step 3). Cut out 20 by 21-inch Back Door opening, as for Front Door. Cut 5 inch by 2½ yards long white corduroy strip for trim; trim Door opening (see Step 4).

9 For Back Door (see photo), cut red corduroy 27 by 25 inches. Cut two 7 by 14-inch window openings centered on door. Bind openings with bias tape (see page 32). Cut a 23-inch-square piece of acetate. Matching tops of acetate and corduroy, mark window openings on acetate. Stitch bias tape to acetate to form window panes; stitch acetate to wrong side of Door around window

openings. Hem sides and bottom; stitch Door to wall (see Step 6).

10 Cut one Side Wall, 27½ by 45 inches, from blue corduroy; hem (see Step 3). Center and cut out a 9½ by 11½-inch window opening (see photo, facing page). Cut 5-inch wide by 2¼ yards white corduroy trim; trim opening as for Door in Step 4.

11 To make window, cut acetate 14 by 16 inches. Draw outline of window centered on acetate. Press bias tape open; stitch to acetate centered along outlines. Stitch folded tape to acetate to form window panes. Center acetate on wrong side of window opening; edgestitch to white trim, ¼ inch from trim edges.

12 Make Shutters from 2 pieces of white corduroy, *each* 9½ by 25 inches. Turn all edges under ½ inch; press. Matching short edges, fold each piece in half, wrong sides together; edgestitch ¼ inch from all edges. Stitch self-gripping fastener tape to each Shutter at top corner, front and back; stitch matching pieces on house wall, and above window (see photo). Stitch Shutters to window's sides. Add tulip appliqués to wall below window (see Step 5).

13 Cut out and hem remaining Side Wall (see Steps 3 and 9). Add pockets made of scraps or nylon netting fabric to inside of wall, if desired.

14 With fabric roof in place on table, pin walls evenly to roof edges so hems touch floor; overlap wall panels at corners. Remove from form; stitch walls to roof on all sides with 2 rows of stitching ¾ inch apart.

Design: Pamela Seifert.

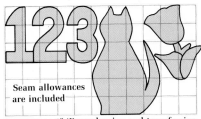

Seam allowances are included

1 square = 2″ (For enlarging and transferring instructions, see page 38)

Index

Machine-appliquéd bunnies (photos above) or apples (below) make these garments one of a kind. Use the "Wardrobe toppers" pattern on pages 62–63 for the jacket and vest. The appliqué patterns appear on page 43.

COMBINED INDEX

A comprehensive index to all three volumes appears on the following pages.
This is in addition to the individual book indexes which appear on page 96 of
each title.

Children's Furniture

STEPHEN MARLEY

Handsome rocking horse meets wild
rocking lion (see page 7).

Children's Rooms & Play Yards

DARROW M. WATT

A storybook mural splashes fantasy on a
child's wall (see page 37).

Children's Clothes & Toys

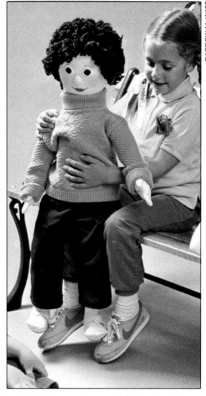

DARROW M. WATT

Child-size doll makes a perfect playmate
(see page 80).

STEPHEN MARLEY

Whimsical animal chair, from *Children's Furniture,* page 34

Combined Index

Puppet menagerie, from
Children's Clothes & Toys,
page 88

DARROW M. WATT

Combined Index

DARROW M. WATT

Shiki-buton, from *Children's Rooms & Play Yards,* page 47

Combined Index